STAR WARS

FROM THE JOURNALS OF OBI-WAN KENOBI

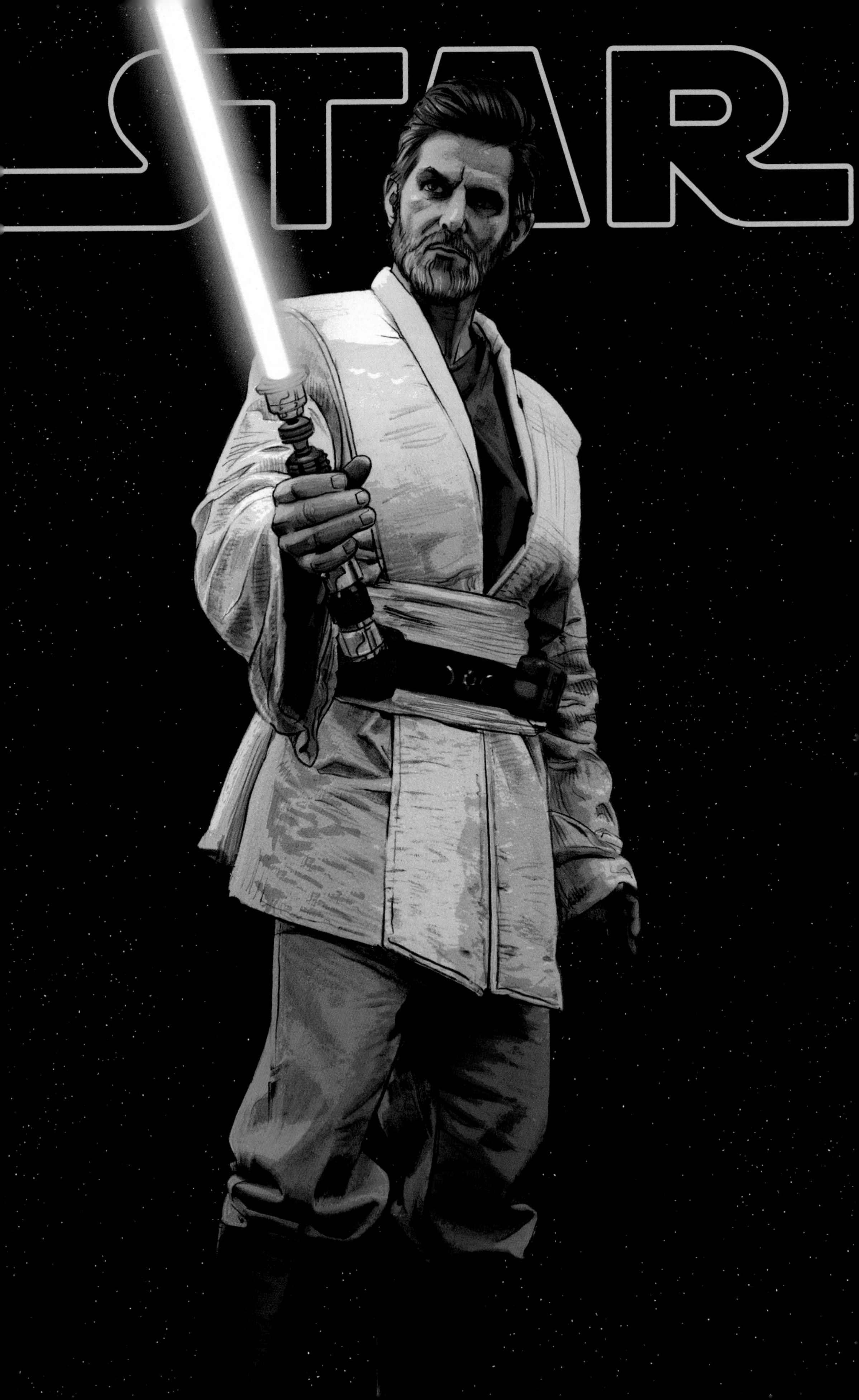
STAR

WARS™

FROM THE JOURNALS OF OBI-WAN KENOBI

Writer **JASON AARON**

STAR WARS #7

Artist **SIMONE BIANCHI**
Color Artist **JUSTIN PONSOR**
Letterer **CHRIS ELIOPOULOS**
Cover Art **JOHN CASSADAY** & **LAURA MARTIN**

STAR WARS #15 & #20

Artist/Cover **MIKE MAYHEW**
Letterer **CHRIS ELIOPOULOS**

STAR WARS #26-30

Artist **SALVADOR LARROCA**
Color Artist **EDGAR DELGADO**
Letterers **CHRIS ELIOPOULOS** (#26) & **CLAYTON COWLES** (#27-30)
Cover Art **STUART IMMONEN**

"THE SAND WILL PROVIDE"

Writers **JASON AARON** & **DASH AARON**
Artist **ANDREA SORRENTINO**
Color Artist **LEE LOUGHRIDGE**

Assistant Editor **HEATHER ANTOS**
Editor **JORDAN D. WHITE**
Editor in Chief **C.B. CEBULSKI**

Collection Editor **JENNIFER GRÜNWALD**
Assistant Managing Editor **MAIA LOY**
Assistant Managing Editor **LISA MONTALBANO**
Editor, Special Projects **MARK D. BEAZLEY**
VP Production & Special Projects **JEFF YOUNGQUIST**
Research **JEPH YORK**
SVP Print, Sales & Marketing **DAVID GABRIEL**
Book Designer **ADAM DEL RE**

FOR LUCASFILM:

Senior Editor **ROBERT SIMPSON**
Creative Director **MICHAEL SIGLAIN**
Lucasfilm Story Group **MATT MARTIN**
PABLO HIDALGO
EMILY SHKOUKANI
Lucasfilm Art Department **PHIL SZOSTAK**

STAR WARS: FROM THE JOURNALS OF OBI-WAN KENOBI. Contains material originally published in magazine form as STAR WARS (2015) #7, #15, #20, #26-30; and STAR WARS (2015) #37. First printing 2020. ISBN 978-1-302-92528-4. Published by MARVEL WORLDWIDE, INC., a subsidiary of MARVEL ENTERTAINMENT, LLC. OFFICE OF PUBLICATION: 1290 Avenue of the Americas, New York, NY 10104.

Printed in the U.S.A. KEVIN FEIGE, Chief Creative Officer; DAN BUCKLEY, President, Marvel Entertainment; JOHN NEE, Publisher; JOE QUESADA, EVP & Creative Director; TOM BREVOORT, SVP of Publishing; DAVID BOGART, Associate Publisher & SVP of Talent Affairs; Publishing & Partnership; DAVID GABRIEL, VP of Print & Digital Publishing; JEFF YOUNGQUIST, VP of Production & Special Projects; DAN CARR, Executive Director of Publishing Technology; ALEX MORALES, Director of Publishing Operations; DAN EDINGTON, Managing Editor; SUSAN CRESPI, Production Manager; STAN LEE, Chairman Emeritus. For information regarding advertising in Marvel Comics or on Marvel.com, please contact Vit DeBellis, Custom Solutions & Integrated Advertising Manager, at vdebellis@marvel.com. For Marvel subscription inquiries, please call 888-511-5480. **Manufactured between 9/4/2020 and 10/6/2020 by LSC COMMUNICATIONS INC., KENDALLVILLE, IN, USA.**

10 9 8 7 6 5 4 3 2 1

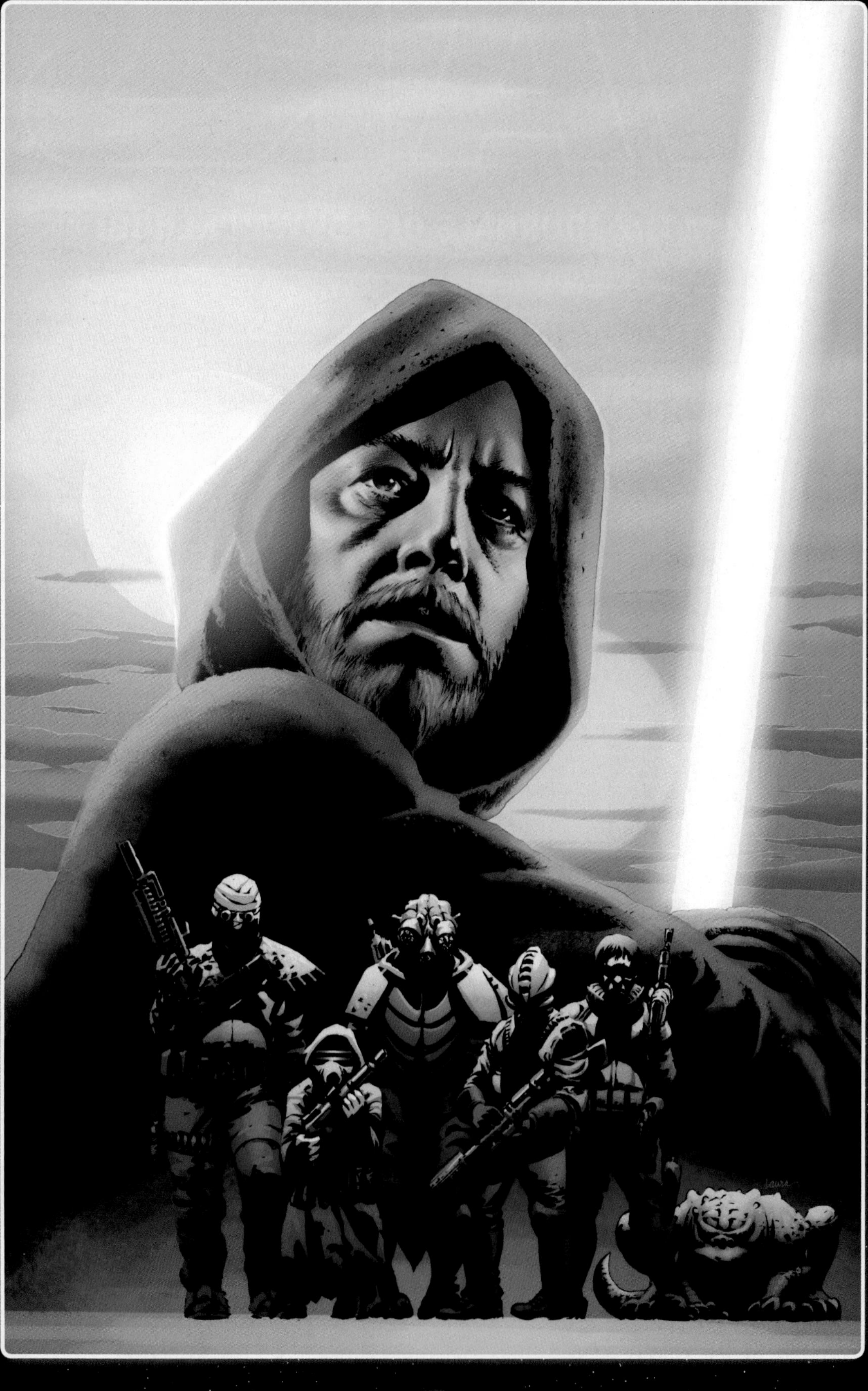

7

FROM THE JOURNALS OF
OLD BEN KENOBI

"THE LAST OF HIS BREED"

WHILE SEARCHING FOR ANSWERS IN HIS

QUEST TO BECOME A JEDI,

LUKE SKYWALKER HAS UNCOVERED A

JOURNAL WRITTEN BY JEDI MASTER

OBI-WAN KENOBI, A JOURNAL THAT KENOBI

SPECIFICALLY LEFT BEHIND

FOR LUKE TO FIND. THE JOURNAL DETAILS

KENOBI'S ADVENTURES DURING THE TIME

HE WAS IN HIDING ON TATOOINE.

WHAT FOLLOWS IS AN EXCERPT

FROM THAT JOURNAL.

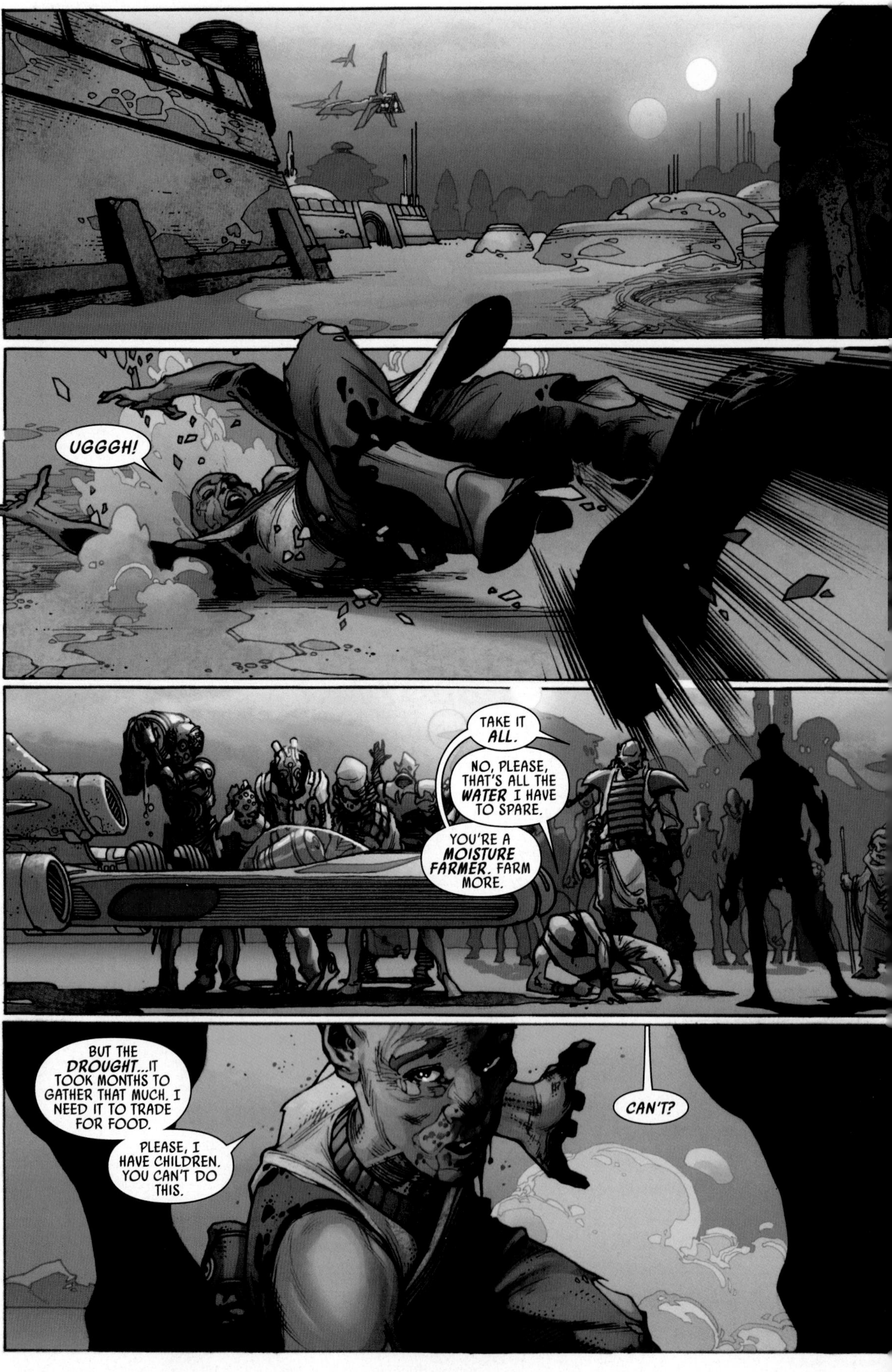
UGGGH!
TAKE IT ALL.
NO, PLEASE, THAT'S ALL THE WATER I HAVE TO SPARE.
YOU'RE A MOISTURE FARMER. FARM MORE.
BUT THE DROUGHT...IT TOOK MONTHS TO GATHER THAT MUCH. I NEED IT TO TRADE FOR FOOD.
PLEASE, I HAVE CHILDREN. YOU CAN'T DO THIS.
CAN'T?

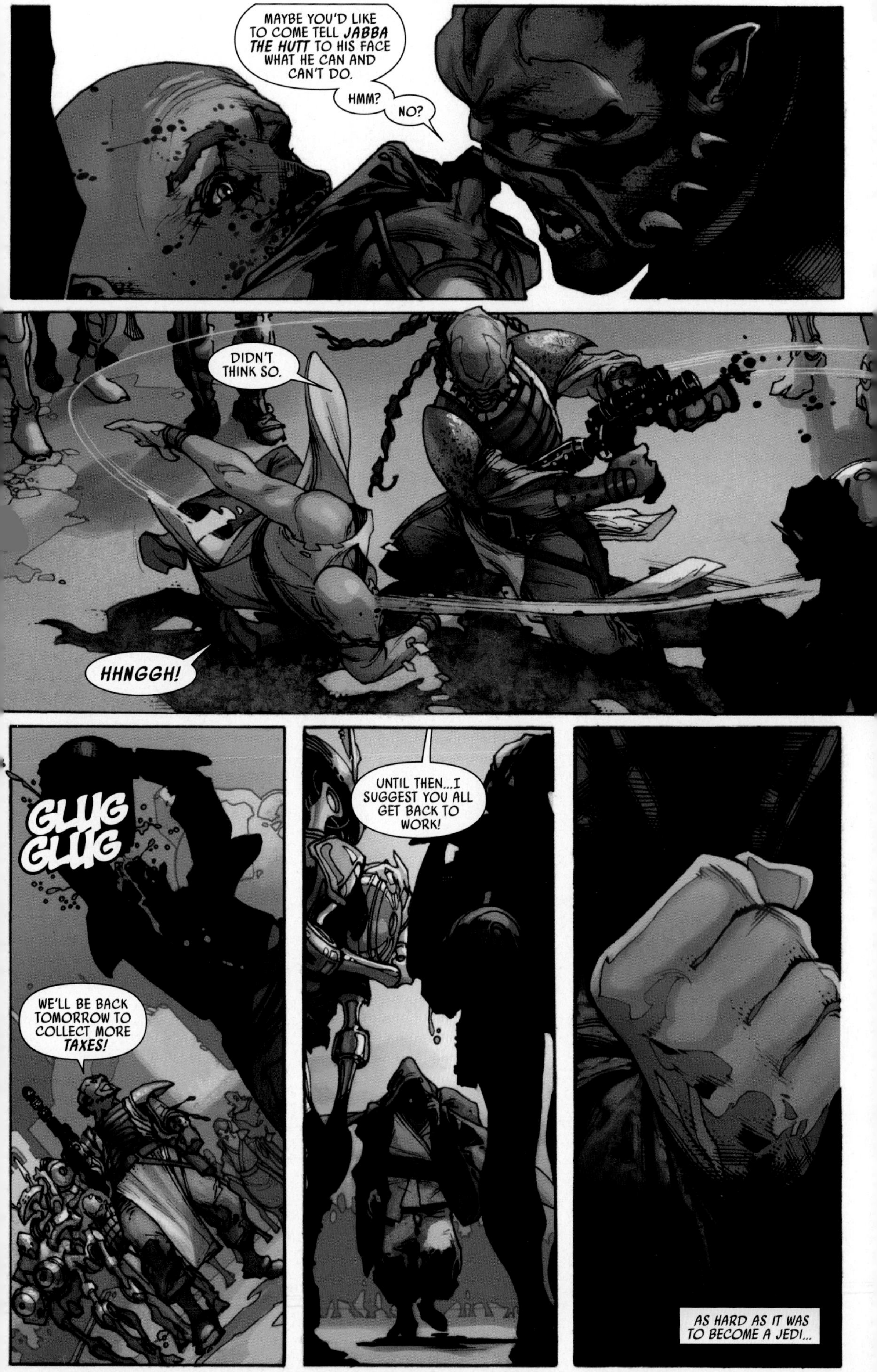
MAYBE YOU'D LIKE TO COME TELL JABBA THE HUTT TO HIS FACE WHAT HE CAN AND CAN'T DO.
HMM?
NO?
DIDN'T THINK SO.
HHNGGH!
GLUG GLUG
WE'LL BE BACK TOMORROW TO COLLECT MORE TAXES!
UNTIL THEN...I SUGGEST YOU ALL GET BACK TO WORK!
AS HARD AS IT WAS TO BECOME A JEDI...

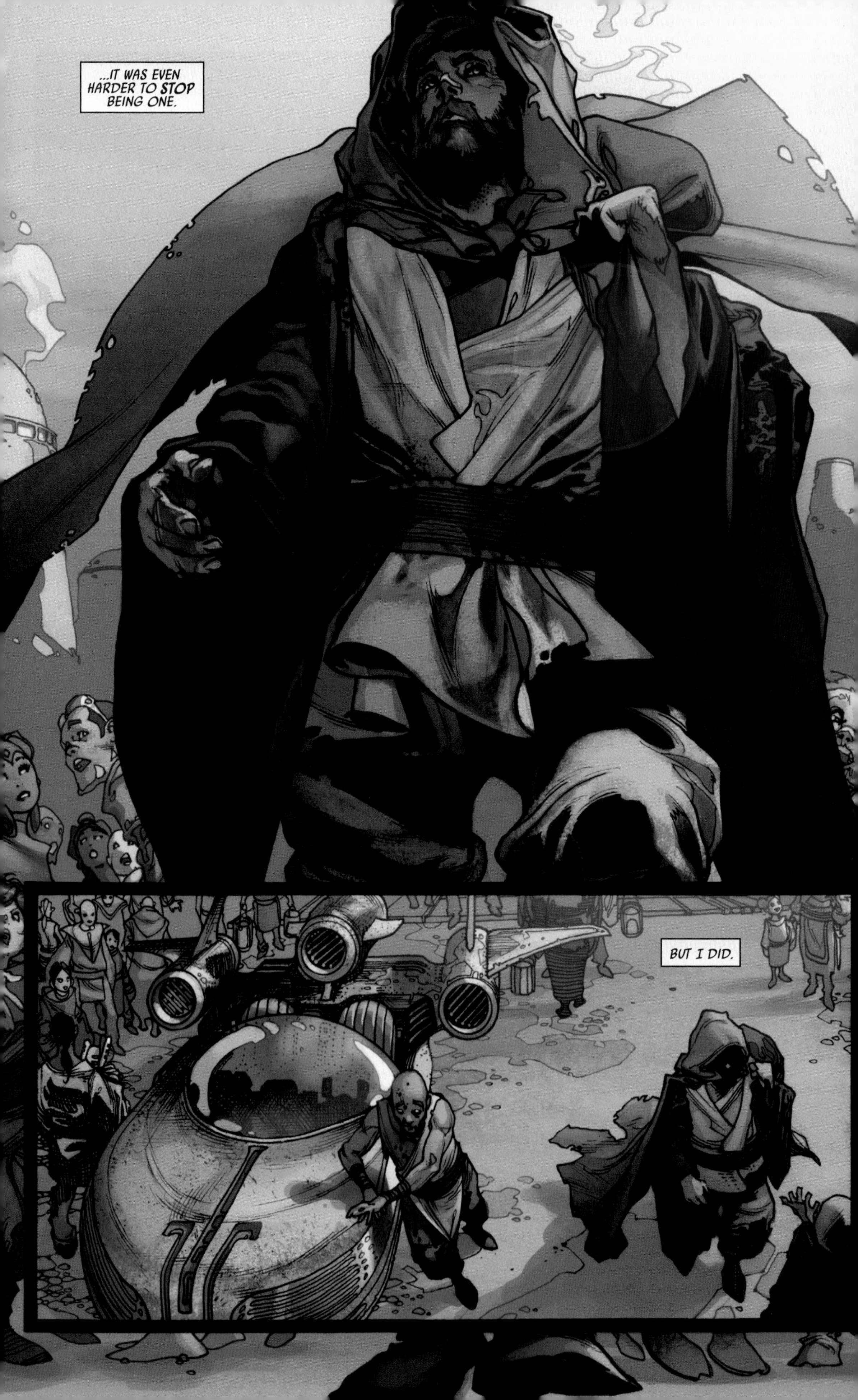
...IT WAS EVEN HARDER TO STOP BEING ONE.
BUT I DID.

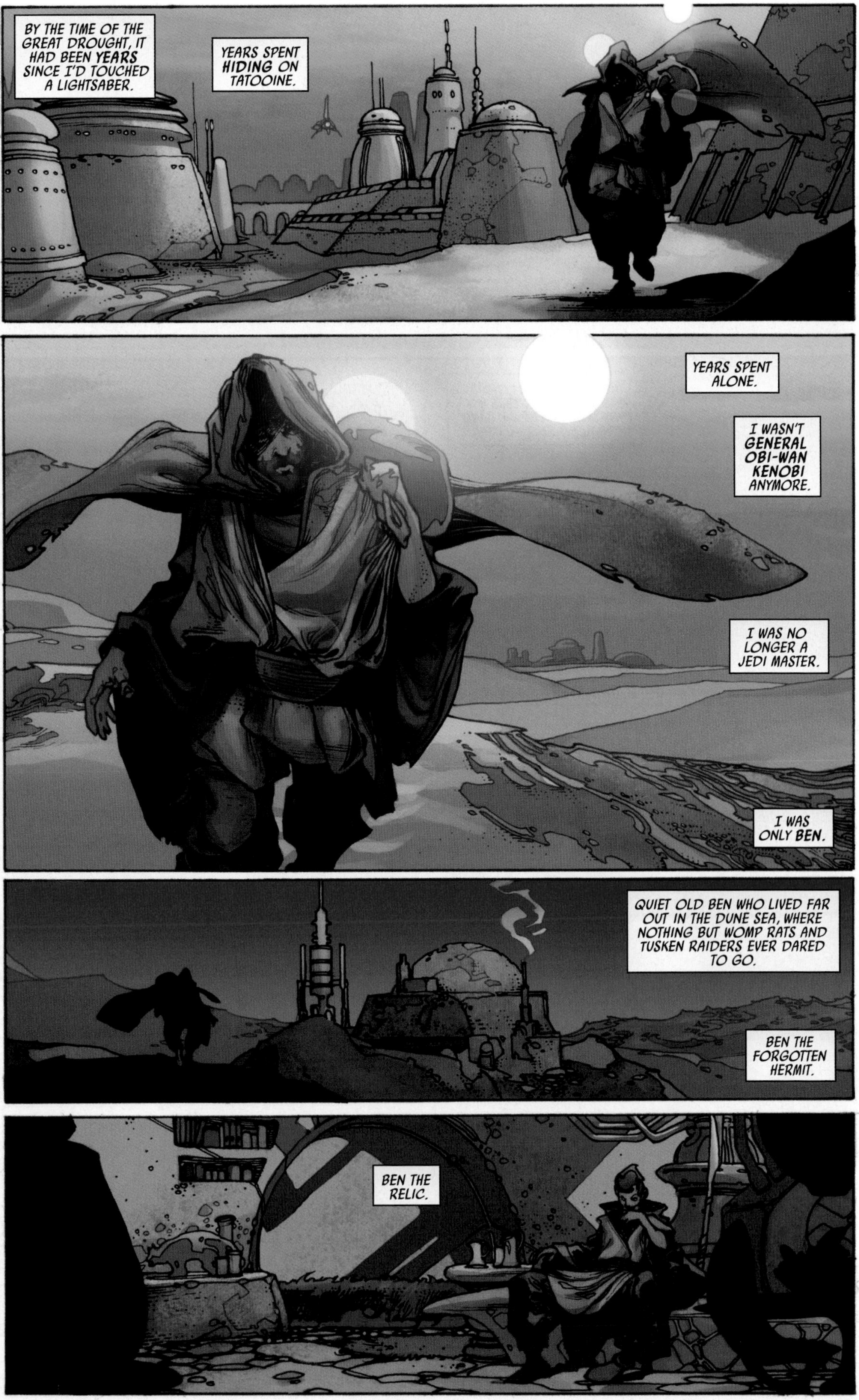
BY THE TIME OF THE GREAT DROUGHT, IT HAD BEEN YEARS SINCE I'D TOUCHED A LIGHTSABER.
YEARS SPENT HIDING ON TATOOINE.
YEARS SPENT ALONE.
I WASN'T GENERAL OBI-WAN KENOBI ANYMORE.
I WAS NO LONGER A JEDI MASTER.
I WAS ONLY BEN.
QUIET OLD BEN WHO LIVED FAR OUT IN THE DUNE SEA, WHERE NOTHING BUT WOMP RATS AND TUSKEN RAIDERS EVER DARED TO GO.
BEN THE FORGOTTEN HERMIT.
BEN THE RELIC.

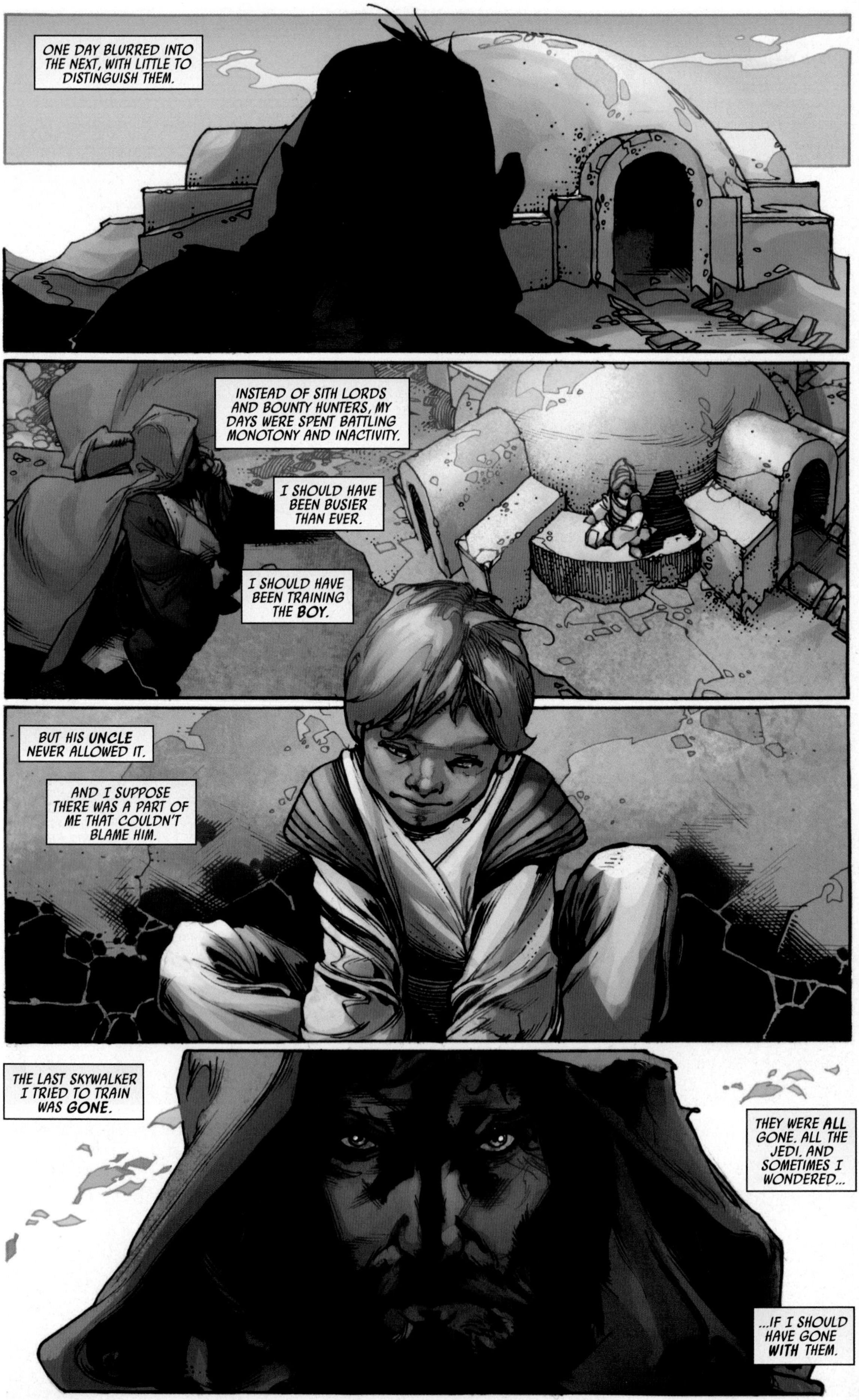
ONE DAY BLURRED INTO THE NEXT, WITH LITTLE TO DISTINGUISH THEM.
INSTEAD OF SITH LORDS AND BOUNTY HUNTERS, MY DAYS WERE SPENT BATTLING MONOTONY AND INACTIVITY.
I SHOULD HAVE BEEN BUSIER THAN EVER.
I SHOULD HAVE BEEN TRAINING THE BOY.
BUT HIS UNCLE NEVER ALLOWED IT.
AND I SUPPOSE THERE WAS A PART OF ME THAT COULDN'T BLAME HIM.
THE LAST SKYWALKER I TRIED TO TRAIN WAS GONE.
THEY WERE ALL GONE. ALL THE JEDI. AND SOMETIMES I WONDERED...
...IF I SHOULD HAVE GONE WITH THEM.

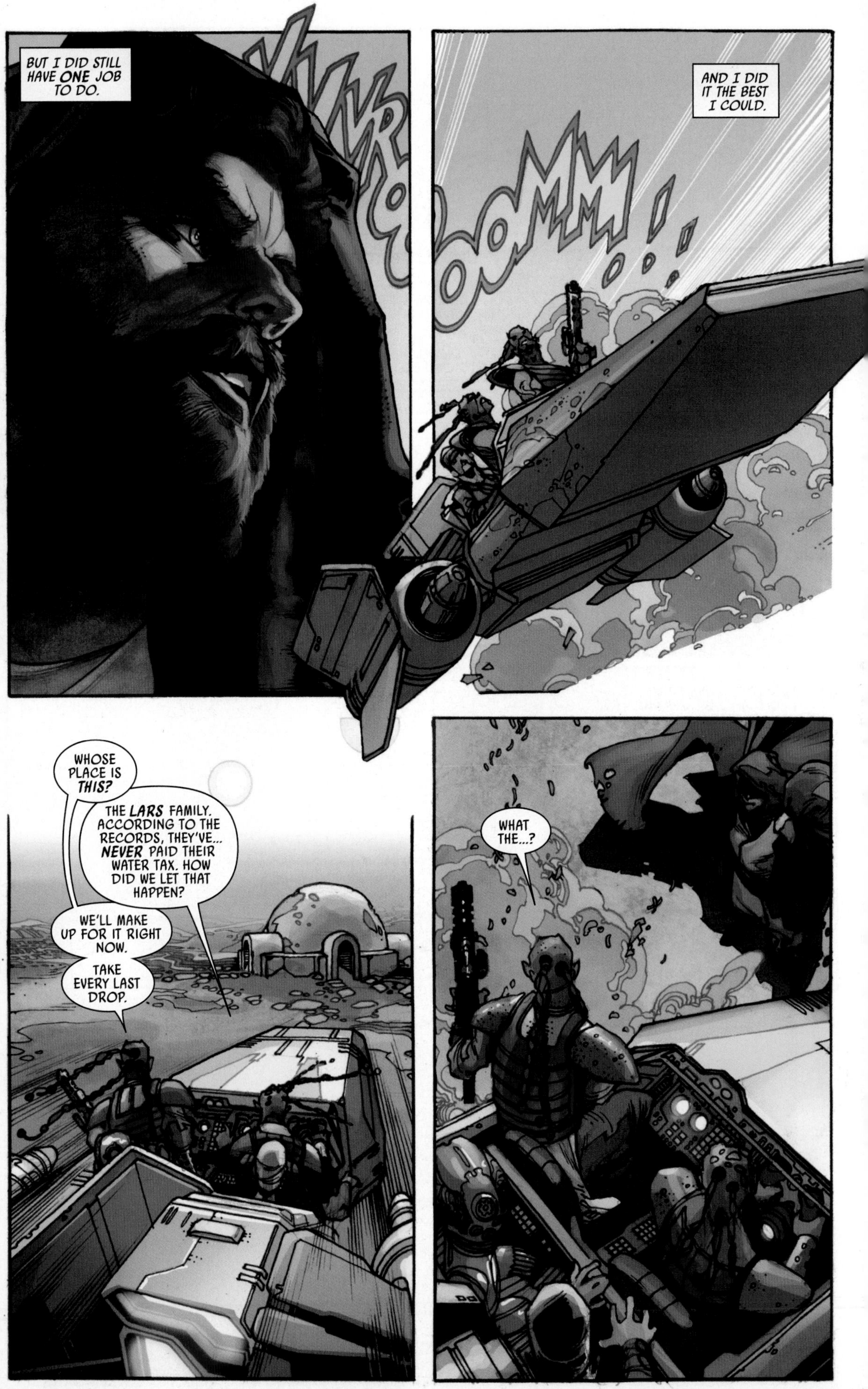
BUT I DID STILL HAVE ONE JOB TO DO.
VVVRRROOOMM!!
AND I DID IT THE BEST I COULD.
WHOSE PLACE IS THIS?
THE LARS FAMILY. ACCORDING TO THE RECORDS, THEY'VE... NEVER PAID THEIR WATER TAX. HOW DID WE LET THAT HAPPEN?
WE'LL MAKE UP FOR IT RIGHT NOW.
TAKE EVERY LAST DROP.
WHAT THE...?

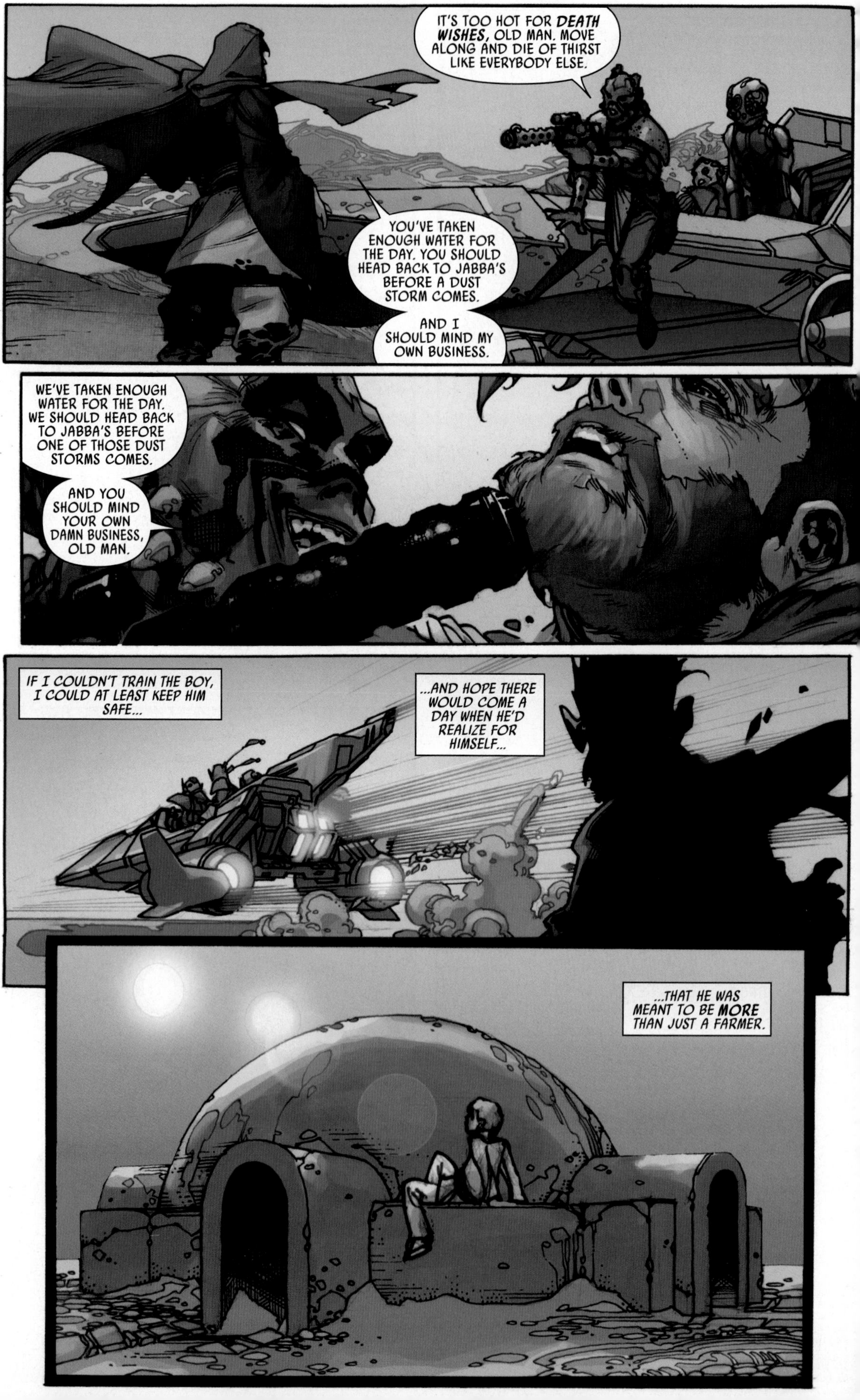
IT'S TOO HOT FOR DEATH WISHES, OLD MAN. MOVE ALONG AND DIE OF THIRST LIKE EVERYBODY ELSE.
YOU'VE TAKEN ENOUGH WATER FOR THE DAY. YOU SHOULD HEAD BACK TO JABBA'S BEFORE A DUST STORM COMES.
AND I SHOULD MIND MY OWN BUSINESS.
WE'VE TAKEN ENOUGH WATER FOR THE DAY. WE SHOULD HEAD BACK TO JABBA'S BEFORE ONE OF THOSE DUST STORMS COMES.
AND YOU SHOULD MIND YOUR OWN DAMN BUSINESS, OLD MAN.
IF I COULDN'T TRAIN THE BOY, I COULD AT LEAST KEEP HIM SAFE...
...AND HOPE THERE WOULD COME A DAY WHEN HE'D REALIZE FOR HIMSELF...
...THAT HE WAS MEANT TO BE MORE THAN JUST A FARMER.

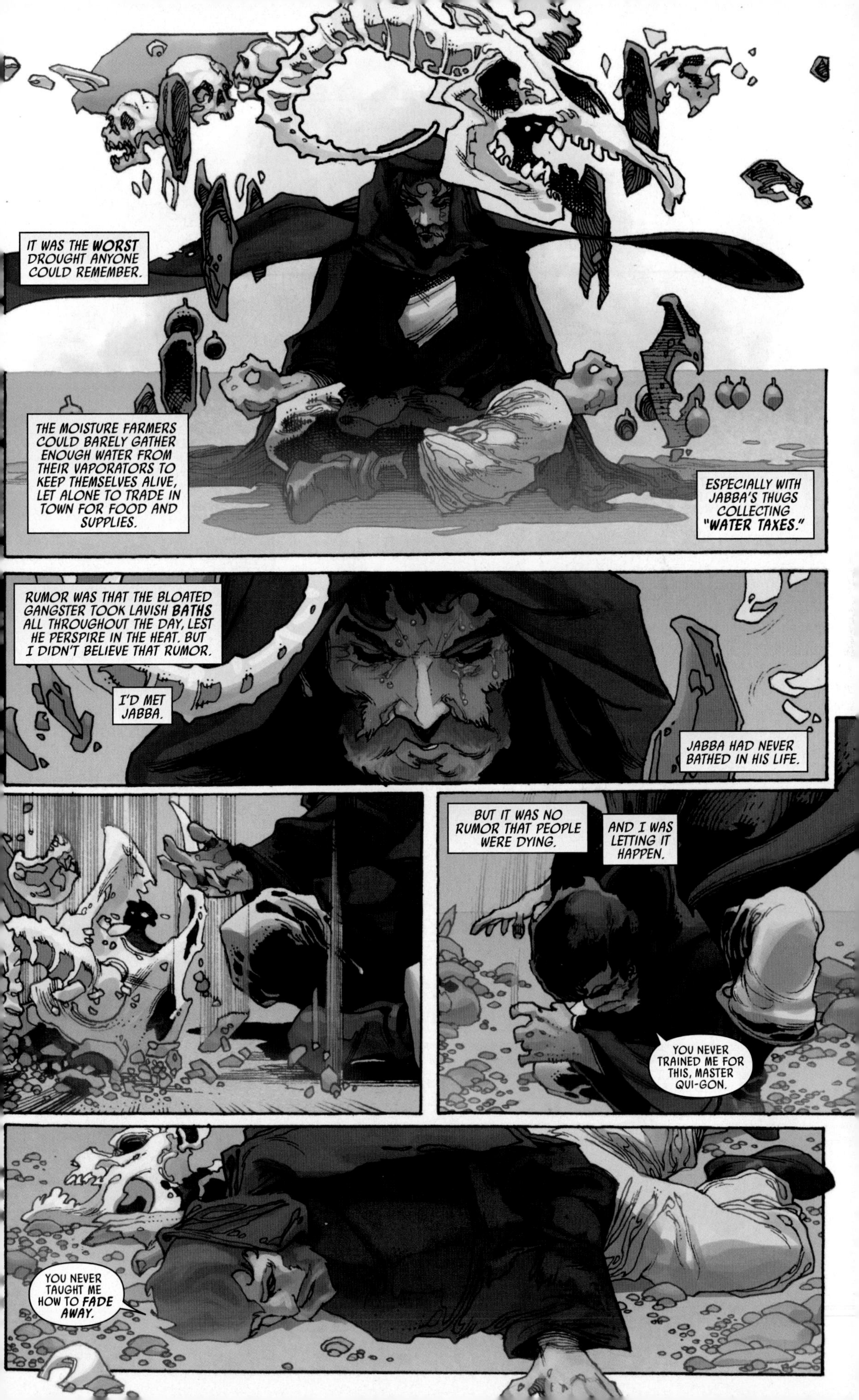
IT WAS THE **WORST** DROUGHT ANYONE COULD REMEMBER.
THE MOISTURE FARMERS COULD BARELY GATHER ENOUGH WATER FROM THEIR VAPORATORS TO KEEP THEMSELVES ALIVE, LET ALONE TO TRADE IN TOWN FOR FOOD AND SUPPLIES.
ESPECIALLY WITH JABBA'S THUGS COLLECTING **"WATER TAXES."**
RUMOR WAS THAT THE BLOATED GANGSTER TOOK LAVISH **BATHS** ALL THROUGHOUT THE DAY, LEST HE PERSPIRE IN THE HEAT. BUT I DIDN'T BELIEVE THAT RUMOR.
I'D MET JABBA.
JABBA HAD NEVER BATHED IN HIS LIFE.
BUT IT WAS NO RUMOR THAT PEOPLE WERE DYING.
AND I WAS LETTING IT HAPPEN.
YOU NEVER TRAINED ME FOR THIS, MASTER QUI-GON.
YOU NEVER TAUGHT ME HOW TO **FADE AWAY.**

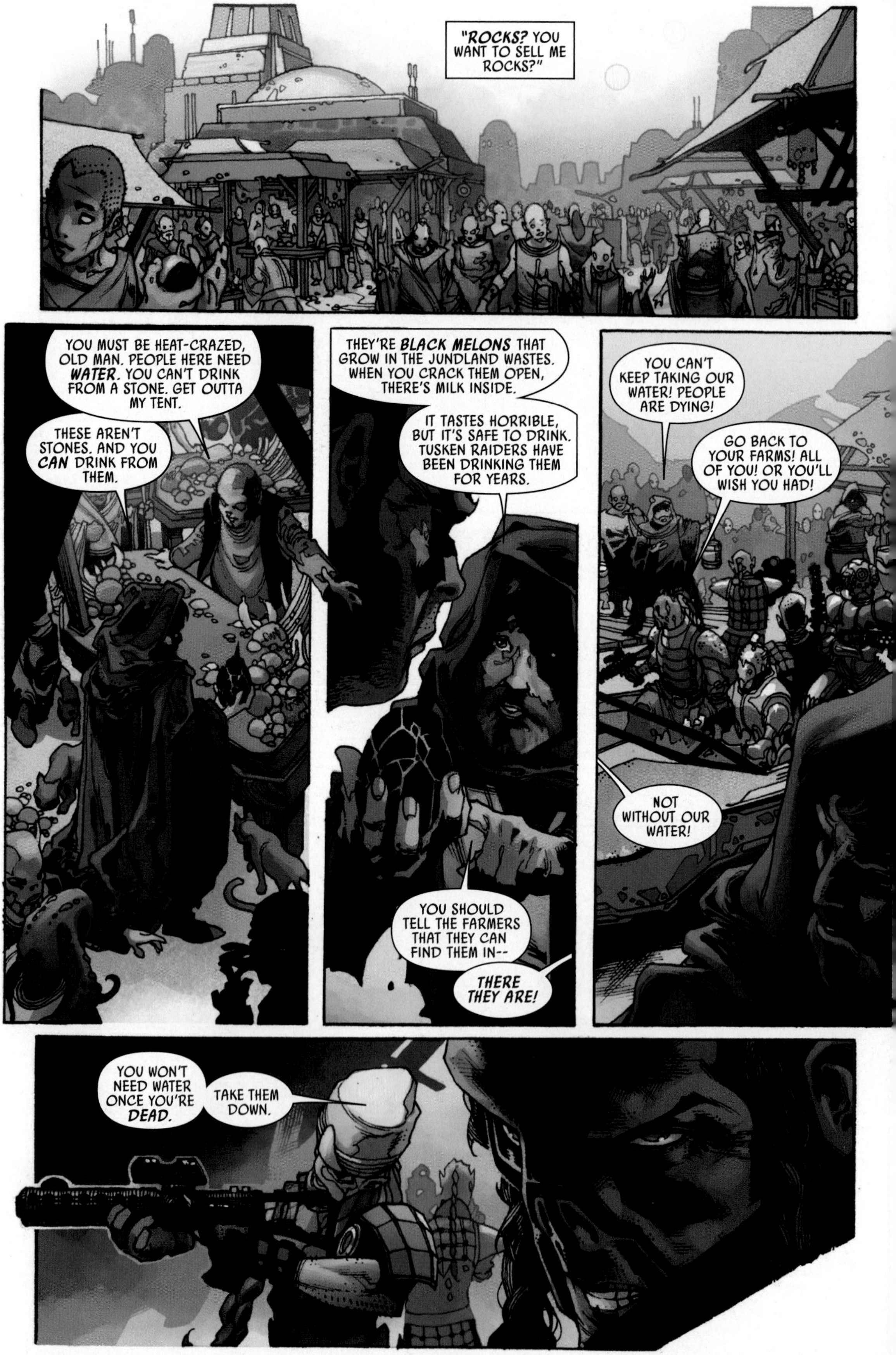
"ROCKS? YOU WANT TO SELL ME ROCKS?"
YOU MUST BE HEAT-CRAZED, OLD MAN. PEOPLE HERE NEED WATER. YOU CAN'T DRINK FROM A STONE. GET OUTTA MY TENT.
THESE AREN'T STONES. AND YOU CAN DRINK FROM THEM.
THEY'RE BLACK MELONS THAT GROW IN THE JUNDLAND WASTES. WHEN YOU CRACK THEM OPEN, THERE'S MILK INSIDE.
IT TASTES HORRIBLE, BUT IT'S SAFE TO DRINK. TUSKEN RAIDERS HAVE BEEN DRINKING THEM FOR YEARS.
YOU SHOULD TELL THE FARMERS THAT THEY CAN FIND THEM IN--
THERE THEY ARE!
YOU CAN'T KEEP TAKING OUR WATER! PEOPLE ARE DYING!
GO BACK TO YOUR FARMS! ALL OF YOU! OR YOU'LL WISH YOU HAD!
NOT WITHOUT OUR WATER!
YOU WON'T NEED WATER ONCE YOU'RE DEAD.
TAKE THEM DOWN.

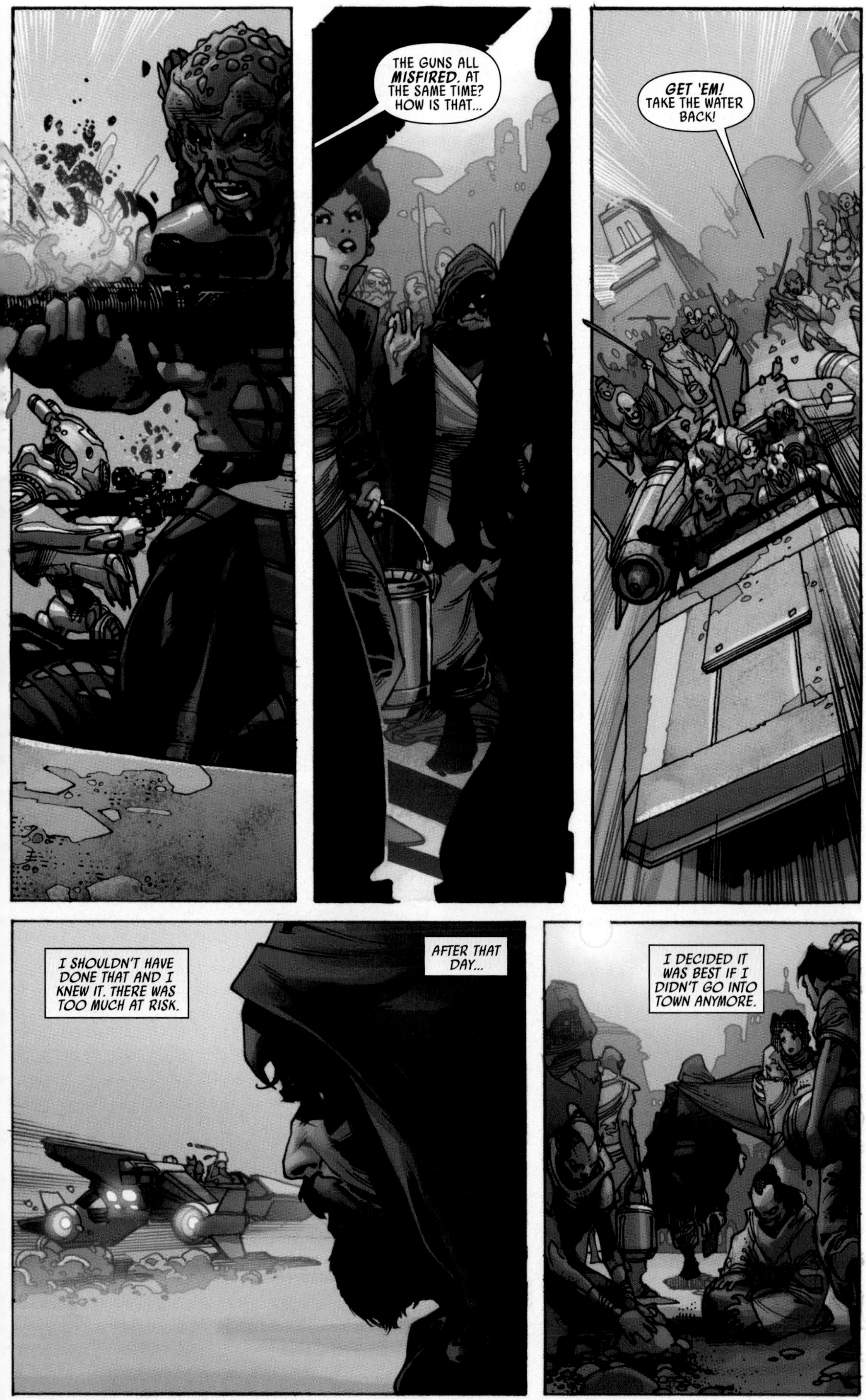
THE GUNS ALL MISFIRED. AT THE SAME TIME? HOW IS THAT...
GET 'EM! TAKE THE WATER BACK!
I SHOULDN'T HAVE DONE THAT AND I KNEW IT. THERE WAS TOO MUCH AT RISK.
AFTER THAT DAY...
I DECIDED IT WAS BEST IF I DIDN'T GO INTO TOWN ANYMORE.

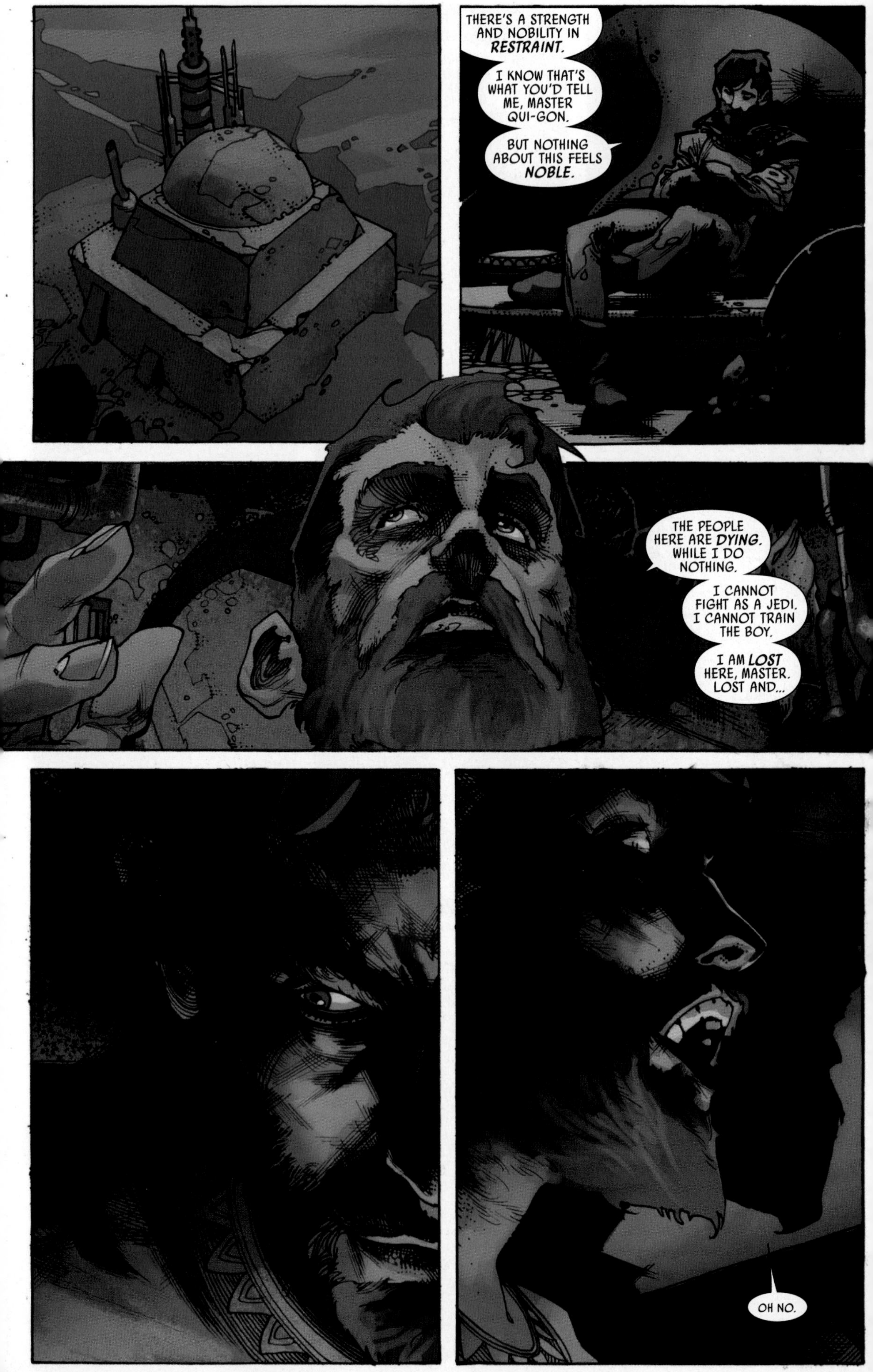
THERE'S A STRENGTH AND NOBILITY IN RESTRAINT.
I KNOW THAT'S WHAT YOU'D TELL ME, MASTER QUI-GON.
BUT NOTHING ABOUT THIS FEELS NOBLE.
THE PEOPLE HERE ARE DYING. WHILE I DO NOTHING.
I CANNOT FIGHT AS A JEDI. I CANNOT TRAIN THE BOY.
I AM LOST HERE, MASTER. LOST AND...
OH NO.

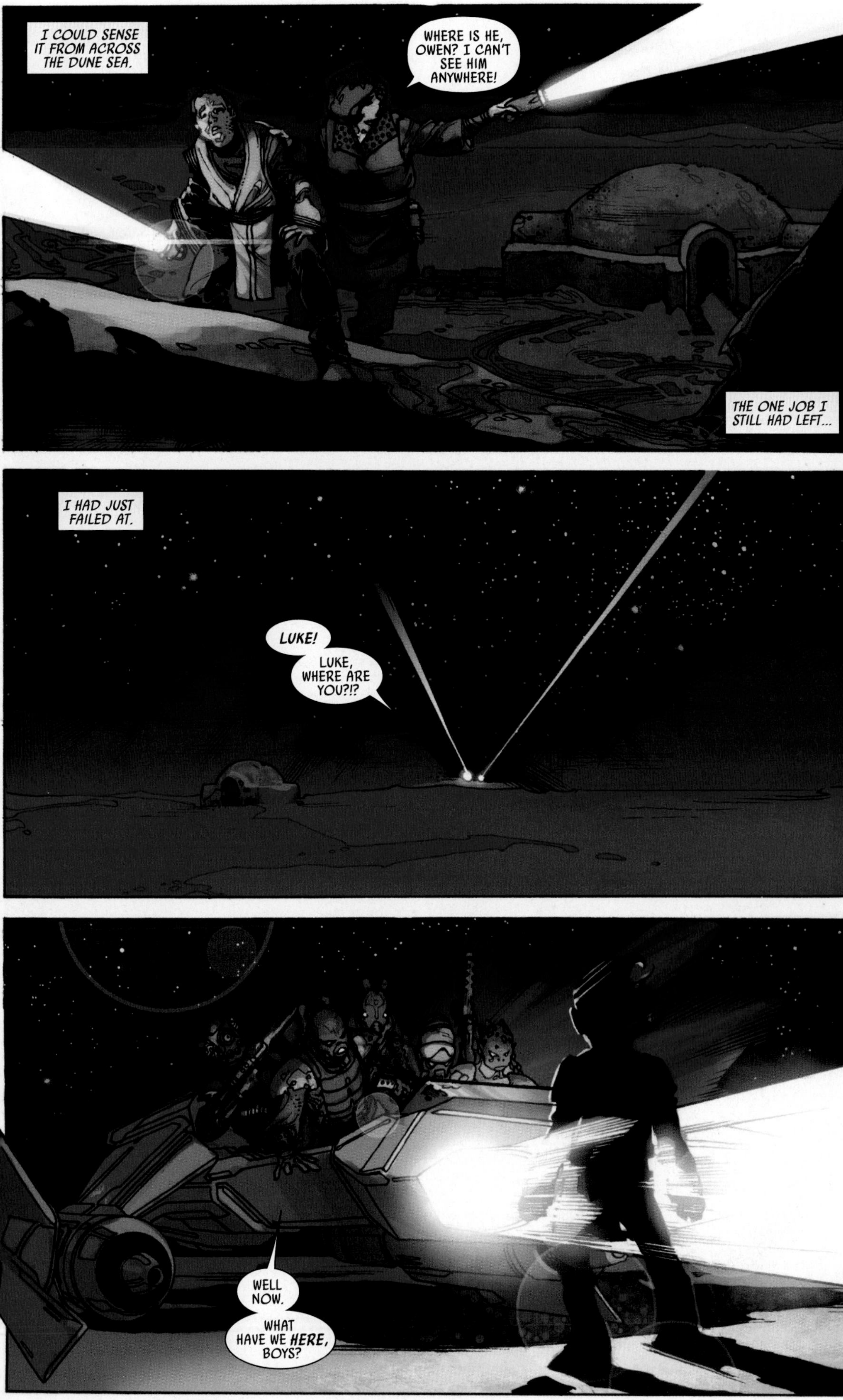
I COULD SENSE IT FROM ACROSS THE DUNE SEA.
WHERE IS HE, OWEN? I CAN'T SEE HIM ANYWHERE!
THE ONE JOB I STILL HAD LEFT...
I HAD JUST FAILED AT.
LUKE!
LUKE, WHERE ARE YOU?!?
WELL NOW.
WHAT HAVE WE HERE, BOYS?

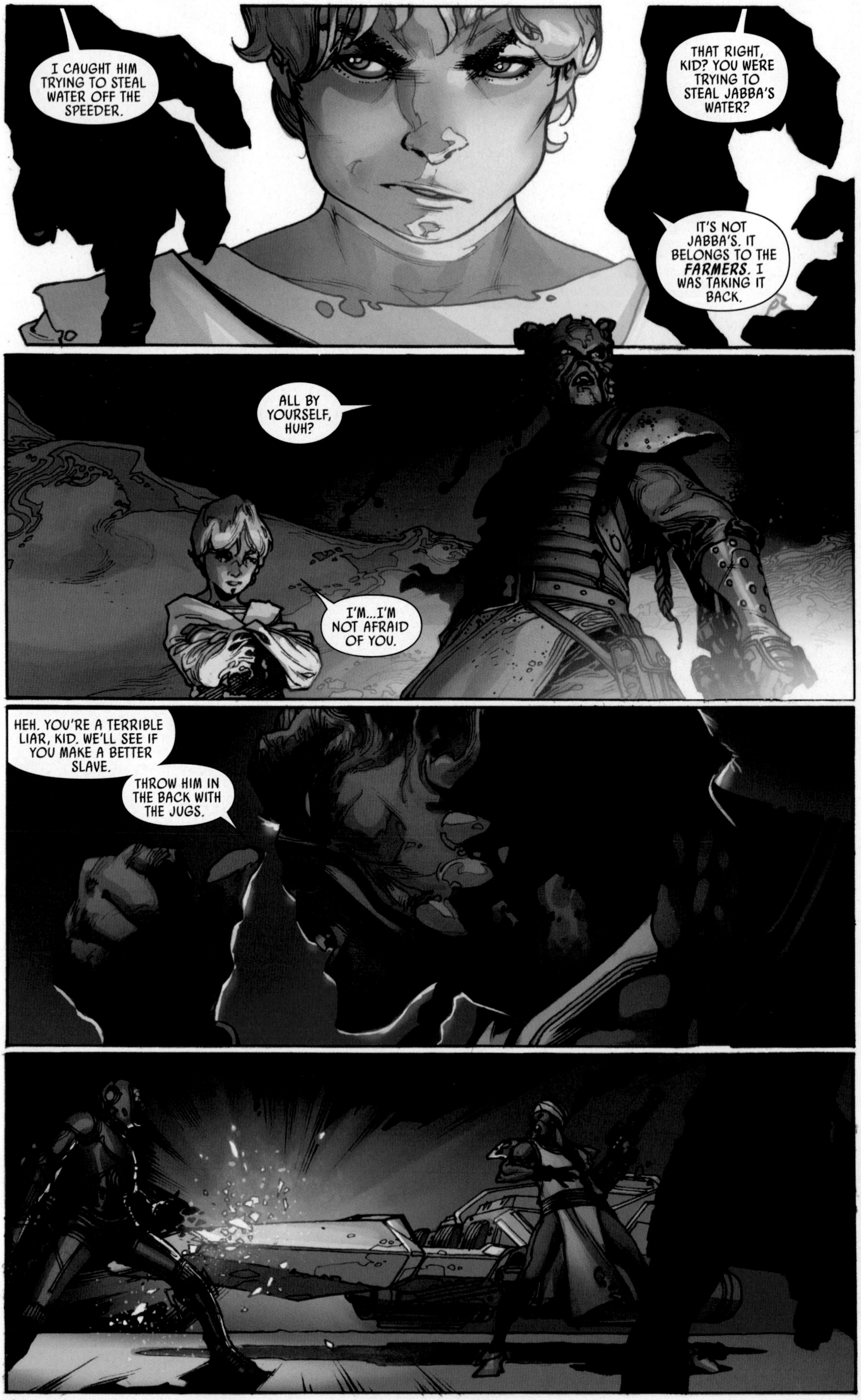
I CAUGHT HIM TRYING TO STEAL WATER OFF THE SPEEDER.
THAT RIGHT, KID? YOU WERE TRYING TO STEAL JABBA'S WATER?
IT'S NOT JABBA'S. IT BELONGS TO THE FARMERS. I WAS TAKING IT BACK.
ALL BY YOURSELF, HUH?
I'M...I'M NOT AFRAID OF YOU.
HEH. YOU'RE A TERRIBLE LIAR, KID. WE'LL SEE IF YOU MAKE A BETTER SLAVE.
THROW HIM IN THE BACK WITH THE JUGS.

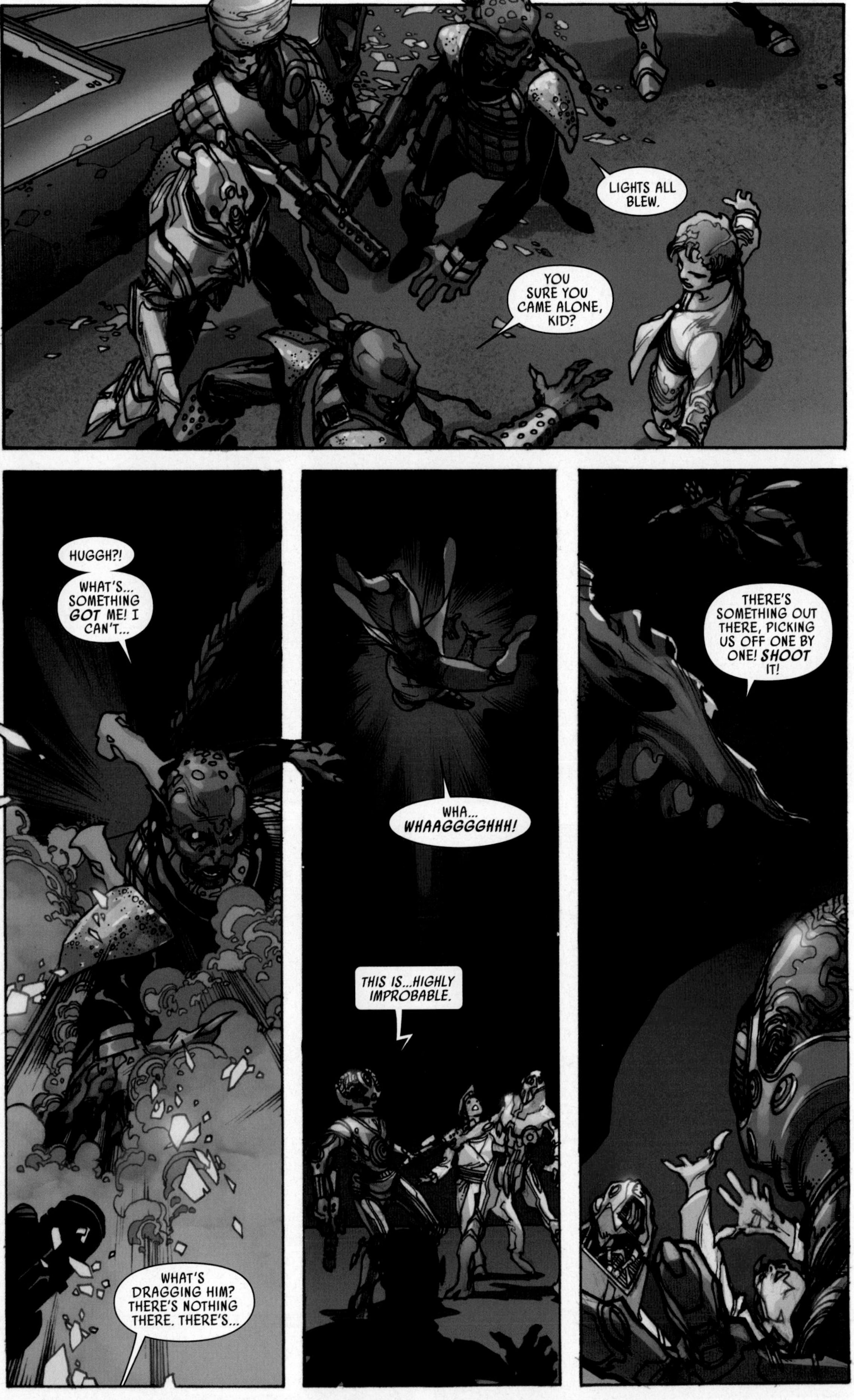
LIGHTS ALL BLEW.
YOU SURE YOU CAME ALONE, KID?
HUGGH?!
WHAT'S... SOMETHING GOT ME! I CAN'T...
WHAT'S DRAGGING HIM? THERE'S NOTHING THERE. THERE'S...
WHA... WHAAGGGGHHH!
THIS IS...HIGHLY IMPROBABLE.
THERE'S SOMETHING OUT THERE, PICKING US OFF ONE BY ONE! SHOOT IT!

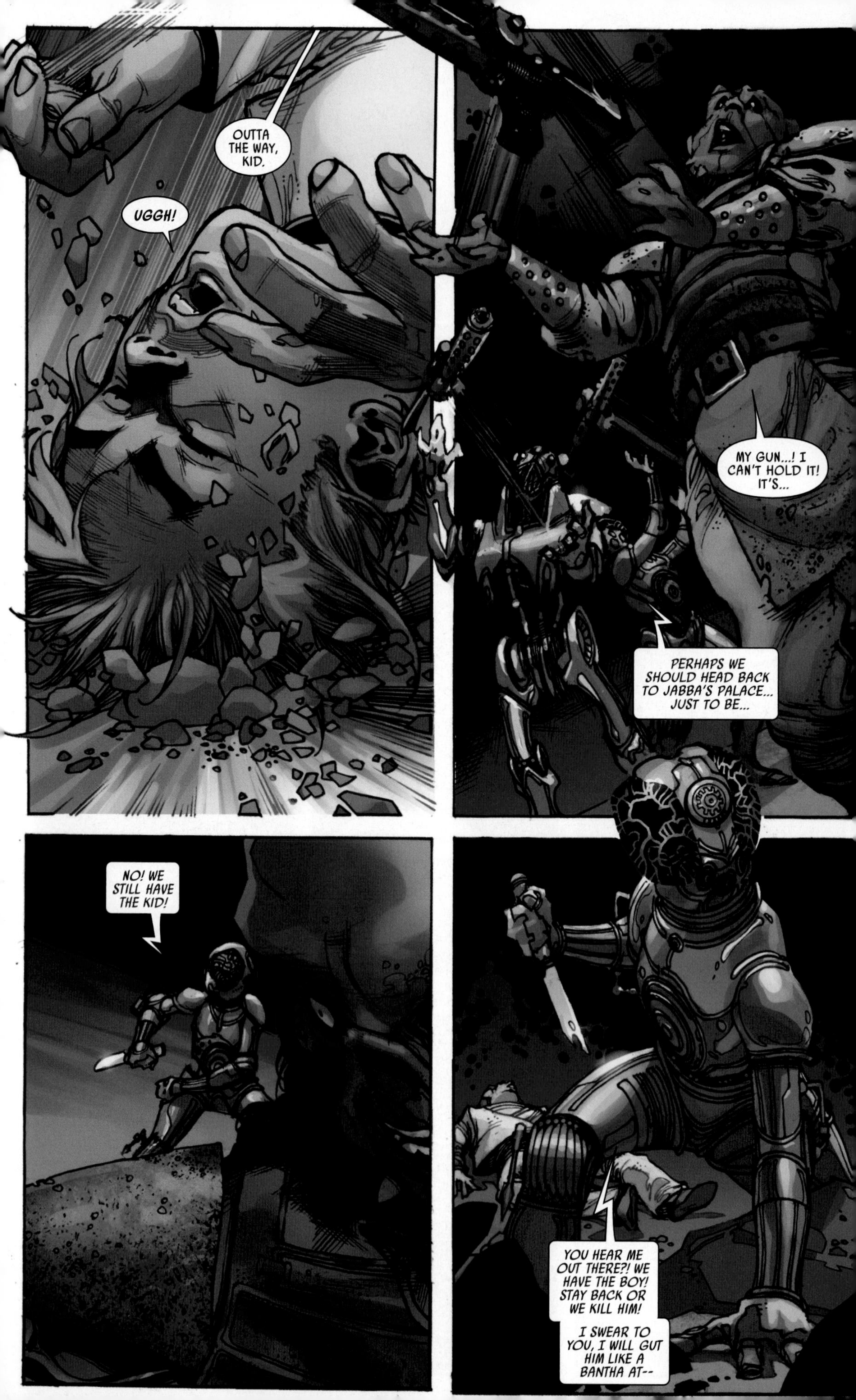
OUTTA THE WAY, KID.
UGGH!
MY GUN...! I CAN'T HOLD IT! IT'S...
PERHAPS WE SHOULD HEAD BACK TO JABBA'S PALACE... JUST TO BE...
NO! WE STILL HAVE THE KID!
YOU HEAR ME OUT THERE?! WE HAVE THE BOY! STAY BACK OR WE KILL HIM!
I SWEAR TO YOU, I WILL GUT HIM LIKE A BANTHA AT--

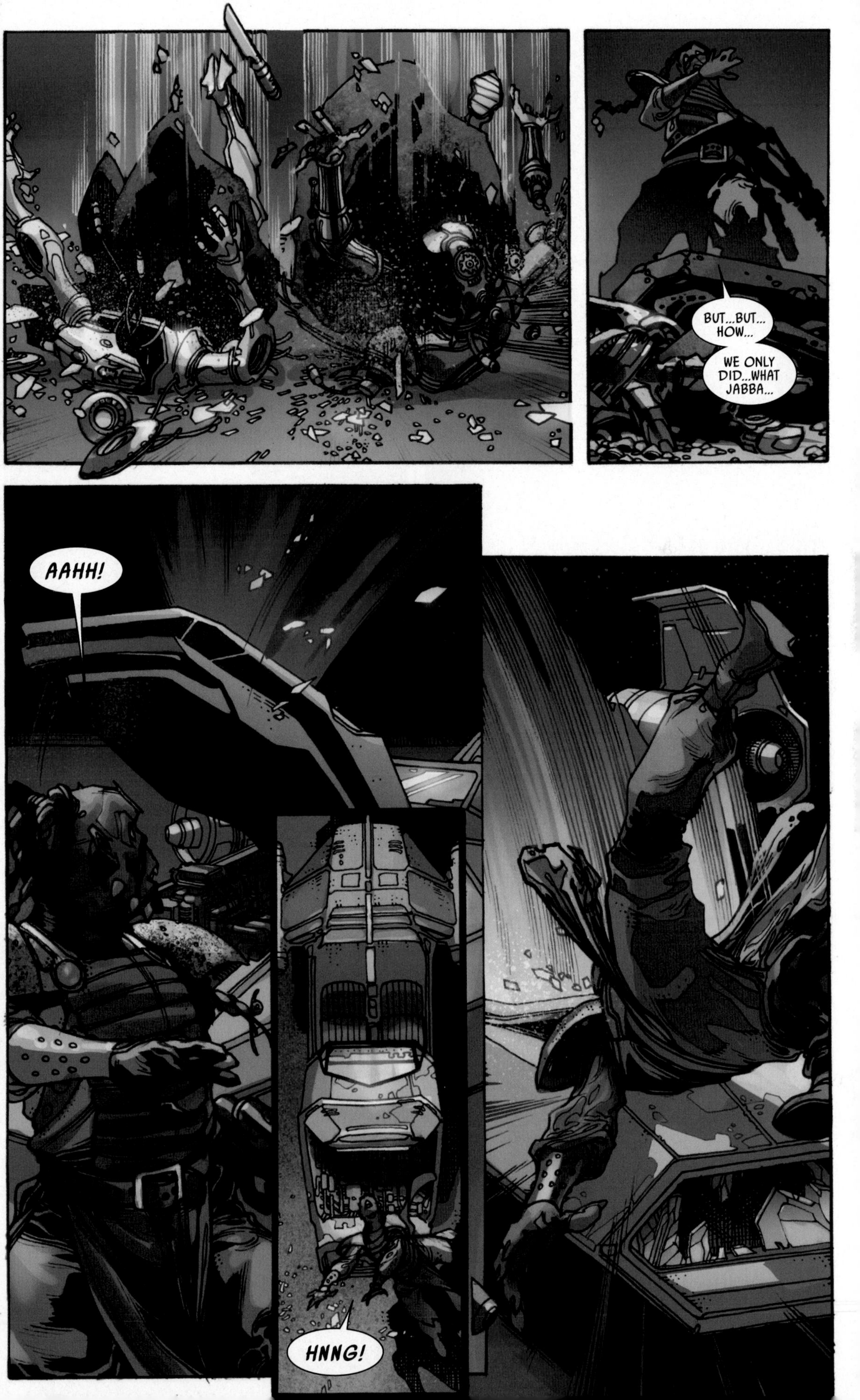
BUT...BUT... HOW...
WE ONLY DID...WHAT JABBA...
AAHH!
HNNG!

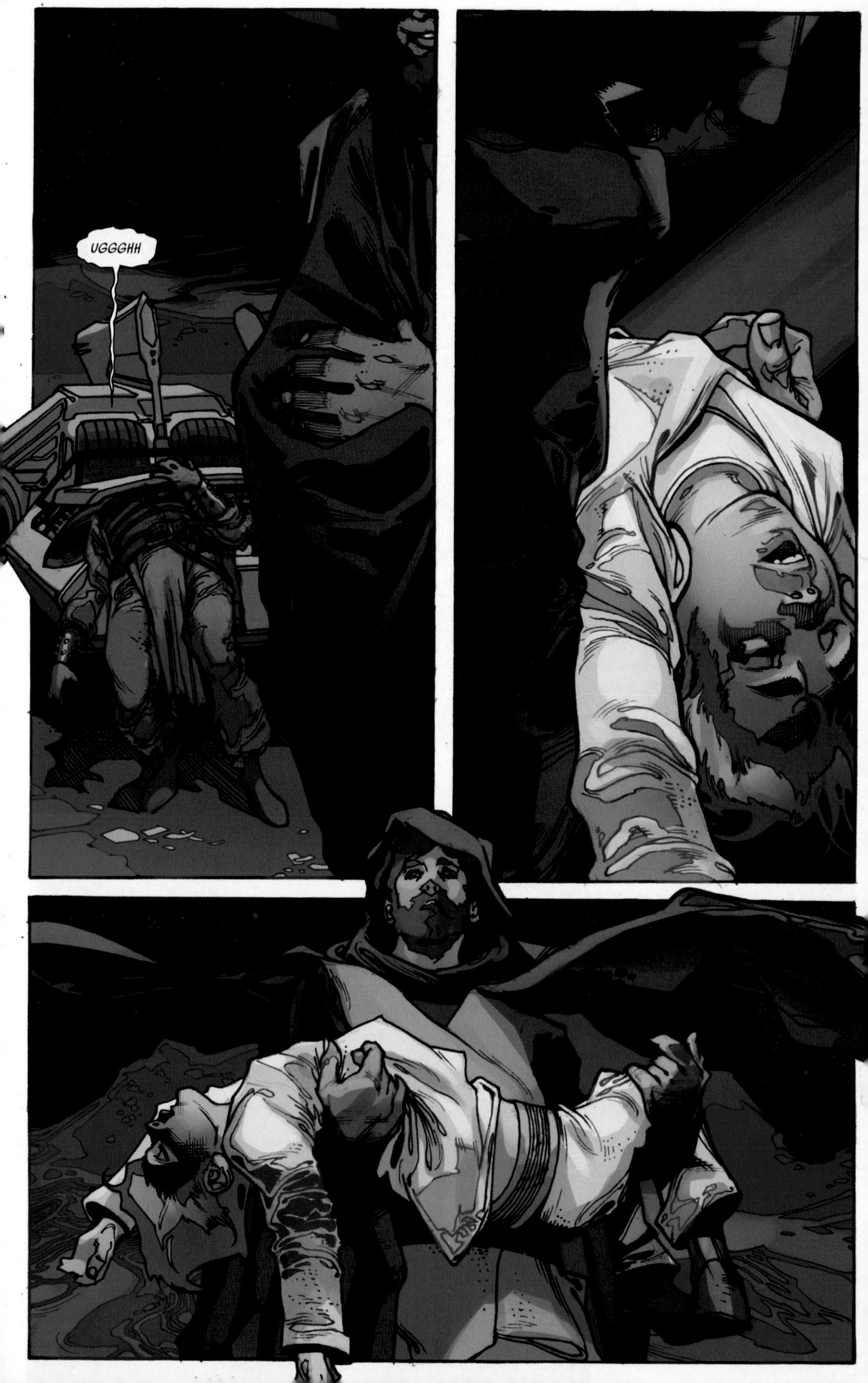
UGGGHH

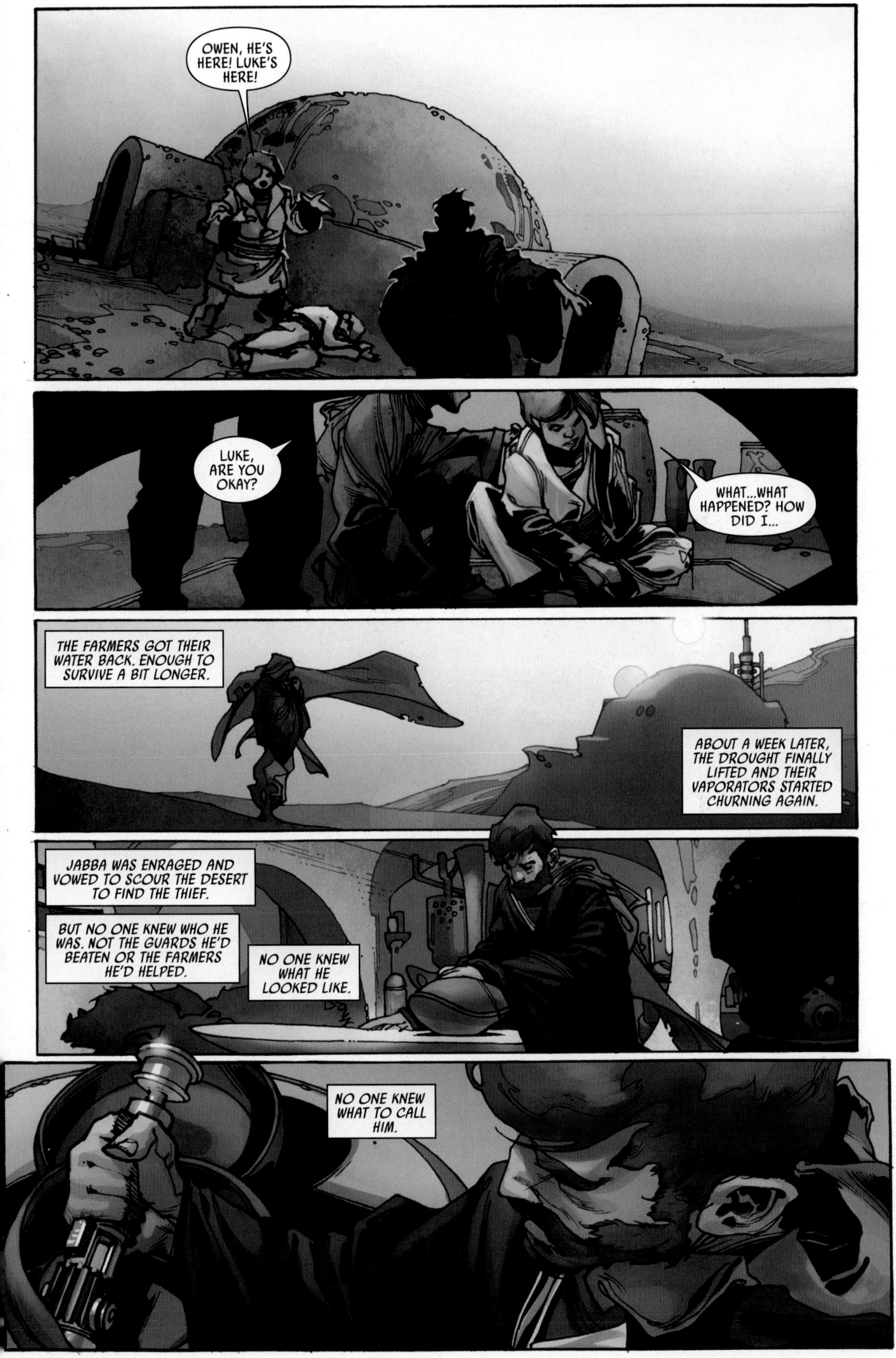
OWEN, HE'S HERE! LUKE'S HERE!
LUKE, ARE YOU OKAY?
WHAT...WHAT HAPPENED? HOW DID I...
THE FARMERS GOT THEIR WATER BACK. ENOUGH TO SURVIVE A BIT LONGER.
ABOUT A WEEK LATER, THE DROUGHT FINALLY LIFTED AND THEIR VAPORATORS STARTED CHURNING AGAIN.
JABBA WAS ENRAGED AND VOWED TO SCOUR THE DESERT TO FIND THE THIEF.
BUT NO ONE KNEW WHO HE WAS. NOT THE GUARDS HE'D BEATEN OR THE FARMERS HE'D HELPED.
NO ONE KNEW WHAT HE LOOKED LIKE.
NO ONE KNEW WHAT TO CALL HIM.

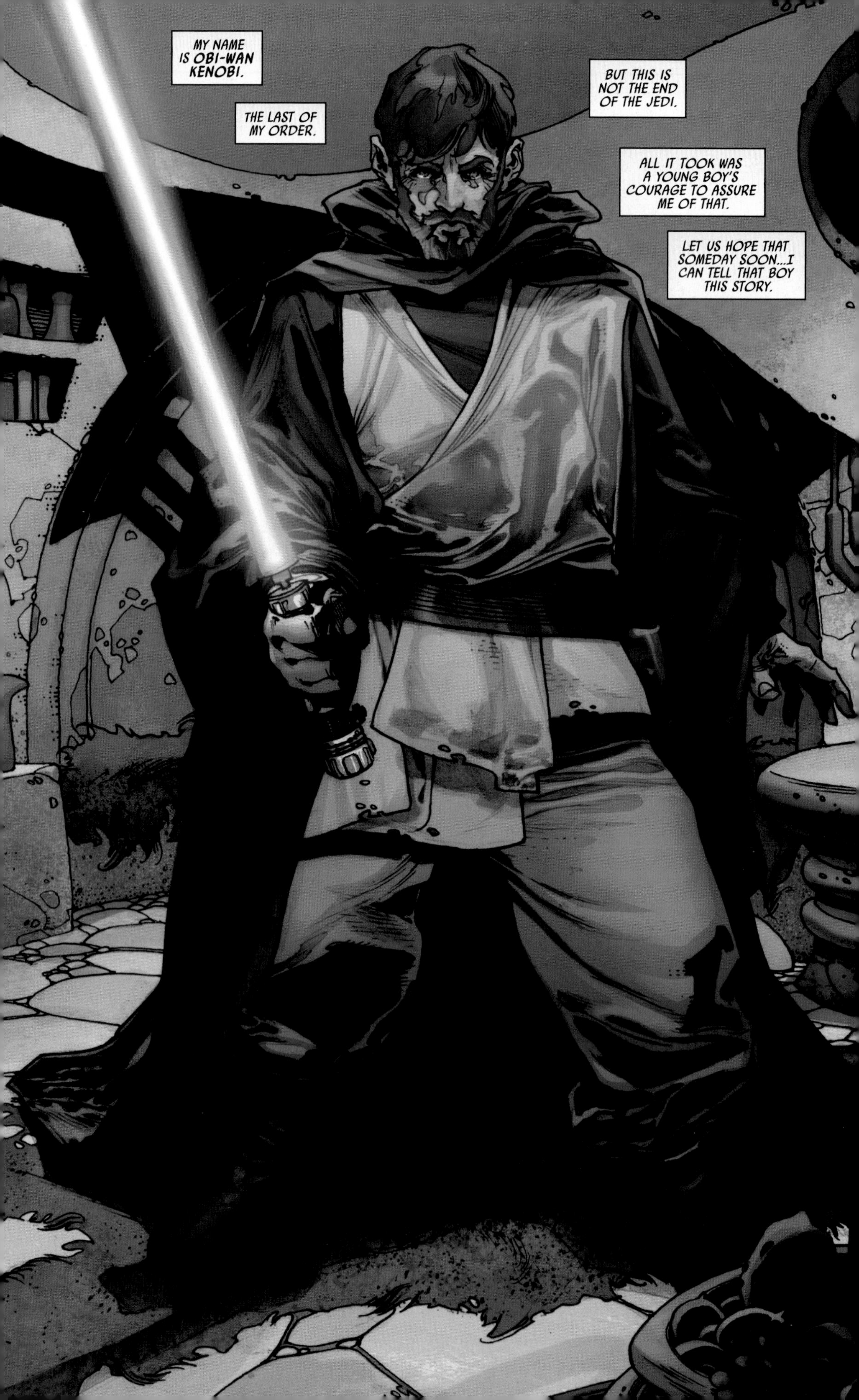
MY NAME IS OBI-WAN KENOBI.
THE LAST OF MY ORDER.
BUT THIS IS NOT THE END OF THE JEDI.
ALL IT TOOK WAS A YOUNG BOY'S COURAGE TO ASSURE ME OF THAT.
LET US HOPE THAT SOMEDAY SOON...I CAN TELL THAT BOY THIS STORY.

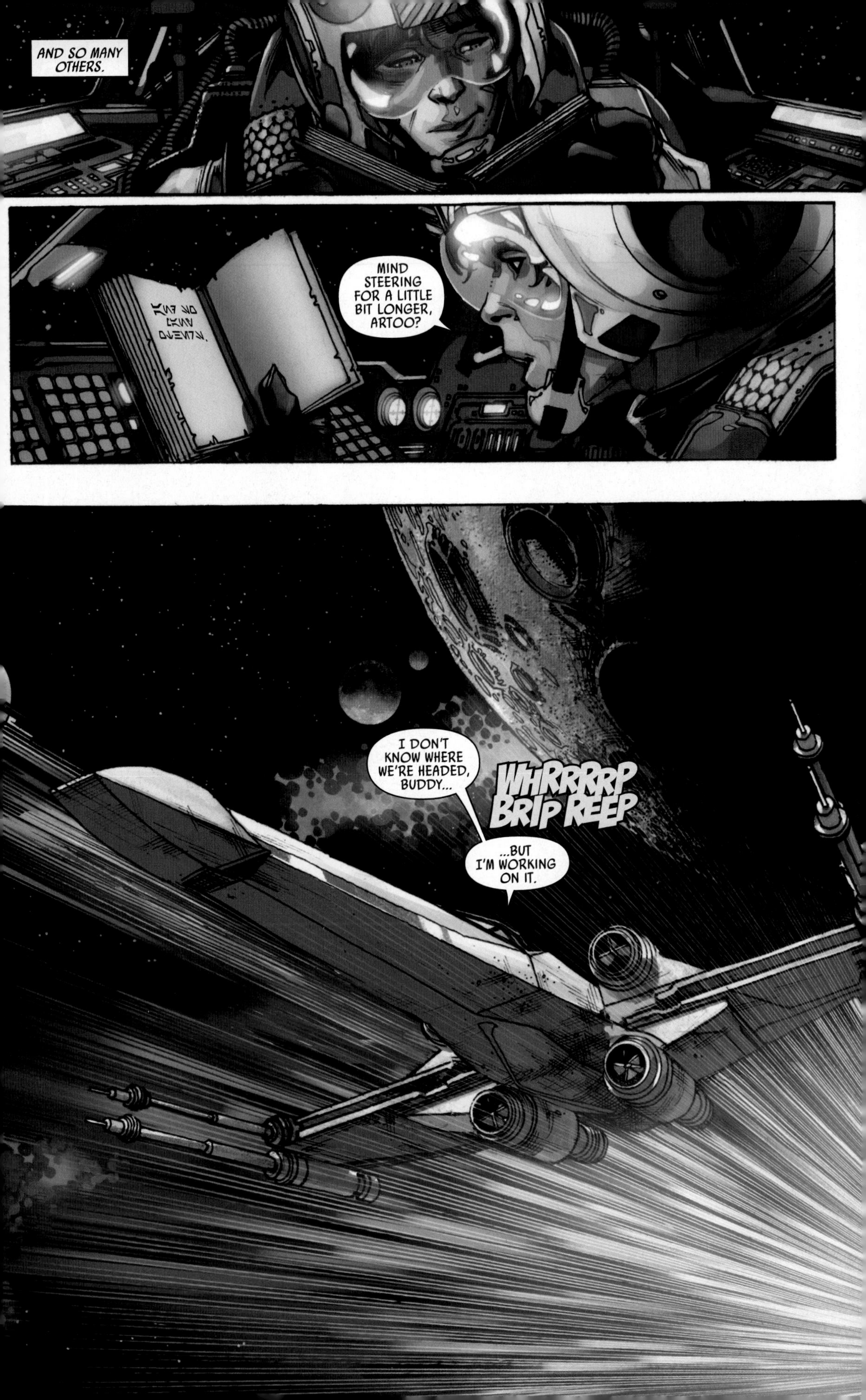
AND SO MANY OTHERS.
MIND STEERING FOR A LITTLE BIT LONGER, ARTOO?
I DON'T KNOW WHERE WE'RE HEADED, BUDDY...
WHRRRRP BRIP REEP
...BUT I'M WORKING ON IT.

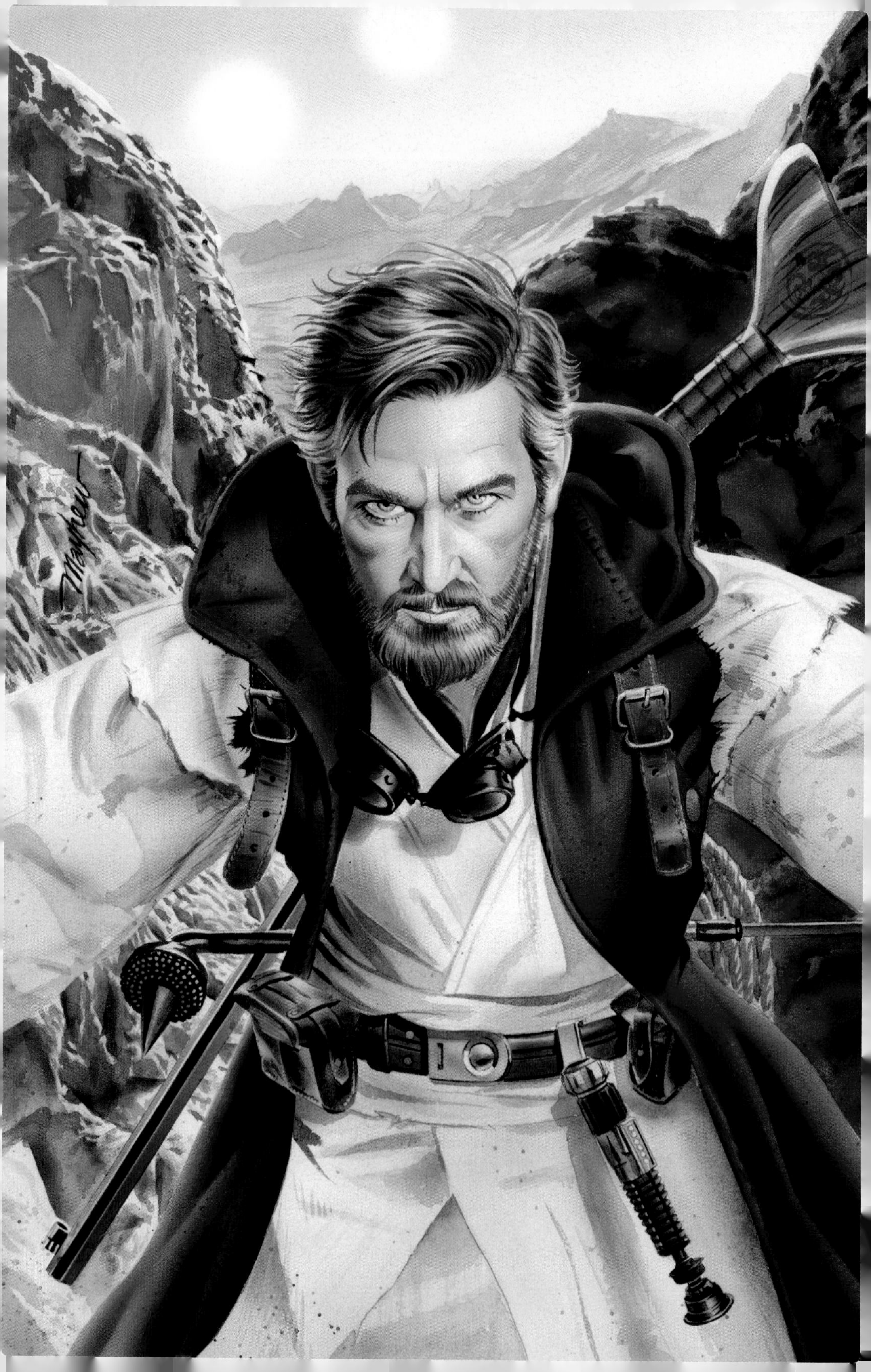

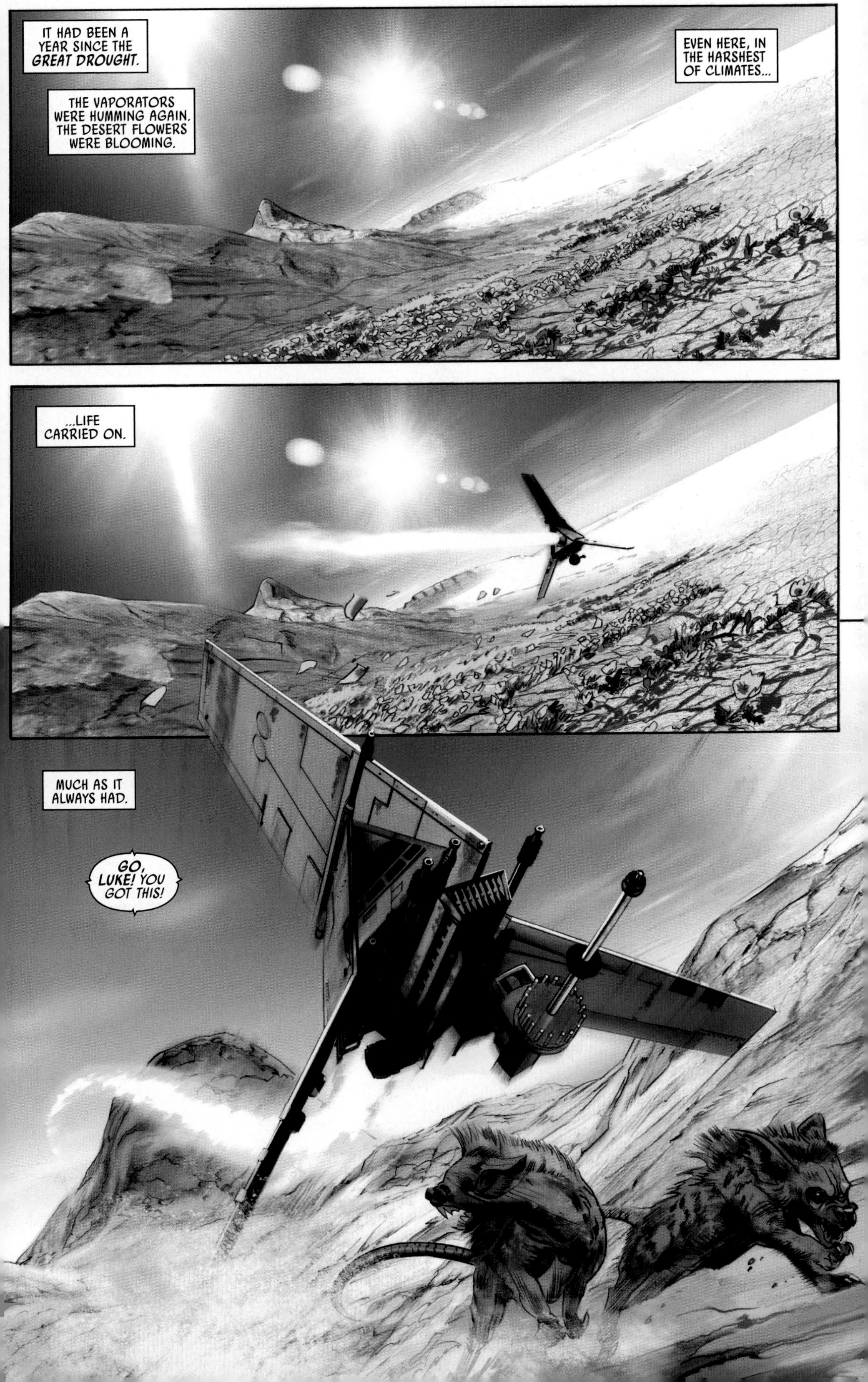
IT HAD BEEN A YEAR SINCE THE GREAT DROUGHT.
THE VAPORATORS WERE HUMMING AGAIN. THE DESERT FLOWERS WERE BLOOMING.
EVEN HERE, IN THE HARSHEST OF CLIMATES...
...LIFE CARRIED ON.
MUCH AS IT ALWAYS HAD.
GO, LUKE! YOU GOT THIS!

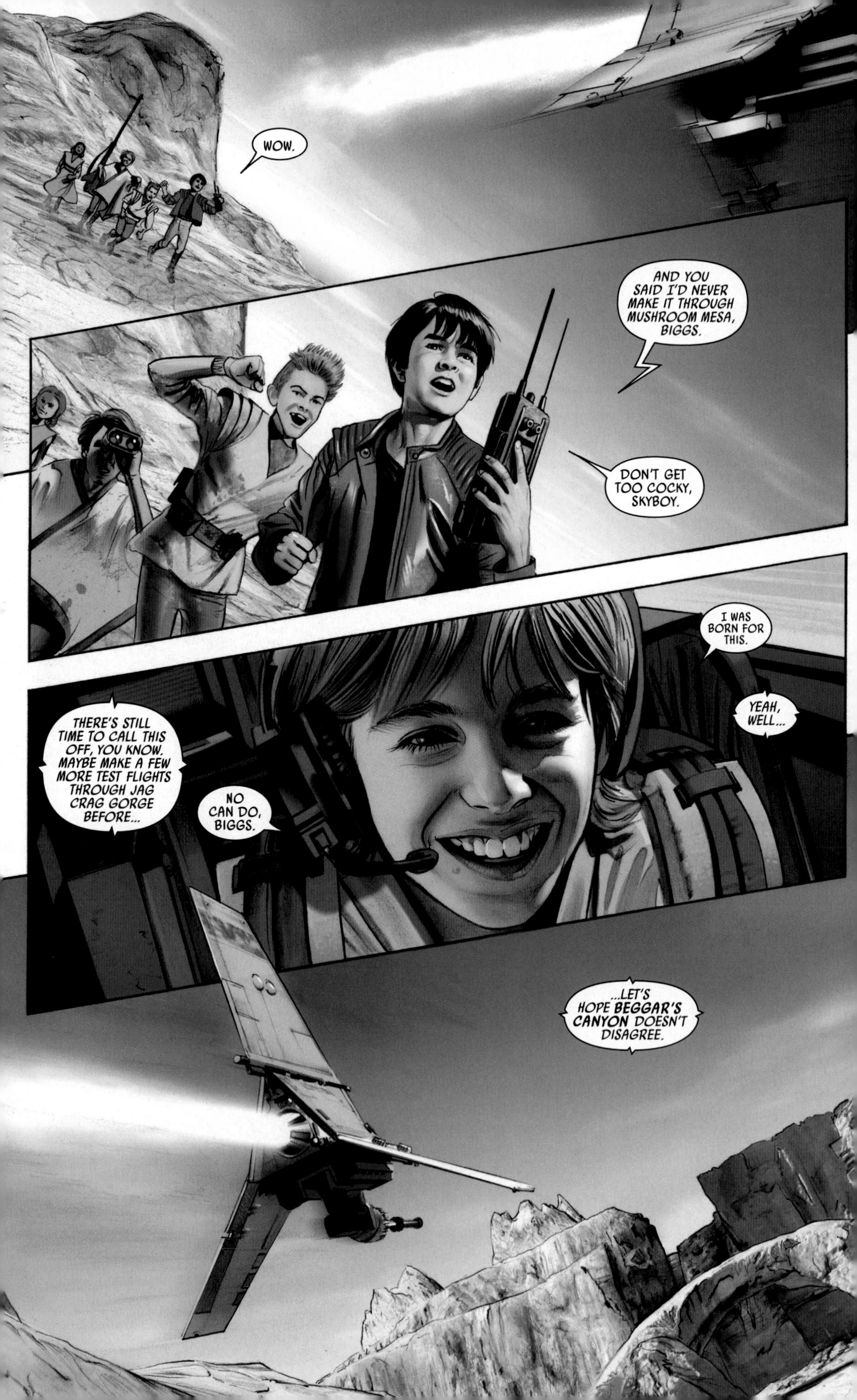
WOW.
AND YOU SAID I'D NEVER MAKE IT THROUGH MUSHROOM MESA, BIGGS.
DON'T GET TOO COCKY, SKYBOY.
I WAS BORN FOR THIS.
THERE'S STILL TIME TO CALL THIS OFF, YOU KNOW. MAYBE MAKE A FEW MORE TEST FLIGHTS THROUGH JAG CRAG GORGE BEFORE...
NO CAN DO, BIGGS.
YEAH, WELL...
...LET'S HOPE BEGGAR'S CANYON DOESN'T DISAGREE.

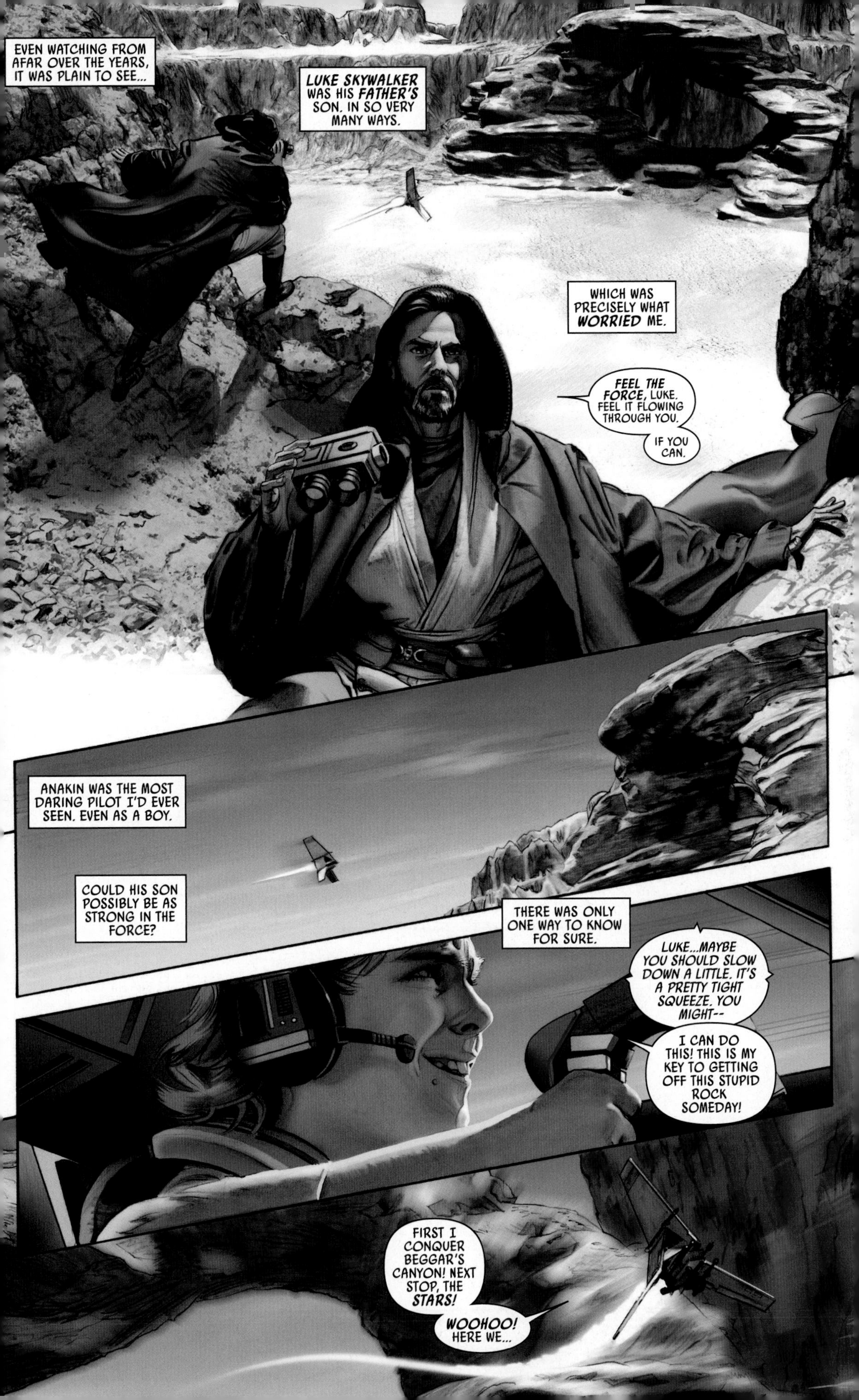
EVEN WATCHING FROM AFAR OVER THE YEARS, IT WAS PLAIN TO SEE...
LUKE SKYWALKER WAS HIS FATHER'S SON. IN SO VERY MANY WAYS.
WHICH WAS PRECISELY WHAT WORRIED ME.
FEEL THE FORCE, LUKE. FEEL IT FLOWING THROUGH YOU.
IF YOU CAN.
ANAKIN WAS THE MOST DARING PILOT I'D EVER SEEN. EVEN AS A BOY.
COULD HIS SON POSSIBLY BE AS STRONG IN THE FORCE?
THERE WAS ONLY ONE WAY TO KNOW FOR SURE.
LUKE...MAYBE YOU SHOULD SLOW DOWN A LITTLE. IT'S A PRETTY TIGHT SQUEEZE. YOU MIGHT--
I CAN DO THIS! THIS IS MY KEY TO GETTING OFF THIS STUPID ROCK SOMEDAY!
FIRST I CONQUER BEGGAR'S CANYON! NEXT STOP, THE STARS!
WOOHOO! HERE WE...

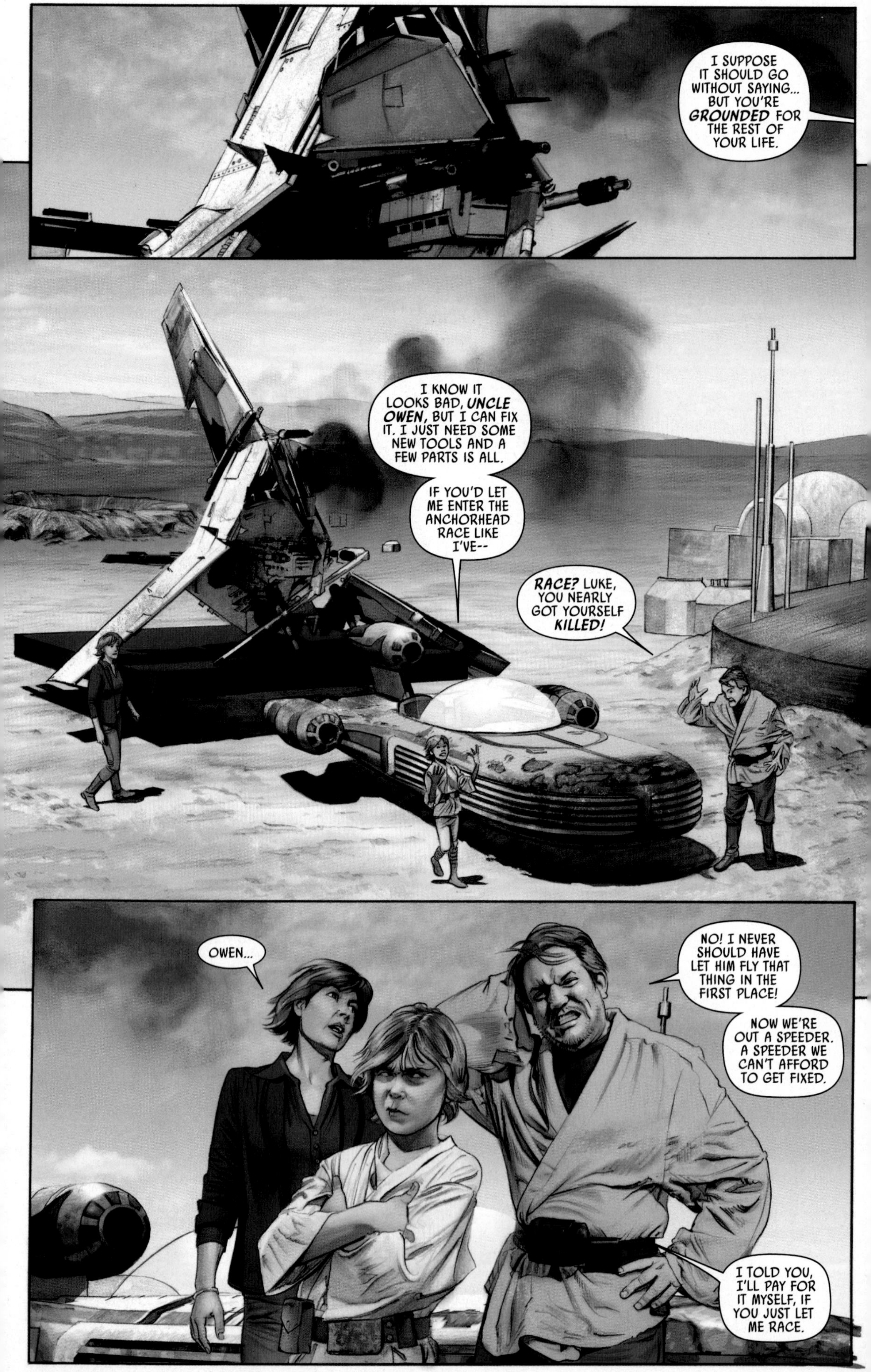
I SUPPOSE IT SHOULD GO WITHOUT SAYING... BUT YOU'RE GROUNDED FOR THE REST OF YOUR LIFE.
I KNOW IT LOOKS BAD, UNCLE OWEN, BUT I CAN FIX IT. I JUST NEED SOME NEW TOOLS AND A FEW PARTS IS ALL.
IF YOU'D LET ME ENTER THE ANCHORHEAD RACE LIKE I'VE--
RACE? LUKE, YOU NEARLY GOT YOURSELF KILLED!
OWEN...
NO! I NEVER SHOULD HAVE LET HIM FLY THAT THING IN THE FIRST PLACE!
NOW WE'RE OUT A SPEEDER. A SPEEDER WE CAN'T AFFORD TO GET FIXED.
I TOLD YOU, I'LL PAY FOR IT MYSELF, IF YOU JUST LET ME RACE.

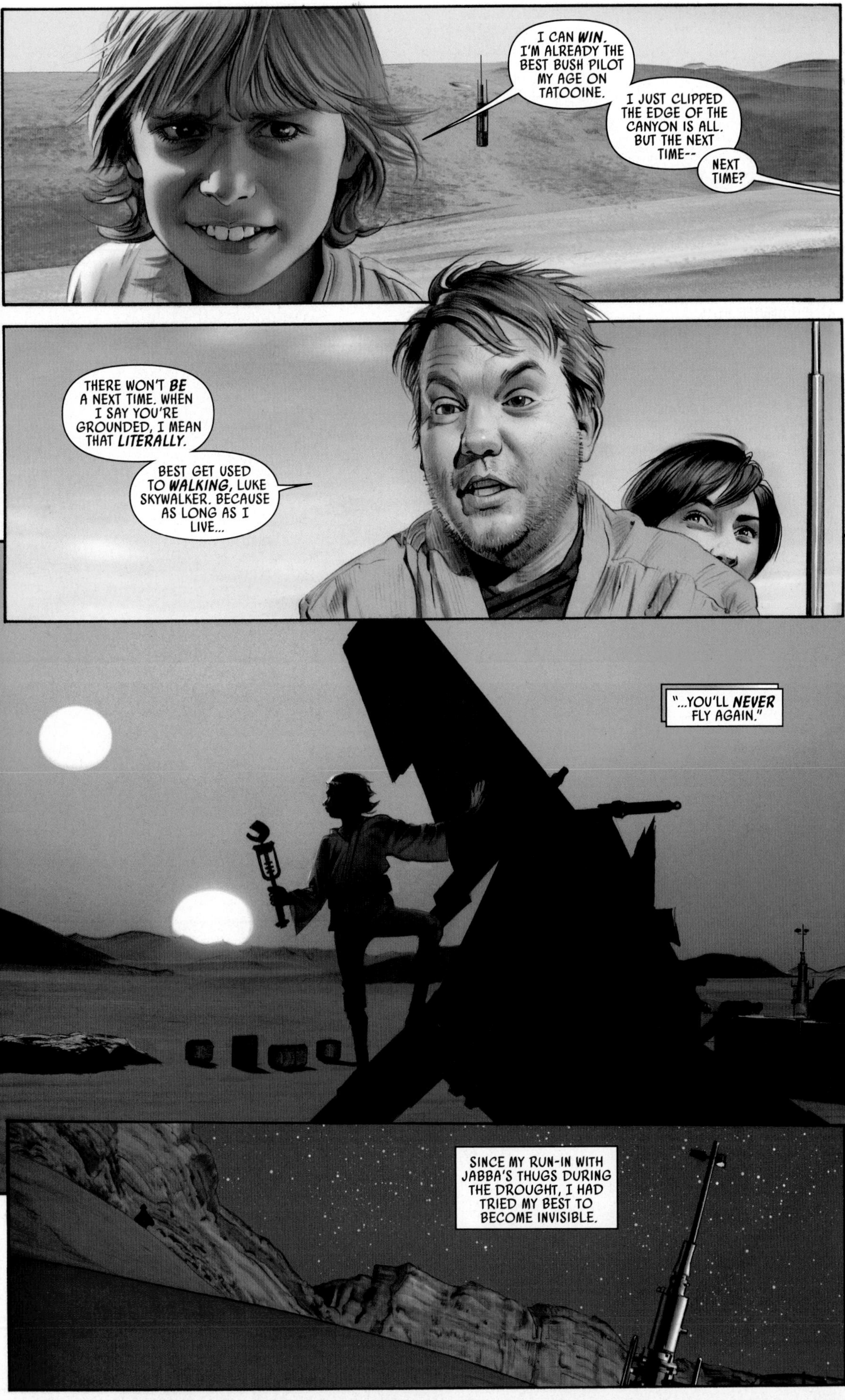
I CAN WIN. I'M ALREADY THE BEST BUSH PILOT MY AGE ON TATOOINE.
I JUST CLIPPED THE EDGE OF THE CANYON IS ALL. BUT THE NEXT TIME--
NEXT TIME?
THERE WON'T BE A NEXT TIME. WHEN I SAY YOU'RE GROUNDED, I MEAN THAT LITERALLY.
BEST GET USED TO WALKING, LUKE SKYWALKER. BECAUSE AS LONG AS I LIVE...
"...YOU'LL NEVER FLY AGAIN."
SINCE MY RUN-IN WITH JABBA'S THUGS DURING THE DROUGHT, I HAD TRIED MY BEST TO BECOME INVISIBLE.

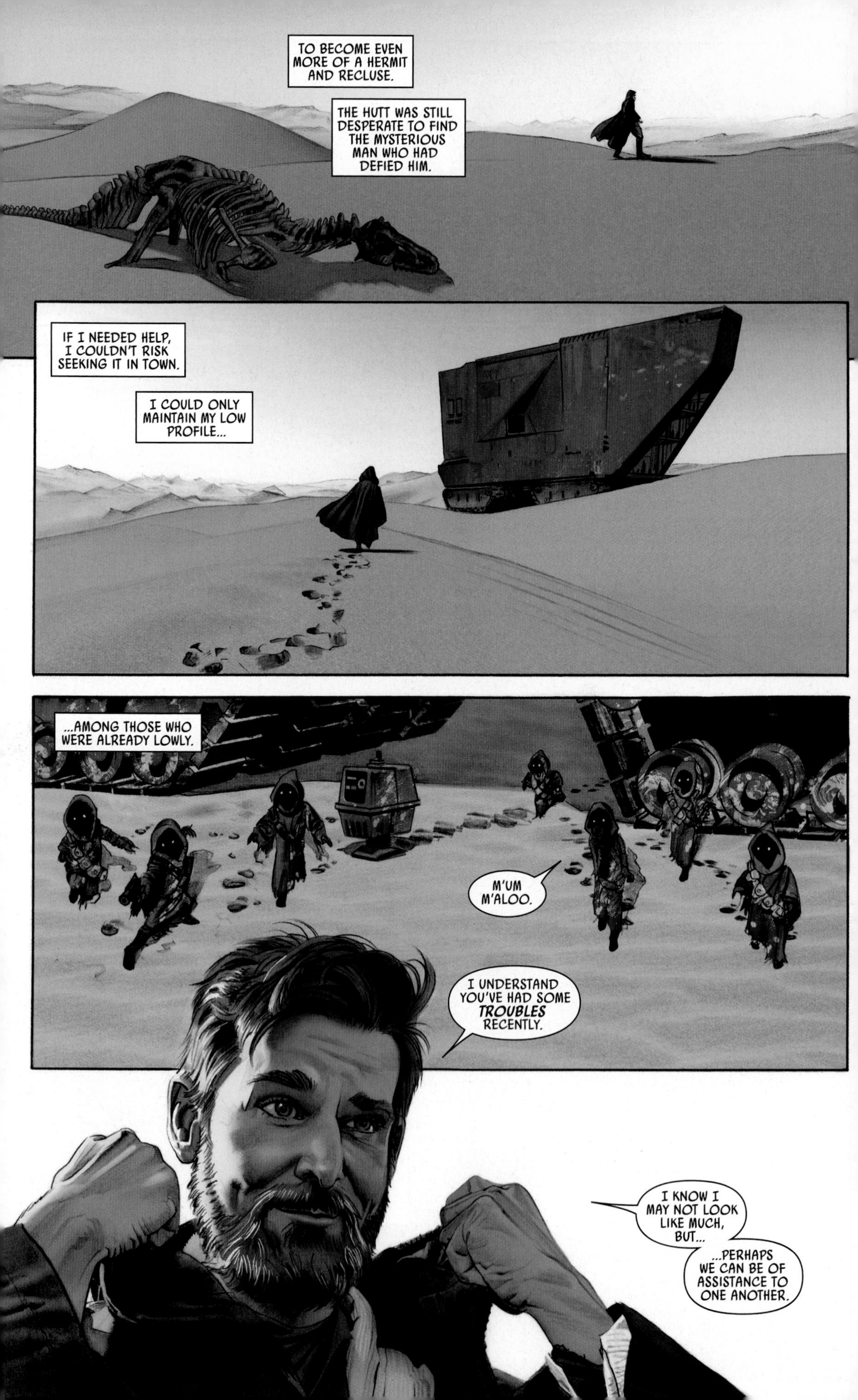
TO BECOME EVEN MORE OF A HERMIT AND RECLUSE.
THE HUTT WAS STILL DESPERATE TO FIND THE MYSTERIOUS MAN WHO HAD DEFIED HIM.
IF I NEEDED HELP, I COULDN'T RISK SEEKING IT IN TOWN.
I COULD ONLY MAINTAIN MY LOW PROFILE...
...AMONG THOSE WHO WERE ALREADY LOWLY.
M'UM M'ALOO.
I UNDERSTAND YOU'VE HAD SOME *TROUBLES* RECENTLY.
I KNOW I MAY NOT LOOK LIKE MUCH, BUT...
...PERHAPS WE CAN BE OF ASSISTANCE TO ONE ANOTHER.

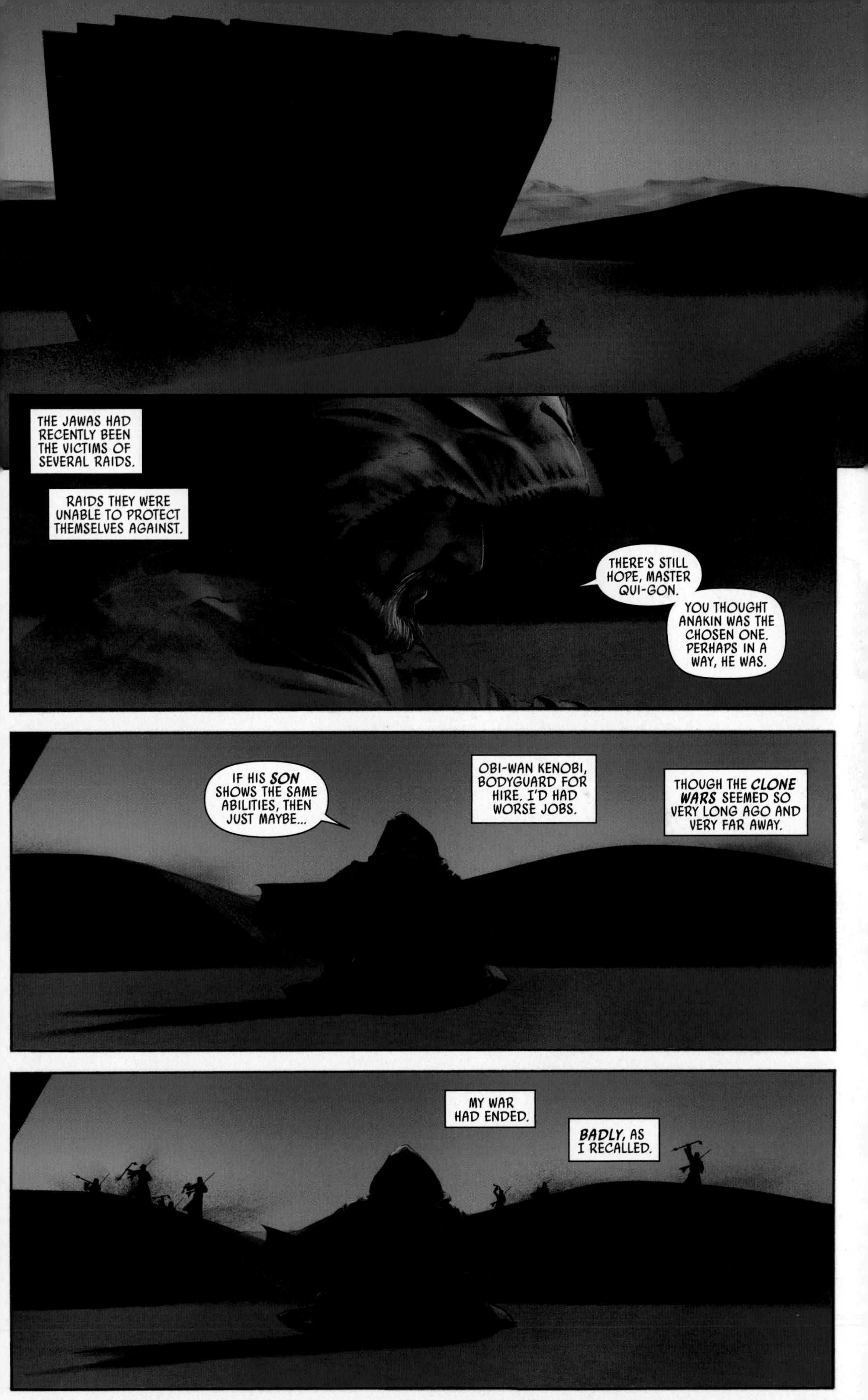
THE JAWAS HAD RECENTLY BEEN THE VICTIMS OF SEVERAL RAIDS.
RAIDS THEY WERE UNABLE TO PROTECT THEMSELVES AGAINST.
THERE'S STILL HOPE, MASTER QUI-GON.
YOU THOUGHT ANAKIN WAS THE CHOSEN ONE. PERHAPS IN A WAY, HE WAS.
IF HIS SON SHOWS THE SAME ABILITIES, THEN JUST MAYBE...
OBI-WAN KENOBI, BODYGUARD FOR HIRE. I'D HAD WORSE JOBS.
THOUGH THE CLONE WARS SEEMED SO VERY LONG AGO AND VERY FAR AWAY.
MY WAR HAD ENDED.
BADLY, AS I RECALLED.

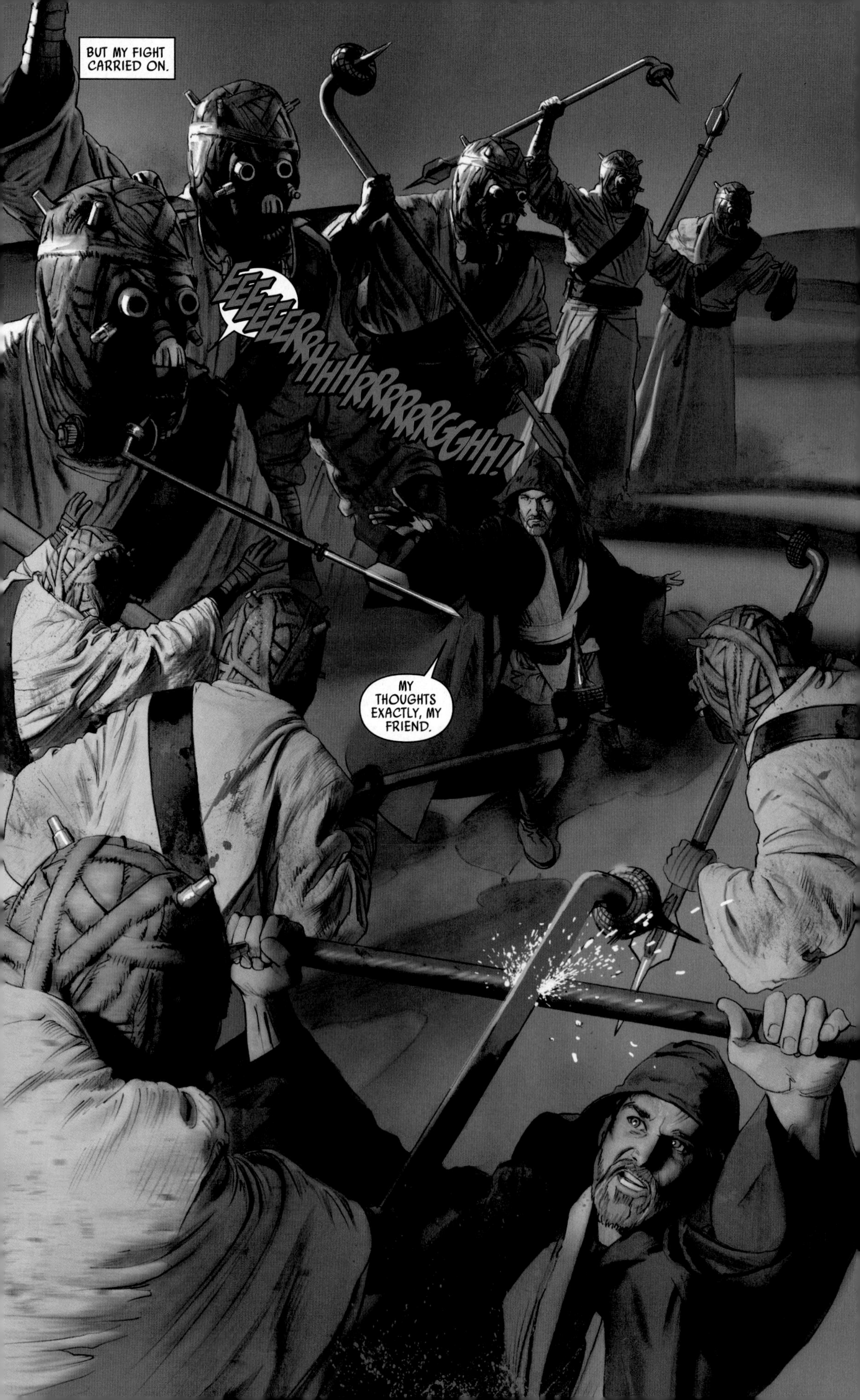
BUT MY FIGHT CARRIED ON.
EEEEEERRHHHRRRRRRGGHH!
MY THOUGHTS EXACTLY, MY FRIEND.

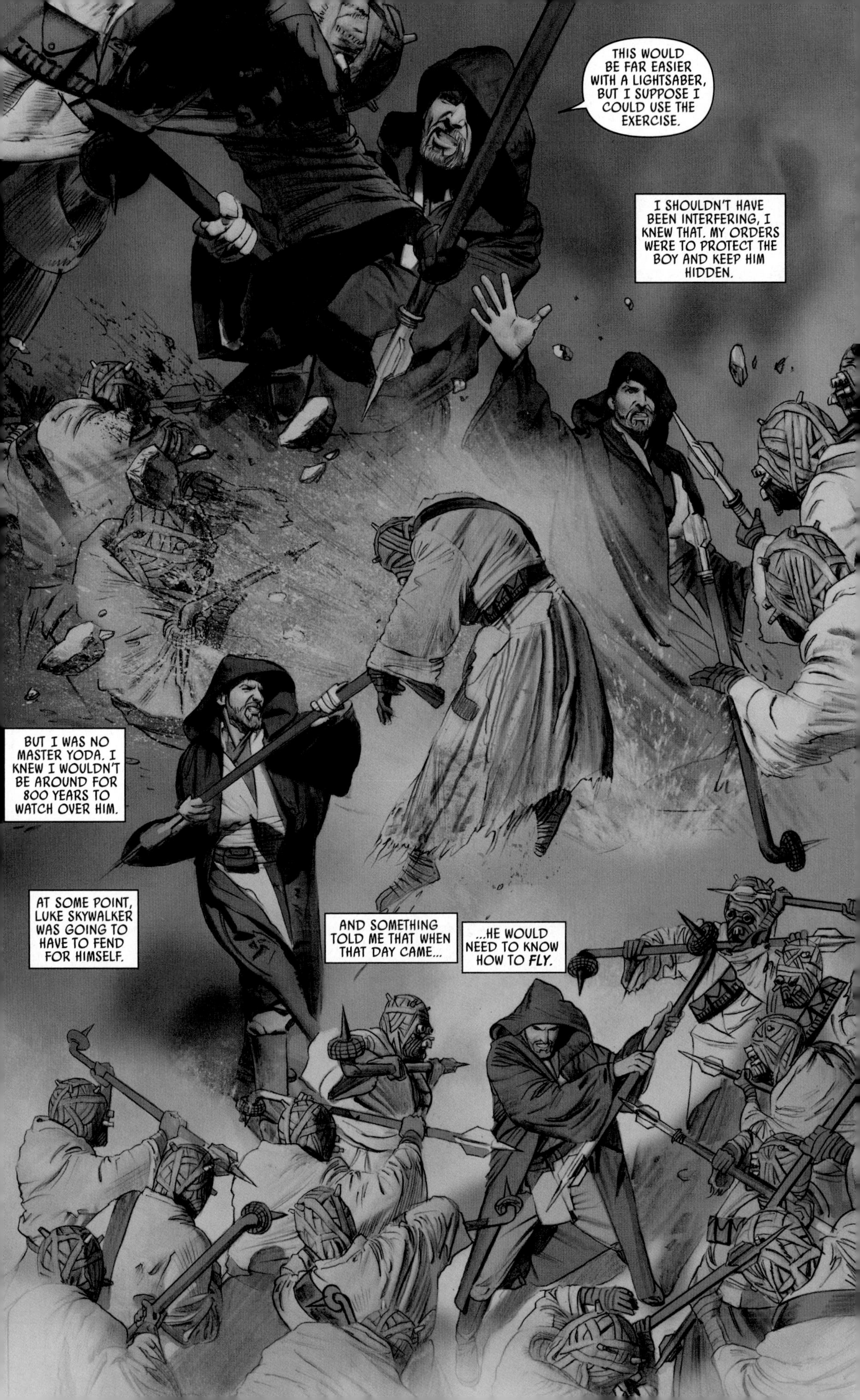
THIS WOULD BE FAR EASIER WITH A LIGHTSABER, BUT I SUPPOSE I COULD USE THE EXERCISE.
I SHOULDN'T HAVE BEEN INTERFERING, I KNEW THAT. MY ORDERS WERE TO PROTECT THE BOY AND KEEP HIM HIDDEN.
BUT I WAS NO MASTER YODA. I KNEW I WOULDN'T BE AROUND FOR 800 YEARS TO WATCH OVER HIM.
AT SOME POINT, LUKE SKYWALKER WAS GOING TO HAVE TO FEND FOR HIMSELF.
AND SOMETHING TOLD ME THAT WHEN THAT DAY CAME...
...HE WOULD NEED TO KNOW HOW TO *FLY*.

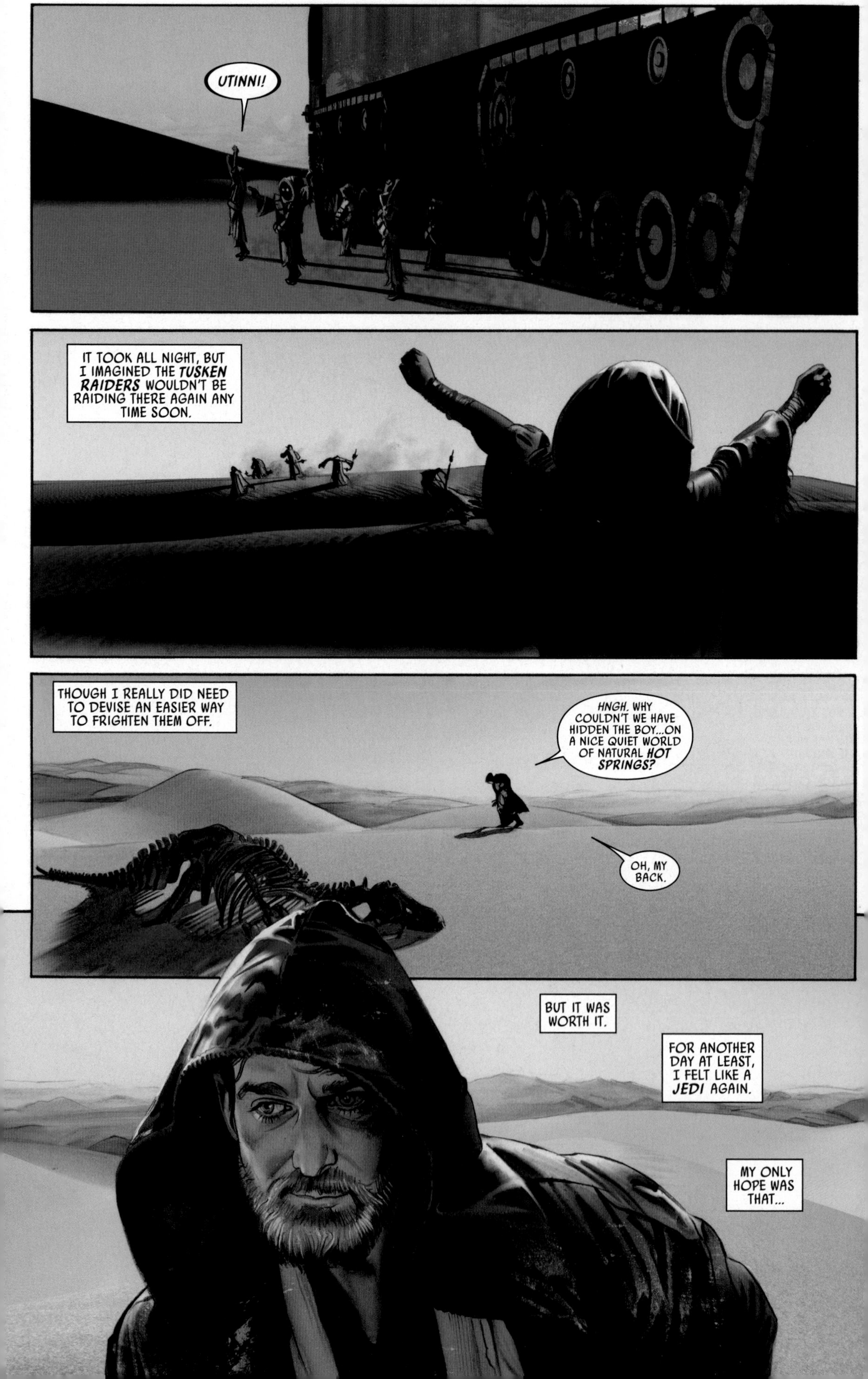
UTINNI!
IT TOOK ALL NIGHT, BUT I IMAGINED THE TUSKEN RAIDERS WOULDN'T BE RAIDING THERE AGAIN ANY TIME SOON.
THOUGH I REALLY DID NEED TO DEVISE AN EASIER WAY TO FRIGHTEN THEM OFF.
HNGH. WHY COULDN'T WE HAVE HIDDEN THE BOY...ON A NICE QUIET WORLD OF NATURAL HOT SPRINGS?
OH, MY BACK.
BUT IT WAS WORTH IT.
FOR ANOTHER DAY AT LEAST, I FELT LIKE A JEDI AGAIN.
MY ONLY HOPE WAS THAT...

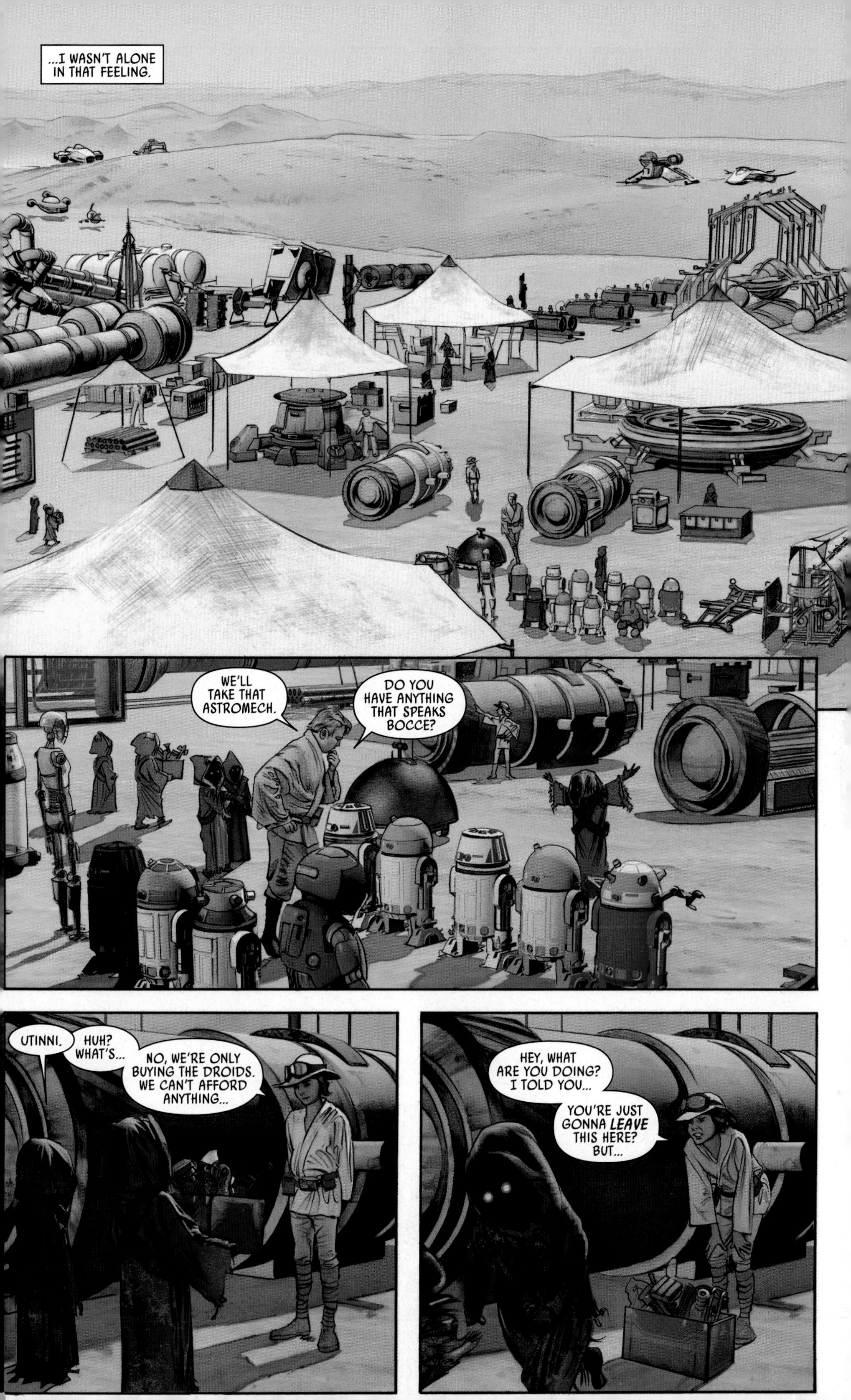
...I WASN'T ALONE IN THAT FEELING.
WE'LL TAKE THAT ASTROMECH.
DO YOU HAVE ANYTHING THAT SPEAKS BOCCE?
UTINNI.
HUH? WHAT'S...
NO, WE'RE ONLY BUYING THE DROIDS. WE CAN'T AFFORD ANYTHING...
HEY, WHAT ARE YOU DOING? I TOLD YOU...
YOU'RE JUST GONNA *LEAVE* THIS HERE? BUT...

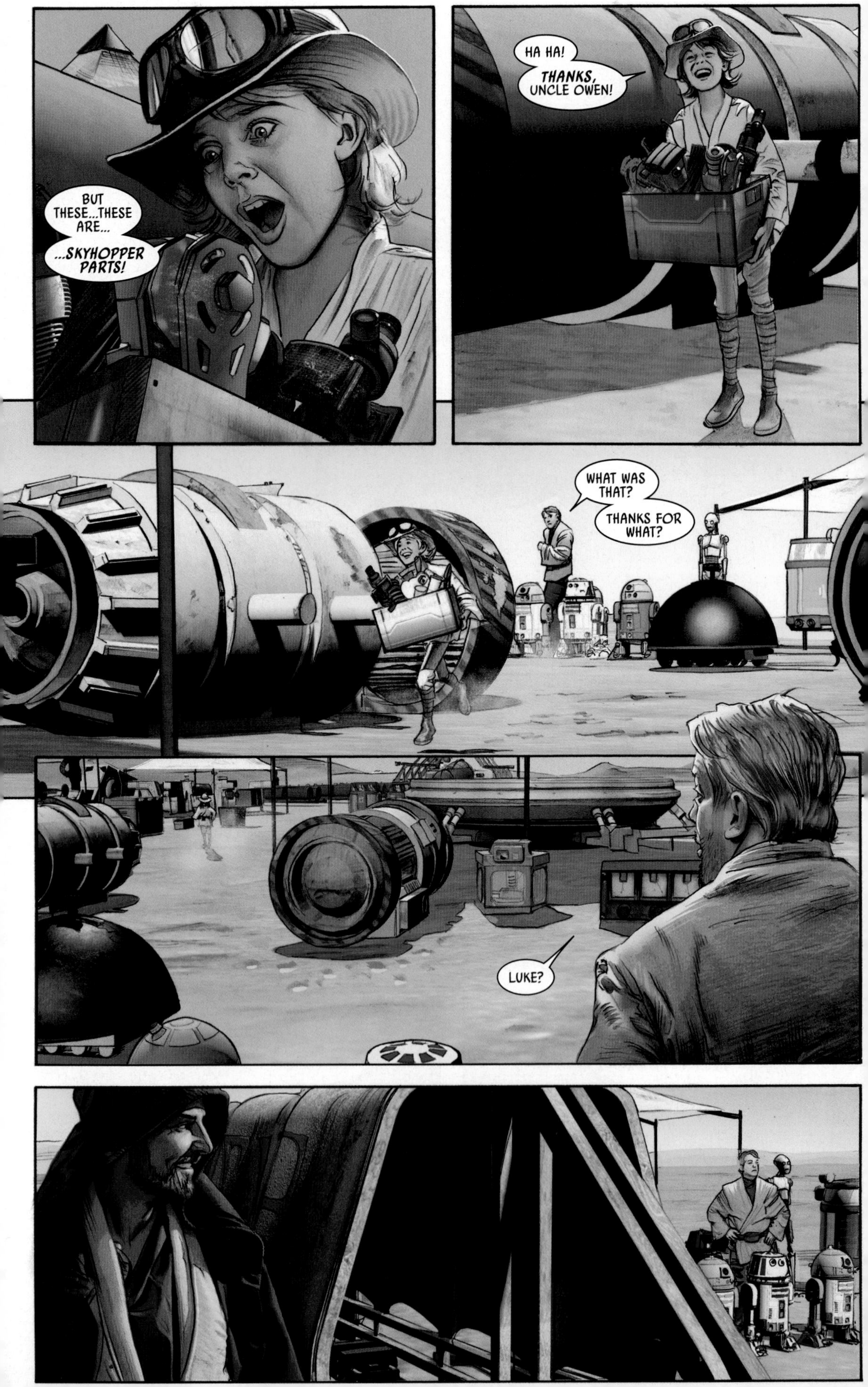
BUT THESE...THESE ARE...
...SKYHOPPER PARTS!
HA HA!
THANKS, UNCLE OWEN!
WHAT WAS THAT?
THANKS FOR WHAT?
LUKE?

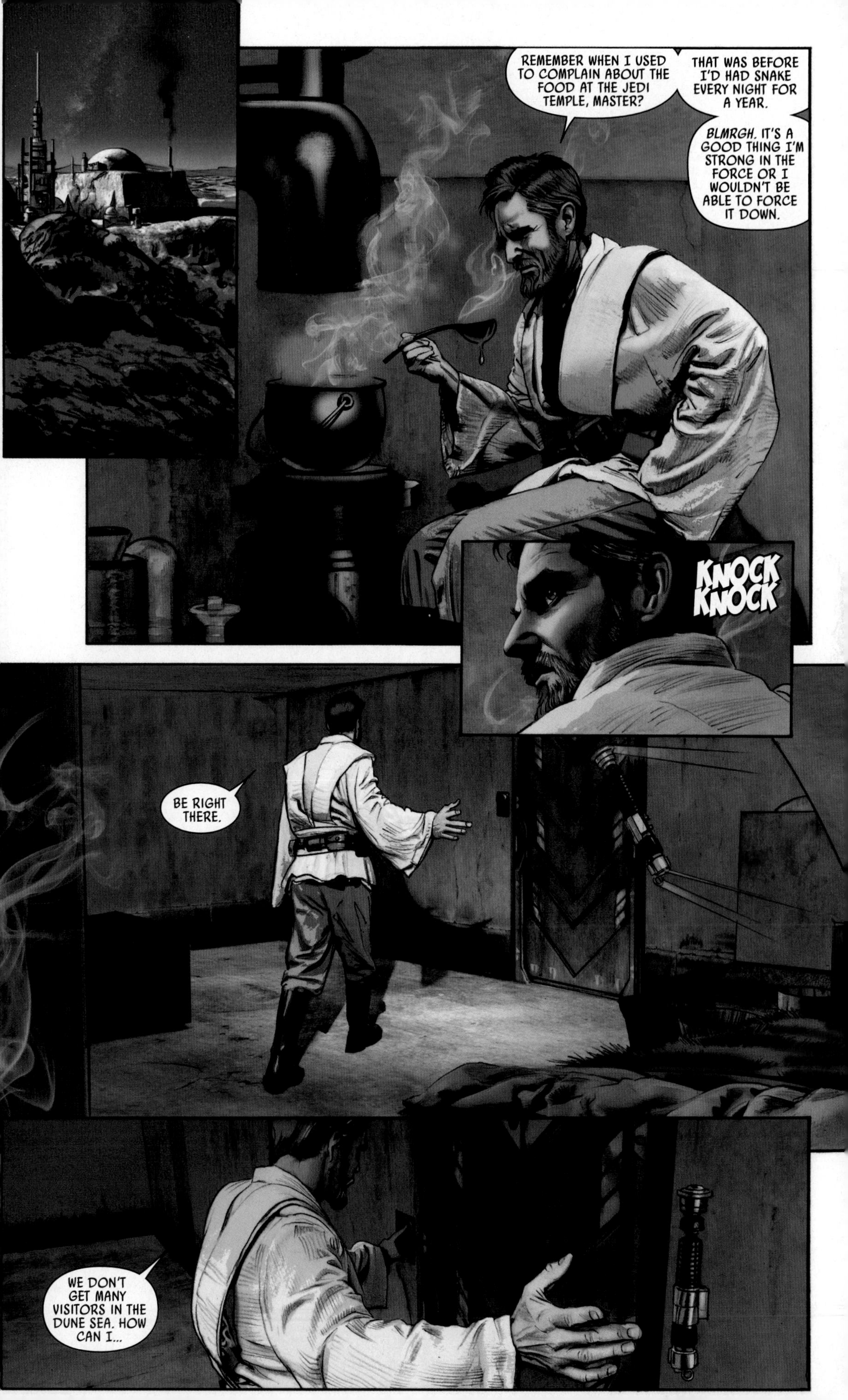
REMEMBER WHEN I USED TO COMPLAIN ABOUT THE FOOD AT THE JEDI TEMPLE, MASTER?
THAT WAS BEFORE I'D HAD SNAKE EVERY NIGHT FOR A YEAR.
BLMRGH. IT'S A GOOD THING I'M STRONG IN THE FORCE OR I WOULDN'T BE ABLE TO FORCE IT DOWN.
KNOCK KNOCK
BE RIGHT THERE.
WE DON'T GET MANY VISITORS IN THE DUNE SEA. HOW CAN I...

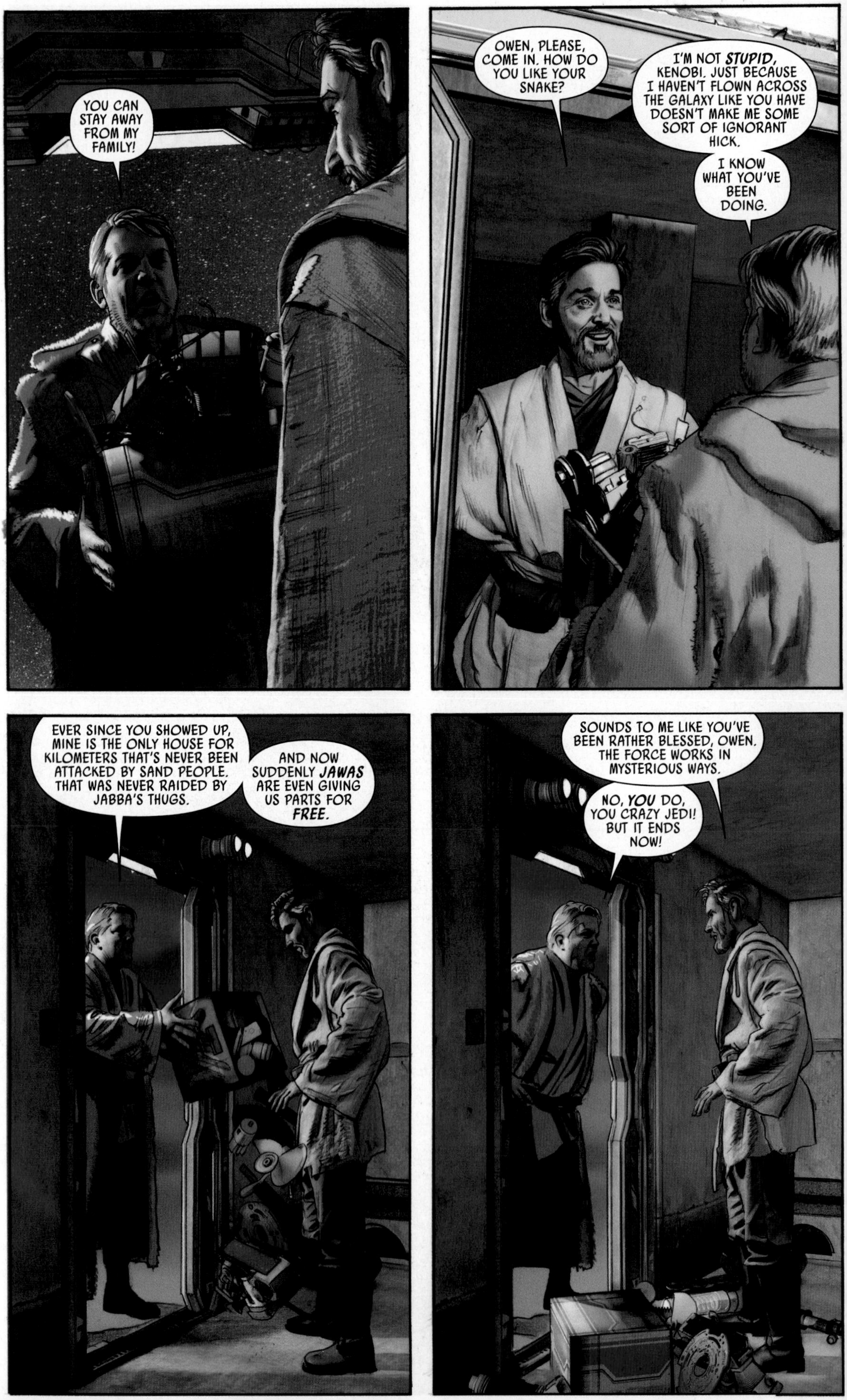
YOU CAN STAY AWAY FROM MY FAMILY!
OWEN, PLEASE, COME IN. HOW DO YOU LIKE YOUR SNAKE?
I'M NOT **STUPID**, KENOBI. JUST BECAUSE I HAVEN'T FLOWN ACROSS THE GALAXY LIKE YOU HAVE DOESN'T MAKE ME SOME SORT OF IGNORANT HICK.
I KNOW WHAT YOU'VE BEEN DOING.
EVER SINCE YOU SHOWED UP, MINE IS THE ONLY HOUSE FOR KILOMETERS THAT'S NEVER BEEN ATTACKED BY SAND PEOPLE. THAT WAS NEVER RAIDED BY JABBA'S THUGS.
AND NOW SUDDENLY **JAWAS** ARE EVEN GIVING US PARTS FOR **FREE**.
SOUNDS TO ME LIKE YOU'VE BEEN RATHER BLESSED, OWEN. THE FORCE WORKS IN MYSTERIOUS WAYS.
NO, **YOU** DO, YOU CRAZY JEDI! BUT IT ENDS NOW!

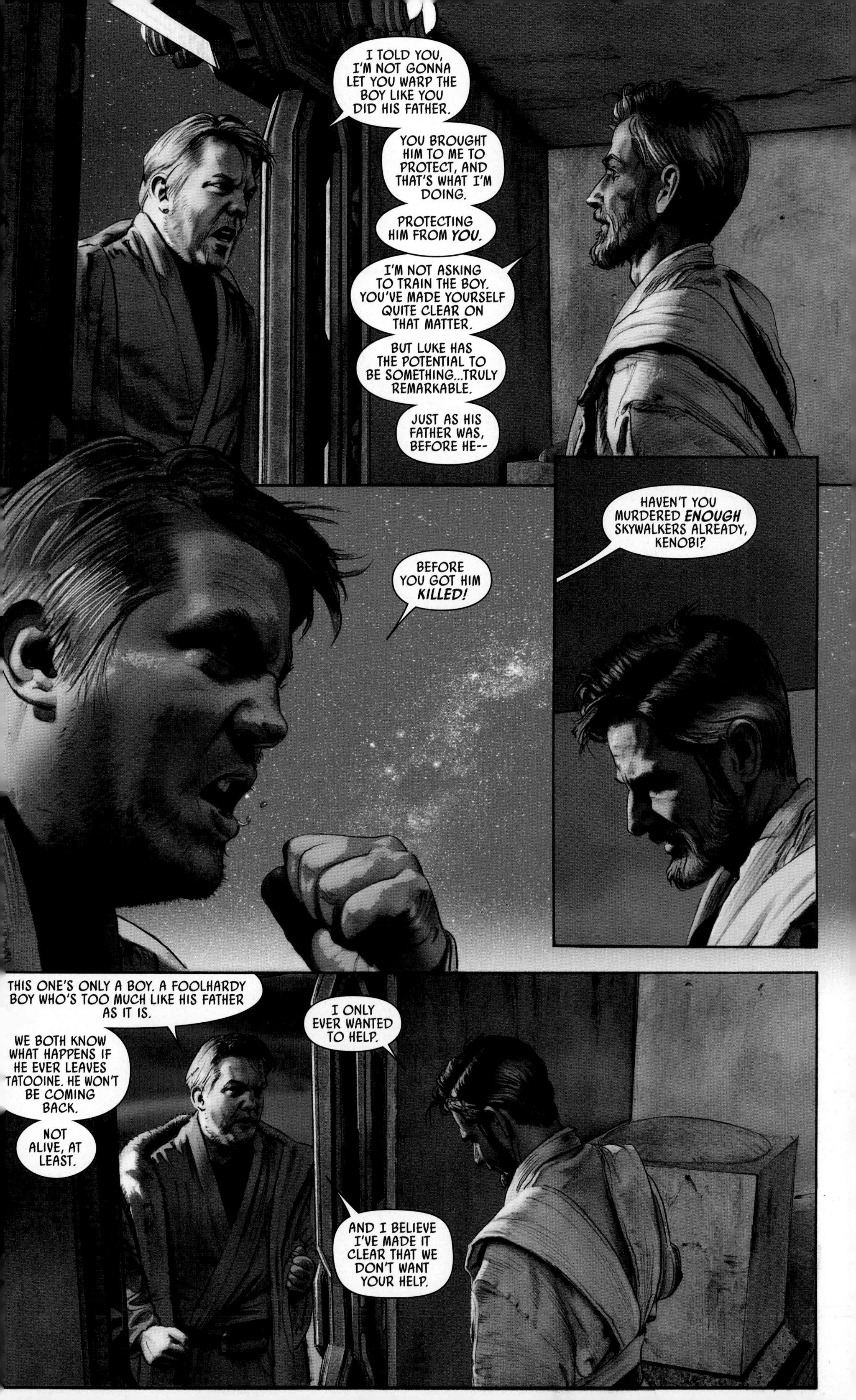
I TOLD YOU, I'M NOT GONNA LET YOU WARP THE BOY LIKE YOU DID HIS FATHER.
YOU BROUGHT HIM TO ME TO PROTECT, AND THAT'S WHAT I'M DOING.
PROTECTING HIM FROM *YOU.*
I'M NOT ASKING TO TRAIN THE BOY. YOU'VE MADE YOURSELF QUITE CLEAR ON THAT MATTER.
BUT LUKE HAS THE POTENTIAL TO BE SOMETHING...TRULY REMARKABLE.
JUST AS HIS FATHER WAS, BEFORE HE--
BEFORE YOU GOT HIM ***KILLED!***
HAVEN'T YOU MURDERED ***ENOUGH*** SKYWALKERS ALREADY, KENOBI?
THIS ONE'S ONLY A BOY. A FOOLHARDY BOY WHO'S TOO MUCH LIKE HIS FATHER AS IT IS.
WE BOTH KNOW WHAT HAPPENS IF HE EVER LEAVES TATOOINE. HE WON'T BE COMING BACK.
NOT ALIVE, AT LEAST.
I ONLY EVER WANTED TO HELP.
AND I BELIEVE I'VE MADE IT CLEAR THAT WE DON'T WANT YOUR HELP.

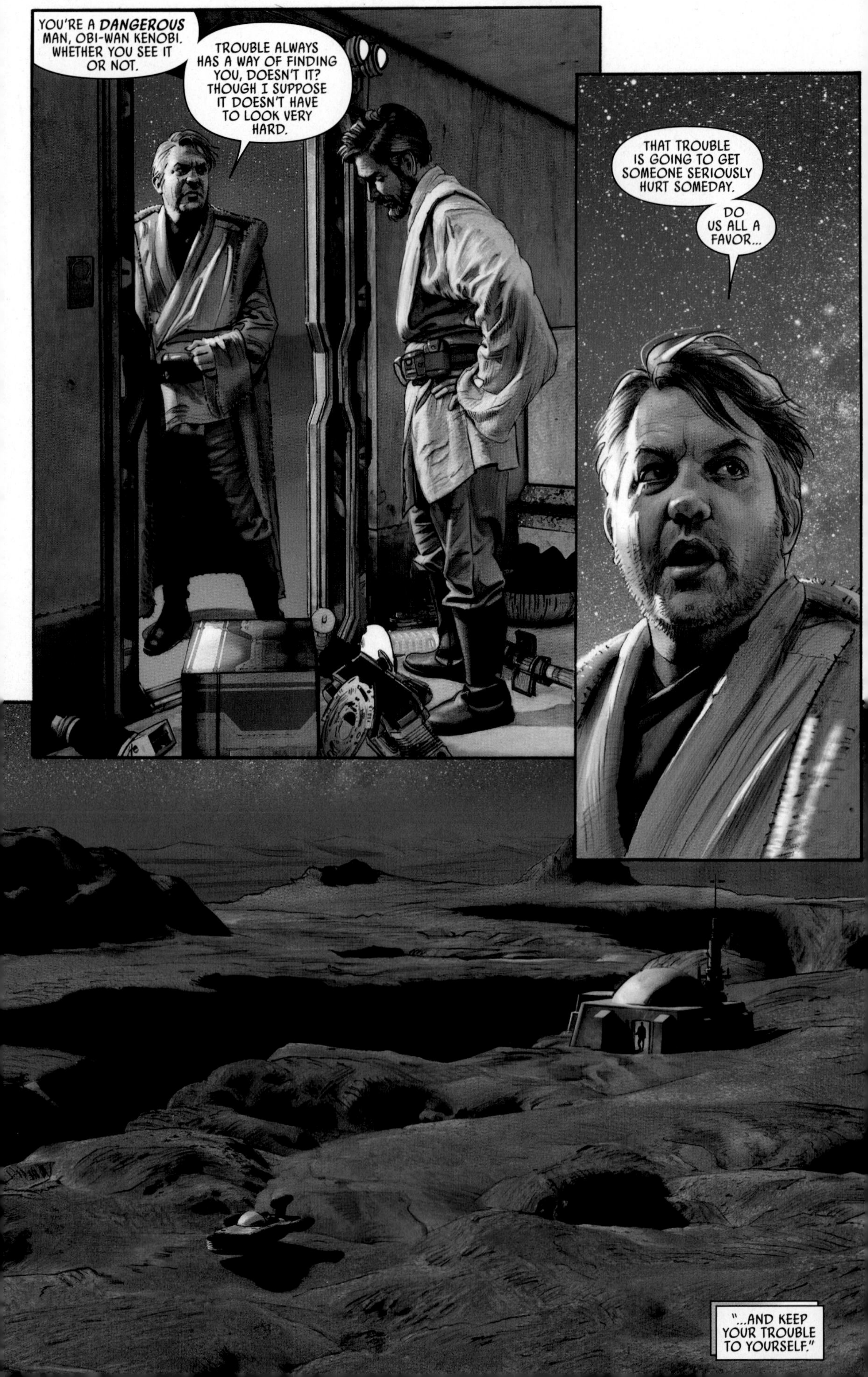
YOU'RE A DANGEROUS MAN, OBI-WAN KENOBI. WHETHER YOU SEE IT OR NOT.
TROUBLE ALWAYS HAS A WAY OF FINDING YOU, DOESN'T IT? THOUGH I SUPPOSE IT DOESN'T HAVE TO LOOK VERY HARD.
THAT TROUBLE IS GOING TO GET SOMEONE SERIOUSLY HURT SOMEDAY.
DO US ALL A FAVOR...
"...AND KEEP YOUR TROUBLE TO YOURSELF."

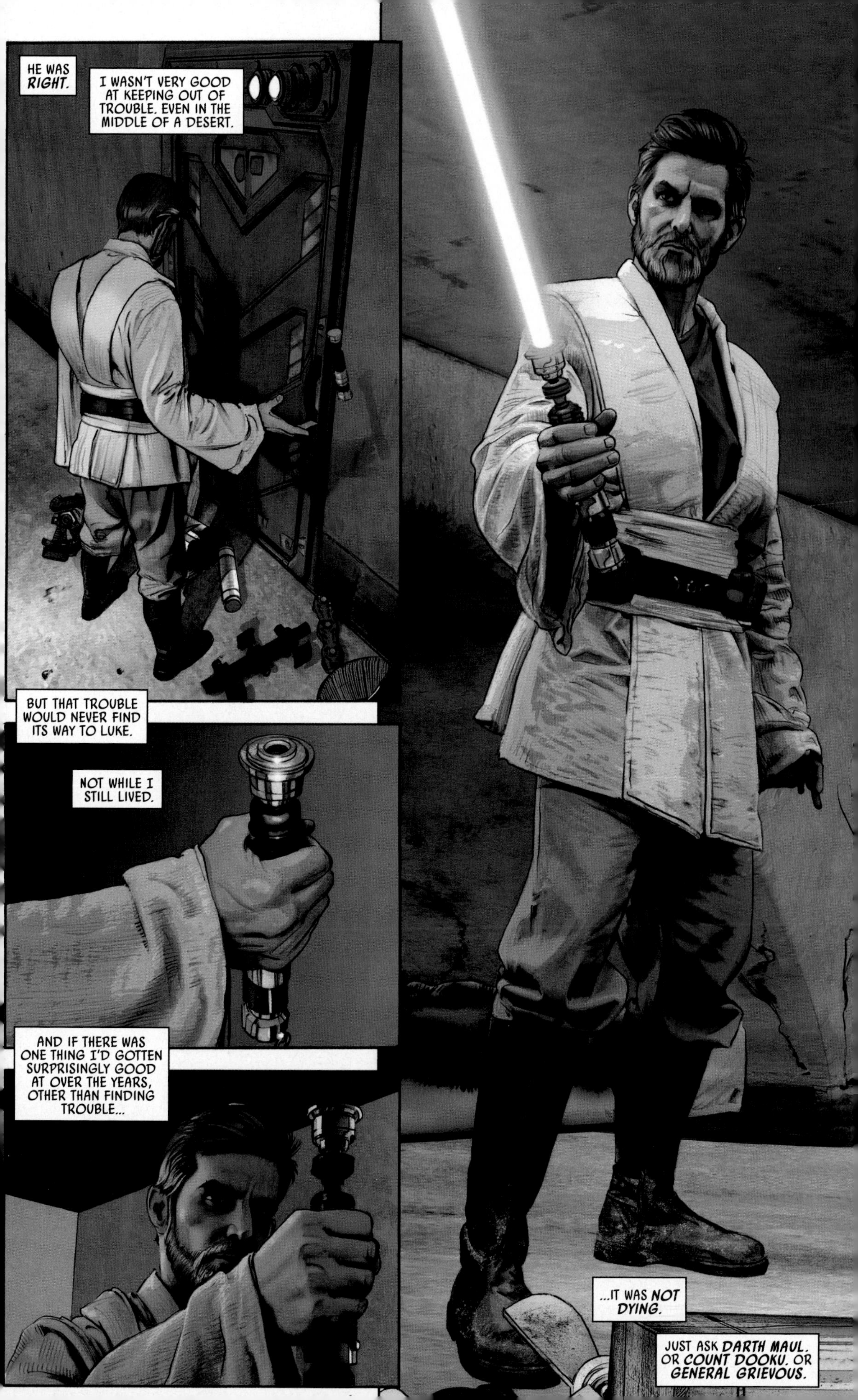
HE WAS RIGHT.
I WASN'T VERY GOOD AT KEEPING OUT OF TROUBLE. EVEN IN THE MIDDLE OF A DESERT.
BUT THAT TROUBLE WOULD NEVER FIND ITS WAY TO LUKE.
NOT WHILE I STILL LIVED.
AND IF THERE WAS ONE THING I'D GOTTEN SURPRISINGLY GOOD AT OVER THE YEARS, OTHER THAN FINDING TROUBLE...
...IT WAS NOT DYING.
JUST ASK DARTH MAUL. OR COUNT DOOKU. OR GENERAL GRIEVOUS.

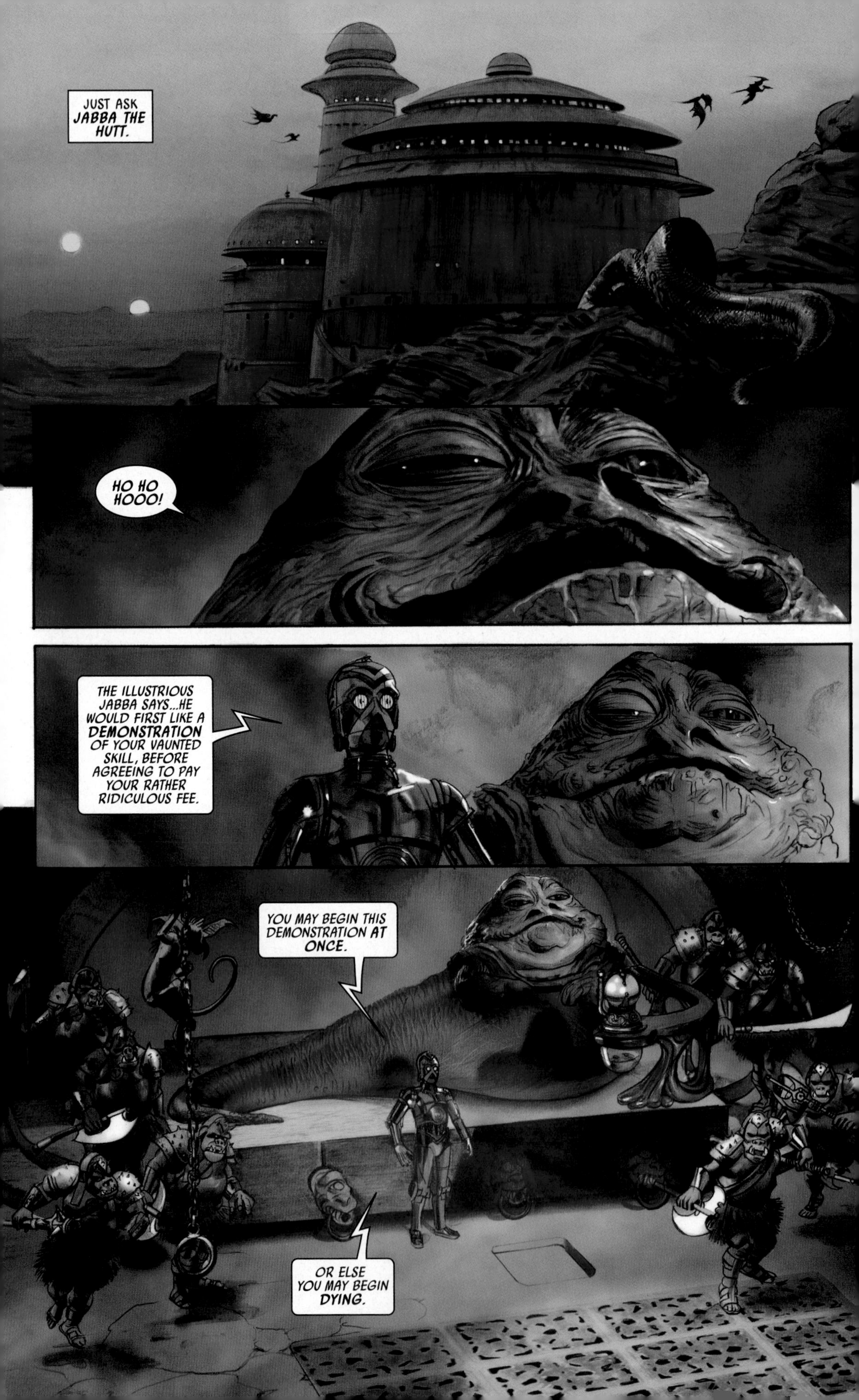
JUST ASK JABBA THE HUTT.
HO HO HOOO!
THE ILLUSTRIOUS JABBA SAYS...HE WOULD FIRST LIKE A DEMONSTRATION OF YOUR VAUNTED SKILL, BEFORE AGREEING TO PAY YOUR RATHER RIDICULOUS FEE.
YOU MAY BEGIN THIS DEMONSTRATION AT ONCE.
OR ELSE YOU MAY BEGIN DYING.

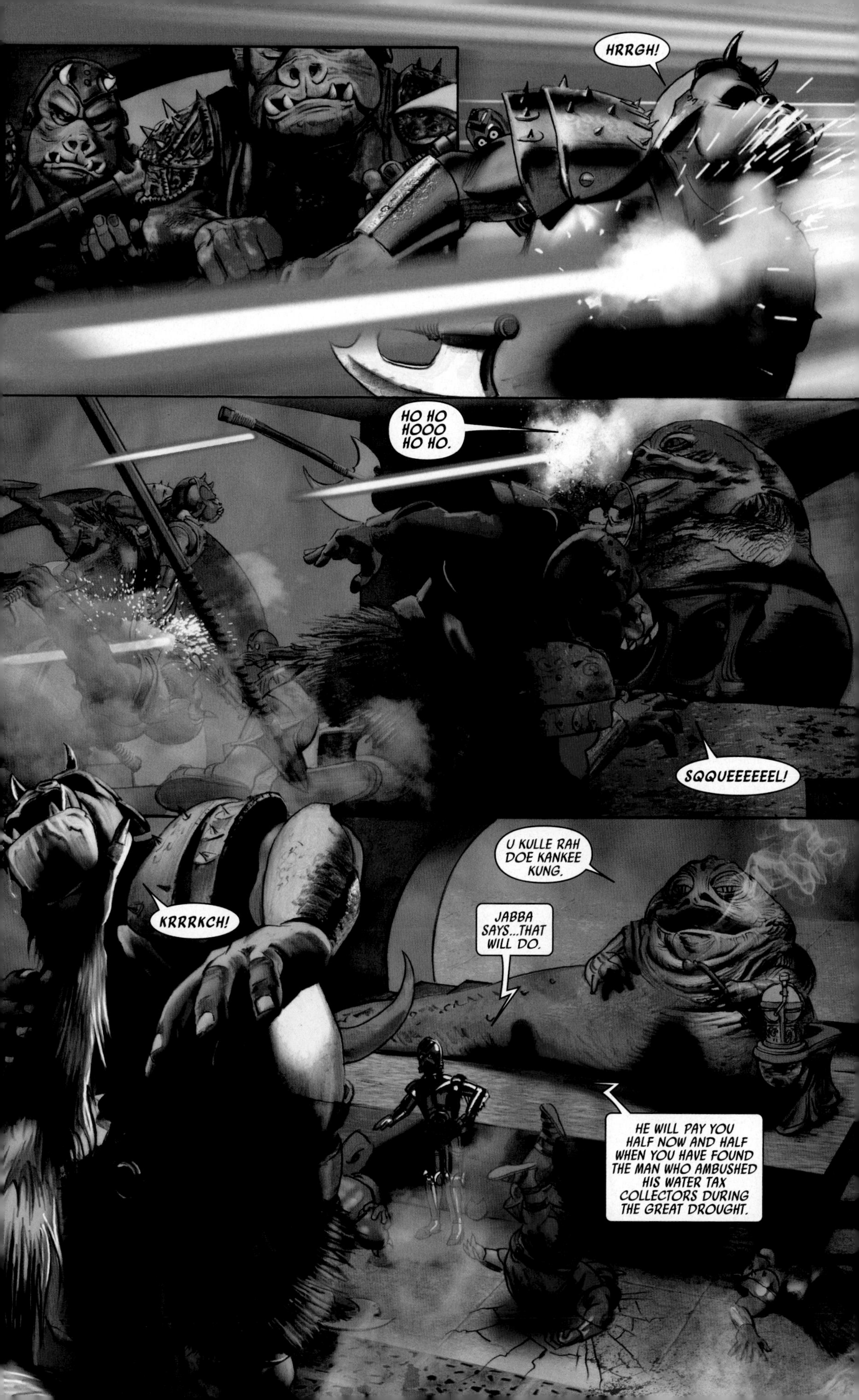
HRRGH!
HO HO HOOO HO HO.
SQQUEEEEEEL!
KRRRKCH!
U KULLE RAH DOE KANKEE KUNG.
JABBA SAYS...THAT WILL DO.
HE WILL PAY YOU HALF NOW AND HALF WHEN YOU HAVE FOUND THE MAN WHO AMBUSHED HIS WATER TAX COLLECTORS DURING THE GREAT DROUGHT.

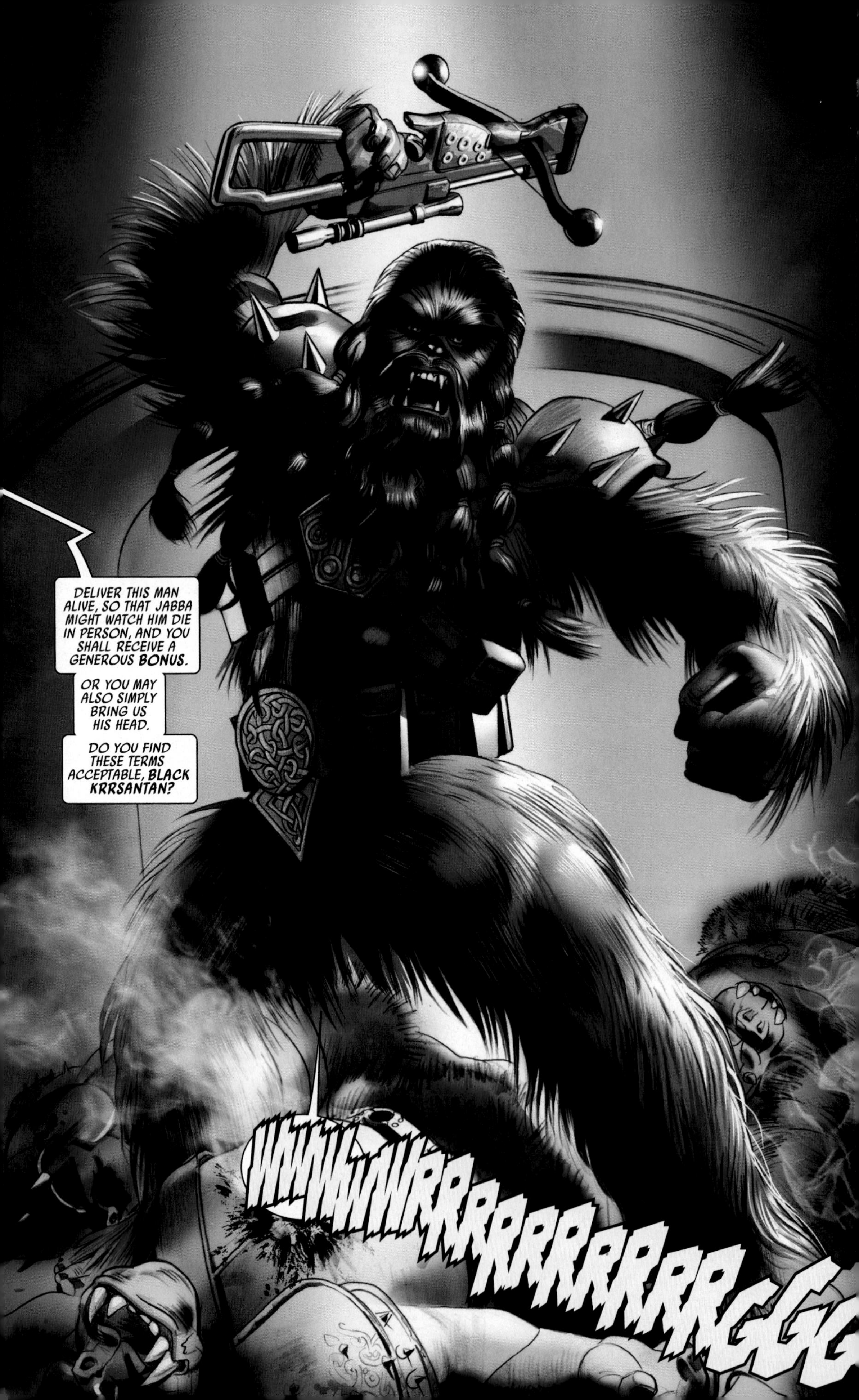
DELIVER THIS MAN ALIVE, SO THAT JABBA MIGHT WATCH HIM DIE IN PERSON, AND YOU SHALL RECEIVE A GENEROUS **BONUS**.
OR YOU MAY ALSO SIMPLY BRING US HIS HEAD.
DO YOU FIND THESE TERMS ACCEPTABLE, **BLACK KRRSANTAN?**
WWWWWRRRRRRRRRRRGG

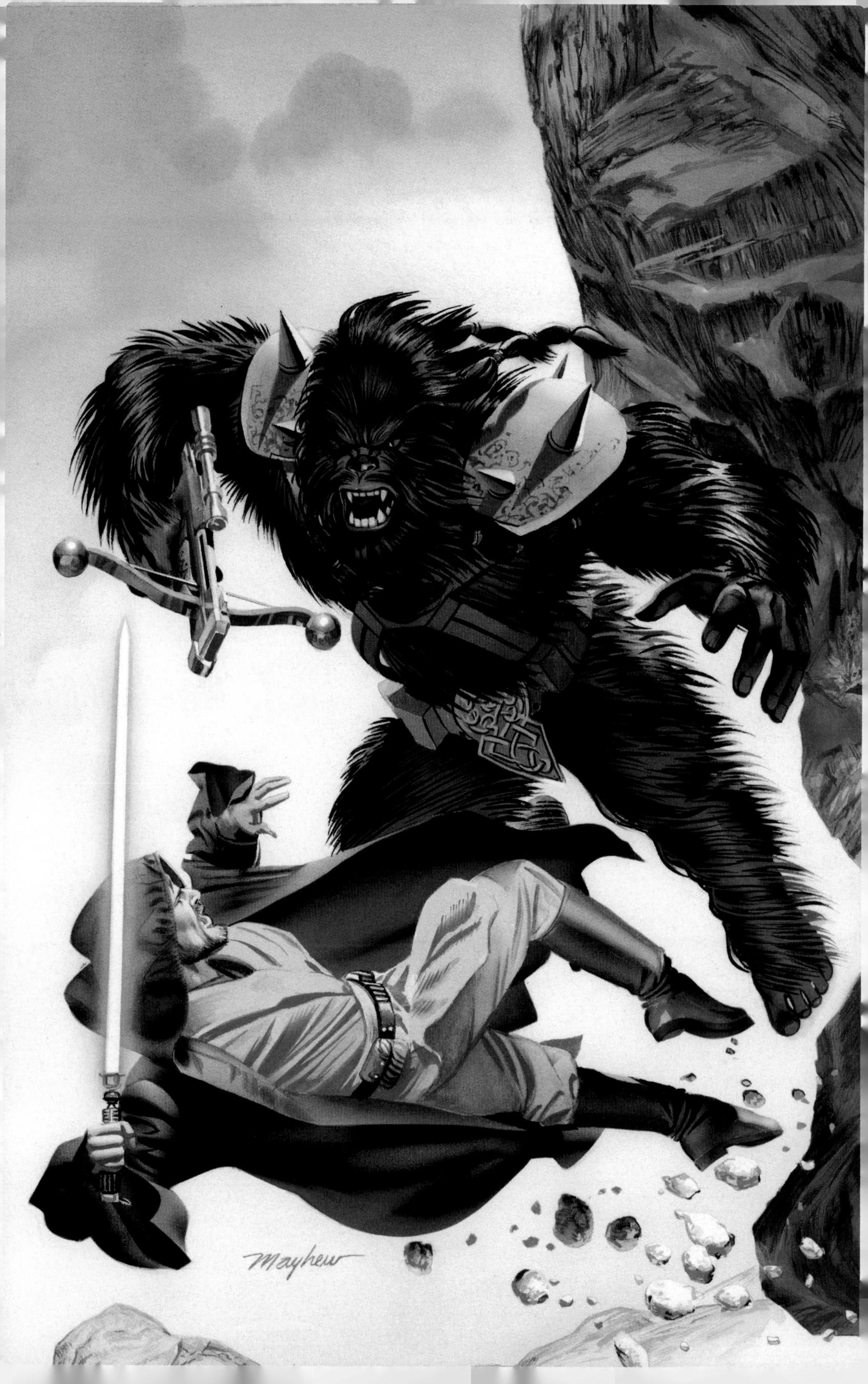
mayhew

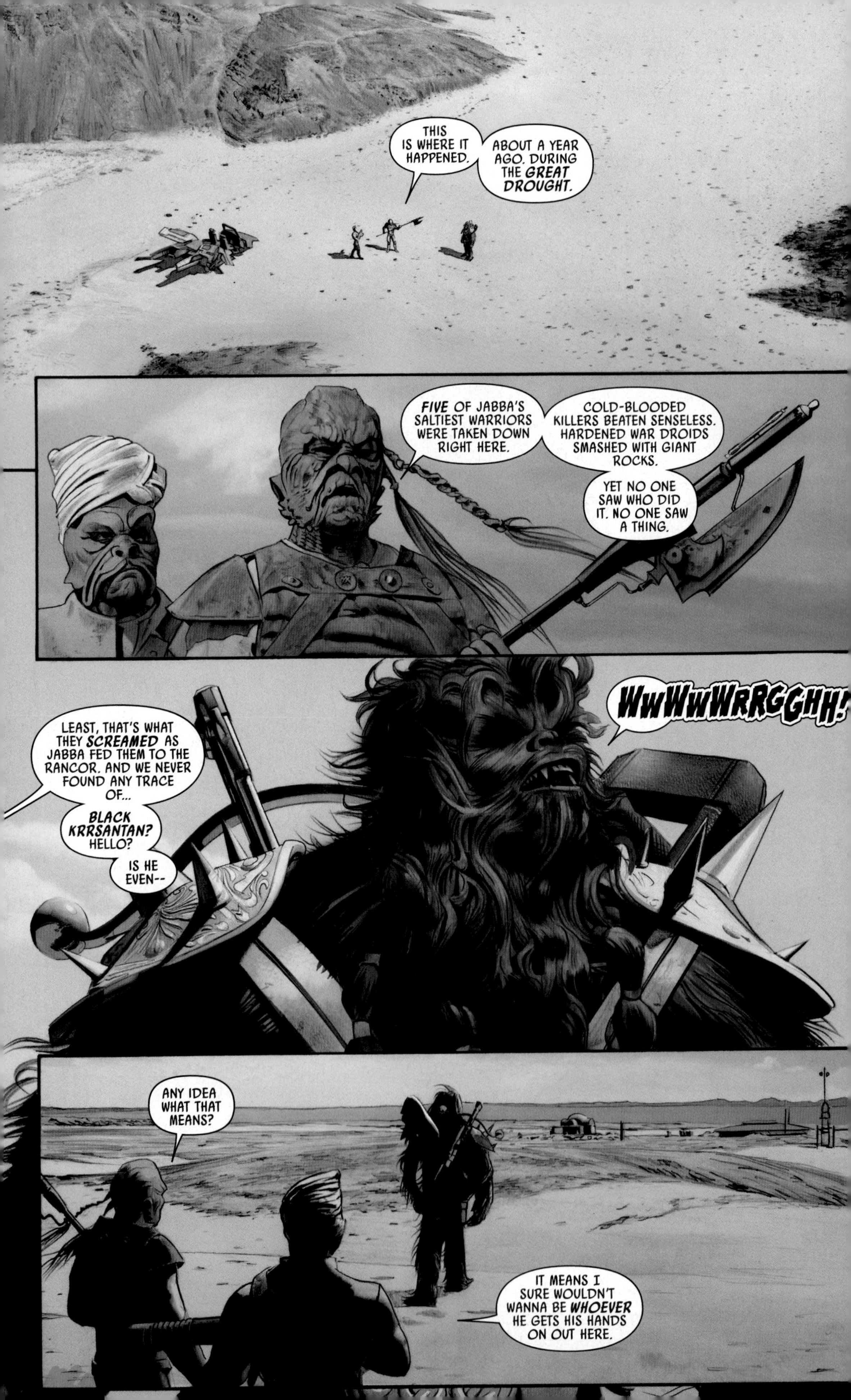
THIS IS WHERE IT HAPPENED.
ABOUT A YEAR AGO. DURING THE GREAT DROUGHT.
FIVE OF JABBA'S SALTIEST WARRIORS WERE TAKEN DOWN RIGHT HERE.
COLD-BLOODED KILLERS BEATEN SENSELESS. HARDENED WAR DROIDS SMASHED WITH GIANT ROCKS.
YET NO ONE SAW WHO DID IT. NO ONE SAW A THING.
LEAST, THAT'S WHAT THEY SCREAMED AS JABBA FED THEM TO THE RANCOR. AND WE NEVER FOUND ANY TRACE OF...
BLACK KRRSANTAN? HELLO?
IS HE EVEN--
WWWWWRRGGHH!
ANY IDEA WHAT THAT MEANS?
IT MEANS I SURE WOULDN'T WANNA BE WHOEVER HE GETS HIS HANDS ON OUT HERE.

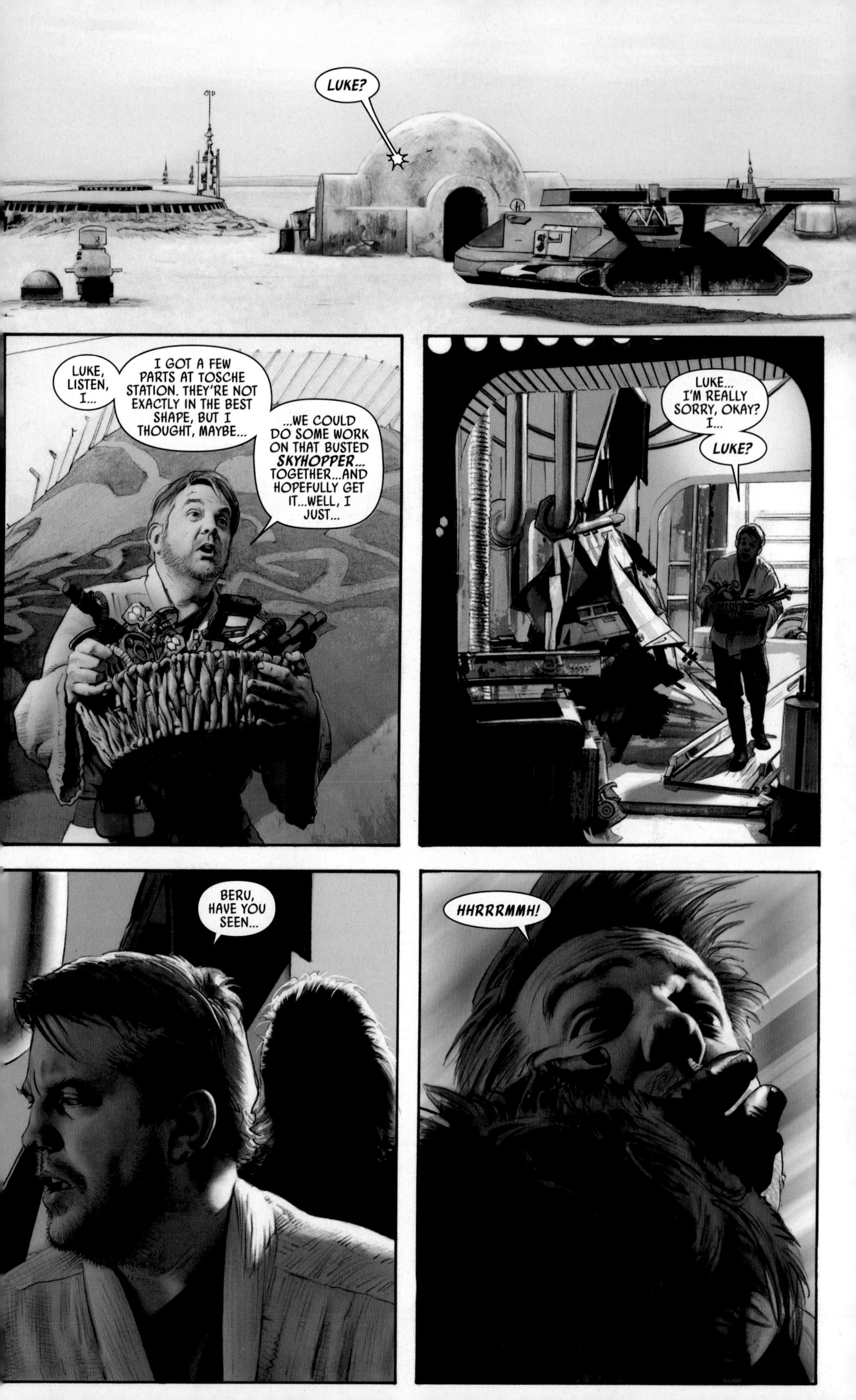
LUKE?
LUKE, LISTEN, I...
I GOT A FEW PARTS AT TOSCHE STATION. THEY'RE NOT EXACTLY IN THE BEST SHAPE, BUT I THOUGHT, MAYBE...
...WE COULD DO SOME WORK ON THAT BUSTED SKYHOPPER... TOGETHER...AND HOPEFULLY GET IT...WELL, I JUST...
LUKE... I'M REALLY SORRY, OKAY? I...
LUKE?
BERU, HAVE YOU SEEN...
HHRRRMMH!

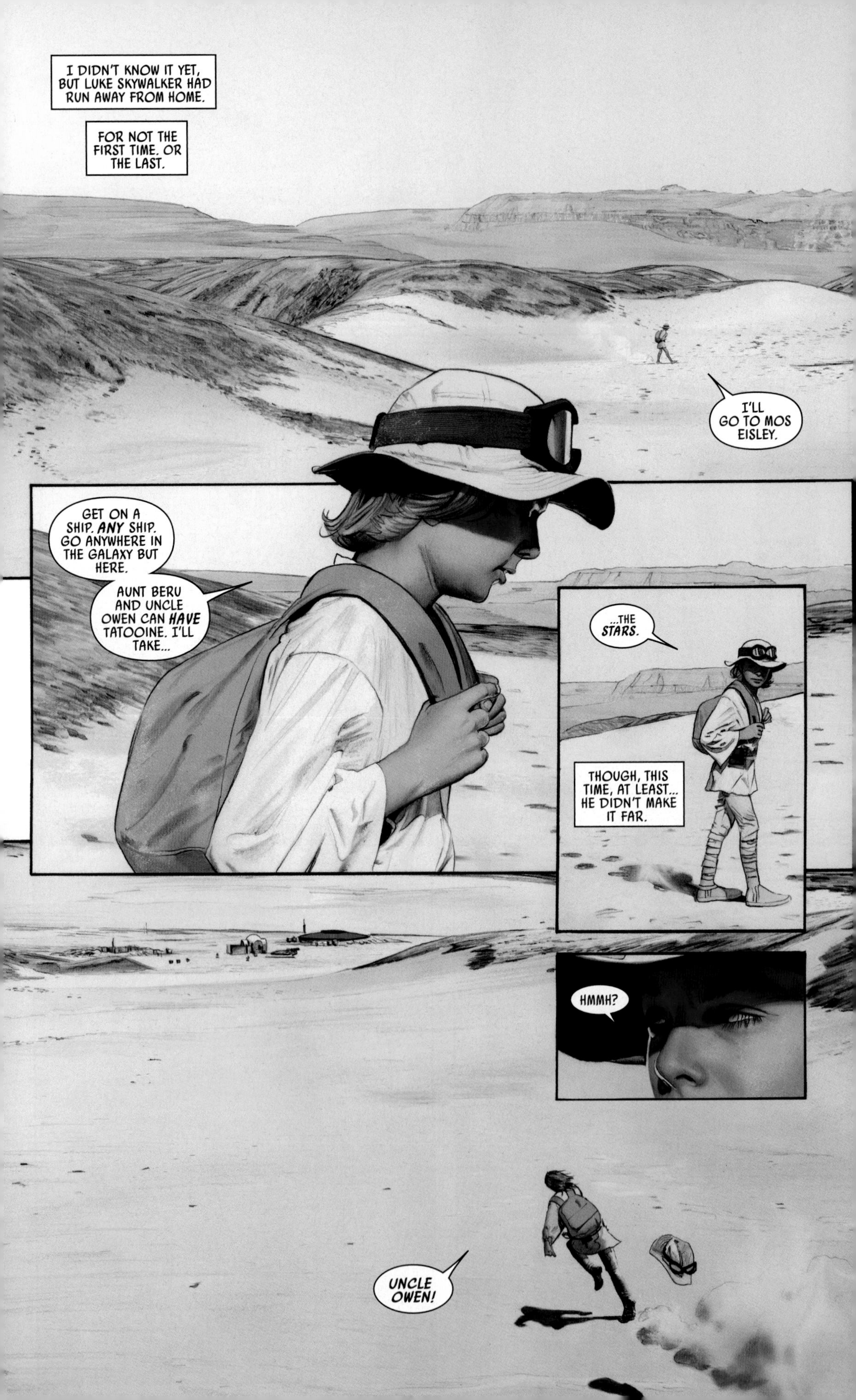

I DIDN'T KNOW IT YET, BUT LUKE SKYWALKER HAD RUN AWAY FROM HOME.
FOR NOT THE FIRST TIME. OR THE LAST.
I'LL GO TO MOS EISLEY.
GET ON A SHIP. ANY SHIP. GO ANYWHERE IN THE GALAXY BUT HERE.
AUNT BERU AND UNCLE OWEN CAN HAVE TATOOINE. I'LL TAKE...
...THE STARS.
THOUGH, THIS TIME, AT LEAST... HE DIDN'T MAKE IT FAR.
HMMH?
UNCLE OWEN!

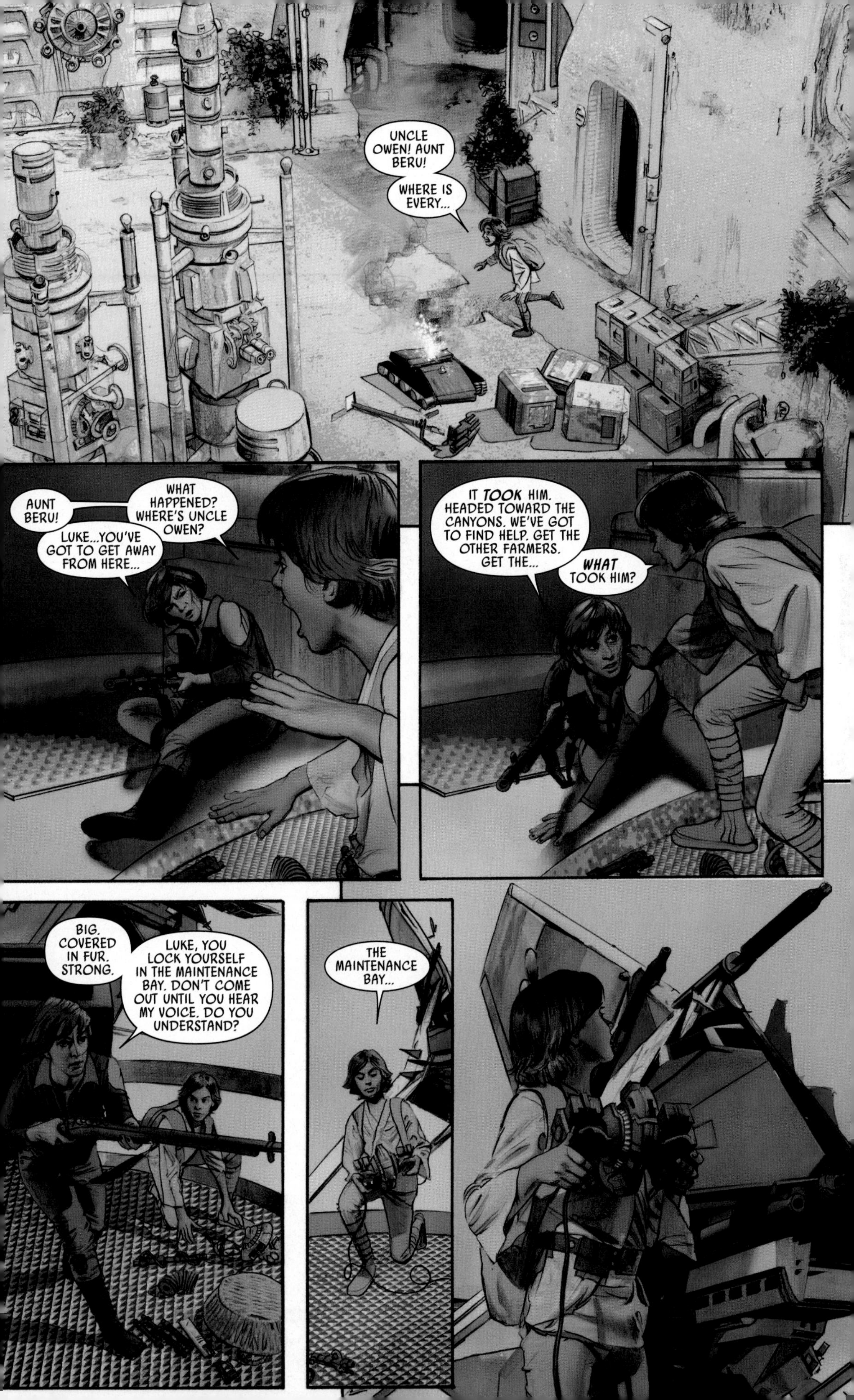
UNCLE OWEN! AUNT BERU!
WHERE IS EVERY...
AUNT BERU!
WHAT HAPPENED? WHERE'S UNCLE OWEN?
LUKE...YOU'VE GOT TO GET AWAY FROM HERE...
IT *TOOK* HIM. HEADED TOWARD THE CANYONS. WE'VE GOT TO FIND HELP. GET THE OTHER FARMERS. GET THE...
WHAT TOOK HIM?
BIG. COVERED IN FUR. STRONG.
LUKE, YOU LOCK YOURSELF IN THE MAINTENANCE BAY. DON'T COME OUT UNTIL YOU HEAR MY VOICE. DO YOU UNDERSTAND?
THE MAINTENANCE BAY...

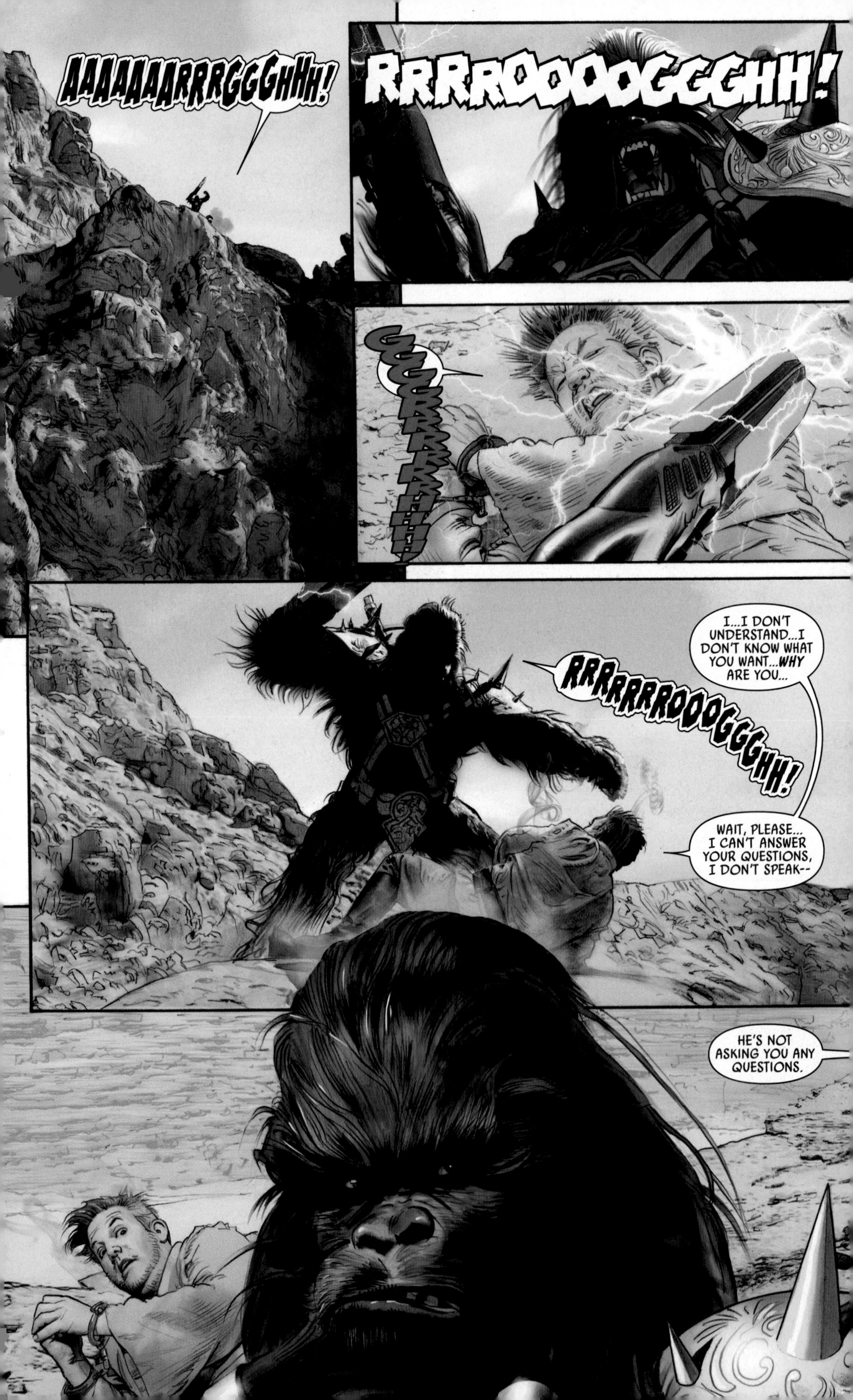
AAAAAAARRRGGGHHH!
RRRROOOOGGGGHH!
GGGGRRRRRRHHH!!
I...I DON'T UNDERSTAND...I DON'T KNOW WHAT YOU WANT...WHY ARE YOU...
RRRRRRRROOOGGGGHH!
WAIT, PLEASE... I CAN'T ANSWER YOUR QUESTIONS, I DON'T SPEAK--
HE'S NOT ASKING YOU ANY QUESTIONS.

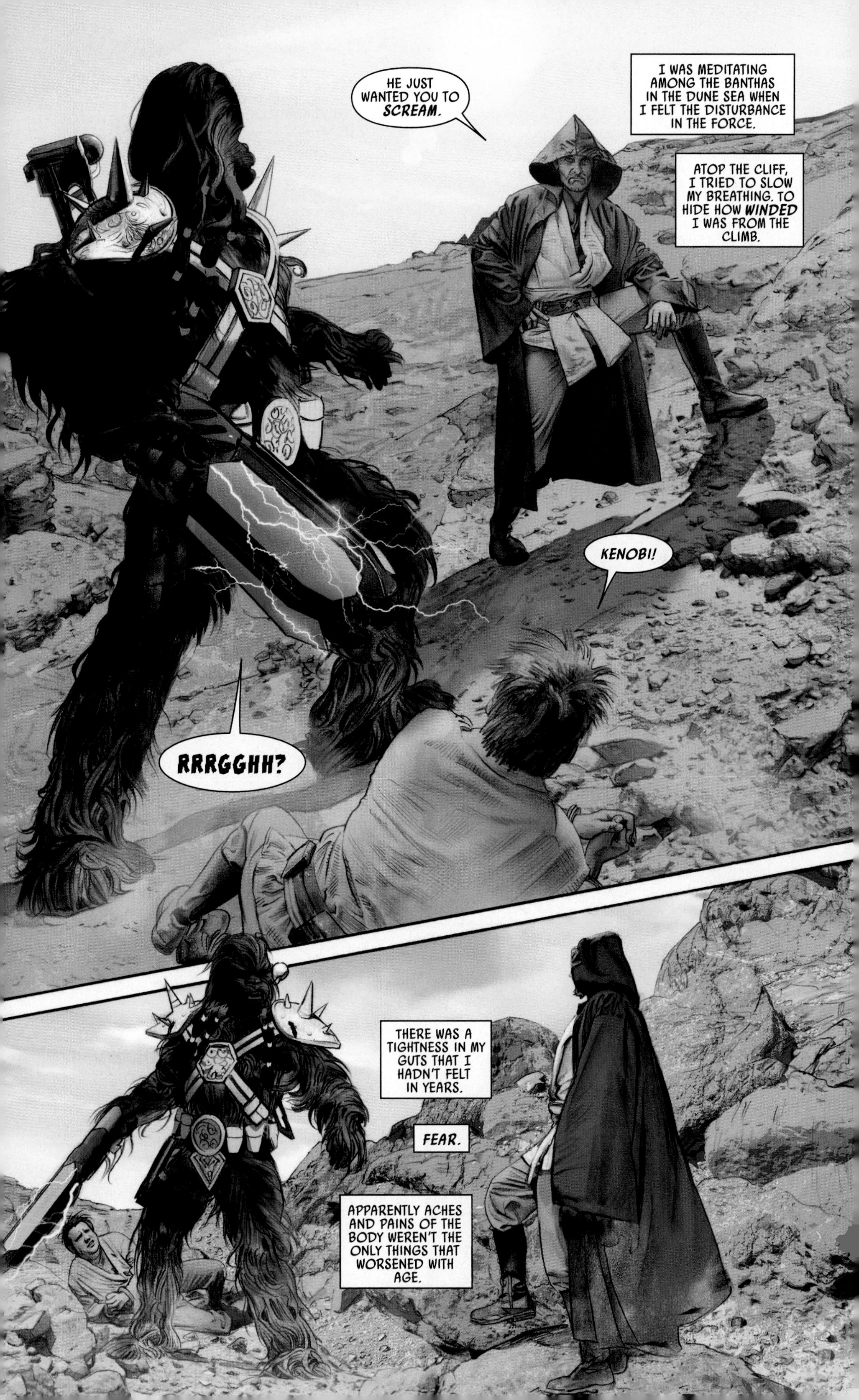
I WAS MEDITATING AMONG THE BANTHAS IN THE DUNE SEA WHEN I FELT THE DISTURBANCE IN THE FORCE.
HE JUST WANTED YOU TO SCREAM.
ATOP THE CLIFF, I TRIED TO SLOW MY BREATHING. TO HIDE HOW WINDED I WAS FROM THE CLIMB.
KENOBI!
RRRGGHH?
THERE WAS A TIGHTNESS IN MY GUTS THAT I HADN'T FELT IN YEARS.
FEAR.
APPARENTLY ACHES AND PAINS OF THE BODY WEREN'T THE ONLY THINGS THAT WORSENED WITH AGE.

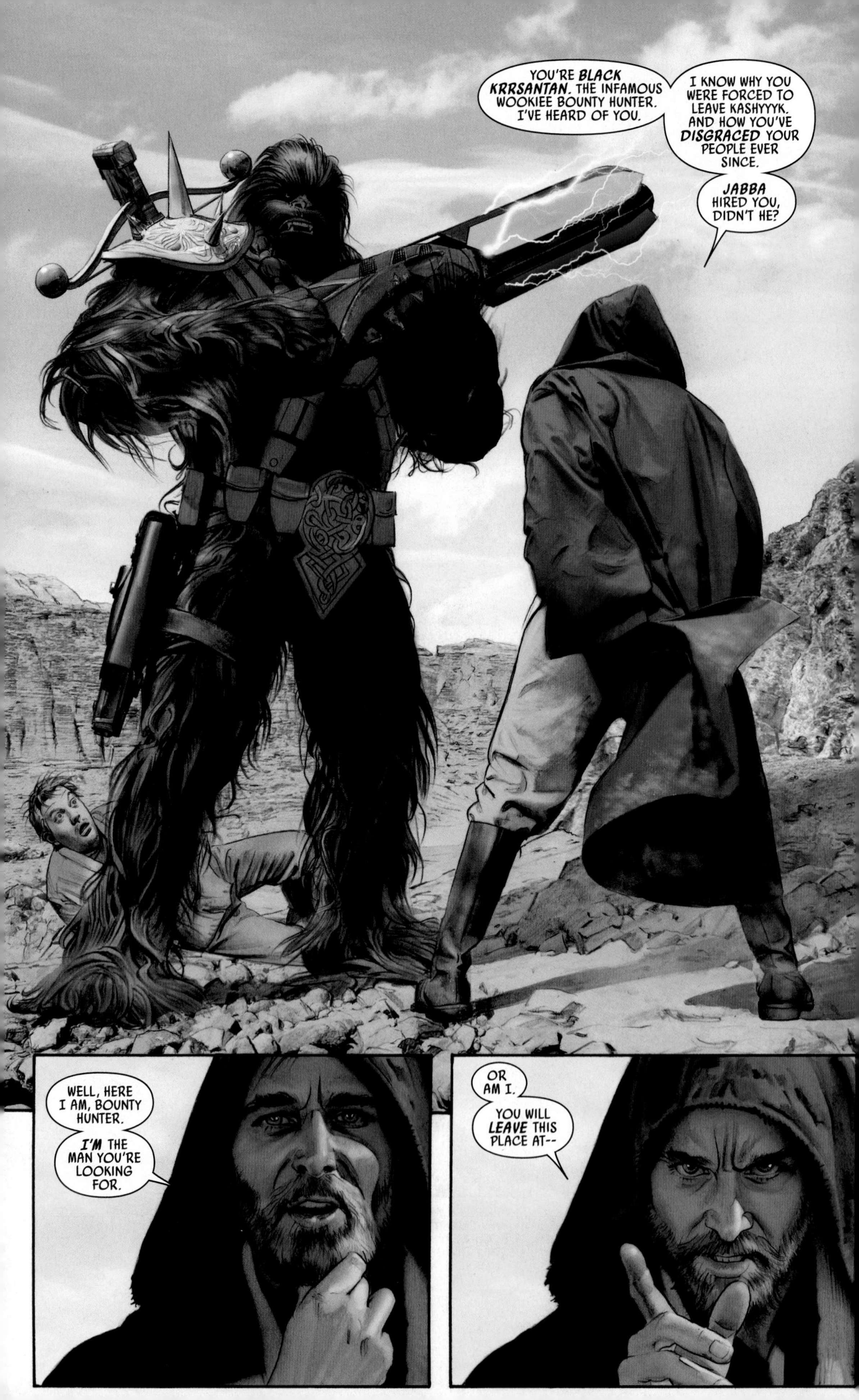
YOU'RE BLACK KRRSANTAN. THE INFAMOUS WOOKIEE BOUNTY HUNTER. I'VE HEARD OF YOU.
I KNOW WHY YOU WERE FORCED TO LEAVE KASHYYYK. AND HOW YOU'VE DISGRACED YOUR PEOPLE EVER SINCE.
JABBA HIRED YOU, DIDN'T HE?
WELL, HERE I AM, BOUNTY HUNTER.
I'M THE MAN YOU'RE LOOKING FOR.
OR AM I.
YOU WILL LEAVE THIS PLACE AT--

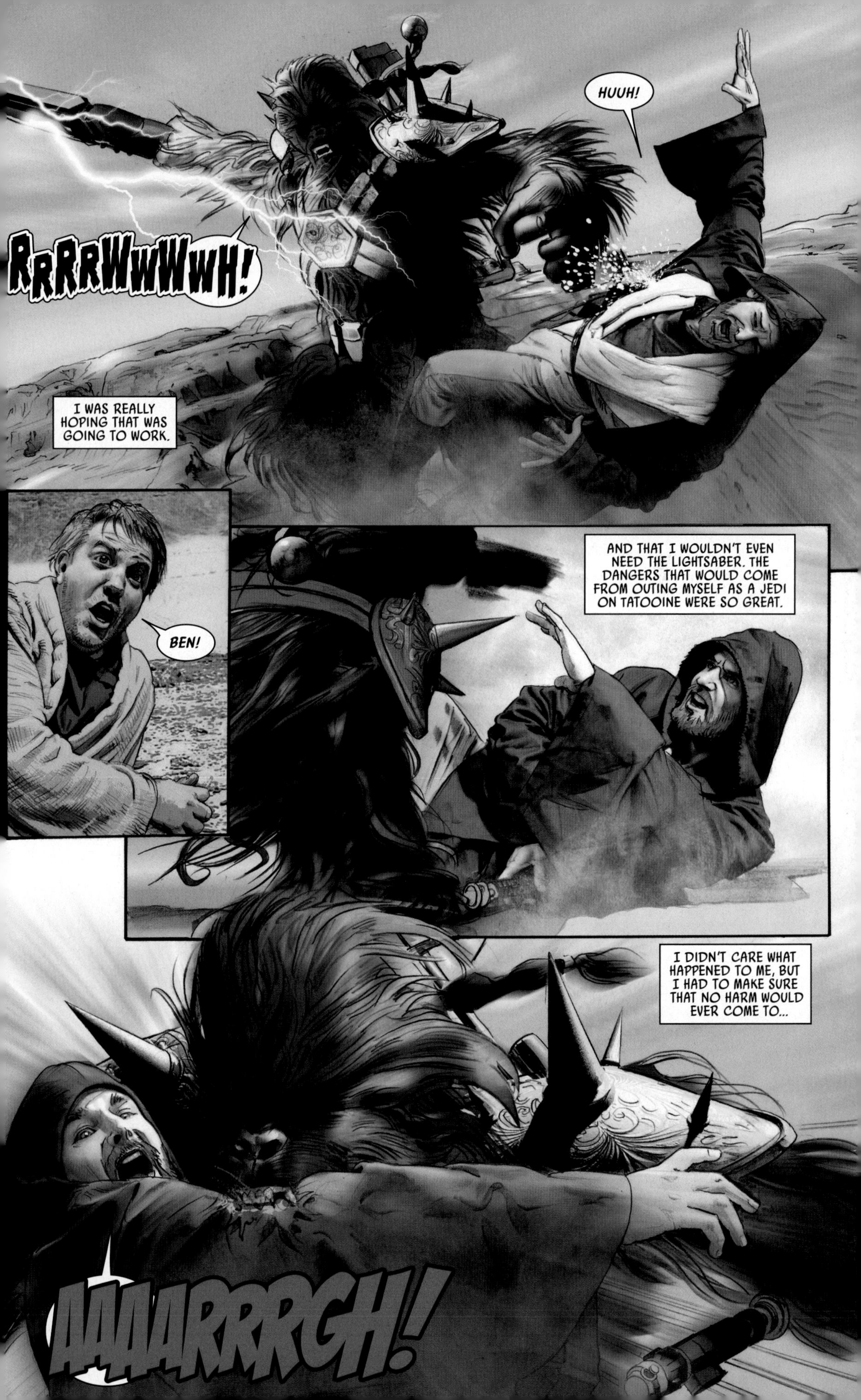

HUUH!
RRRRWWWWWH!
I WAS REALLY HOPING THAT WAS GOING TO WORK.
BEN!
AND THAT I WOULDN'T EVEN NEED THE LIGHTSABER. THE DANGERS THAT WOULD COME FROM OUTING MYSELF AS A JEDI ON TATOOINE WERE SO GREAT.
I DIDN'T CARE WHAT HAPPENED TO ME, BUT I HAD TO MAKE SURE THAT NO HARM WOULD EVER COME TO...
AAAARRRRGH!

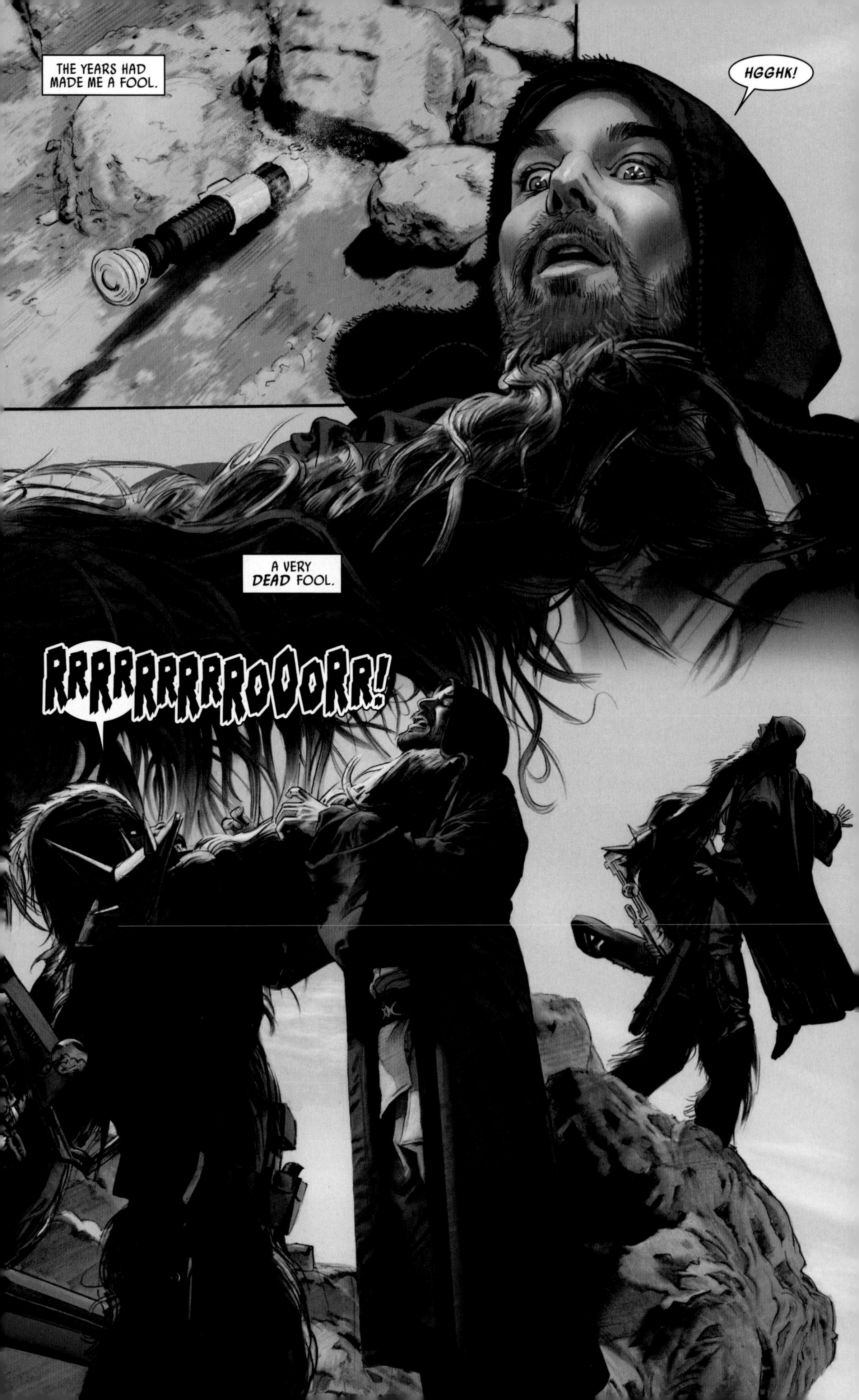
THE YEARS HAD MADE ME A FOOL.
HGGHK!
A VERY DEAD FOOL.
RRRRRRRRROOORR!

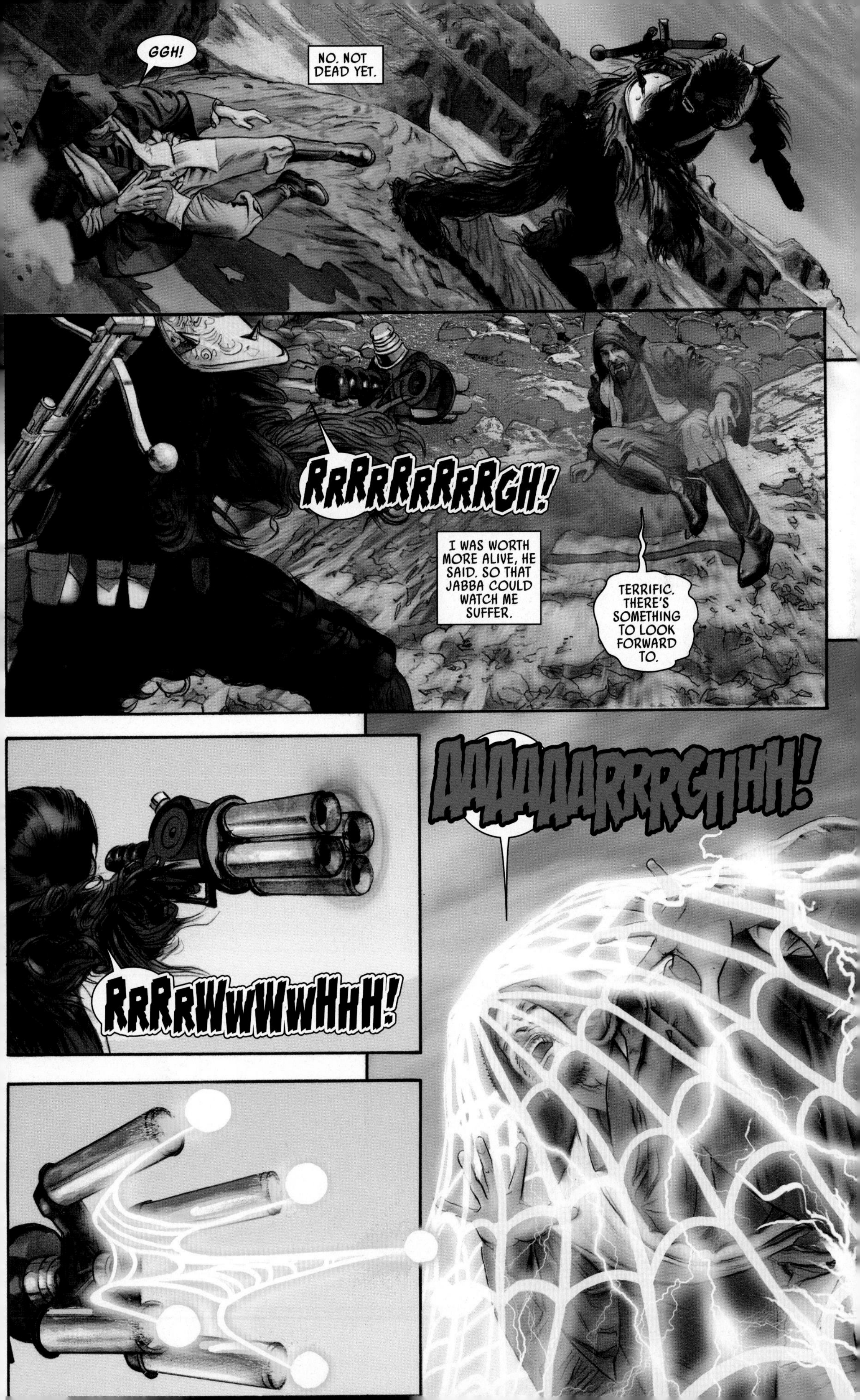
GGH!
NO. NOT DEAD YET.
RRRRRRRRRGH!
I WAS WORTH MORE ALIVE, HE SAID. SO THAT JABBA COULD WATCH ME SUFFER.
TERRIFIC. THERE'S SOMETHING TO LOOK FORWARD TO.
RRRRWWWWHHH!
AAAAAARRRGHHH!

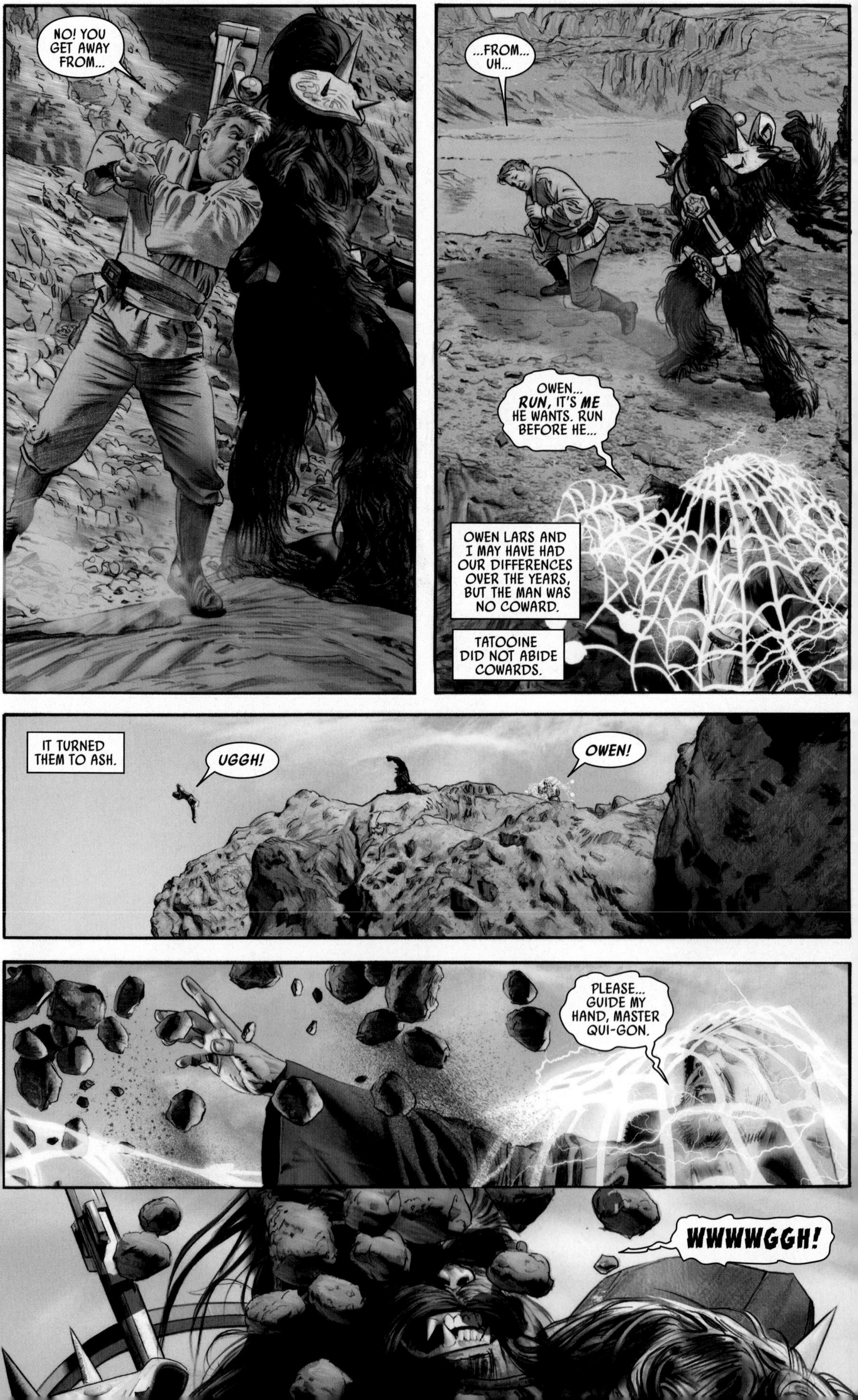
NO! YOU GET AWAY FROM...
...FROM... UH...
OWEN... RUN, IT'S ME HE WANTS. RUN BEFORE HE...
OWEN LARS AND I MAY HAVE HAD OUR DIFFERENCES OVER THE YEARS, BUT THE MAN WAS NO COWARD.
TATOOINE DID NOT ABIDE COWARDS.
IT TURNED THEM TO ASH.
UGGH!
OWEN!
PLEASE... GUIDE MY HAND, MASTER QUI-GON.
WWWWGGH!

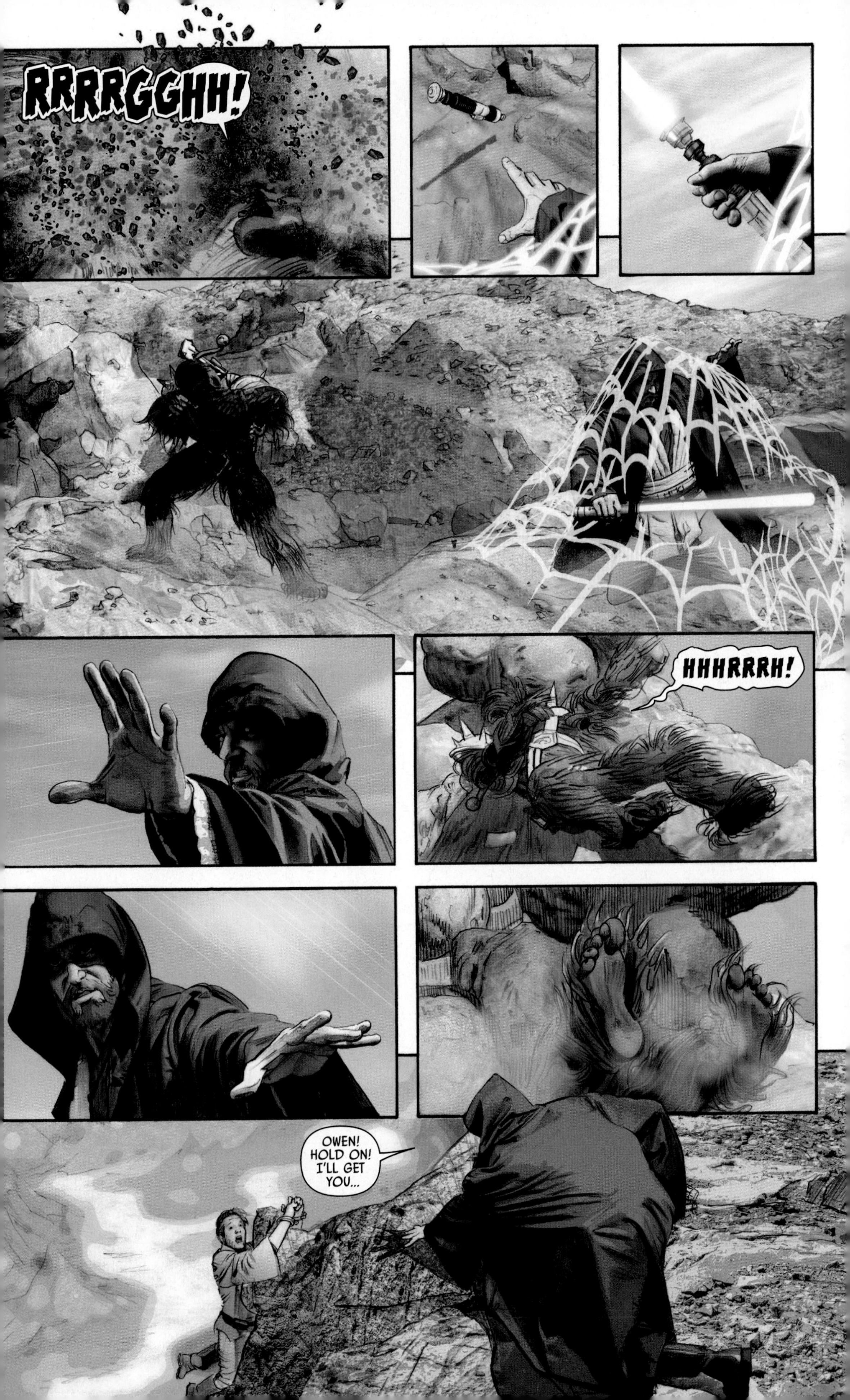
RRRRGGHH!
HHHRRRH!
OWEN! HOLD ON! I'LL GET YOU...

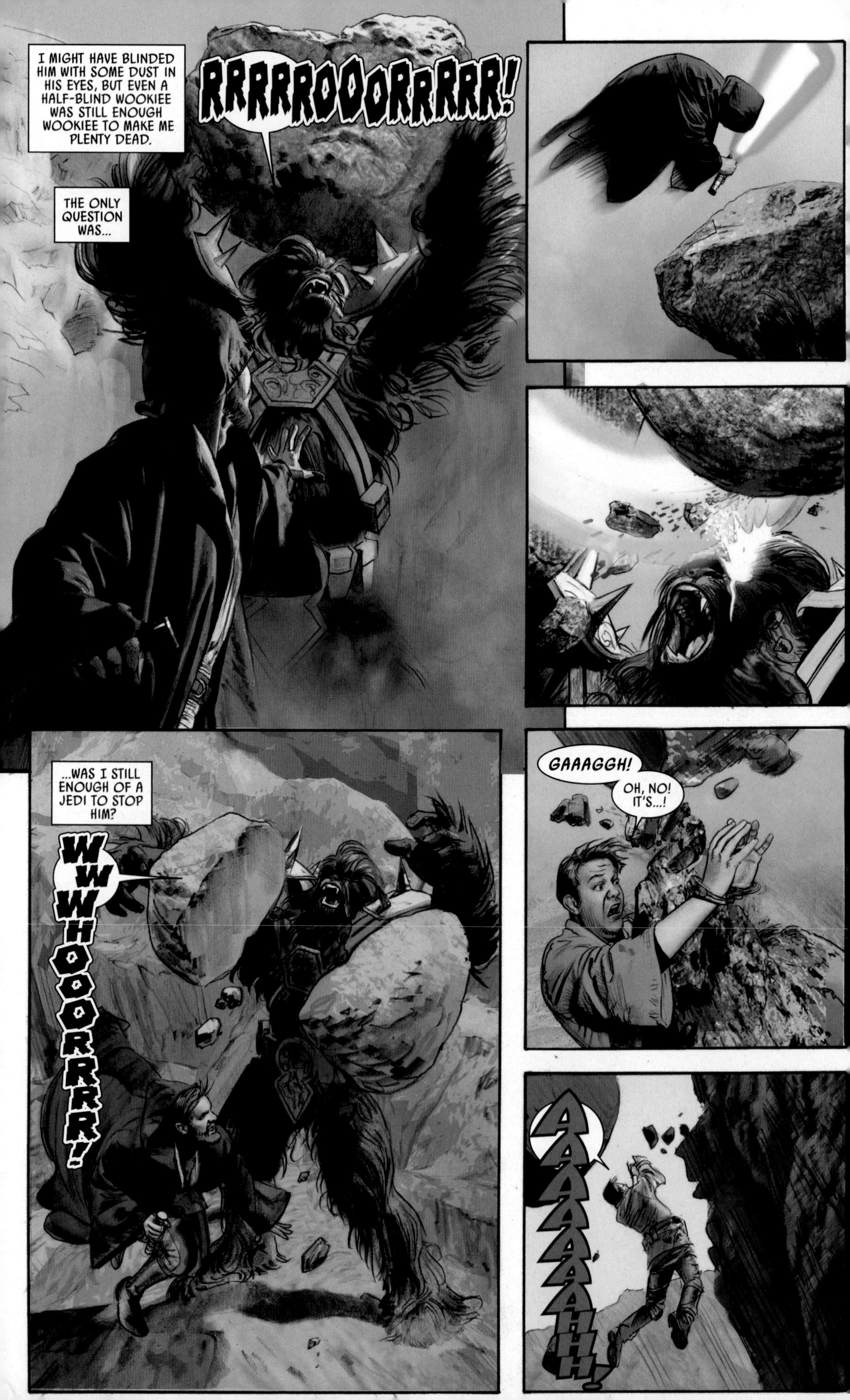

I MIGHT HAVE BLINDED HIM WITH SOME DUST IN HIS EYES, BUT EVEN A HALF-BLIND WOOKIEE WAS STILL ENOUGH WOOKIEE TO MAKE ME PLENTY DEAD.
RRRRROOORRRRR!
THE ONLY QUESTION WAS...
...WAS I STILL ENOUGH OF A JEDI TO STOP HIM?
WWWHOOOORRRRR!
GAAAGGH!
OH, NO! IT'S...!
AAAAAAAHHH!

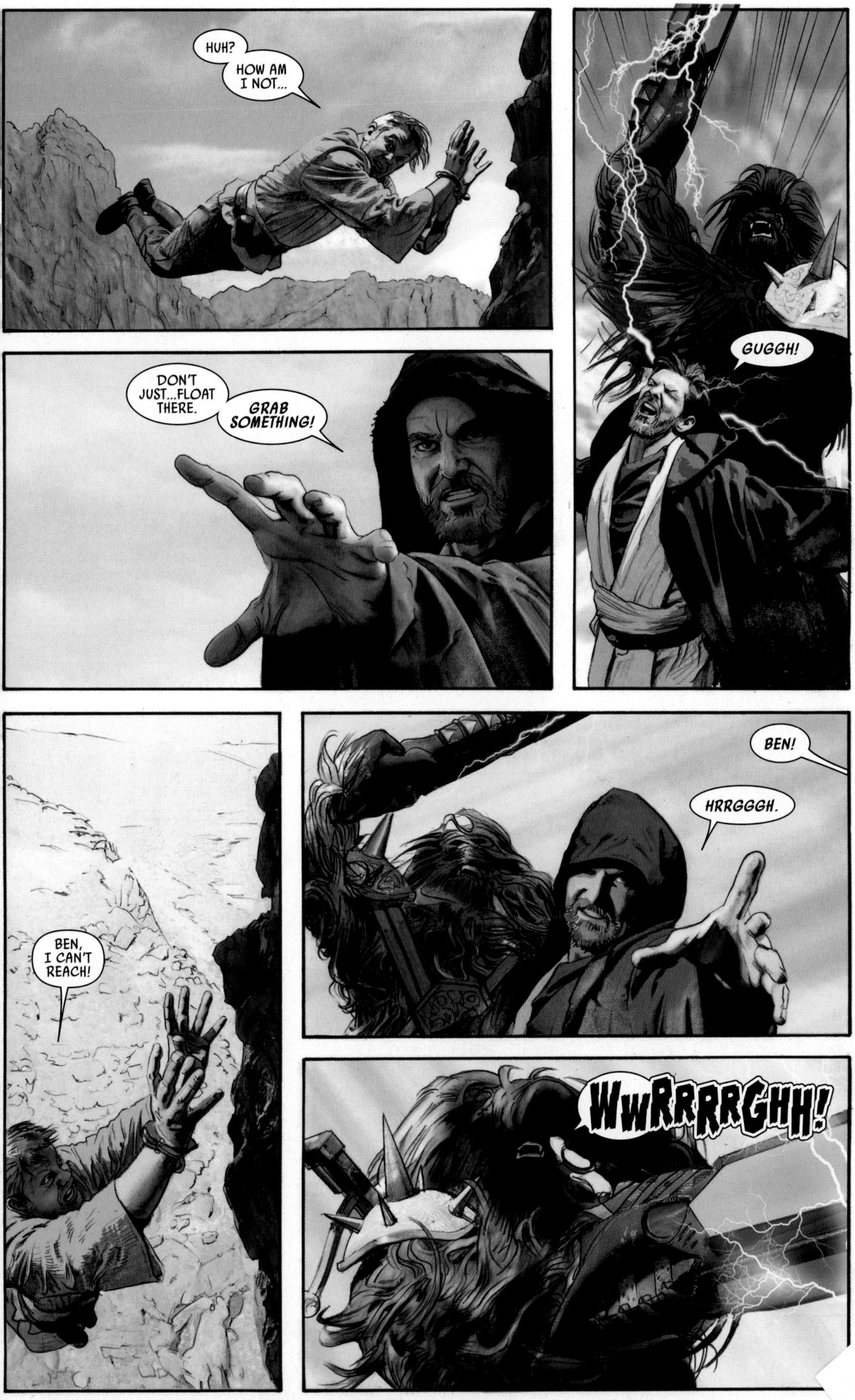
HUH?
HOW AM I NOT...
GUGGH!
DON'T JUST...FLOAT THERE.
GRAB SOMETHING!
BEN, I CAN'T REACH!
BEN!
HRRGGGH.
WwRRRRRGHH!

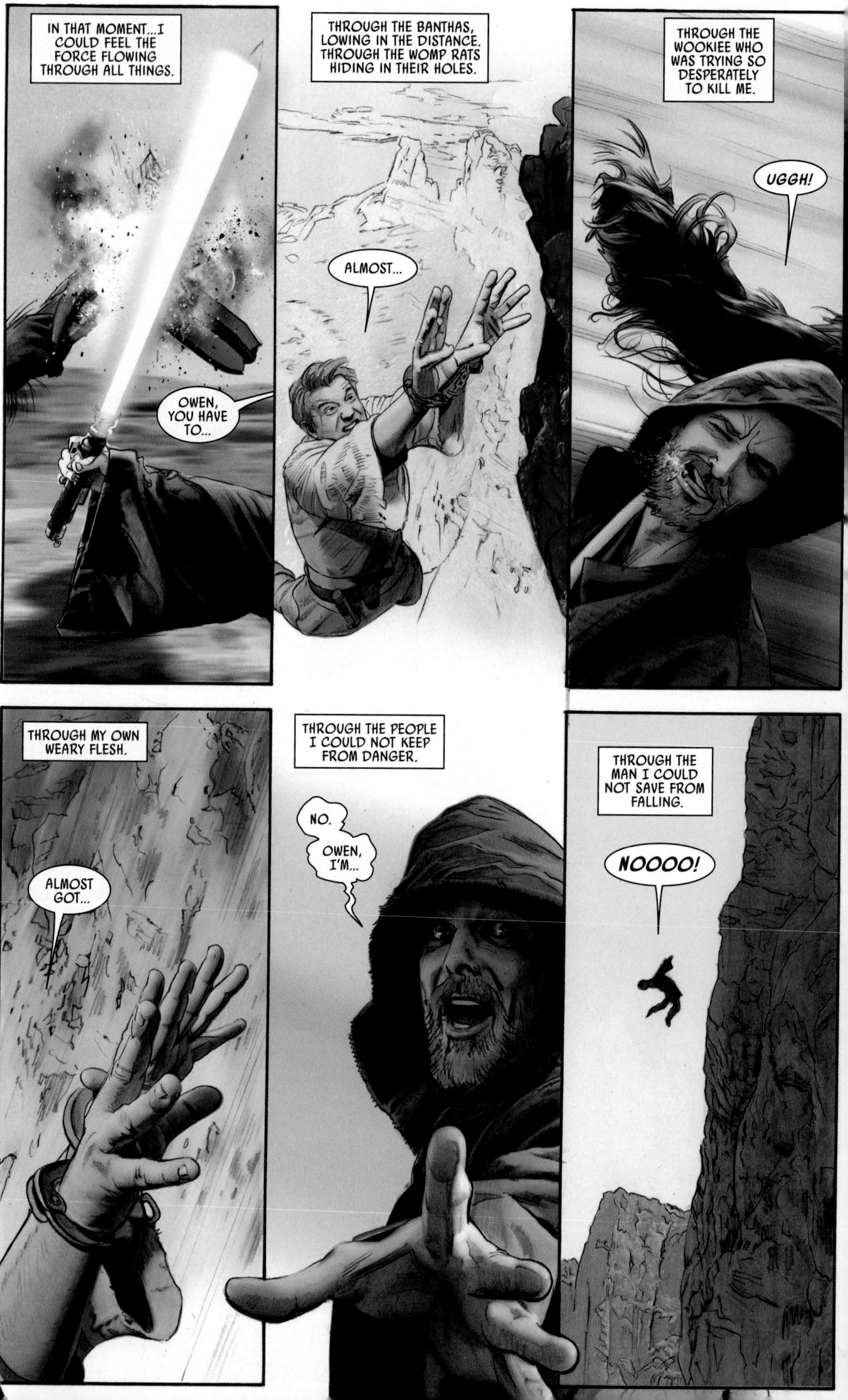
IN THAT MOMENT...I COULD FEEL THE FORCE FLOWING THROUGH ALL THINGS.
OWEN, YOU HAVE TO...
THROUGH THE BANTHAS, LOWING IN THE DISTANCE. THROUGH THE WOMP RATS HIDING IN THEIR HOLES.
ALMOST...
THROUGH THE WOOKIEE WHO WAS TRYING SO DESPERATELY TO KILL ME.
UGGH!
THROUGH MY OWN WEARY FLESH.
ALMOST GOT...
THROUGH THE PEOPLE I COULD NOT KEEP FROM DANGER.
NO.
OWEN, I'M...
THROUGH THE MAN I COULD NOT SAVE FROM FALLING.
NOOOO!

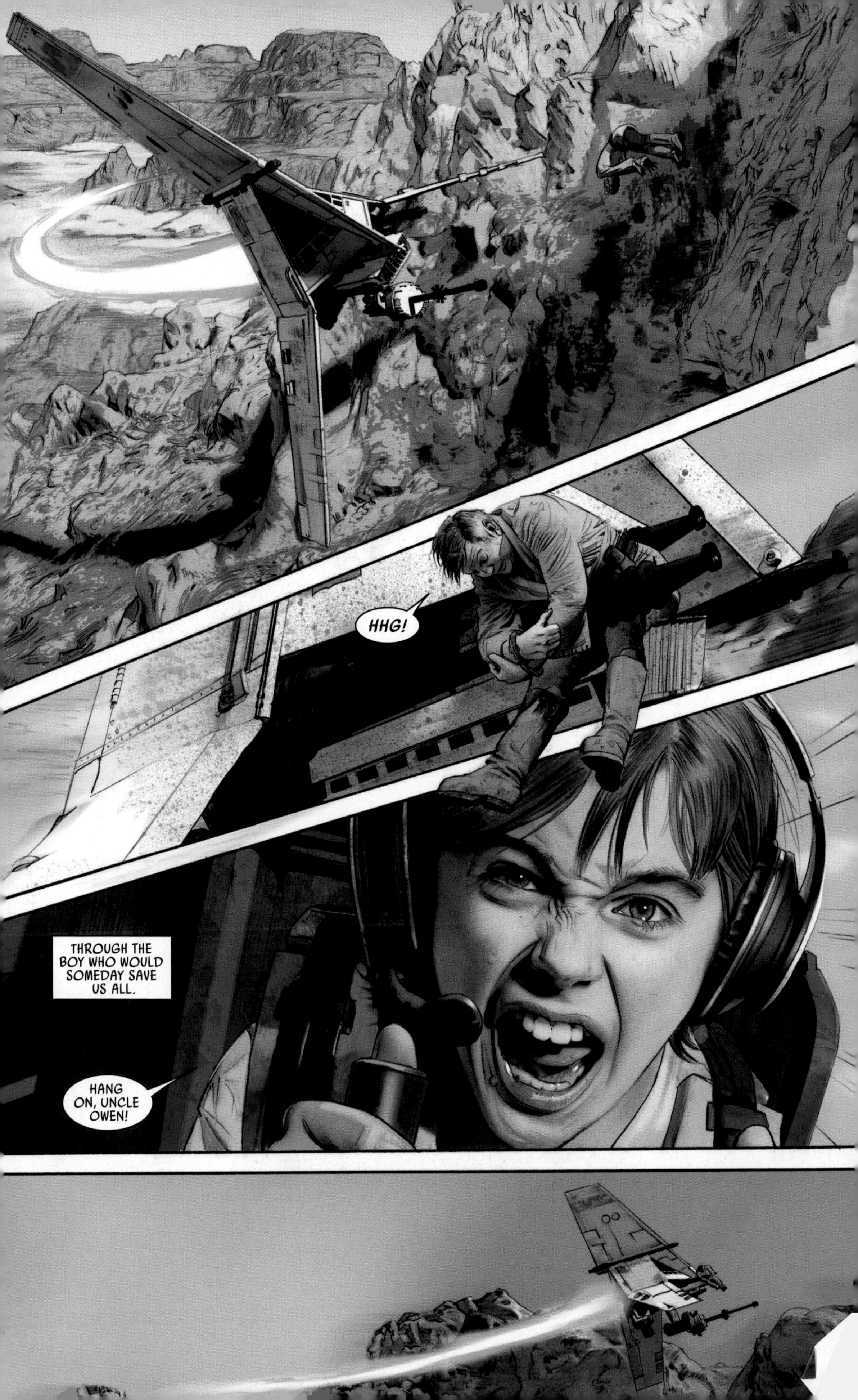
HHG!
THROUGH THE BOY WHO WOULD SOMEDAY SAVE US ALL.
HANG ON, UNCLE OWEN!

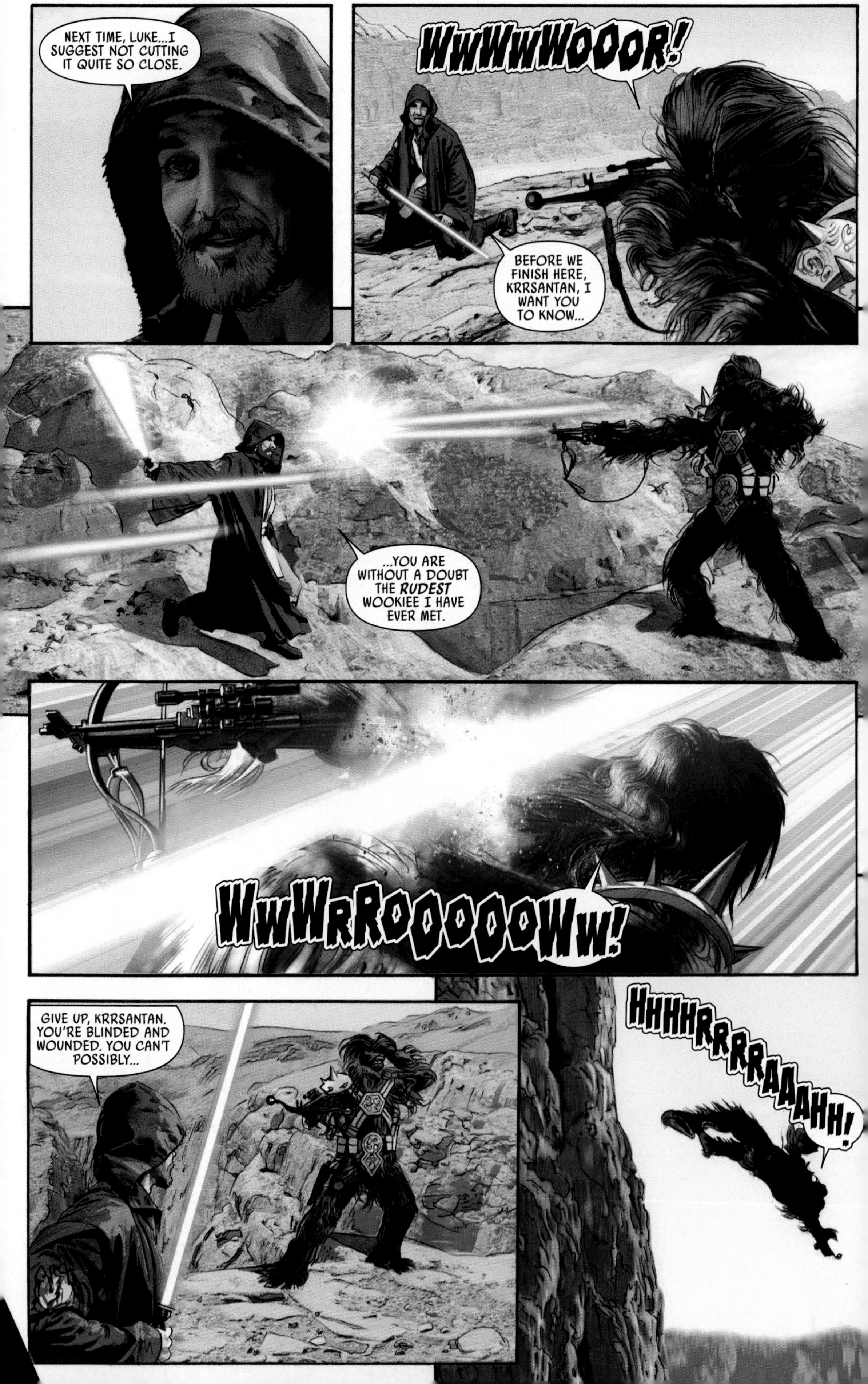
NEXT TIME, LUKE...I SUGGEST NOT CUTTING IT QUITE SO CLOSE.
WWWWWWOOOR!
BEFORE WE FINISH HERE, KRRSANTAN, I WANT YOU TO KNOW...
...YOU ARE WITHOUT A DOUBT THE RUDEST WOOKIEE I HAVE EVER MET.
WWWRROOOOOWW!
GIVE UP, KRRSANTAN. YOU'RE BLINDED AND WOUNDED. YOU CAN'T POSSIBLY...
HHHHRRRRAAAHH!

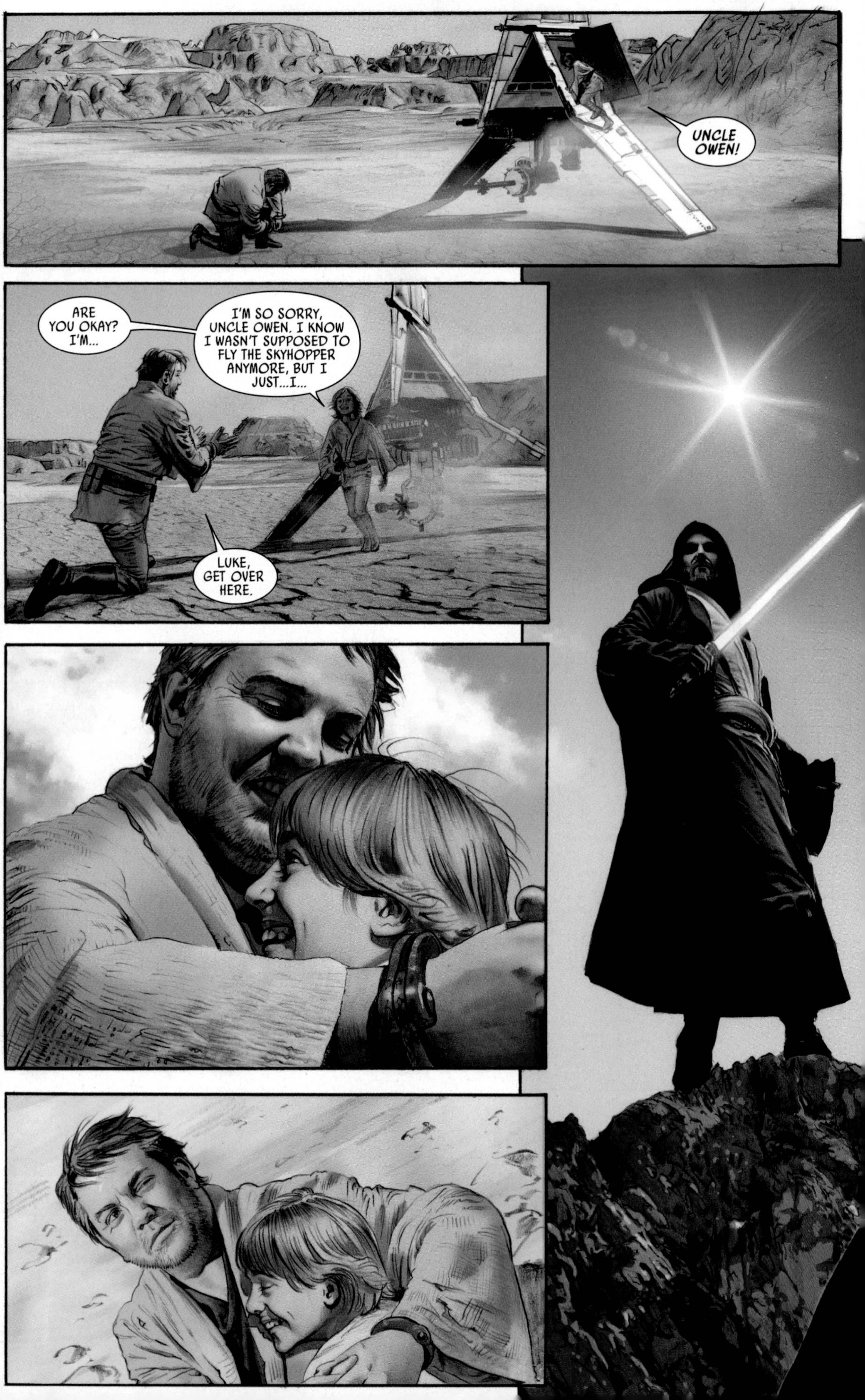
UNCLE OWEN!
ARE YOU OKAY? I'M...
I'M SO SORRY, UNCLE OWEN. I KNOW I WASN'T SUPPOSED TO FLY THE SKYHOPPER ANYMORE, BUT I JUST...I...
LUKE, GET OVER HERE.

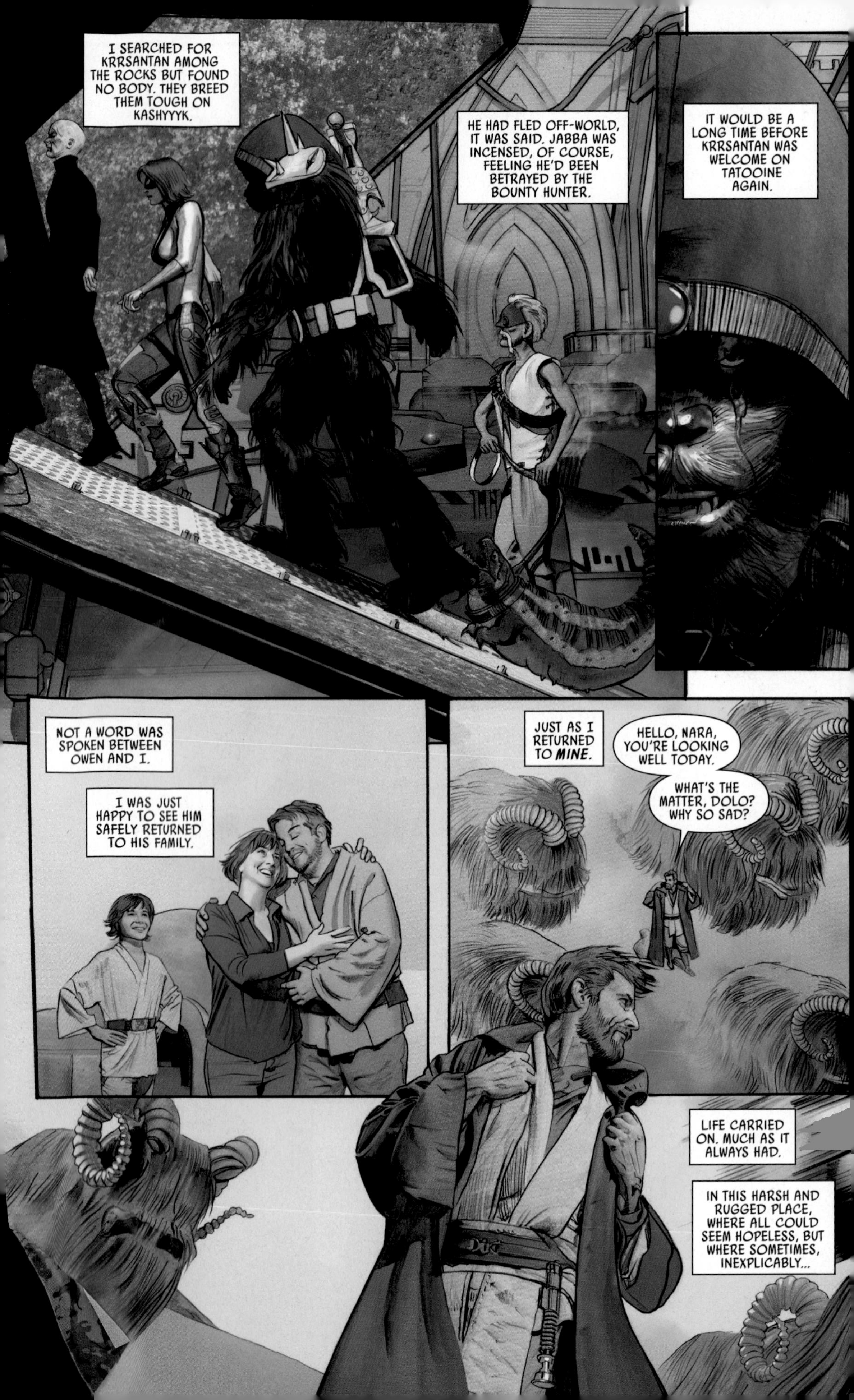
I SEARCHED FOR KRRSANTAN AMONG THE ROCKS BUT FOUND NO BODY. THEY BREED THEM TOUGH ON KASHYYYK.
HE HAD FLED OFF-WORLD, IT WAS SAID. JABBA WAS INCENSED, OF COURSE, FEELING HE'D BEEN BETRAYED BY THE BOUNTY HUNTER.
IT WOULD BE A LONG TIME BEFORE KRRSANTAN WAS WELCOME ON TATOOINE AGAIN.
NOT A WORD WAS SPOKEN BETWEEN OWEN AND I.
I WAS JUST HAPPY TO SEE HIM SAFELY RETURNED TO HIS FAMILY.
JUST AS I RETURNED TO *MINE.*
HELLO, NARA, YOU'RE LOOKING WELL TODAY.
WHAT'S THE MATTER, DOLO? WHY SO SAD?
LIFE CARRIED ON. MUCH AS IT ALWAYS HAD.
IN THIS HARSH AND RUGGED PLACE, WHERE ALL COULD SEEM HOPELESS, BUT WHERE SOMETIMES, INEXPLICABLY...

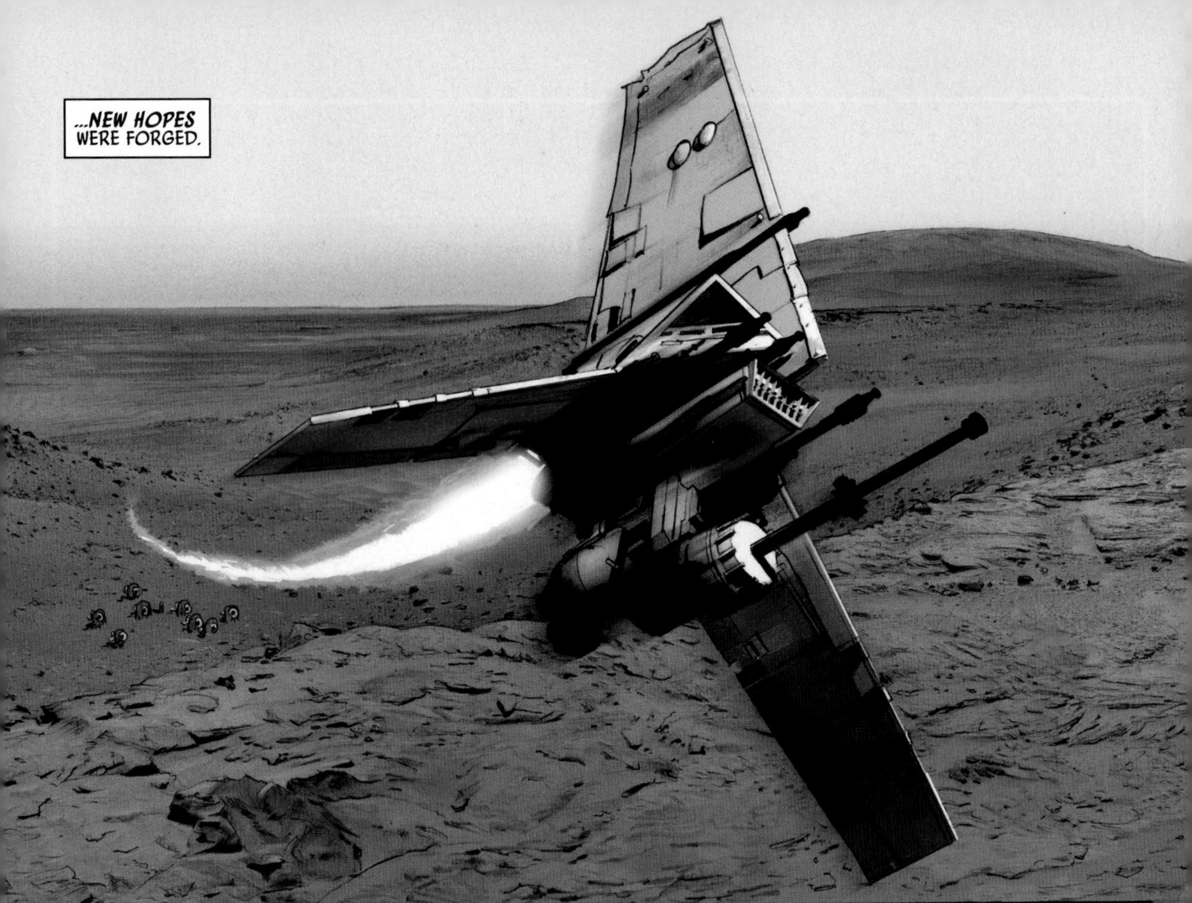
...NEW HOPES
WERE FORGED.

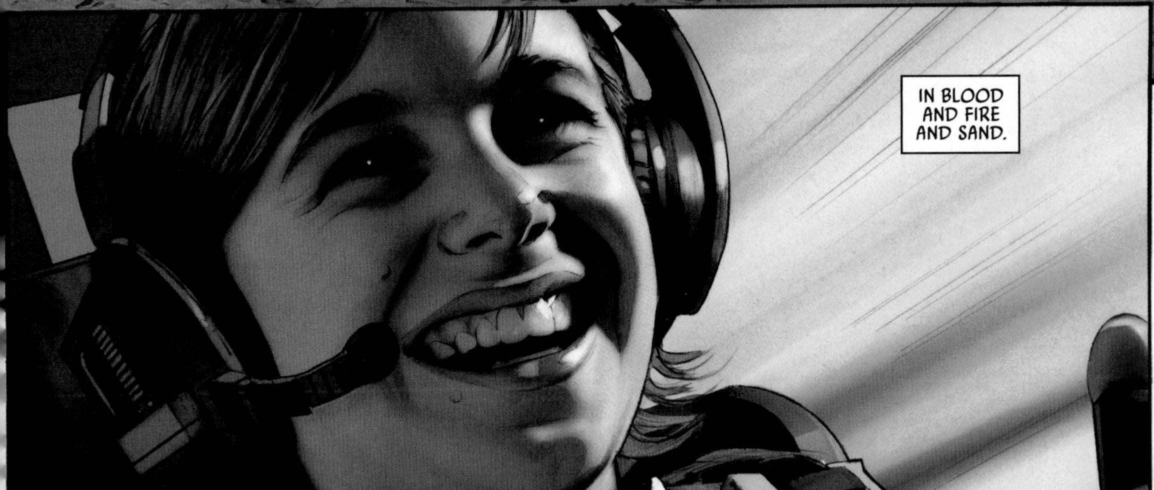
IN BLOOD
AND FIRE
AND SAND.

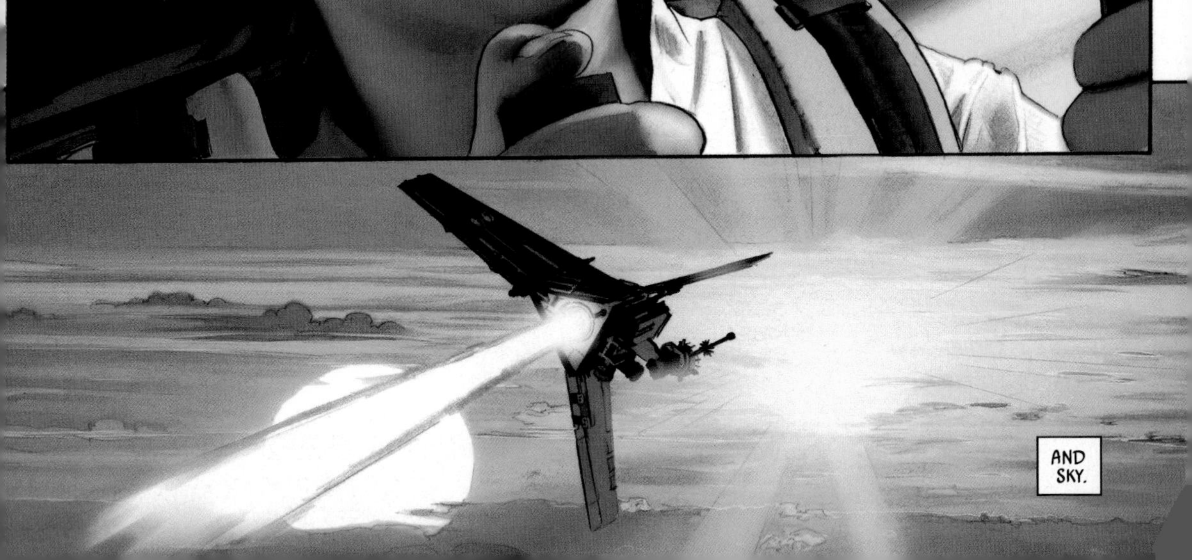
AND
SKY.

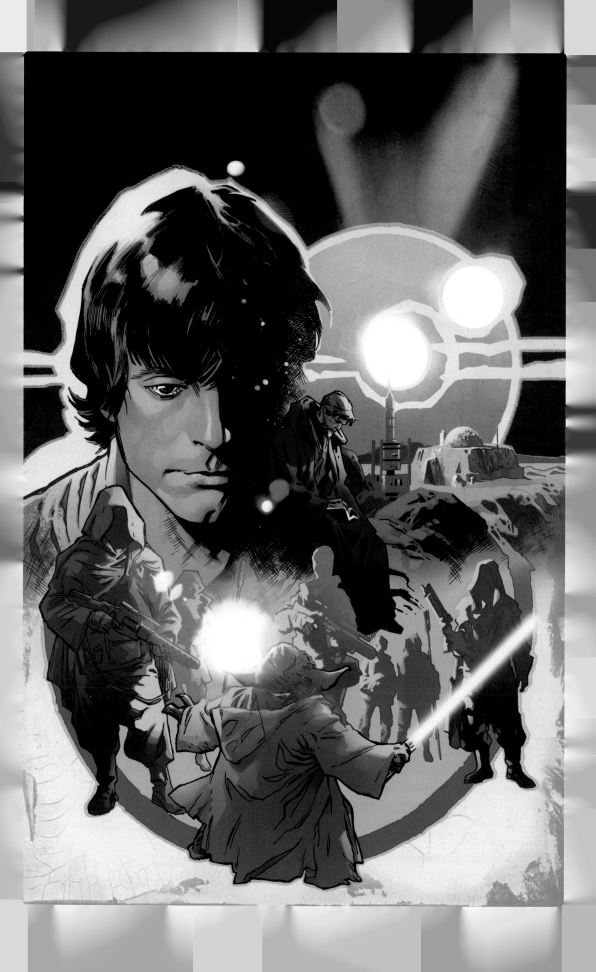

YODA'S SECRET WAR

It is a time of renewed hope for the Rebel Alliance. but the Galactic Empire continues to hold its domination and has doubled its efforts to eliminate any who would stand against its rule.

The Alliance's heroes, pilot Luke Skywalker, Princess Leia, and smuggler-turned-soldier Han Solo, have just succeeded in stealing a massive Star Destroyer to deliver supplies to an ally planet.

However, their success does not come without cost — Darth Vader enlists a group of ultra-dangerous stormtroopers, Scar Squadron, to destroy the rebels. Even though Luke, Leia, and Han escape victorious, the stormtroopers, humiliated in their defeat, vow retribution. In order to force another battle, Scar Squadron turns its focus on its new prisoner: C-3PO....

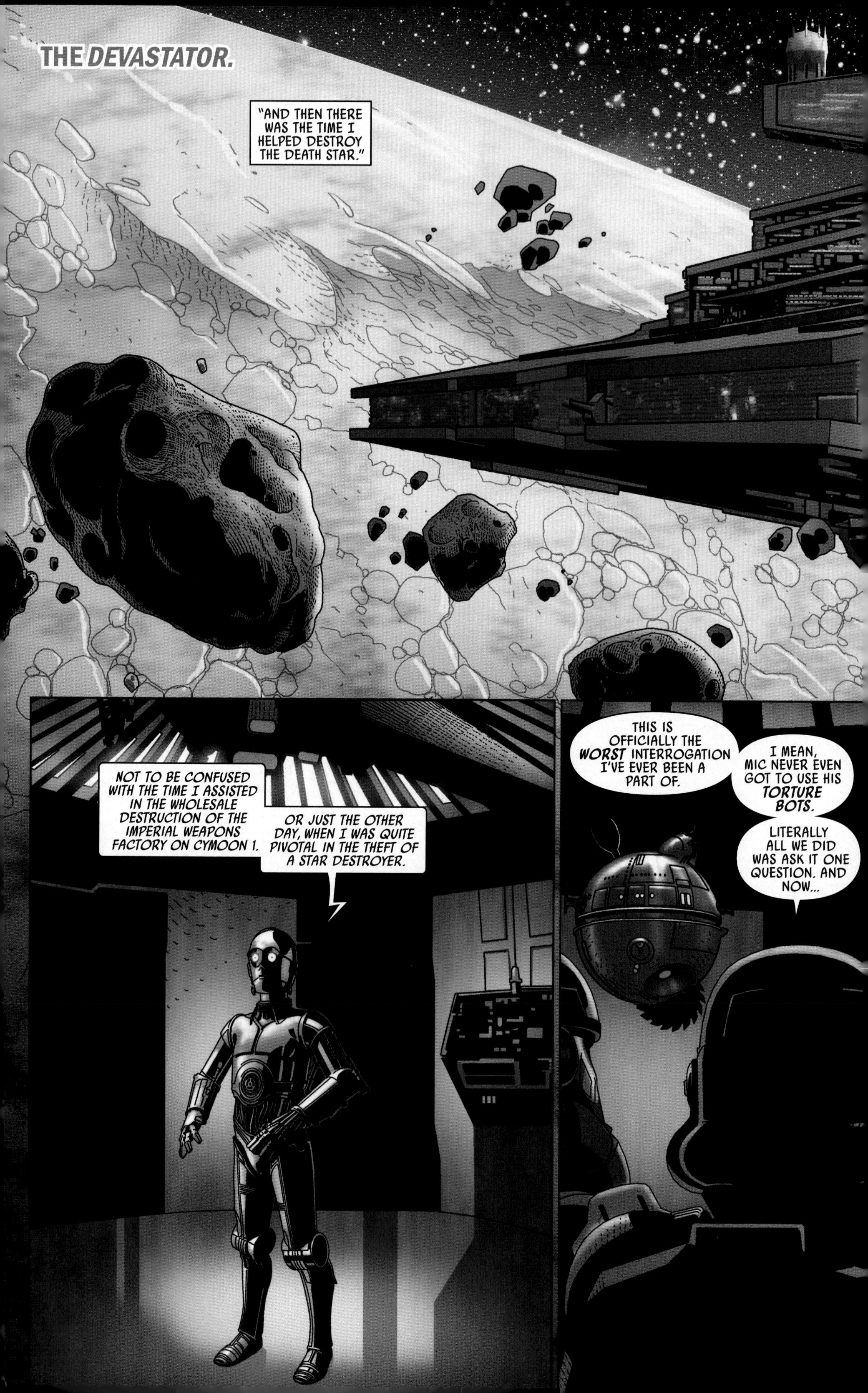
THE DEVASTATOR.
"AND THEN THERE WAS THE TIME I HELPED DESTROY THE DEATH STAR."
NOT TO BE CONFUSED WITH THE TIME I ASSISTED IN THE WHOLESALE DESTRUCTION OF THE IMPERIAL WEAPONS FACTORY ON CYMOON 1.
OR JUST THE OTHER DAY, WHEN I WAS QUITE PIVOTAL IN THE THEFT OF A STAR DESTROYER.
THIS IS OFFICIALLY THE WORST INTERROGATION I'VE EVER BEEN A PART OF.
I MEAN, MIC NEVER EVEN GOT TO USE HIS TORTURE BOTS.
LITERALLY ALL WE DID WAS ASK IT ONE QUESTION. AND NOW...

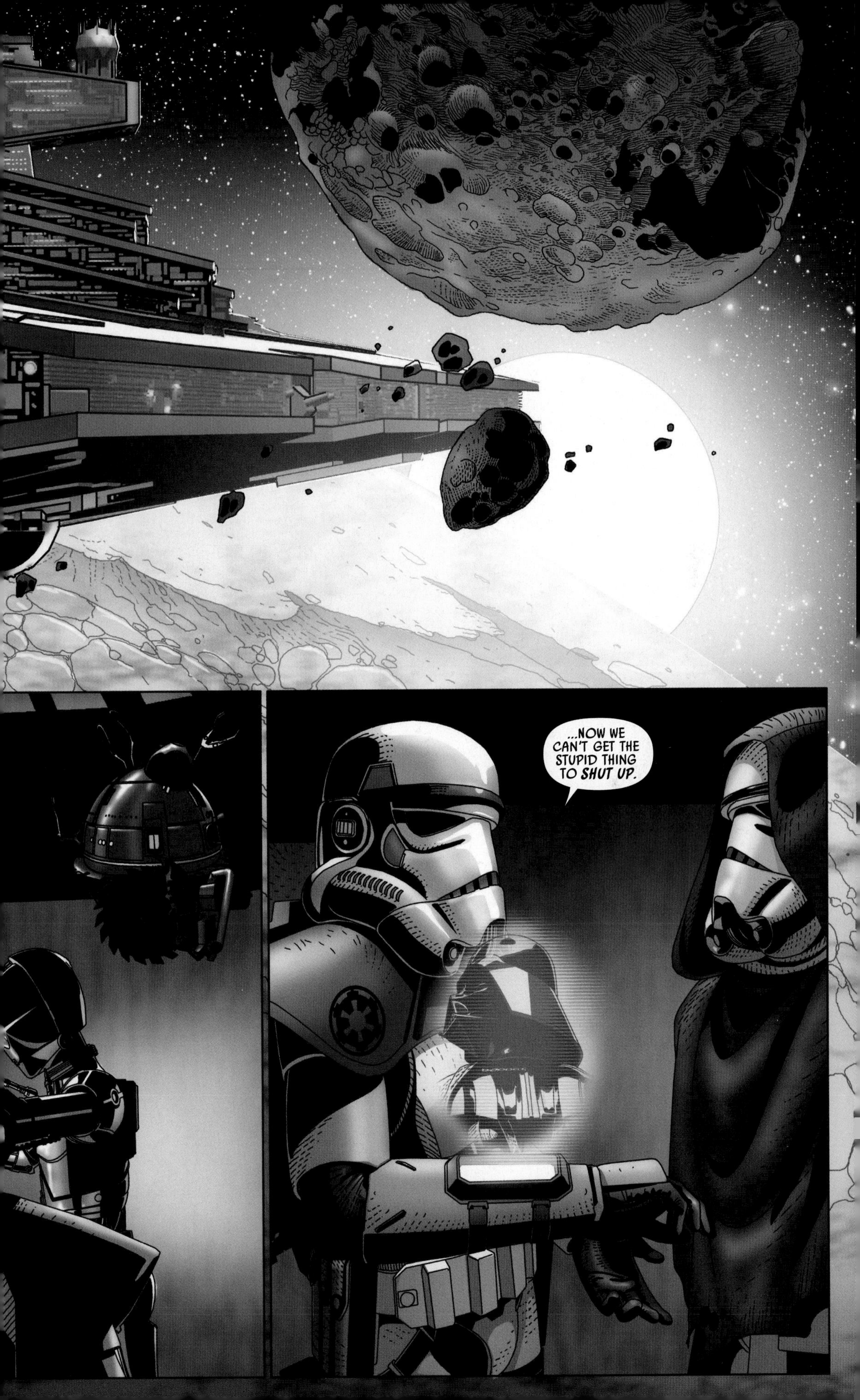
...NOW WE CAN'T GET THE STUPID THING TO SHUT UP.

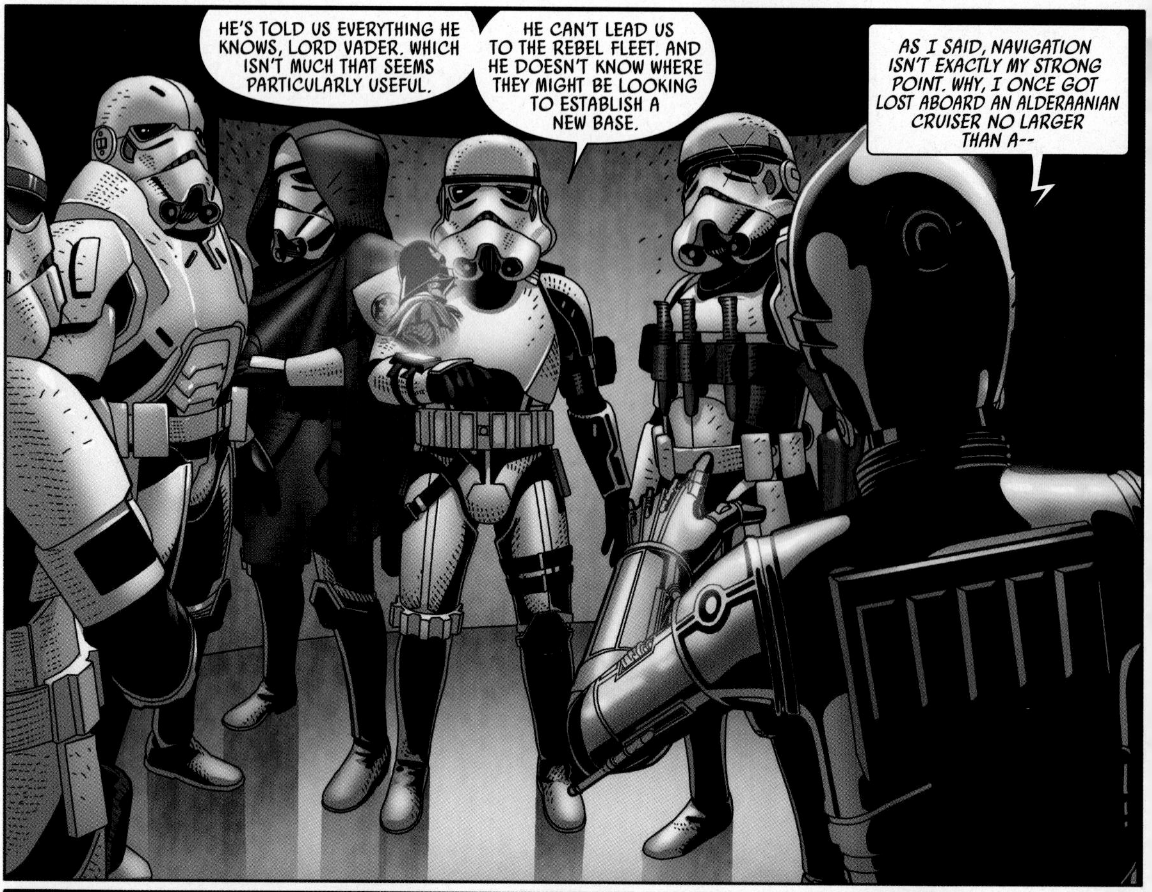
HE'S TOLD US EVERYTHING HE KNOWS, LORD VADER. WHICH ISN'T MUCH THAT SEEMS PARTICULARLY USEFUL.
HE CAN'T LEAD US TO THE REBEL FLEET. AND HE DOESN'T KNOW WHERE THEY MIGHT BE LOOKING TO ESTABLISH A NEW BASE.
AS I SAID, NAVIGATION ISN'T EXACTLY MY STRONG POINT. WHY, I ONCE GOT LOST ABOARD AN ALDERAANIAN CRUISER NO LARGER THAN A--

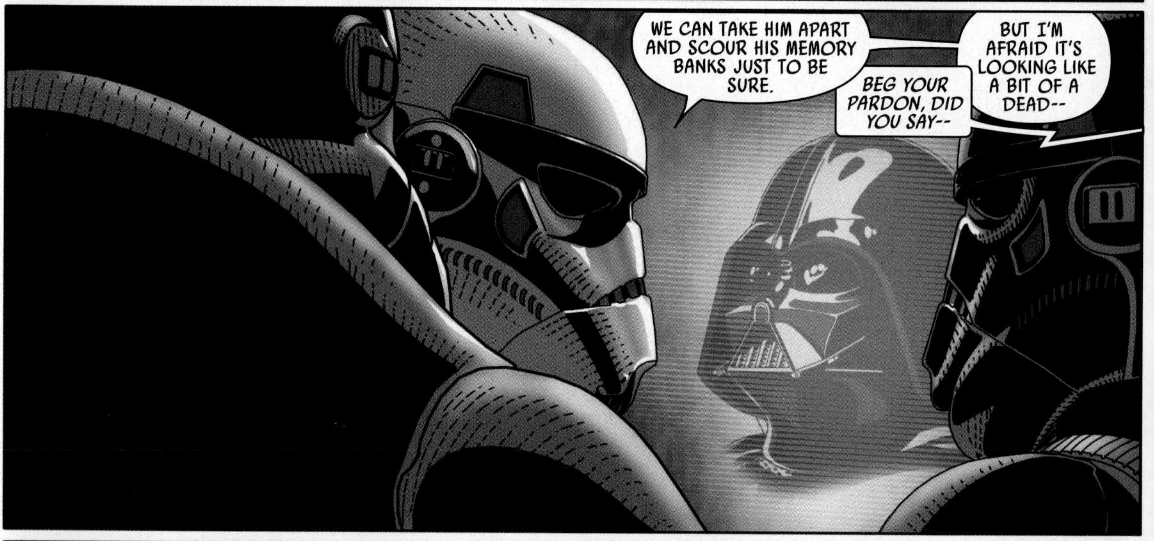
WE CAN TAKE HIM APART AND SCOUR HIS MEMORY BANKS JUST TO BE SURE.
BUT I'M AFRAID IT'S LOOKING LIKE A BIT OF A DEAD--
BEG YOUR PARDON, DID YOU SAY--

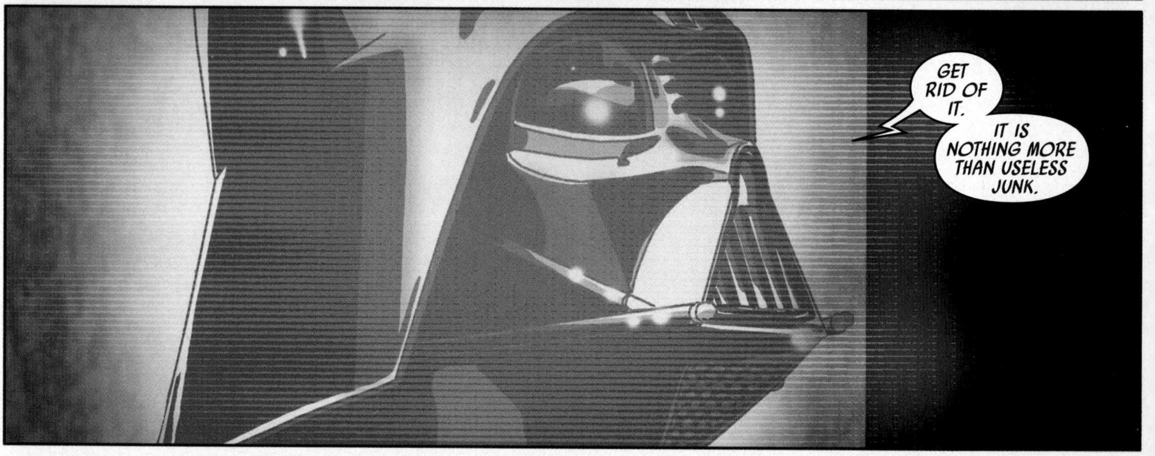
GET RID OF IT.
IT IS NOTHING MORE THAN USELESS JUNK.

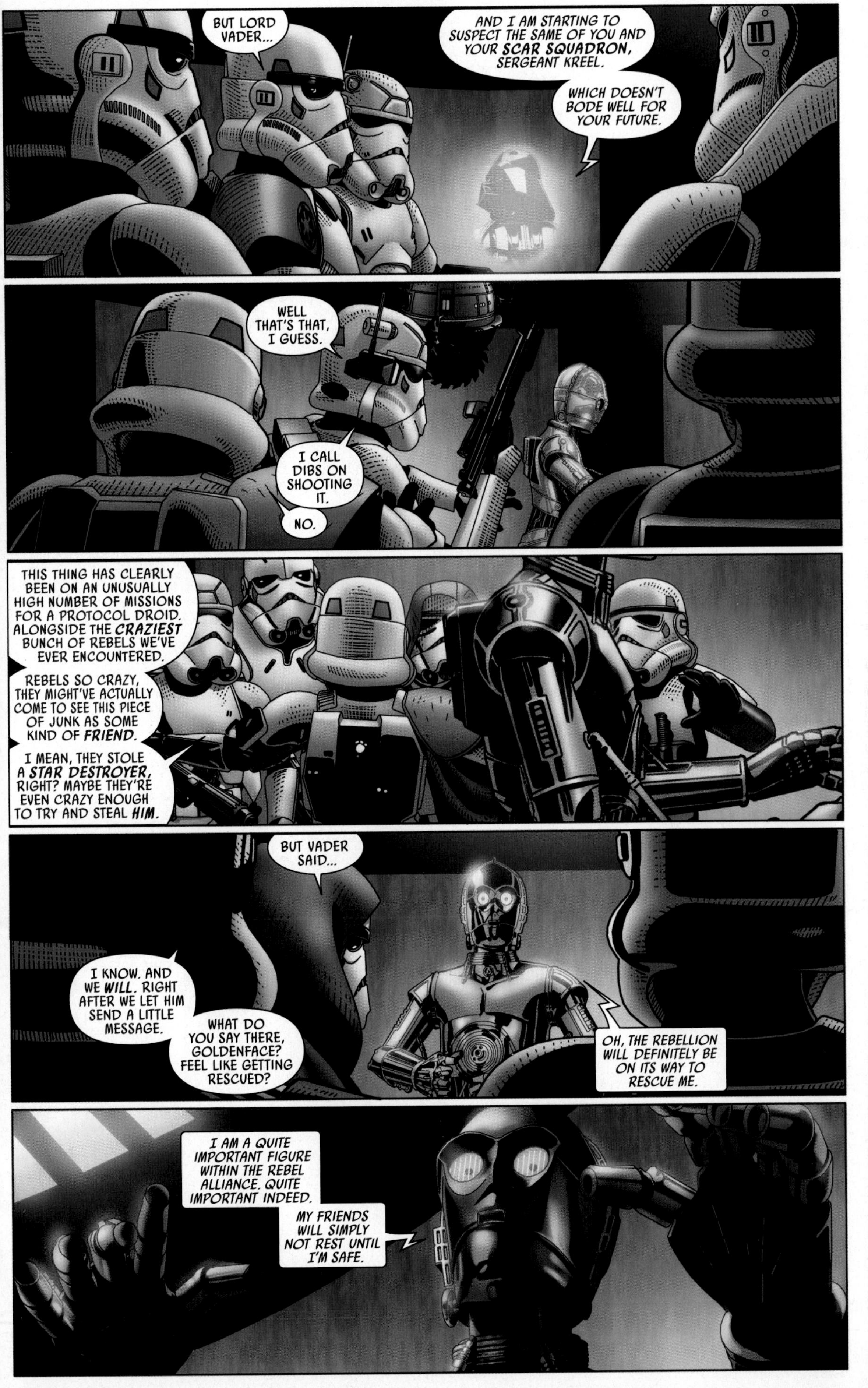
BUT LORD VADER...
AND I AM STARTING TO SUSPECT THE SAME OF YOU AND YOUR SCAR SQUADRON, SERGEANT KREEL.
WHICH DOESN'T BODE WELL FOR YOUR FUTURE.
WELL THAT'S THAT, I GUESS.
I CALL DIBS ON SHOOTING IT.
NO.
THIS THING HAS CLEARLY BEEN ON AN UNUSUALLY HIGH NUMBER OF MISSIONS FOR A PROTOCOL DROID. ALONGSIDE THE CRAZIEST BUNCH OF REBELS WE'VE EVER ENCOUNTERED.
REBELS SO CRAZY, THEY MIGHT'VE ACTUALLY COME TO SEE THIS PIECE OF JUNK AS SOME KIND OF FRIEND.
I MEAN, THEY STOLE A STAR DESTROYER, RIGHT? MAYBE THEY'RE EVEN CRAZY ENOUGH TO TRY AND STEAL HIM.
BUT VADER SAID...
I KNOW. AND WE WILL. RIGHT AFTER WE LET HIM SEND A LITTLE MESSAGE.
WHAT DO YOU SAY THERE, GOLDENFACE? FEEL LIKE GETTING RESCUED?
OH, THE REBELLION WILL DEFINITELY BE ON ITS WAY TO RESCUE ME.
I AM A QUITE IMPORTANT FIGURE WITHIN THE REBEL ALLIANCE. QUITE IMPORTANT INDEED.
MY FRIENDS WILL SIMPLY NOT REST UNTIL I'M SAFE.

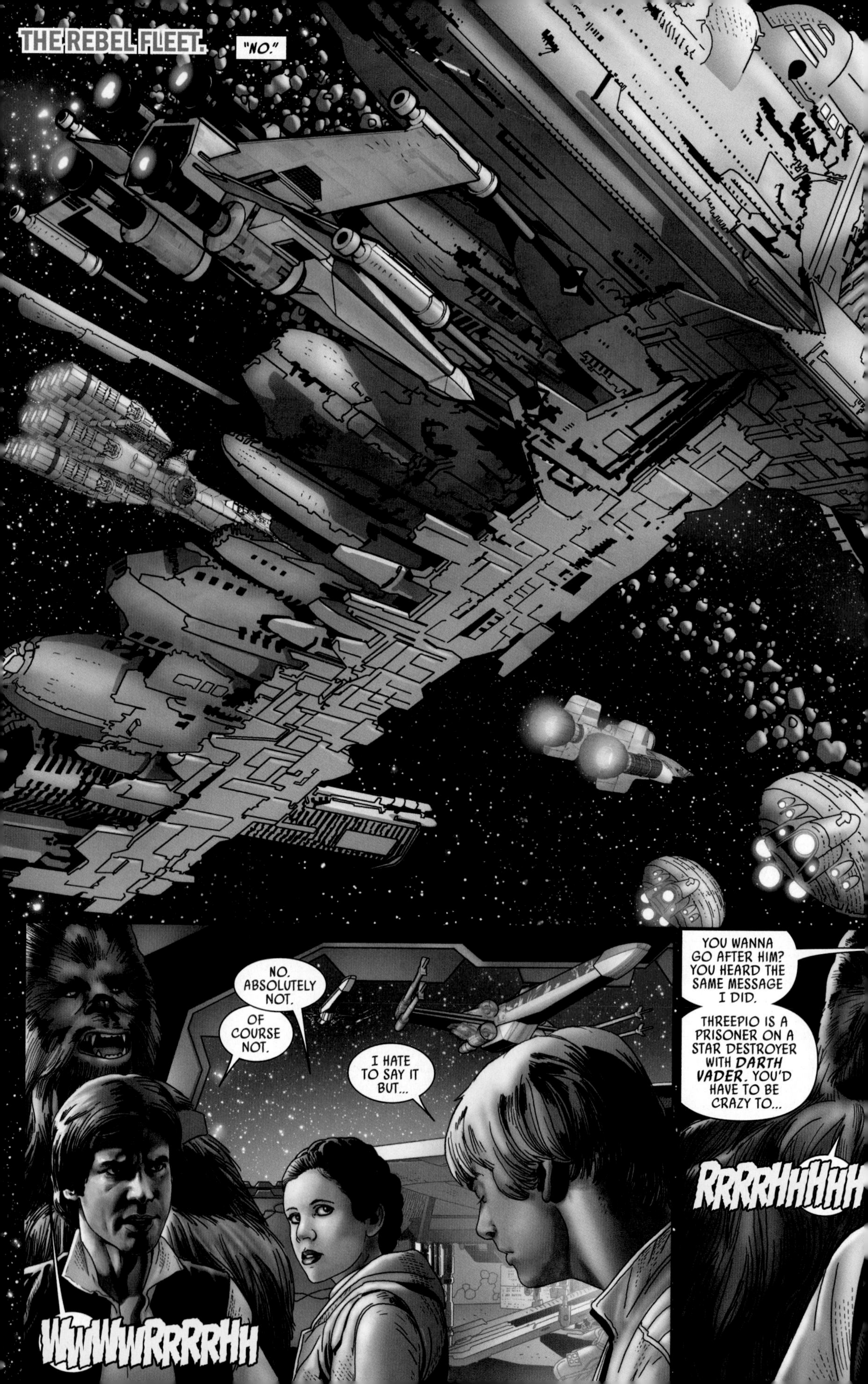
THE REBEL FLEET.
"NO."
NO. ABSOLUTELY NOT.
OF COURSE NOT.
I HATE TO SAY IT BUT...
WWWWWRRRRHH
YOU WANNA GO AFTER HIM? YOU HEARD THE SAME MESSAGE I DID.
THREEPIO IS A PRISONER ON A STAR DESTROYER WITH DARTH VADER. YOU'D HAVE TO BE CRAZY TO...
RRRRHHHHH

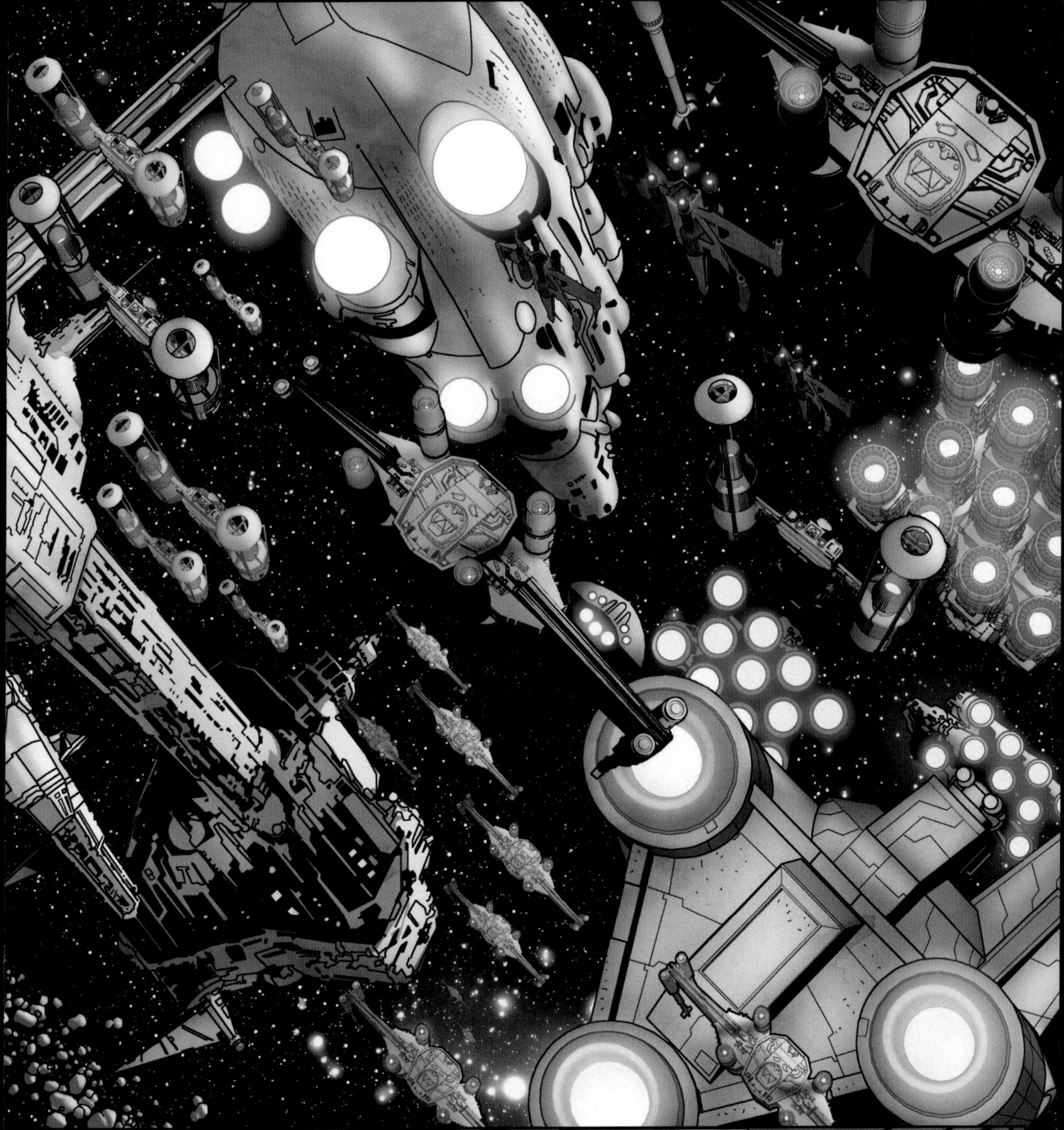

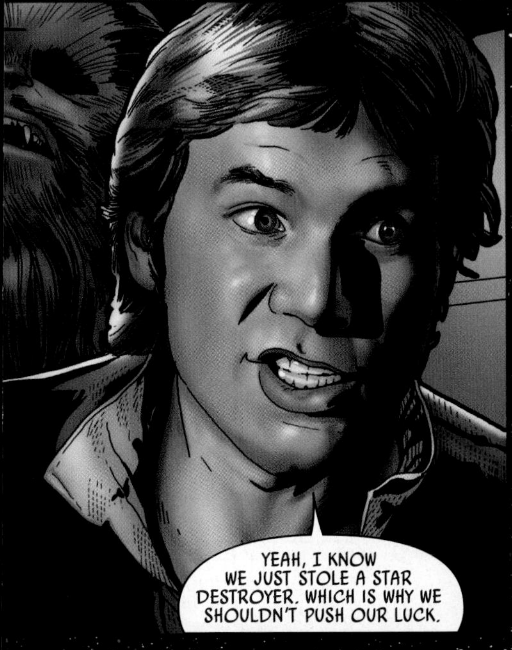
YEAH, I KNOW WE JUST STOLE A STAR DESTROYER. WHICH IS WHY WE SHOULDN'T PUSH OUR LUCK.

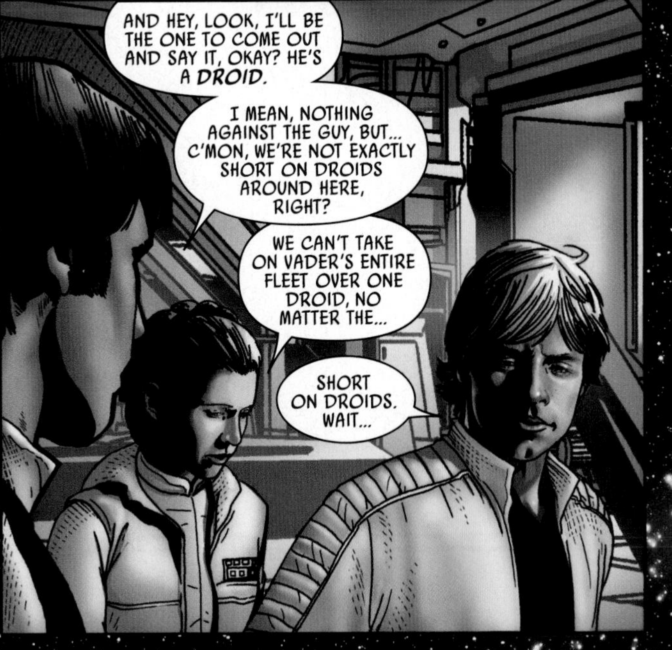
AND HEY, LOOK, I'LL BE THE ONE TO COME OUT AND SAY IT, OKAY? HE'S A *DROID*.
I MEAN, NOTHING AGAINST THE GUY, BUT... C'MON, WE'RE NOT EXACTLY SHORT ON DROIDS AROUND HERE, RIGHT?
WE CAN'T TAKE ON VADER'S ENTIRE FLEET OVER ONE DROID, NO MATTER THE...
SHORT ON DROIDS. WAIT...

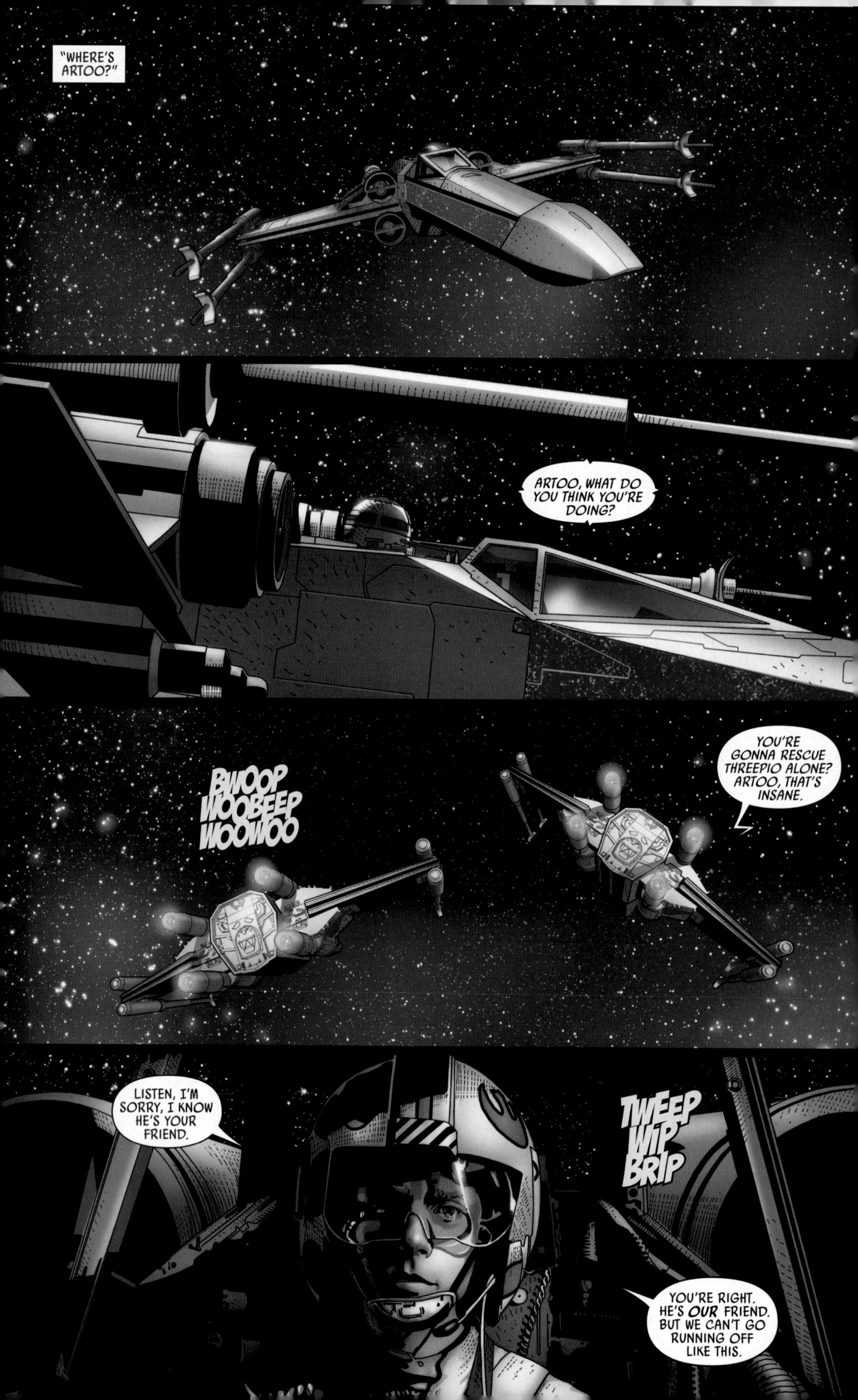
"WHERE'S ARTOO?"
ARTOO, WHAT DO YOU THINK YOU'RE DOING?
BWOOP WOOBEEP WOOWOO
YOU'RE GONNA RESCUE THREEPIO ALONE? ARTOO, THAT'S INSANE.
LISTEN, I'M SORRY, I KNOW HE'S YOUR FRIEND.
TWEEP WIP BRIP
YOU'RE RIGHT. HE'S OUR FRIEND. BUT WE CAN'T GO RUNNING OFF LIKE THIS.

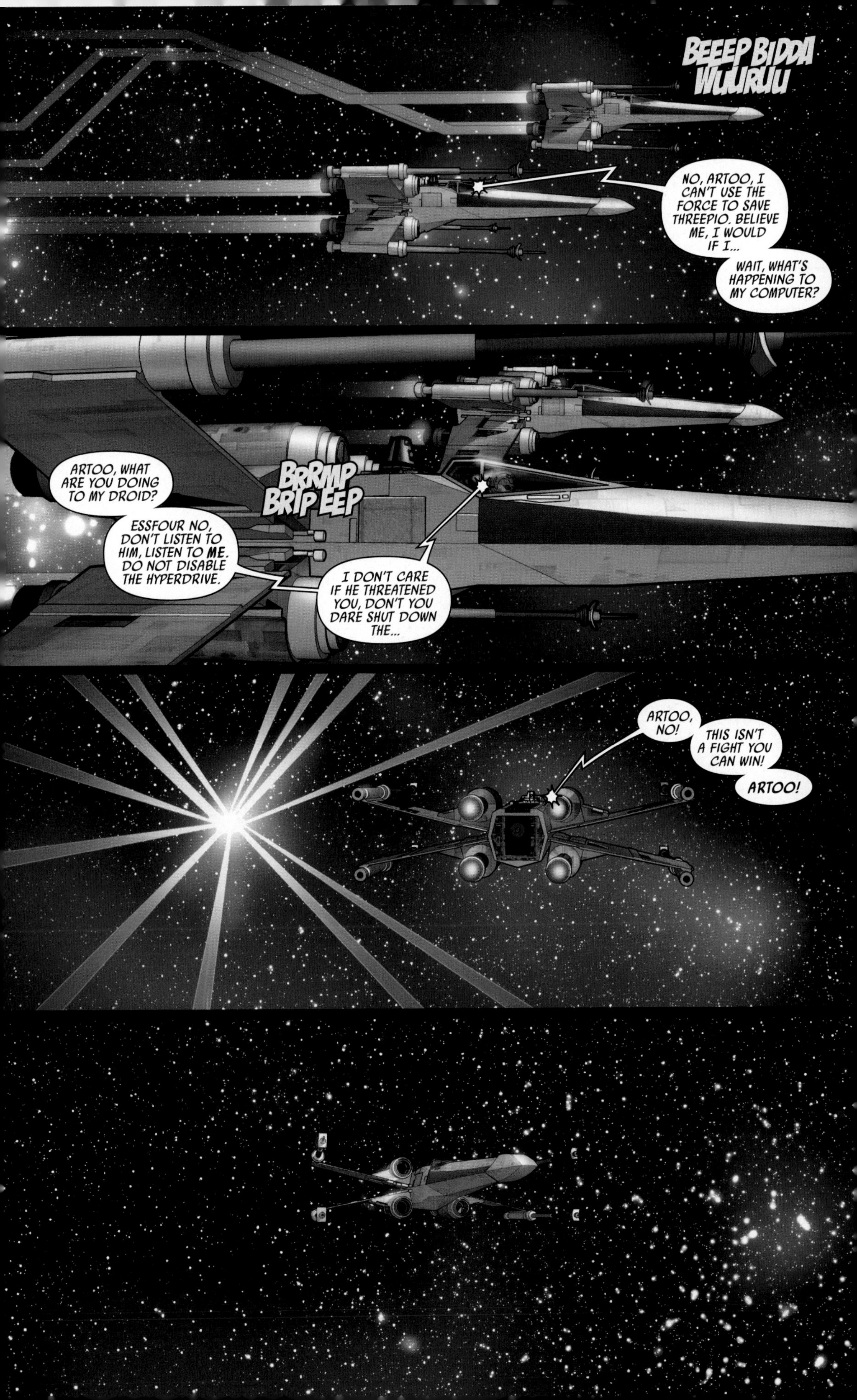
BEEEP BIDDA WUURUU
NO, ARTOO, I CAN'T USE THE FORCE TO SAVE THREEPIO. BELIEVE ME, I WOULD IF I...
WAIT, WHAT'S HAPPENING TO MY COMPUTER?
BRRMP BRIP EEP
ARTOO, WHAT ARE YOU DOING TO MY DROID?
ESSFOUR NO, DON'T LISTEN TO HIM, LISTEN TO ME. DO NOT DISABLE THE HYPERDRIVE.
I DON'T CARE IF HE THREATENED YOU, DON'T YOU DARE SHUT DOWN THE...
ARTOO, NO!
THIS ISN'T A FIGHT YOU CAN WIN!
ARTOO!

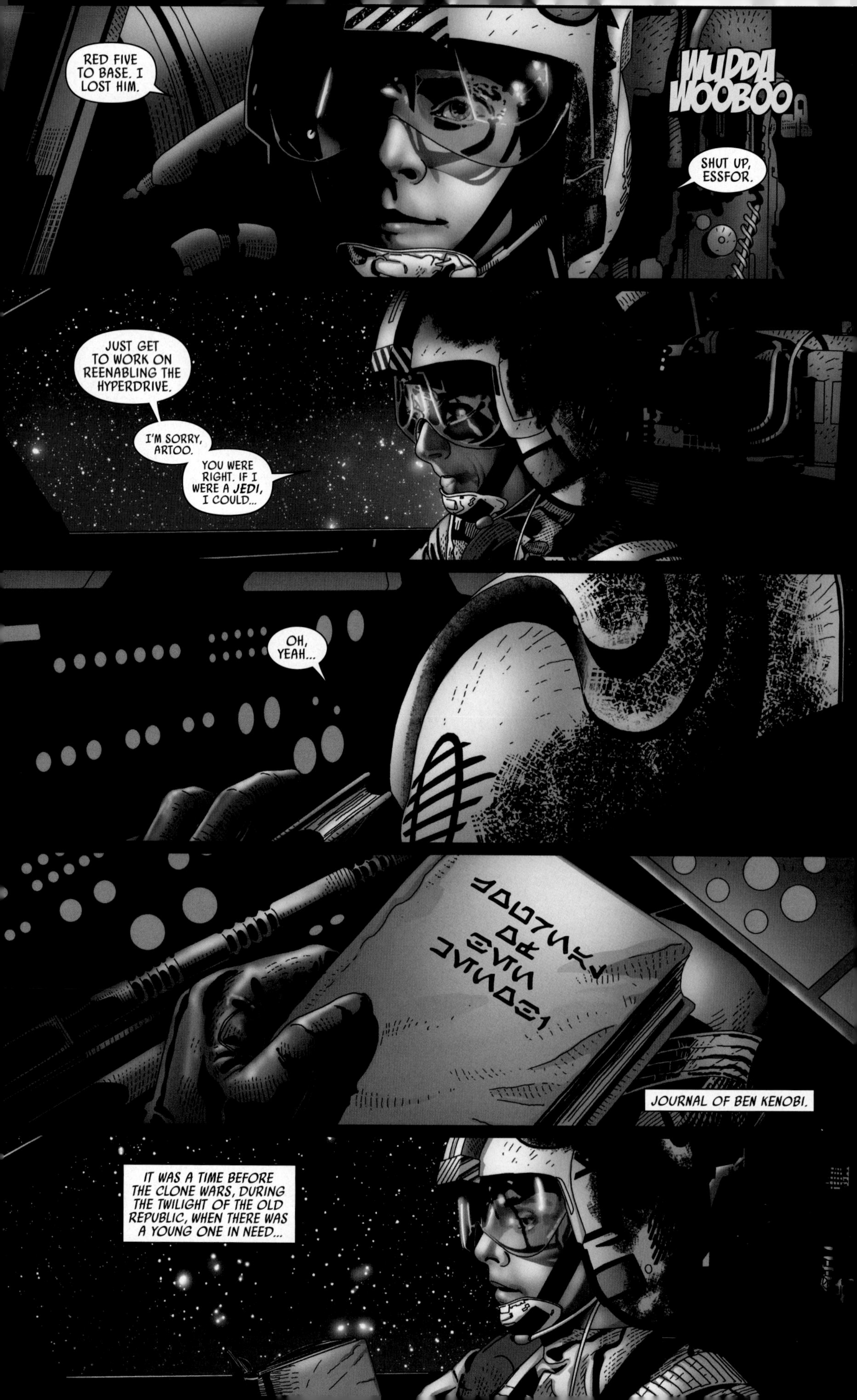
RED FIVE TO BASE. I LOST HIM.
WUDDA WOOBOO
SHUT UP, ESSFOR.
JUST GET TO WORK ON REENABLING THE HYPERDRIVE.
I'M SORRY, ARTOO.
YOU WERE RIGHT. IF I WERE A JEDI, I COULD...
OH, YEAH...
JOURNAL OF BEN KENOBI.
IT WAS A TIME BEFORE THE CLONE WARS, DURING THE TWILIGHT OF THE OLD REPUBLIC, WHEN THERE WAS A YOUNG ONE IN NEED...

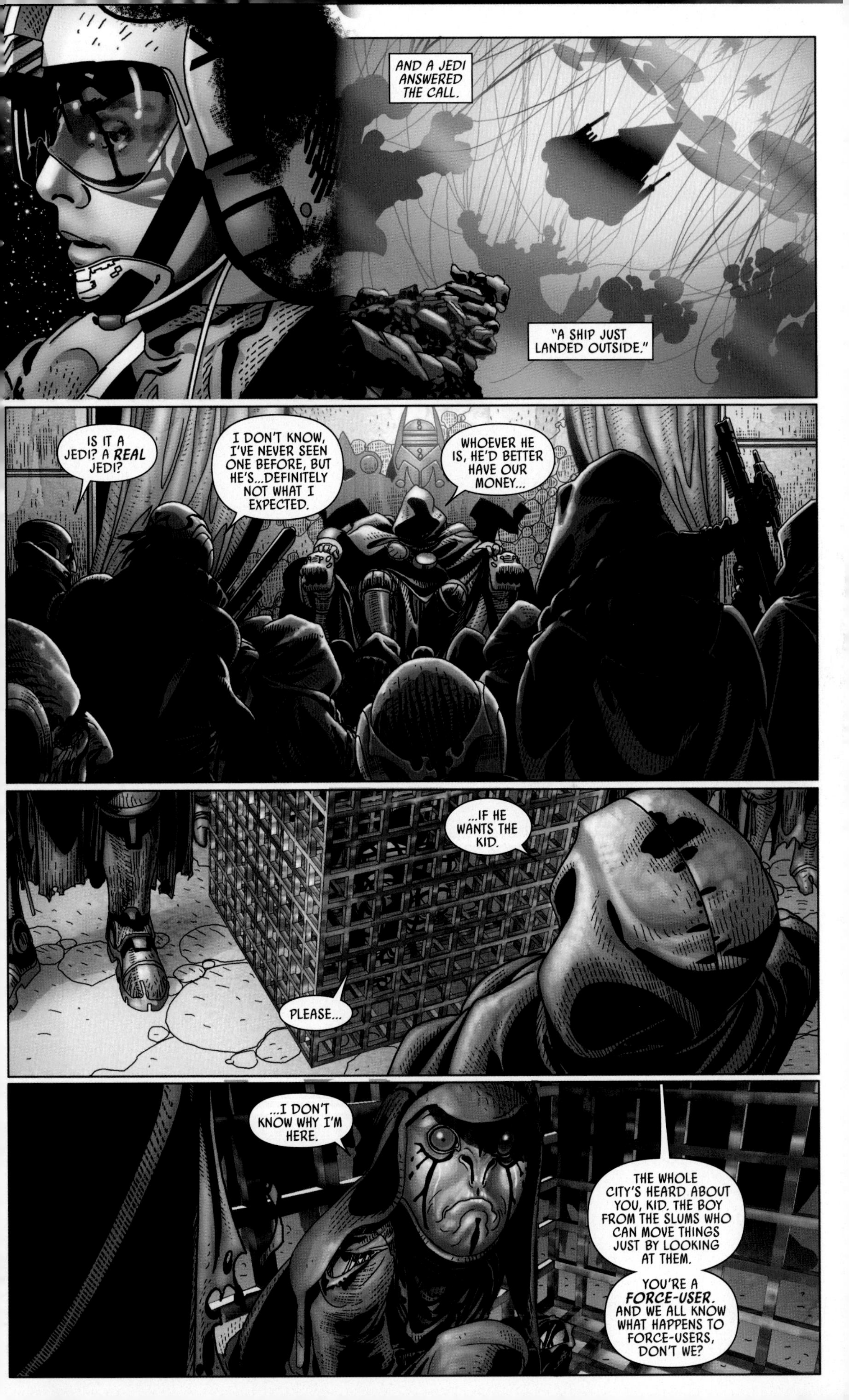
AND A JEDI ANSWERED THE CALL.
"A SHIP JUST LANDED OUTSIDE."
IS IT A JEDI? A REAL JEDI?
I DON'T KNOW, I'VE NEVER SEEN ONE BEFORE, BUT HE'S...DEFINITELY NOT WHAT I EXPECTED.
WHOEVER HE IS, HE'D BETTER HAVE OUR MONEY...
...IF HE WANTS THE KID.
PLEASE...
...I DON'T KNOW WHY I'M HERE.
THE WHOLE CITY'S HEARD ABOUT YOU, KID. THE BOY FROM THE SLUMS WHO CAN MOVE THINGS JUST BY LOOKING AT THEM.
YOU'RE A FORCE-USER. AND WE ALL KNOW WHAT HAPPENS TO FORCE-USERS, DON'T WE?

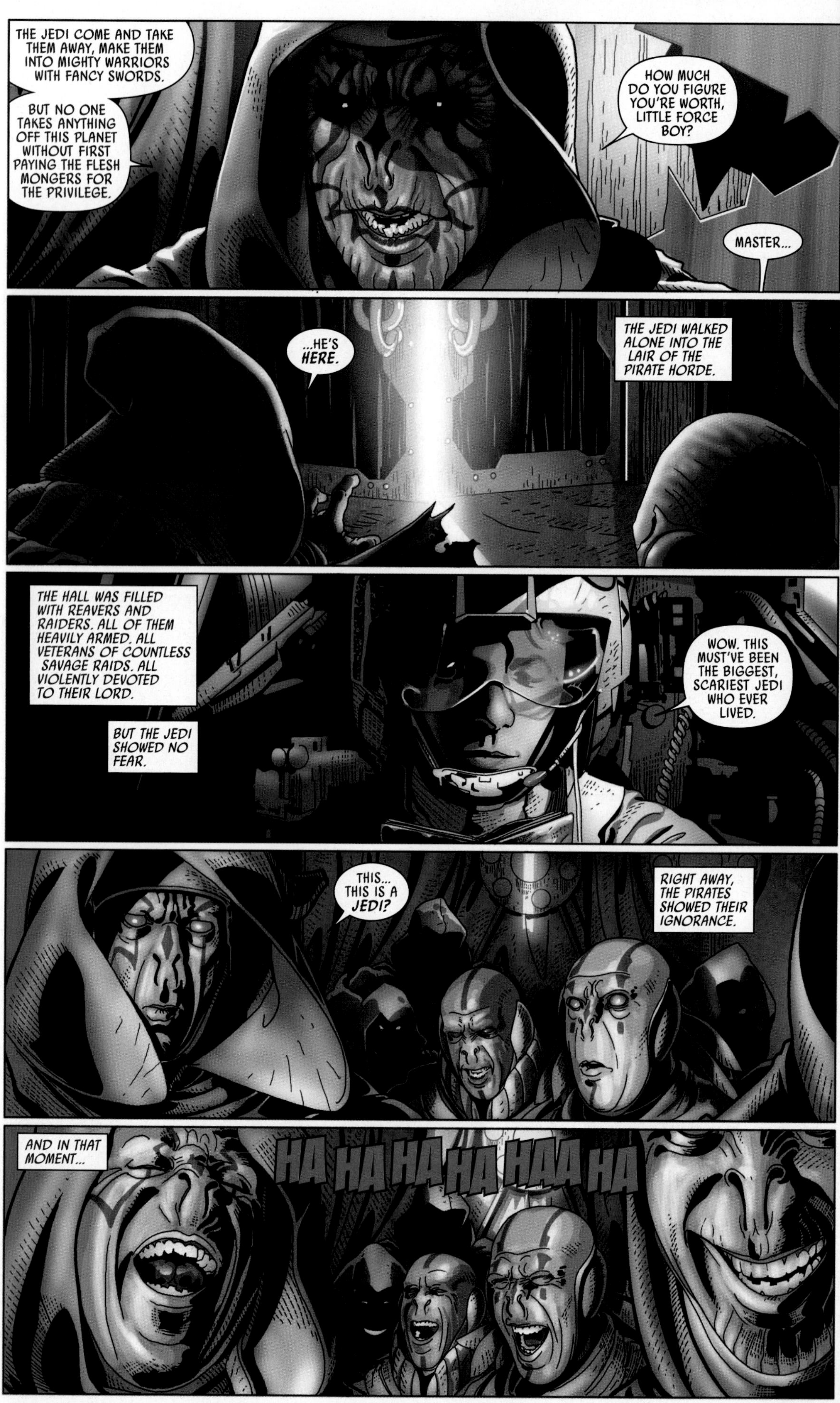
THE JEDI COME AND TAKE THEM AWAY, MAKE THEM INTO MIGHTY WARRIORS WITH FANCY SWORDS.
BUT NO ONE TAKES ANYTHING OFF THIS PLANET WITHOUT FIRST PAYING THE FLESH MONGERS FOR THE PRIVILEGE.
HOW MUCH DO YOU FIGURE YOU'RE WORTH, LITTLE FORCE BOY?
MASTER...
...HE'S HERE.
THE JEDI WALKED ALONE INTO THE LAIR OF THE PIRATE HORDE.
THE HALL WAS FILLED WITH REAVERS AND RAIDERS. ALL OF THEM HEAVILY ARMED. ALL VETERANS OF COUNTLESS SAVAGE RAIDS. ALL VIOLENTLY DEVOTED TO THEIR LORD.
BUT THE JEDI SHOWED NO FEAR.
WOW. THIS MUST'VE BEEN THE BIGGEST, SCARIEST JEDI WHO EVER LIVED.
THIS... THIS IS A JEDI?
RIGHT AWAY, THE PIRATES SHOWED THEIR IGNORANCE.
AND IN THAT MOMENT...
HA HA HA HA HAA HA

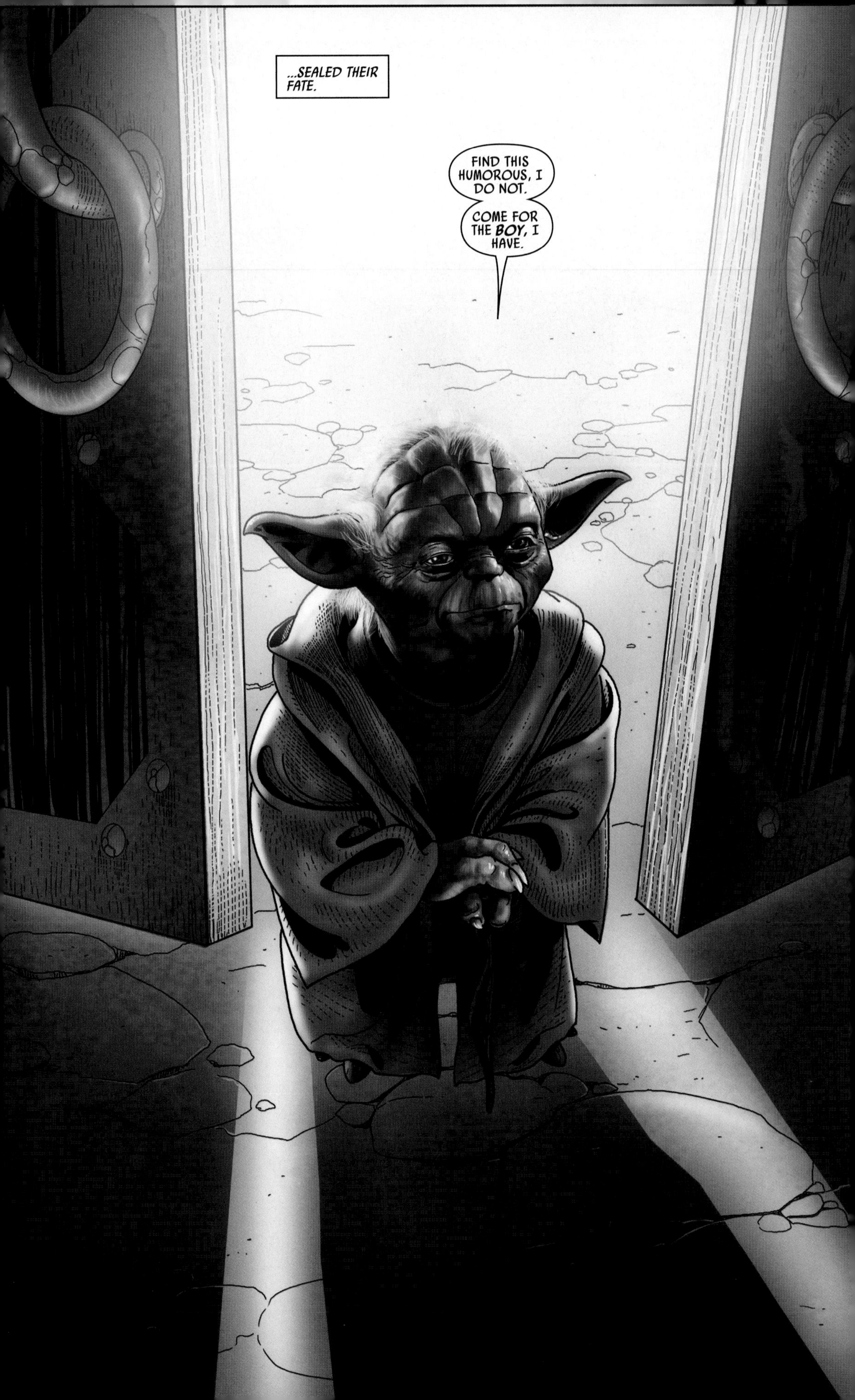
...SEALED THEIR FATE.
FIND THIS HUMOROUS, I DO NOT.
COME FOR THE BOY, I HAVE.

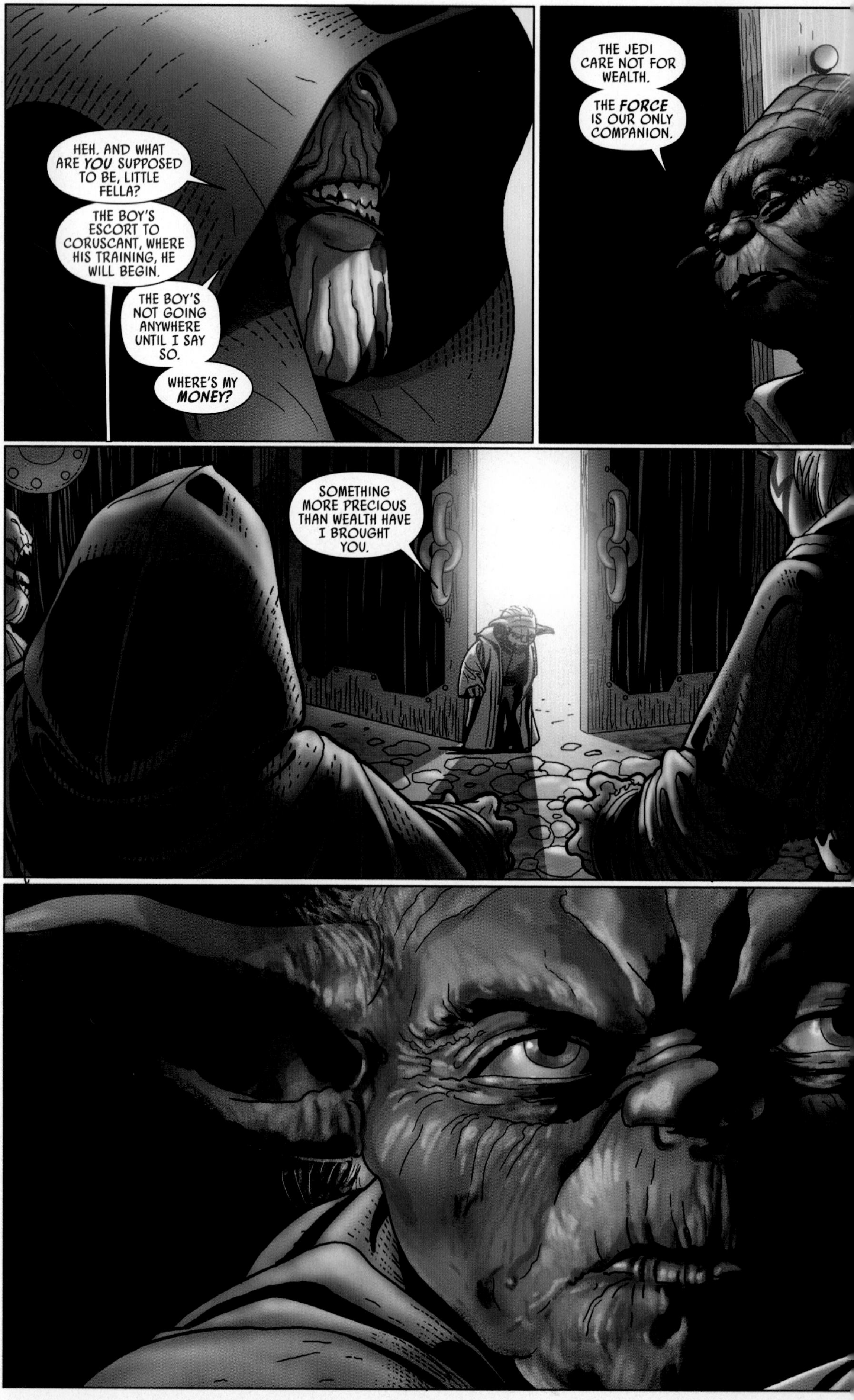
HEH. AND WHAT ARE YOU SUPPOSED TO BE, LITTLE FELLA?
THE BOY'S ESCORT TO CORUSCANT, WHERE HIS TRAINING, HE WILL BEGIN.
THE BOY'S NOT GOING ANYWHERE UNTIL I SAY SO.
WHERE'S MY MONEY?
THE JEDI CARE NOT FOR WEALTH.
THE FORCE IS OUR ONLY COMPANION.
SOMETHING MORE PRECIOUS THAN WEALTH HAVE I BROUGHT YOU.

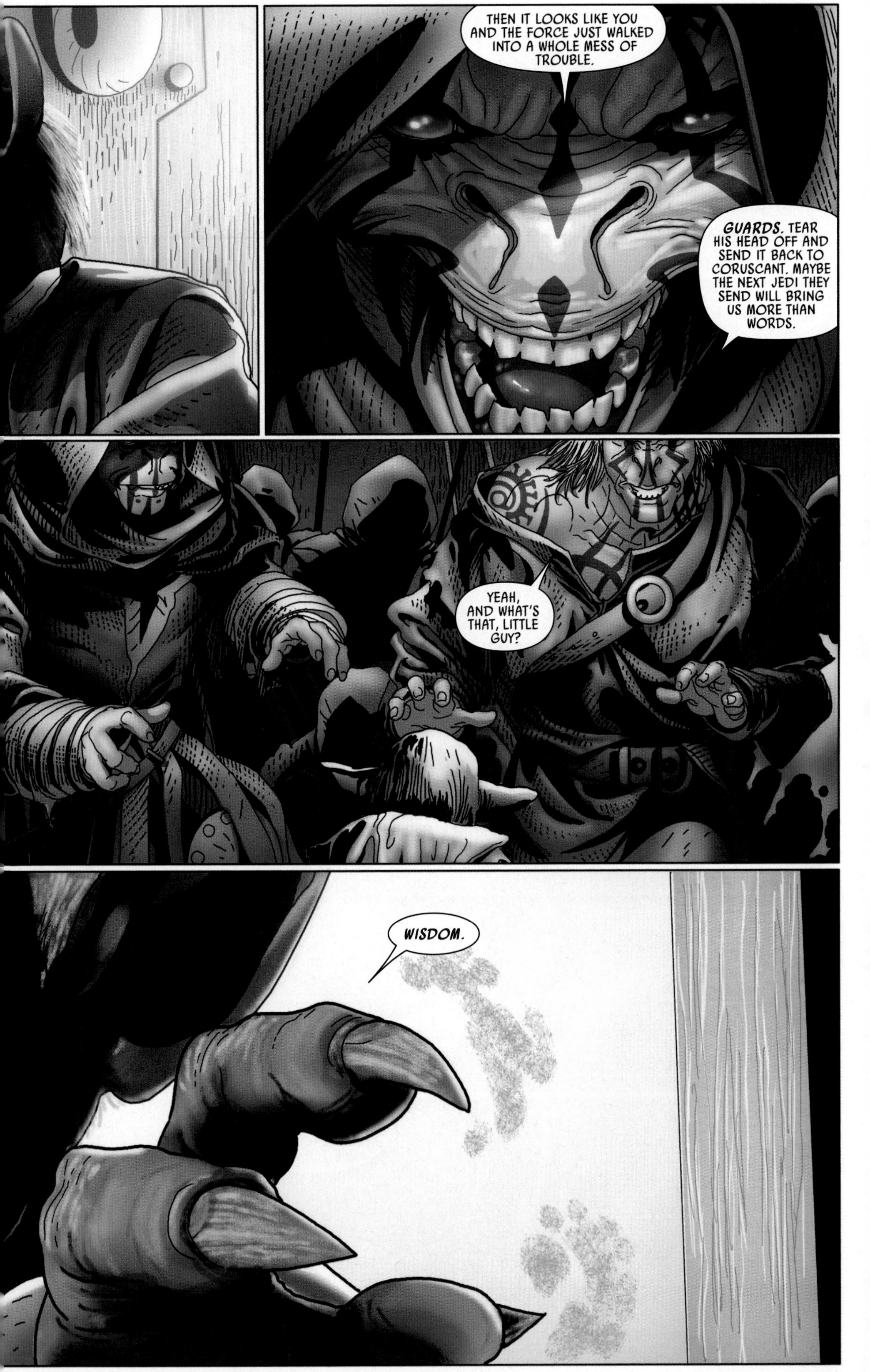
THEN IT LOOKS LIKE YOU AND THE FORCE JUST WALKED INTO A WHOLE MESS OF TROUBLE.
GUARDS. TEAR HIS HEAD OFF AND SEND IT BACK TO CORUSCANT. MAYBE THE NEXT JEDI THEY SEND WILL BRING US MORE THAN WORDS.
YEAH, AND WHAT'S THAT, LITTLE GUY?
WISDOM.

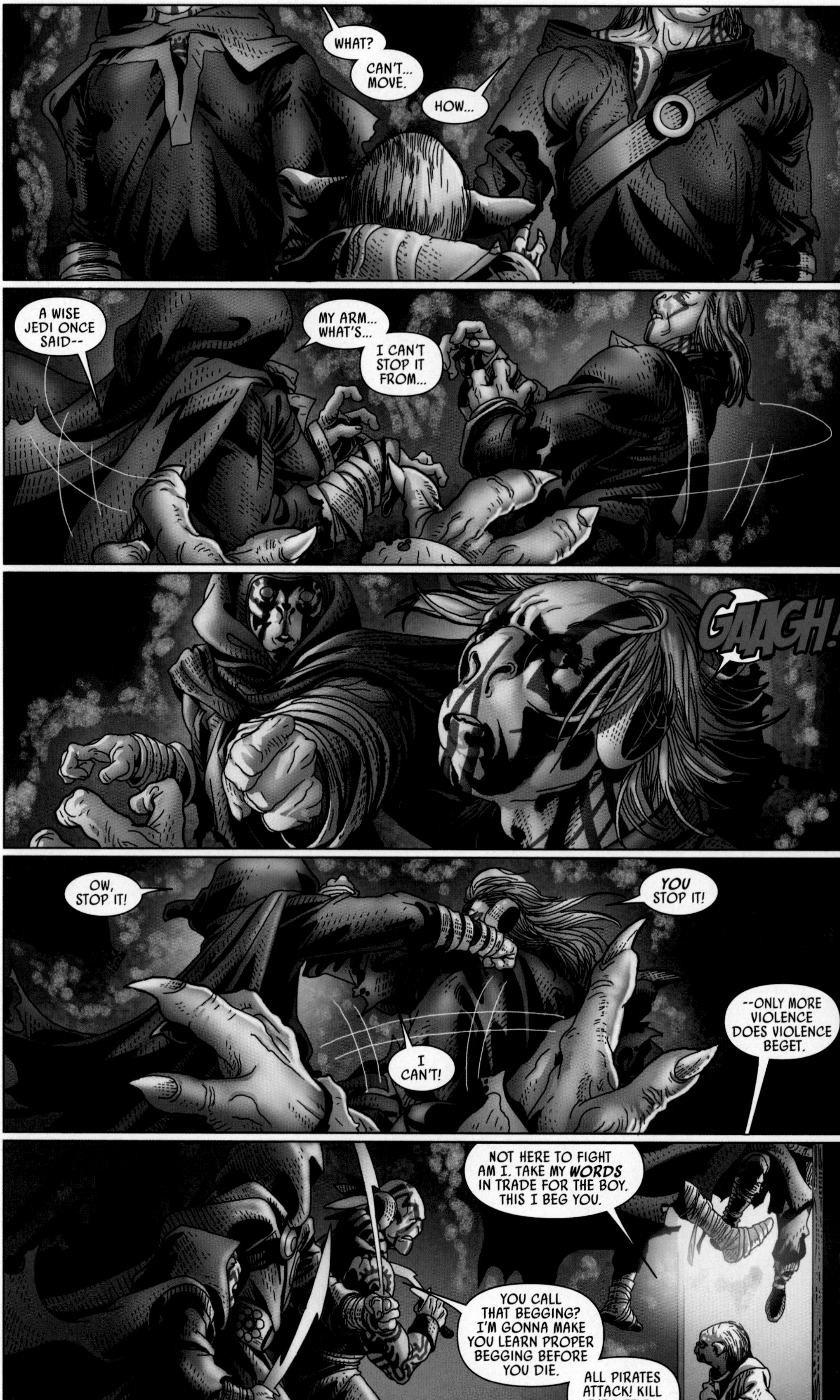

WHAT?
CAN'T... MOVE.
HOW...
A WISE JEDI ONCE SAID--
MY ARM... WHAT'S...
I CAN'T STOP IT FROM...
GAAGH!
OW, STOP IT!
YOU STOP IT!
I CAN'T!
--ONLY MORE VIOLENCE DOES VIOLENCE BEGET.
NOT HERE TO FIGHT AM I. TAKE MY WORDS IN TRADE FOR THE BOY. THIS I BEG YOU.
YOU CALL THAT BEGGING? I'M GONNA MAKE YOU LEARN PROPER BEGGING BEFORE YOU DIE.
ALL PIRATES ATTACK! KILL THE LITTLE--

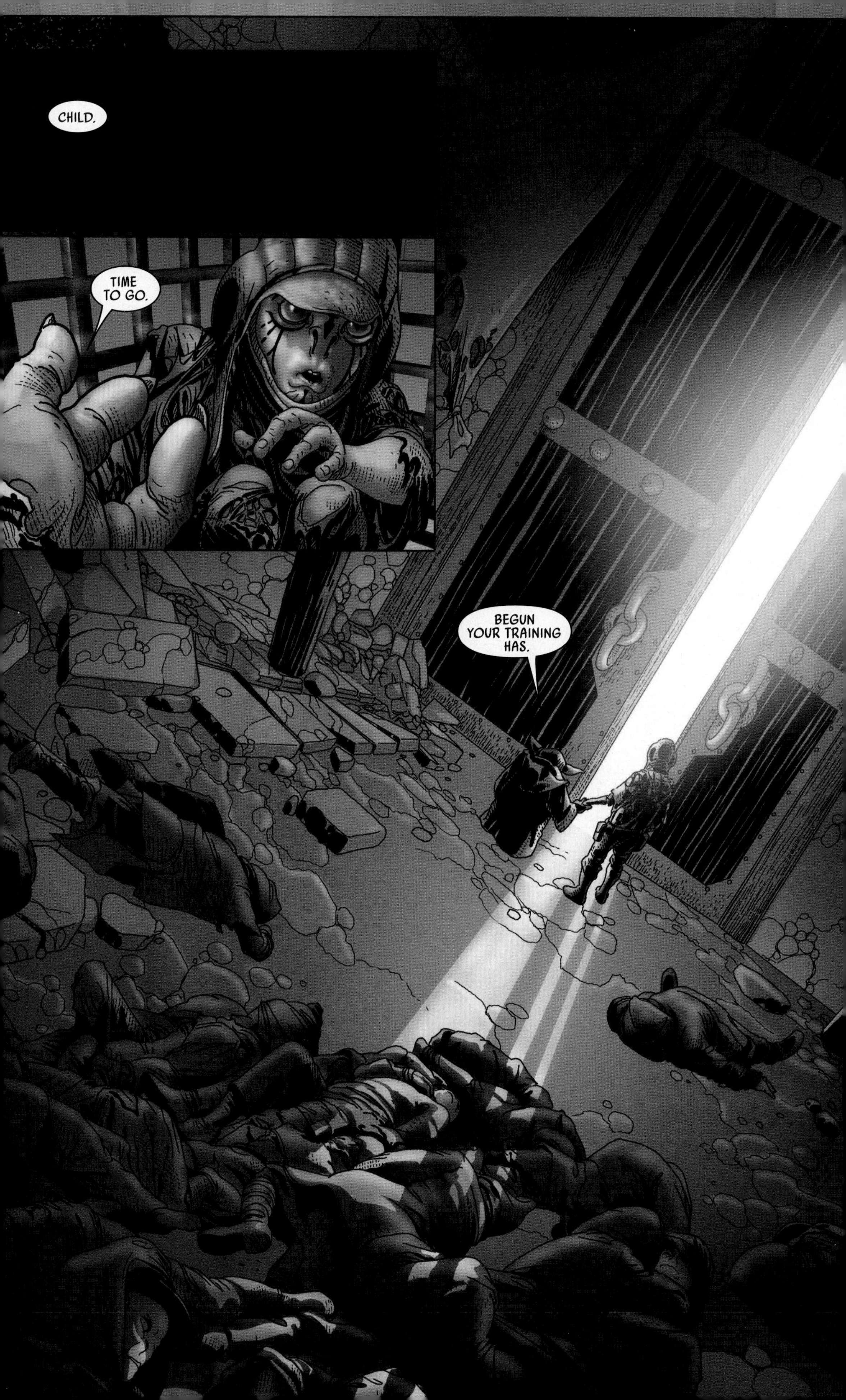
CHILD.
TIME TO GO.
BEGUN YOUR TRAINING HAS.

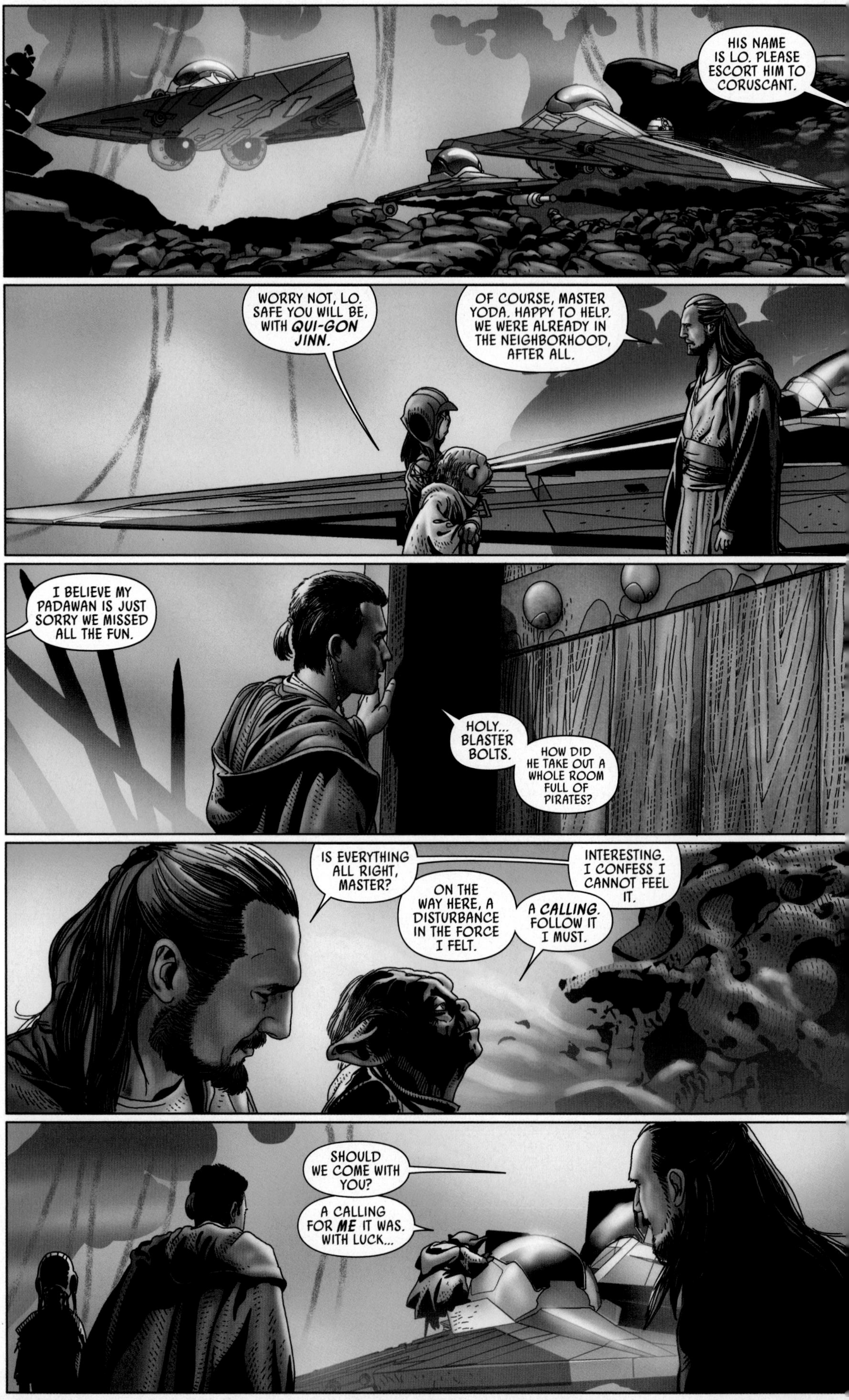
HIS NAME IS LO. PLEASE ESCORT HIM TO CORUSCANT.
WORRY NOT, LO. SAFE YOU WILL BE, WITH QUI-GON JINN.
OF COURSE, MASTER YODA. HAPPY TO HELP. WE WERE ALREADY IN THE NEIGHBORHOOD, AFTER ALL.
I BELIEVE MY PADAWAN IS JUST SORRY WE MISSED ALL THE FUN.
HOLY... BLASTER BOLTS.
HOW DID HE TAKE OUT A WHOLE ROOM FULL OF PIRATES?
IS EVERYTHING ALL RIGHT, MASTER?
ON THE WAY HERE, A DISTURBANCE IN THE FORCE I FELT.
A CALLING. FOLLOW IT I MUST.
INTERESTING. I CONFESS I CANNOT FEEL IT.
SHOULD WE COME WITH YOU?
A CALLING FOR ME IT WAS. WITH LUCK...

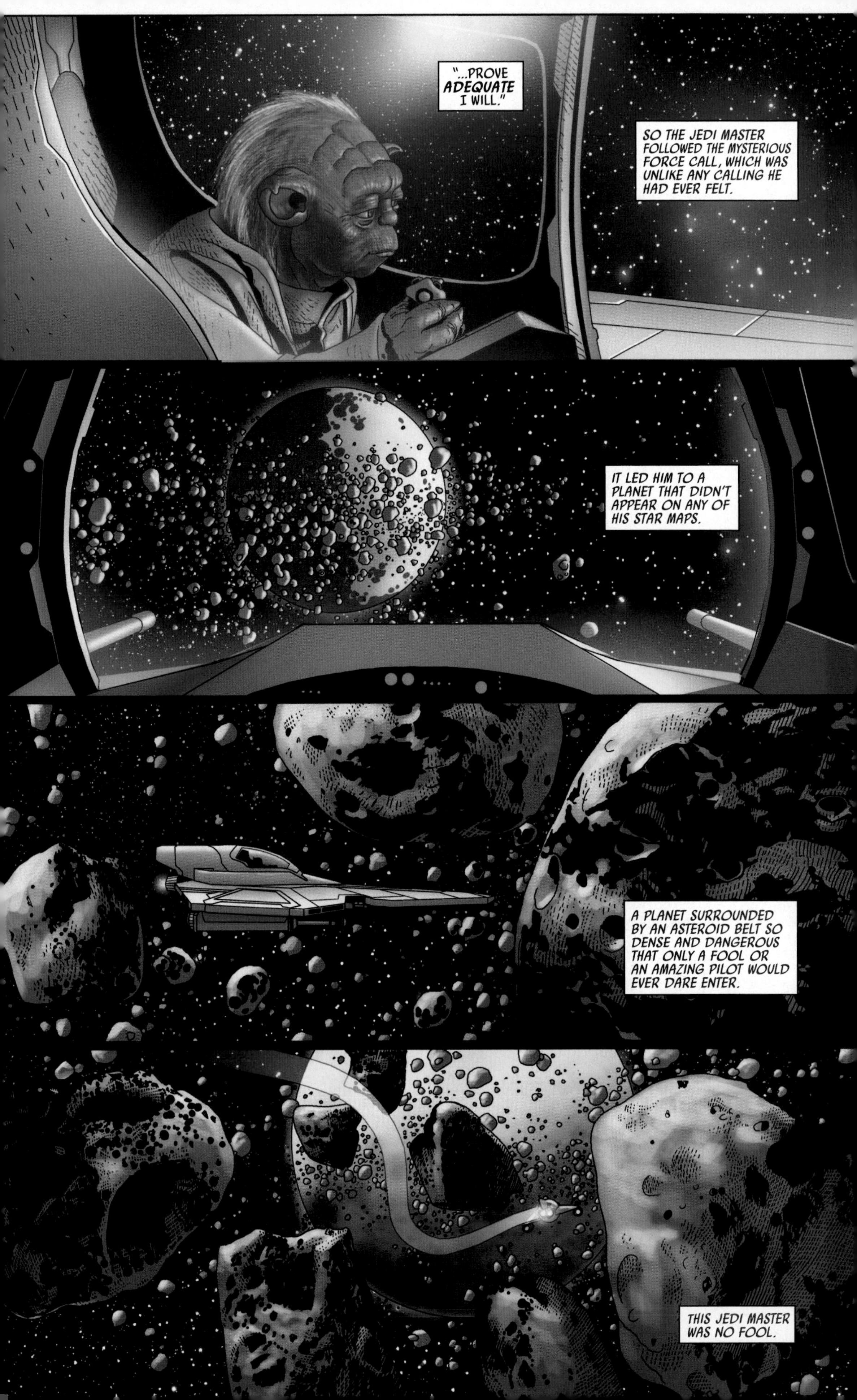
"...PROVE ADEQUATE I WILL."
SO THE JEDI MASTER FOLLOWED THE MYSTERIOUS FORCE CALL, WHICH WAS UNLIKE ANY CALLING HE HAD EVER FELT.
IT LED HIM TO A PLANET THAT DIDN'T APPEAR ON ANY OF HIS STAR MAPS.
A PLANET SURROUNDED BY AN ASTEROID BELT SO DENSE AND DANGEROUS THAT ONLY A FOOL OR AN AMAZING PILOT WOULD EVER DARE ENTER.
THIS JEDI MASTER WAS NO FOOL.

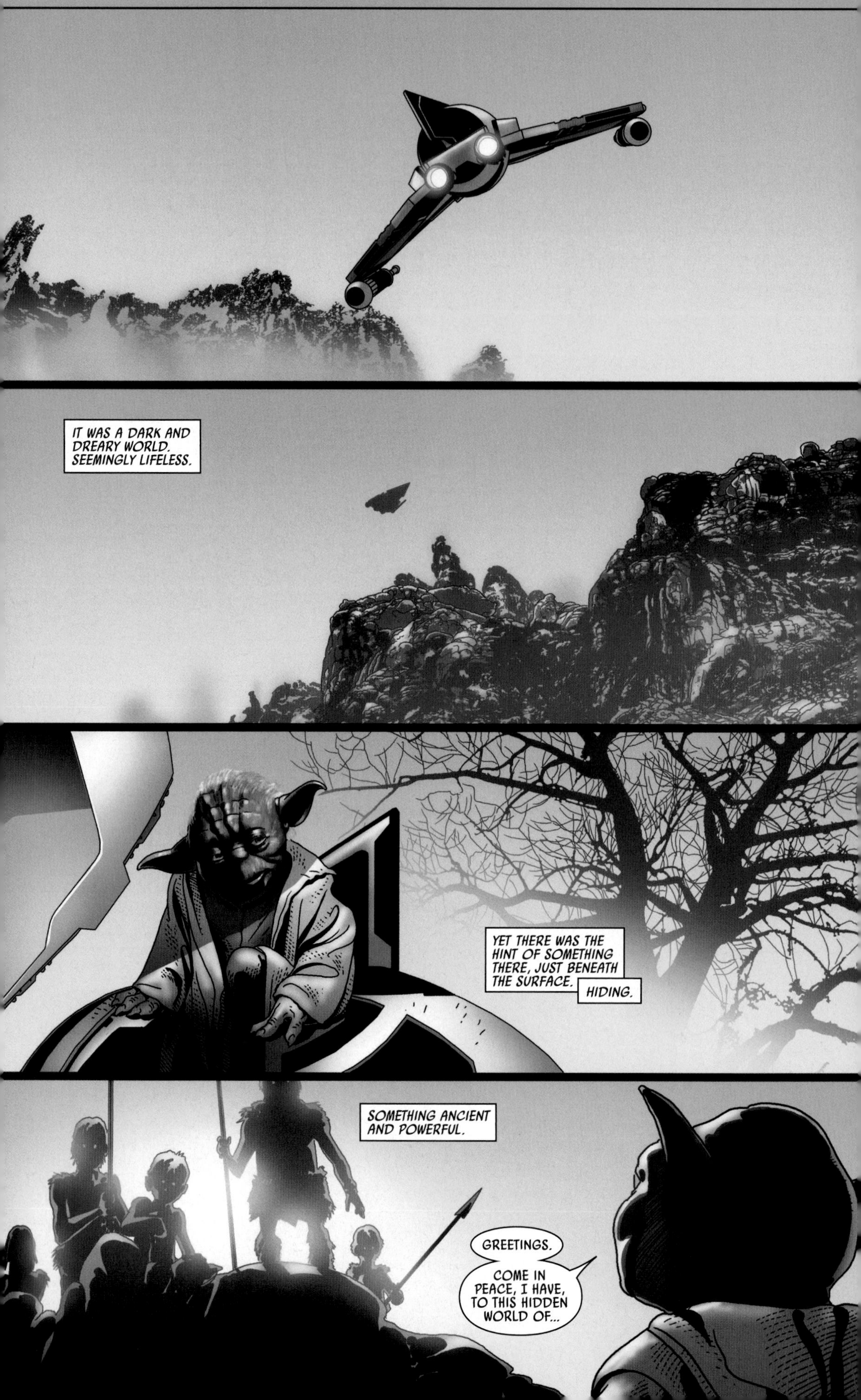
IT WAS A DARK AND DREARY WORLD. SEEMINGLY LIFELESS.
YET THERE WAS THE HINT OF SOMETHING THERE, JUST BENEATH THE SURFACE.
HIDING.
SOMETHING ANCIENT AND POWERFUL.
GREETINGS.
COME IN PEACE, I HAVE, TO THIS HIDDEN WORLD OF...

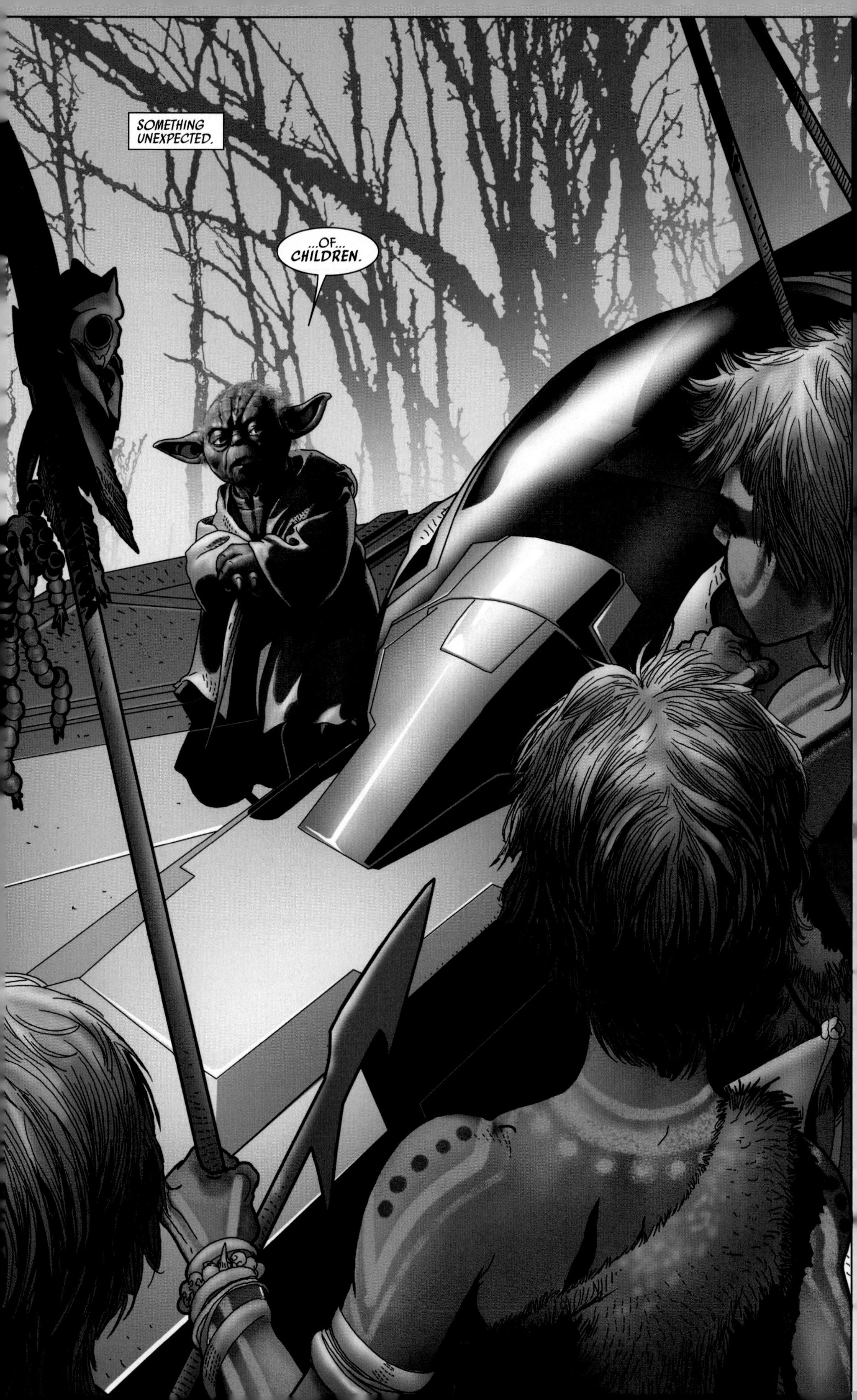
SOMETHING UNEXPECTED.
...OF... CHILDREN.

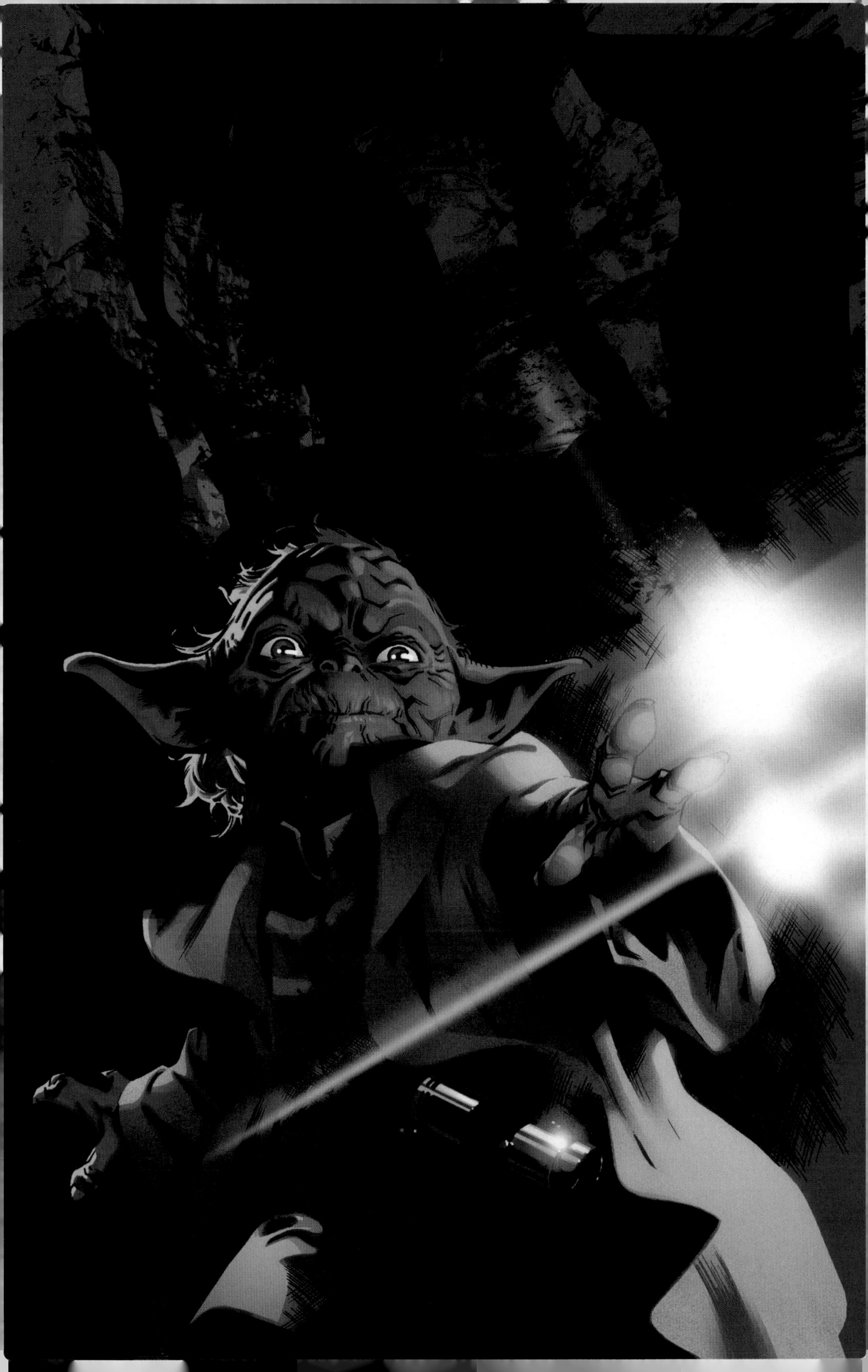

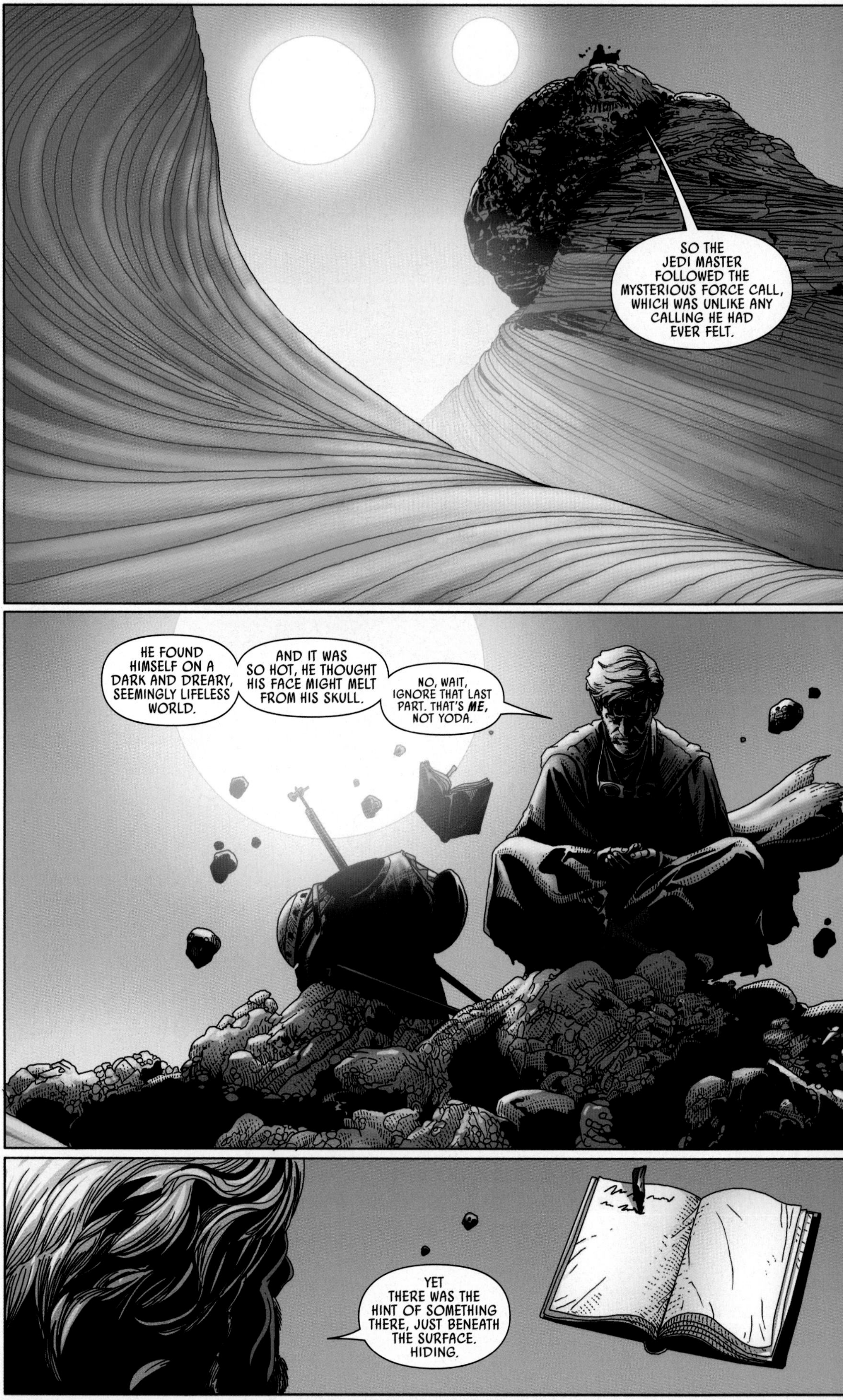
SO THE JEDI MASTER FOLLOWED THE MYSTERIOUS FORCE CALL, WHICH WAS UNLIKE ANY CALLING HE HAD EVER FELT.
HE FOUND HIMSELF ON A DARK AND DREARY, SEEMINGLY LIFELESS WORLD.
AND IT WAS SO HOT, HE THOUGHT HIS FACE MIGHT MELT FROM HIS SKULL.
NO, WAIT, IGNORE THAT LAST PART. THAT'S *ME*, NOT YODA.
YET THERE WAS THE HINT OF SOMETHING THERE, JUST BENEATH THE SURFACE. HIDING.

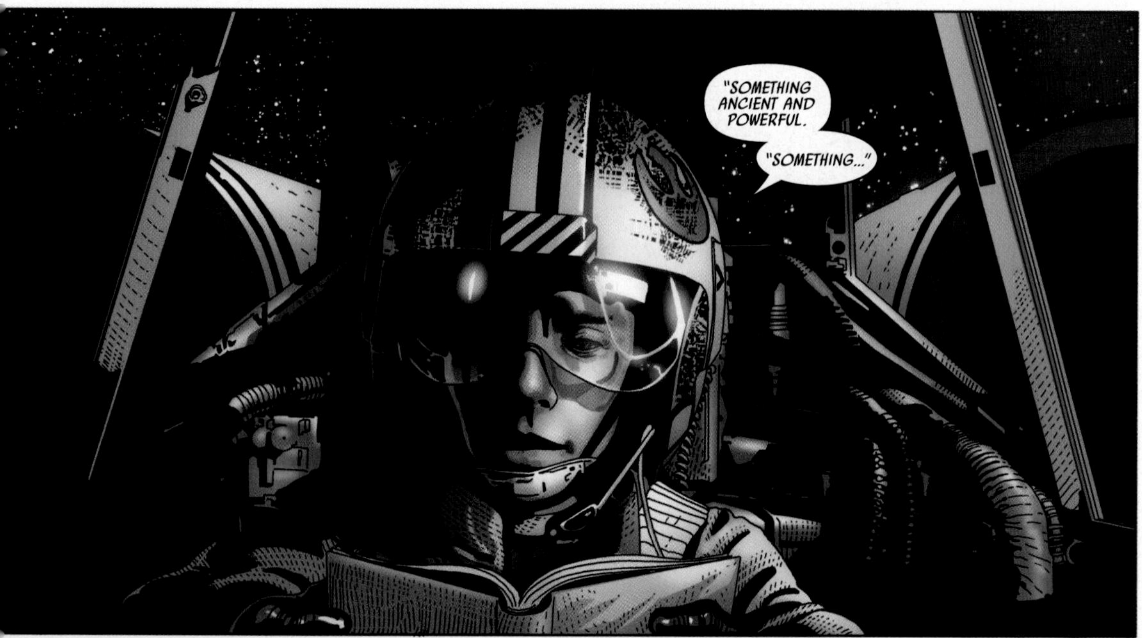
"SOMETHING ANCIENT AND POWERFUL.
"SOMETHING..."

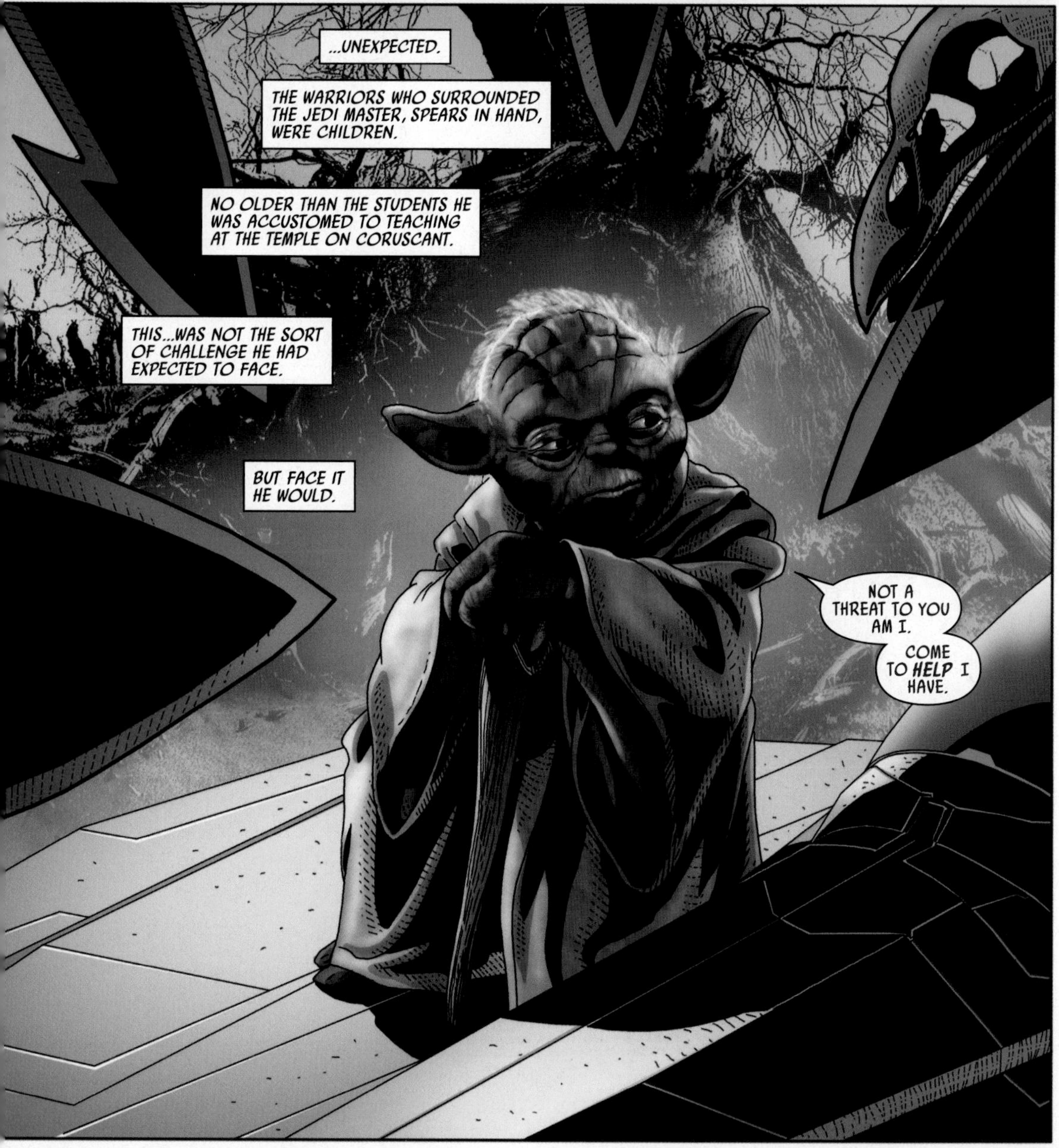
...UNEXPECTED.
THE WARRIORS WHO SURROUNDED THE JEDI MASTER, SPEARS IN HAND, WERE CHILDREN.
NO OLDER THAN THE STUDENTS HE WAS ACCUSTOMED TO TEACHING AT THE TEMPLE ON CORUSCANT.
THIS...WAS NOT THE SORT OF CHALLENGE HE HAD EXPECTED TO FACE.
BUT FACE IT HE WOULD.
NOT A THREAT TO YOU AM I.
COME TO HELP I HAVE.

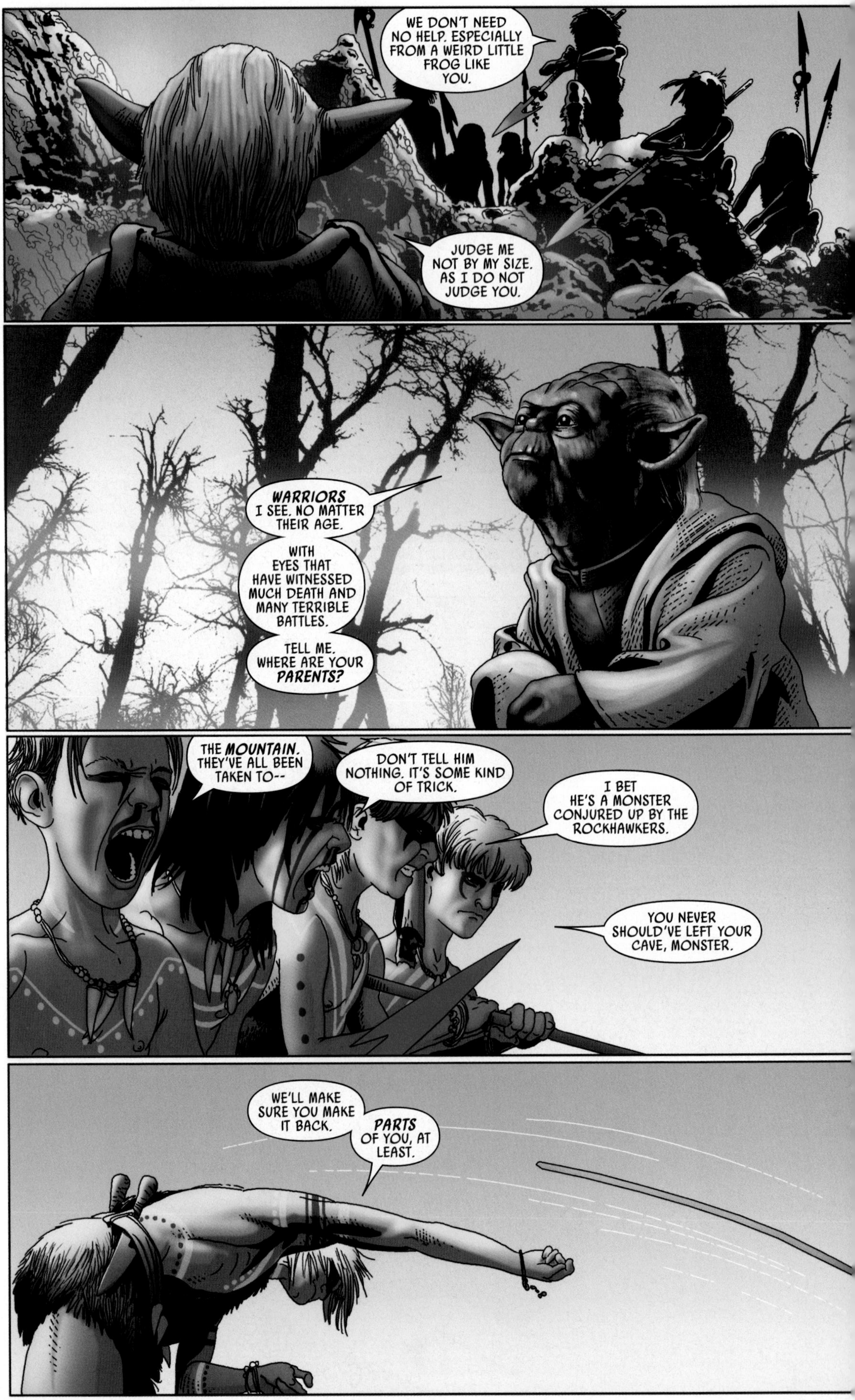
WE DON'T NEED NO HELP. ESPECIALLY FROM A WEIRD LITTLE FROG LIKE YOU.
JUDGE ME NOT BY MY SIZE. AS I DO NOT JUDGE YOU.
WARRIORS I SEE. NO MATTER THEIR AGE.
WITH EYES THAT HAVE WITNESSED MUCH DEATH AND MANY TERRIBLE BATTLES.
TELL ME. WHERE ARE YOUR PARENTS?
THE MOUNTAIN. THEY'VE ALL BEEN TAKEN TO--
DON'T TELL HIM NOTHING. IT'S SOME KIND OF TRICK.
I BET HE'S A MONSTER CONJURED UP BY THE ROCKHAWKERS.
YOU NEVER SHOULD'VE LEFT YOUR CAVE, MONSTER.
WE'LL MAKE SURE YOU MAKE IT BACK.
PARTS OF YOU, AT LEAST.

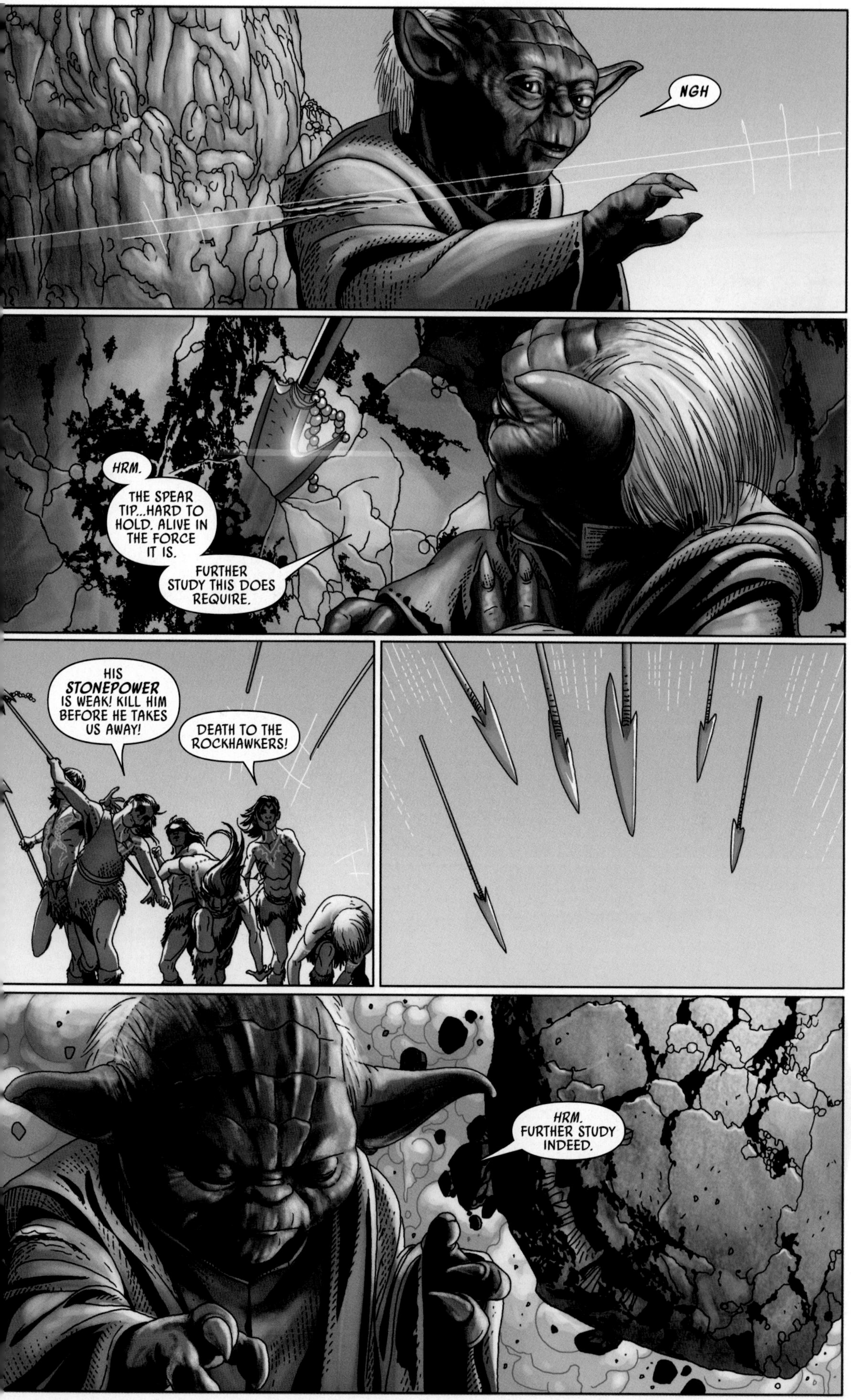
NGH
HRM.
THE SPEAR TIP...HARD TO HOLD. ALIVE IN THE FORCE IT IS.
FURTHER STUDY THIS DOES REQUIRE.
HIS STONEPOWER IS WEAK! KILL HIM BEFORE HE TAKES US AWAY!
DEATH TO THE ROCKHAWKERS!
HRM. FURTHER STUDY INDEED.

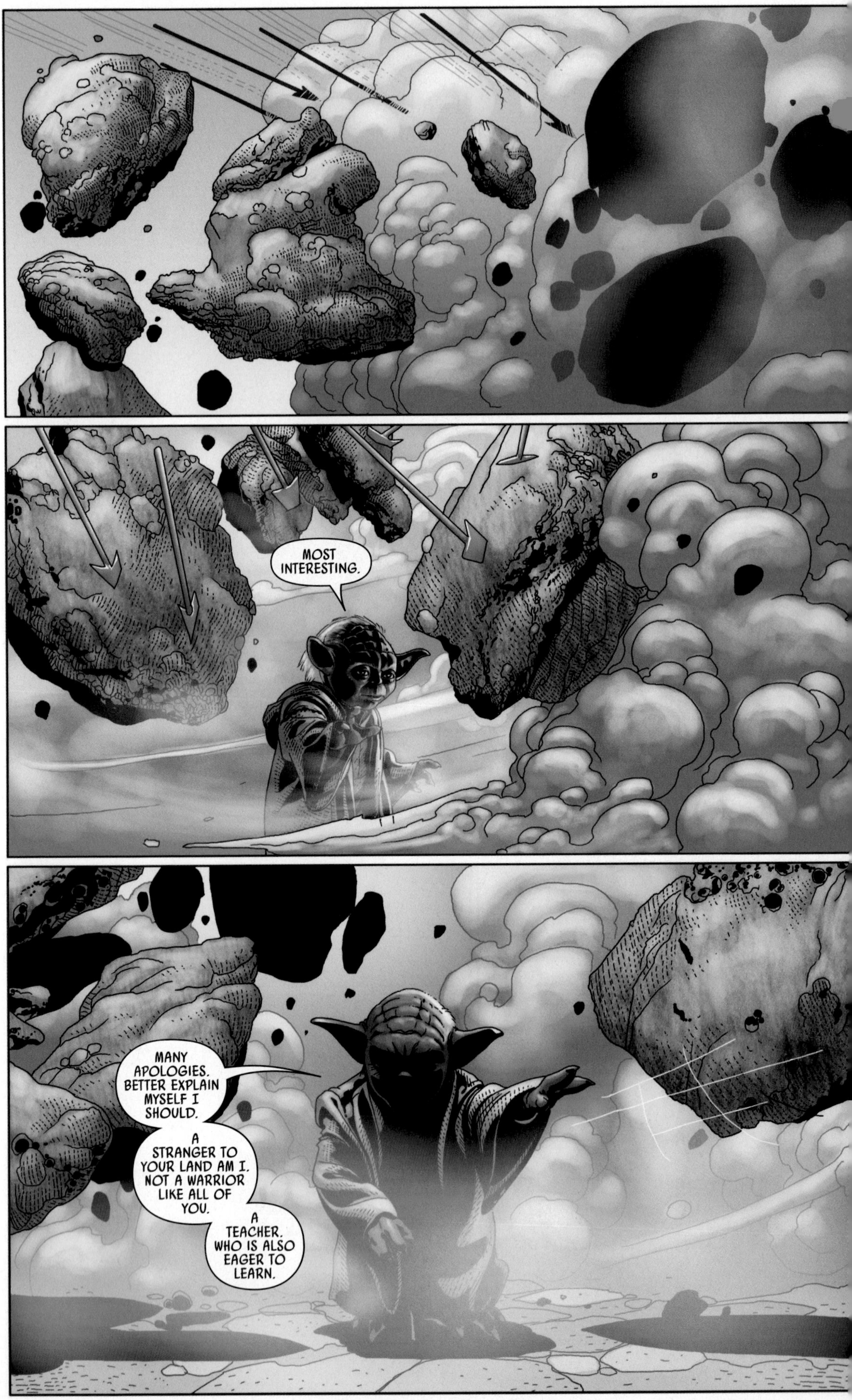
MOST INTERESTING.
MANY APOLOGIES. BETTER EXPLAIN MYSELF I SHOULD.
A STRANGER TO YOUR LAND AM I. NOT A WARRIOR LIKE ALL OF YOU.
A TEACHER. WHO IS ALSO EAGER TO LEARN.

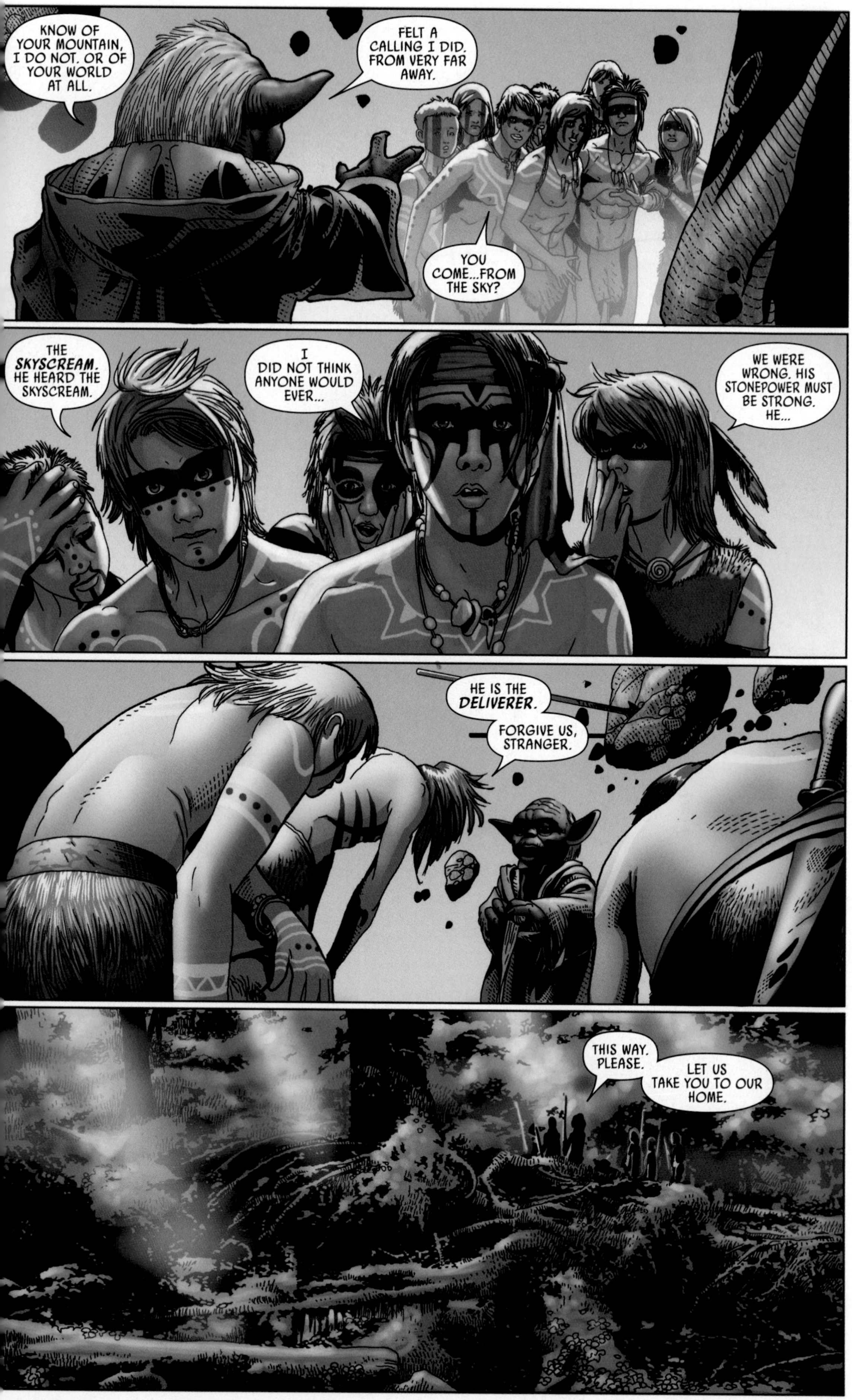
KNOW OF YOUR MOUNTAIN, I DO NOT. OR OF YOUR WORLD AT ALL.
FELT A CALLING I DID. FROM VERY FAR AWAY.
YOU COME...FROM THE SKY?
THE **SKYSCREAM.** HE HEARD THE SKYSCREAM.
I DID NOT THINK ANYONE WOULD EVER...
WE WERE WRONG. HIS STONEPOWER MUST BE STRONG. HE...
HE IS THE **DELIVERER.**
FORGIVE US, STRANGER.
THIS WAY. PLEASE.
LET US TAKE YOU TO OUR HOME.

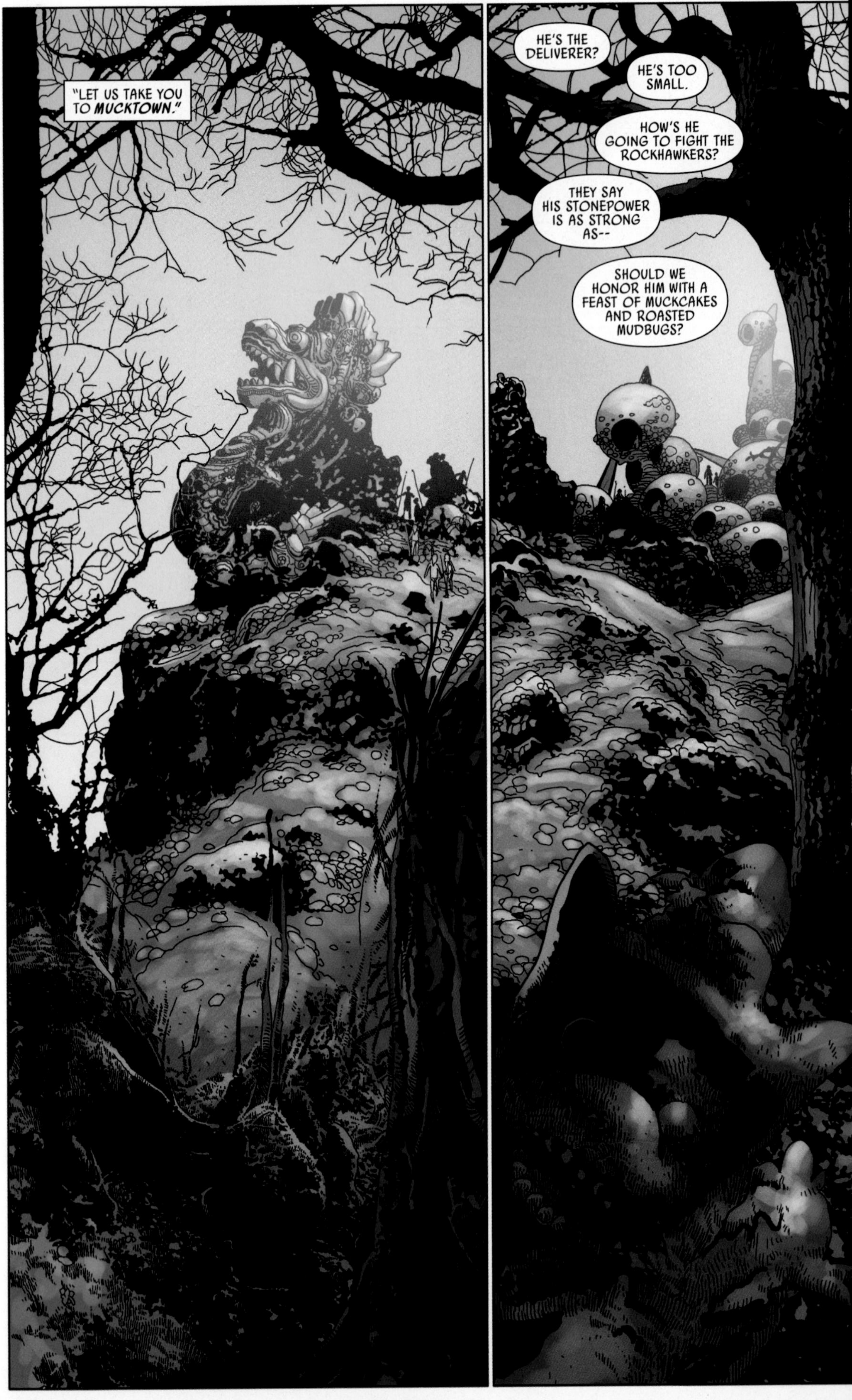
"LET US TAKE YOU TO MUCKTOWN."
HE'S THE DELIVERER?
HE'S TOO SMALL.
HOW'S HE GOING TO FIGHT THE ROCKHAWKERS?
THEY SAY HIS STONEPOWER IS AS STRONG AS--
SHOULD WE HONOR HIM WITH A FEAST OF MUCKCAKES AND ROASTED MUDBUGS?

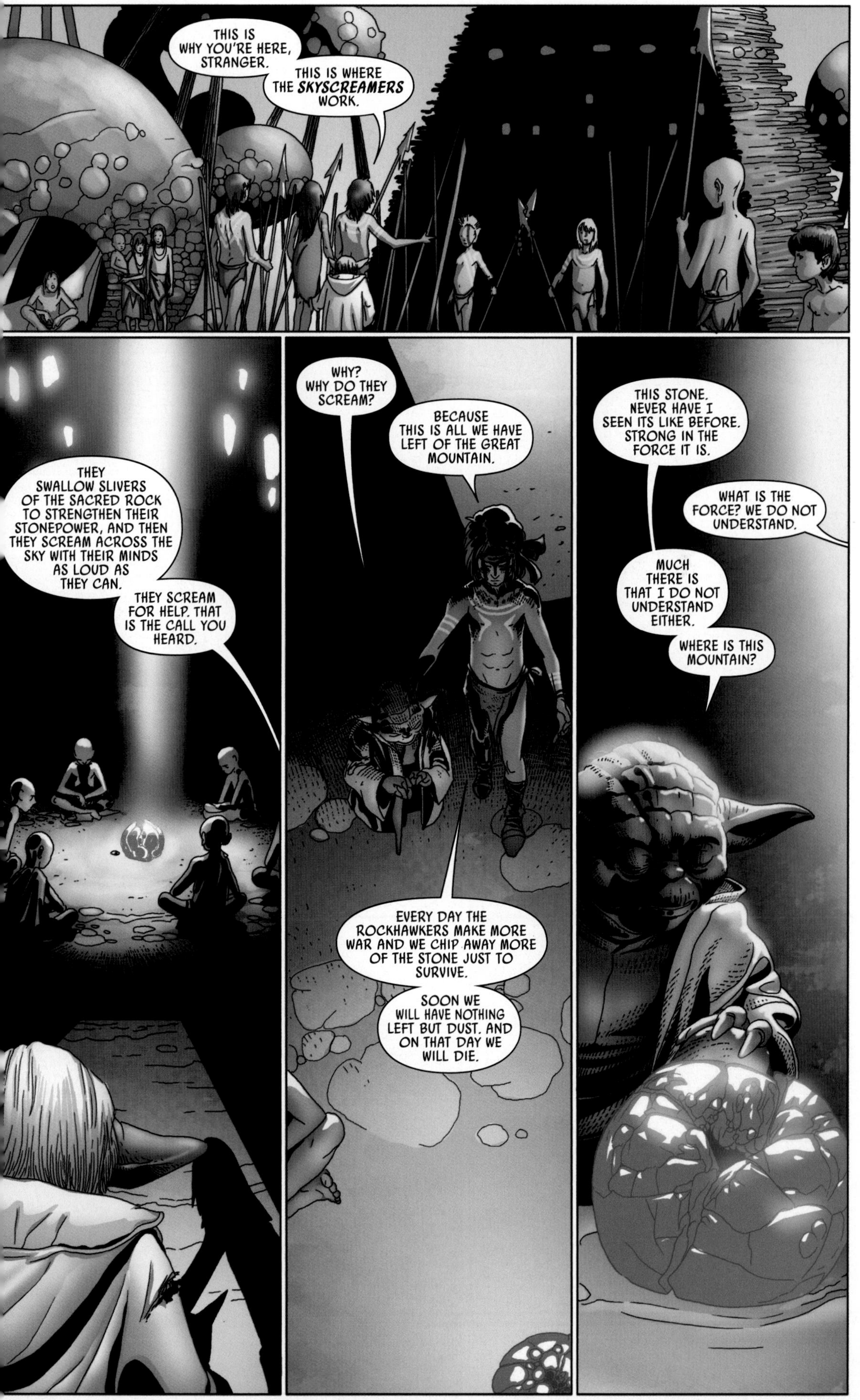
THIS IS WHY YOU'RE HERE, STRANGER.
THIS IS WHERE THE SKYSCREAMERS WORK.
THEY SWALLOW SLIVERS OF THE SACRED ROCK TO STRENGTHEN THEIR STONEPOWER, AND THEN THEY SCREAM ACROSS THE SKY WITH THEIR MINDS AS LOUD AS THEY CAN.
THEY SCREAM FOR HELP. THAT IS THE CALL YOU HEARD.
WHY? WHY DO THEY SCREAM?
BECAUSE THIS IS ALL WE HAVE LEFT OF THE GREAT MOUNTAIN.
EVERY DAY THE ROCKHAWKERS MAKE MORE WAR AND WE CHIP AWAY MORE OF THE STONE JUST TO SURVIVE.
SOON WE WILL HAVE NOTHING LEFT BUT DUST. AND ON THAT DAY WE WILL DIE.
THIS STONE. NEVER HAVE I SEEN ITS LIKE BEFORE. STRONG IN THE FORCE IT IS.
WHAT IS THE FORCE? WE DO NOT UNDERSTAND.
MUCH THERE IS THAT I DO NOT UNDERSTAND EITHER.
WHERE IS THIS MOUNTAIN?

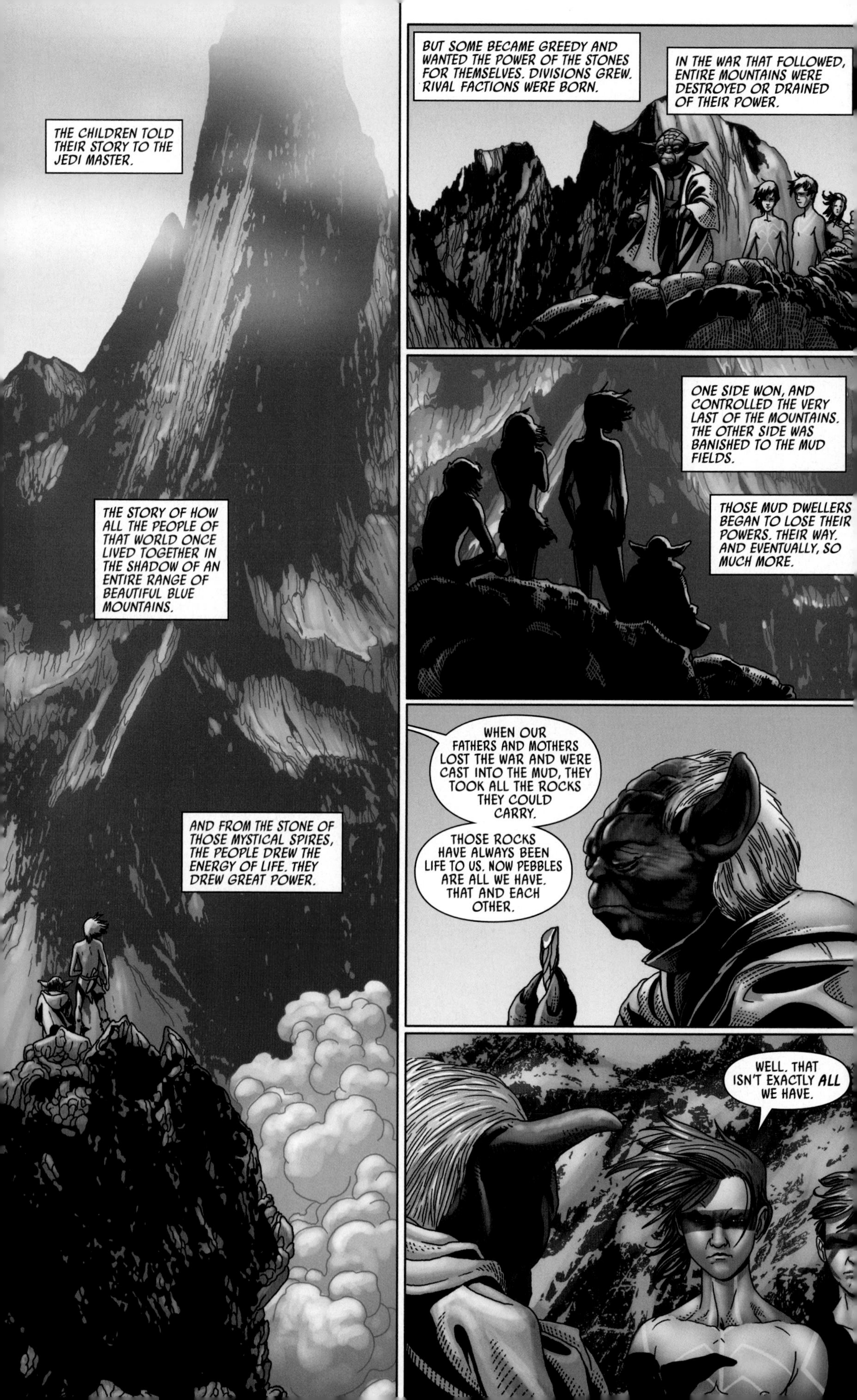
THE CHILDREN TOLD THEIR STORY TO THE JEDI MASTER.
THE STORY OF HOW ALL THE PEOPLE OF THAT WORLD ONCE LIVED TOGETHER IN THE SHADOW OF AN ENTIRE RANGE OF BEAUTIFUL BLUE MOUNTAINS.
AND FROM THE STONE OF THOSE MYSTICAL SPIRES, THE PEOPLE DREW THE ENERGY OF LIFE. THEY DREW GREAT POWER.
BUT SOME BECAME GREEDY AND WANTED THE POWER OF THE STONES FOR THEMSELVES. DIVISIONS GREW. RIVAL FACTIONS WERE BORN.
IN THE WAR THAT FOLLOWED, ENTIRE MOUNTAINS WERE DESTROYED OR DRAINED OF THEIR POWER.
ONE SIDE WON, AND CONTROLLED THE VERY LAST OF THE MOUNTAINS. THE OTHER SIDE WAS BANISHED TO THE MUD FIELDS.
THOSE MUD DWELLERS BEGAN TO LOSE THEIR POWERS. THEIR WAY. AND EVENTUALLY, SO MUCH MORE.
WHEN OUR FATHERS AND MOTHERS LOST THE WAR AND WERE CAST INTO THE MUD, THEY TOOK ALL THE ROCKS THEY COULD CARRY.
THOSE ROCKS HAVE ALWAYS BEEN LIFE TO US. NOW PEBBLES ARE ALL WE HAVE. THAT AND EACH OTHER.
WELL. THAT ISN'T EXACTLY ALL WE HAVE.

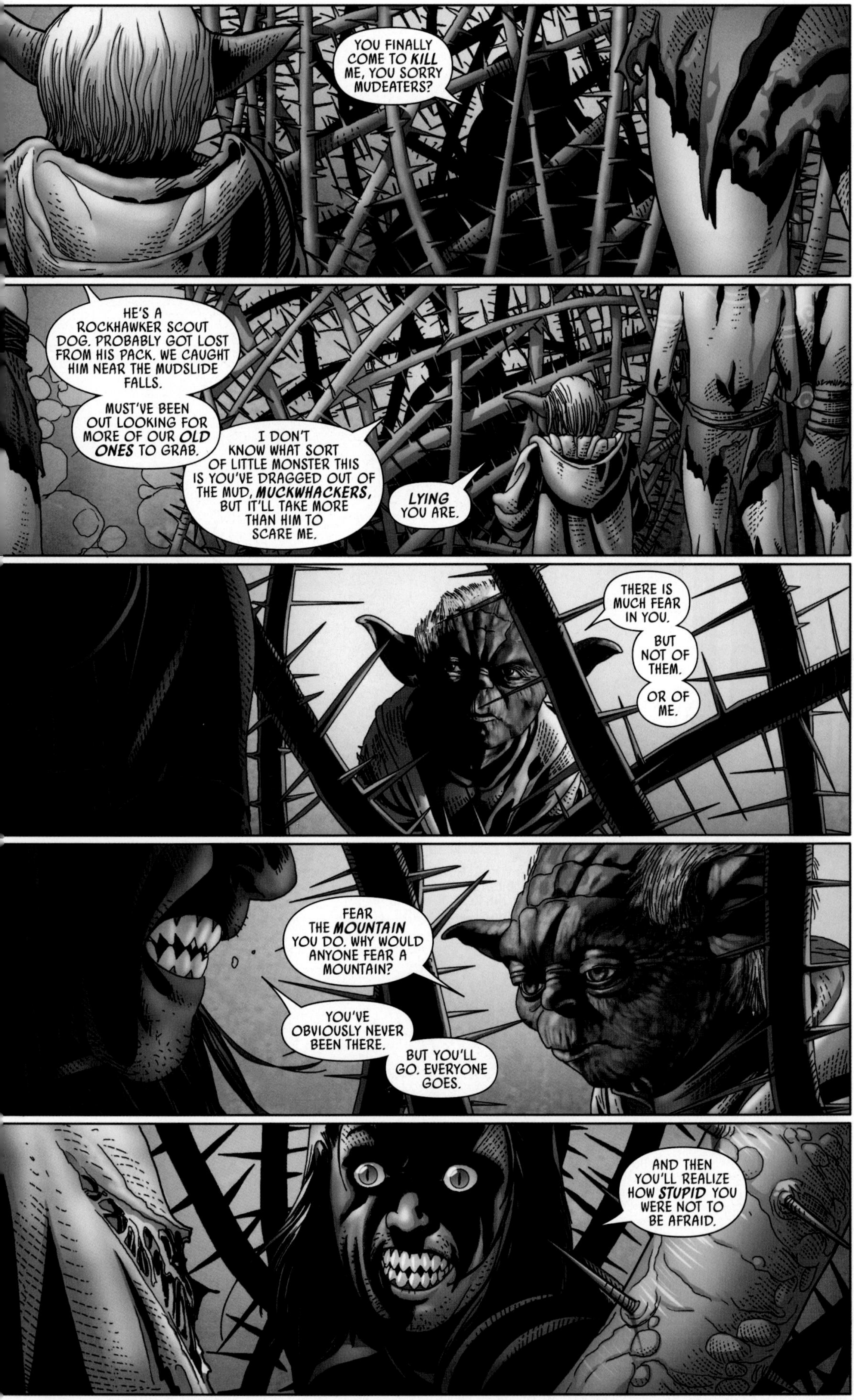
YOU FINALLY COME TO KILL ME, YOU SORRY MUDEATERS?
HE'S A ROCKHAWKER SCOUT DOG. PROBABLY GOT LOST FROM HIS PACK. WE CAUGHT HIM NEAR THE MUDSLIDE FALLS.
MUST'VE BEEN OUT LOOKING FOR MORE OF OUR OLD ONES TO GRAB.
I DON'T KNOW WHAT SORT OF LITTLE MONSTER THIS IS YOU'VE DRAGGED OUT OF THE MUD, MUCKWHACKERS, BUT IT'LL TAKE MORE THAN HIM TO SCARE ME.
LYING YOU ARE.
THERE IS MUCH FEAR IN YOU.
BUT NOT OF THEM.
OR OF ME.
FEAR THE MOUNTAIN YOU DO. WHY WOULD ANYONE FEAR A MOUNTAIN?
YOU'VE OBVIOUSLY NEVER BEEN THERE.
BUT YOU'LL GO. EVERYONE GOES.
AND THEN YOU'LL REALIZE HOW STUPID YOU WERE NOT TO BE AFRAID.

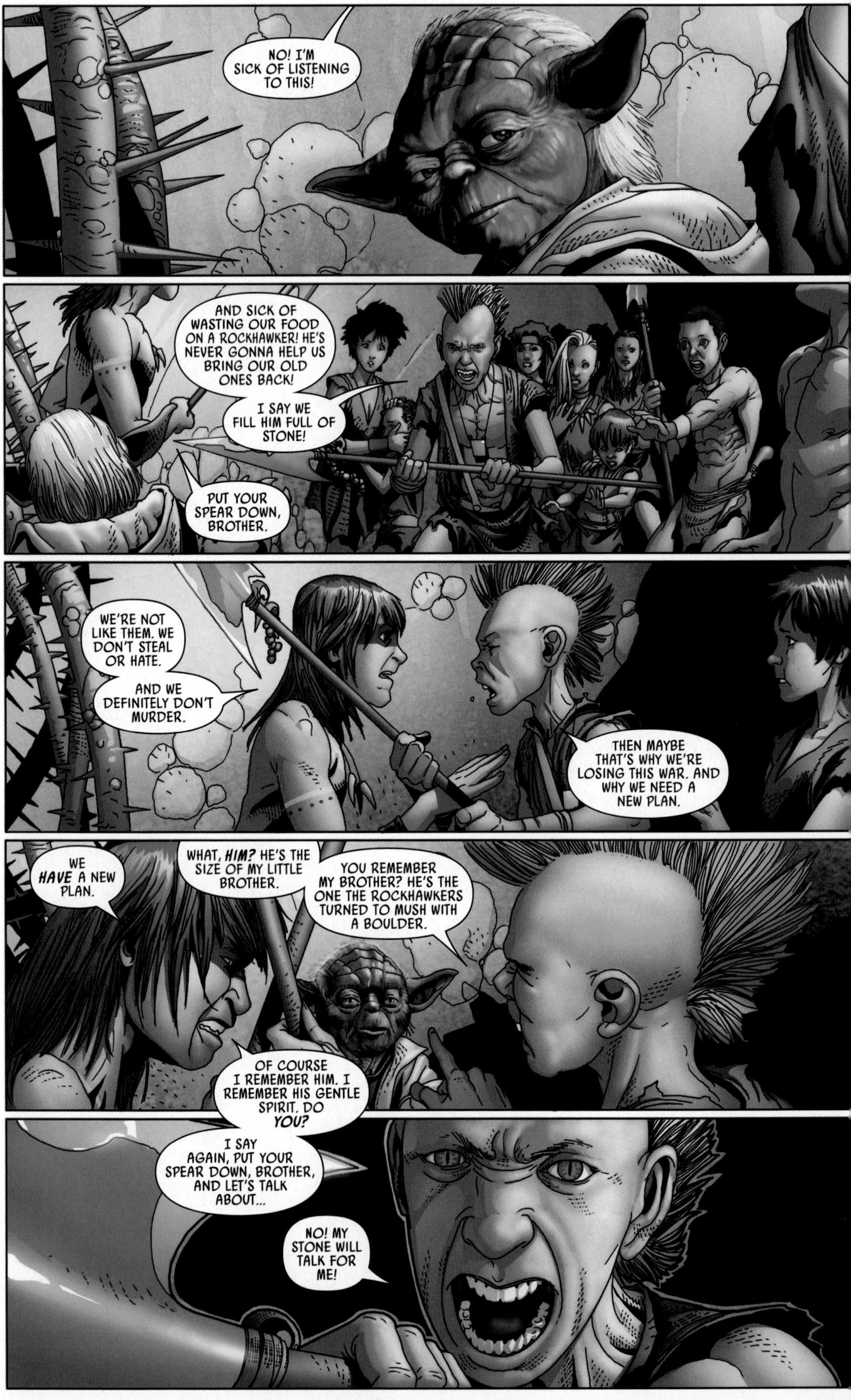
NO! I'M SICK OF LISTENING TO THIS!
AND SICK OF WASTING OUR FOOD ON A ROCKHAWKER! HE'S NEVER GONNA HELP US BRING OUR OLD ONES BACK!
I SAY WE FILL HIM FULL OF STONE!
PUT YOUR SPEAR DOWN, BROTHER.
WE'RE NOT LIKE THEM. WE DON'T STEAL OR HATE.
AND WE DEFINITELY DON'T MURDER.
THEN MAYBE THAT'S WHY WE'RE LOSING THIS WAR. AND WHY WE NEED A NEW PLAN.
WE *HAVE* A NEW PLAN.
WHAT, *HIM?* HE'S THE SIZE OF MY LITTLE BROTHER.
YOU REMEMBER MY BROTHER? HE'S THE ONE THE ROCKHAWKERS TURNED TO MUSH WITH A BOULDER.
OF COURSE I REMEMBER HIM. I REMEMBER HIS GENTLE SPIRIT. DO *YOU?*
I SAY AGAIN, PUT YOUR SPEAR DOWN, BROTHER, AND LET'S TALK ABOUT...
NO! MY STONE WILL TALK FOR ME!

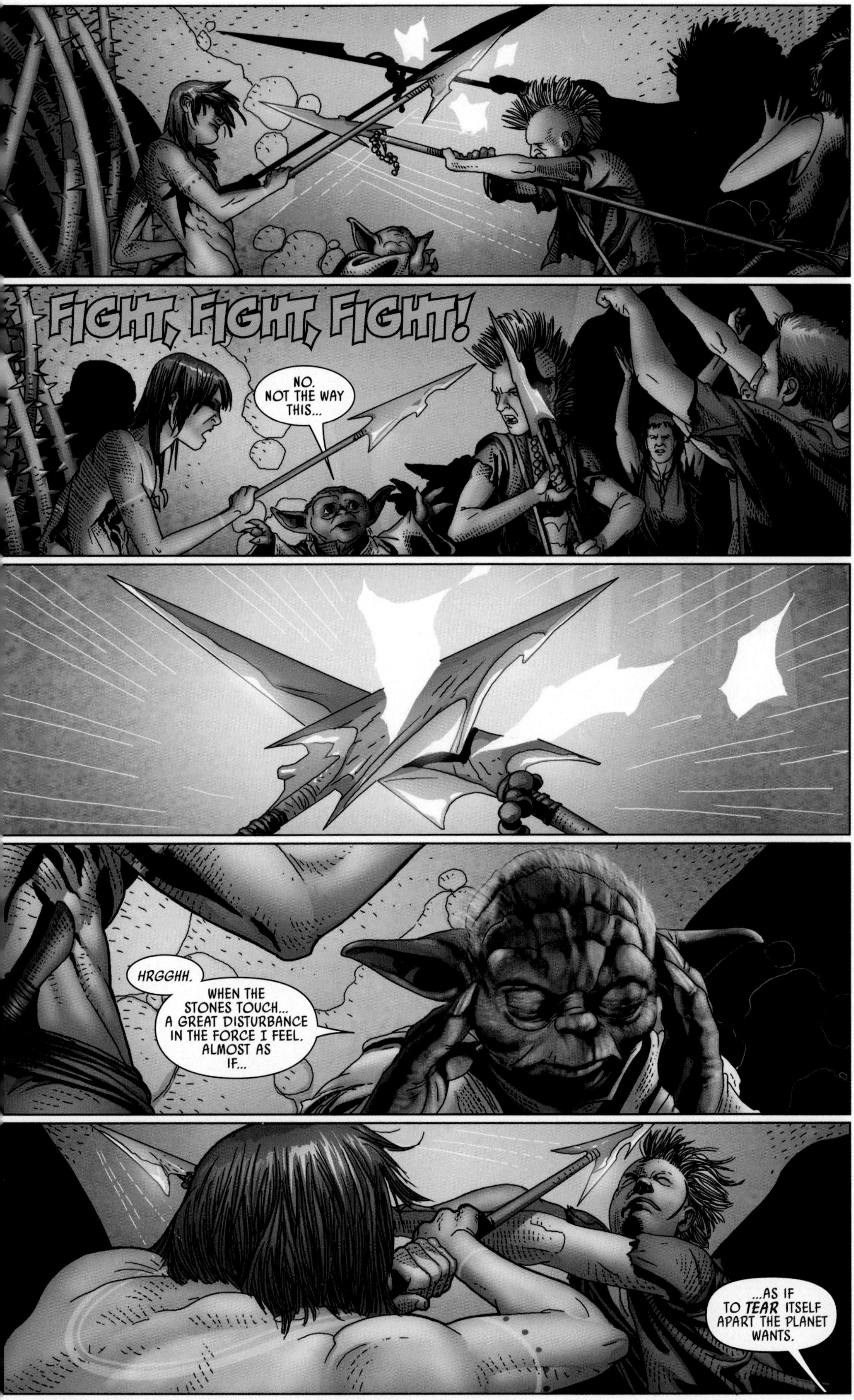
FIGHT, FIGHT, FIGHT!
NO. NOT THE WAY THIS...
HRGGHH.
WHEN THE STONES TOUCH... A GREAT DISTURBANCE IN THE FORCE I FEEL. ALMOST AS IF...
...AS IF TO TEAR ITSELF APART THE PLANET WANTS.

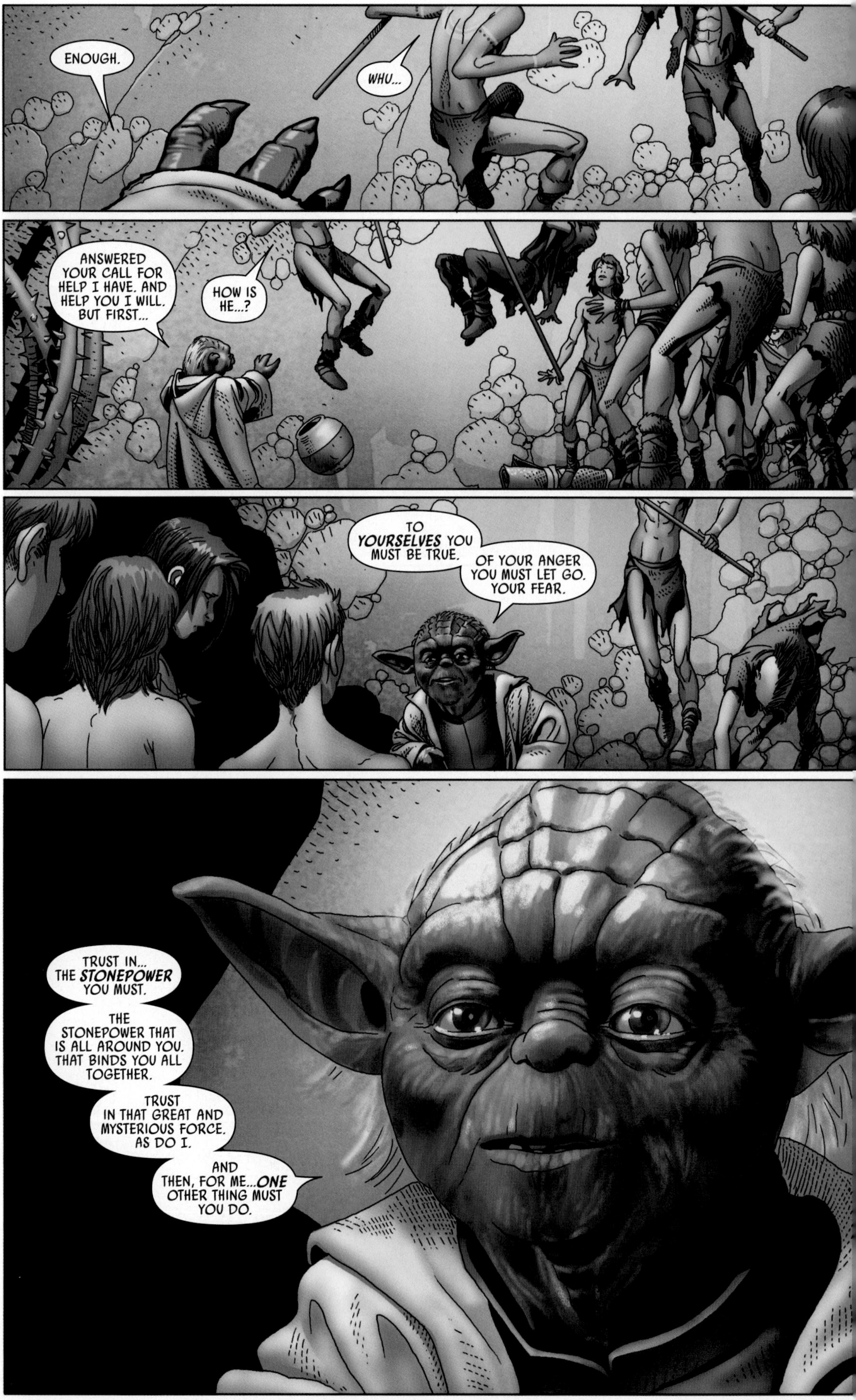
ENOUGH.
WHU...
ANSWERED YOUR CALL FOR HELP I HAVE. AND HELP YOU I WILL. BUT FIRST...
HOW IS HE...?
TO *YOURSELVES* YOU MUST BE TRUE.
OF YOUR ANGER YOU MUST LET GO. YOUR FEAR.
TRUST IN... THE *STONEPOWER* YOU MUST.
THE STONEPOWER THAT IS ALL AROUND YOU. THAT BINDS YOU ALL TOGETHER.
TRUST IN THAT GREAT AND MYSTERIOUS FORCE, AS DO I.
AND THEN, FOR ME...*ONE* OTHER THING MUST YOU DO.

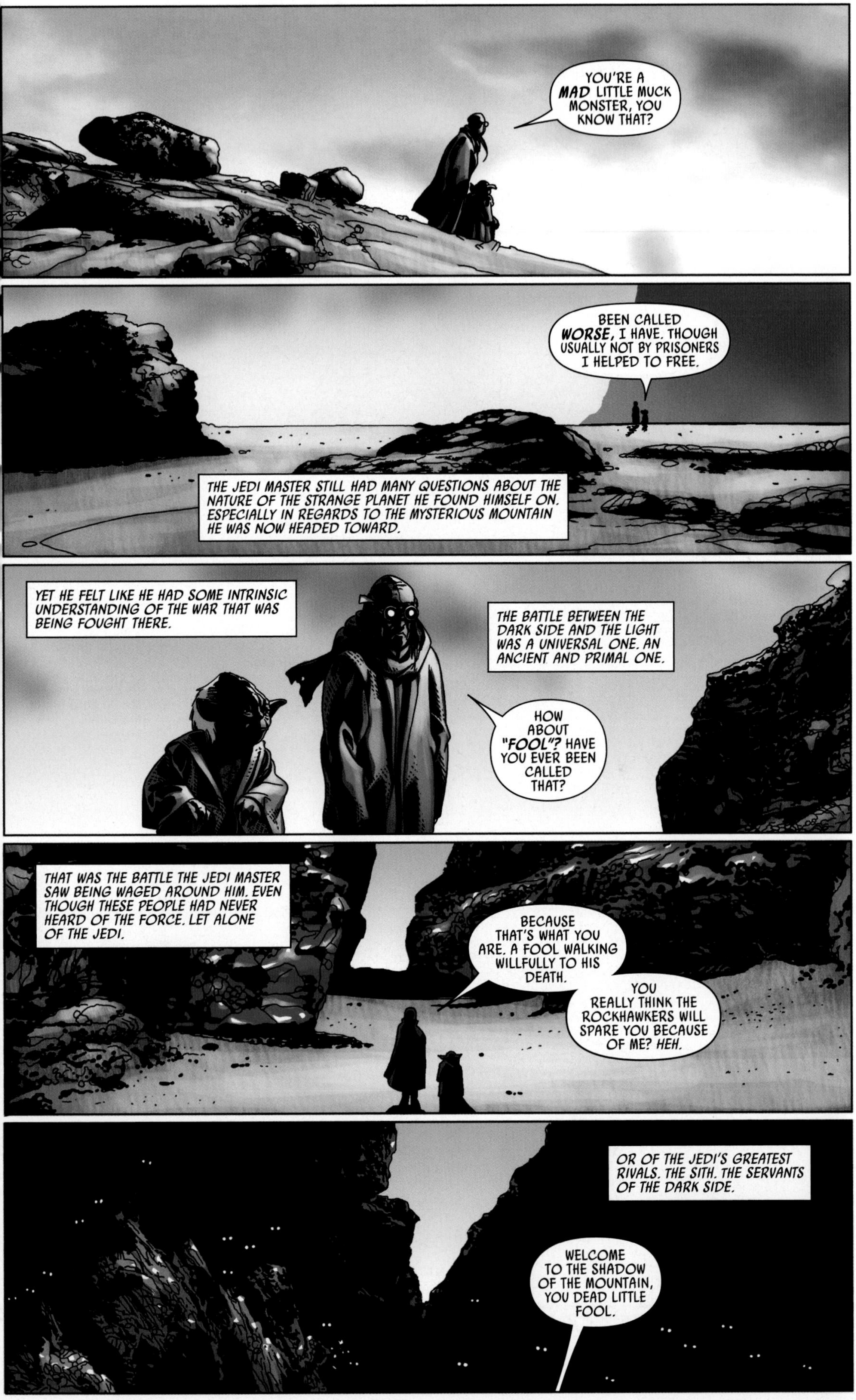
YOU'RE A MAD LITTLE MUCK MONSTER, YOU KNOW THAT?
BEEN CALLED WORSE, I HAVE. THOUGH USUALLY NOT BY PRISONERS I HELPED TO FREE.
THE JEDI MASTER STILL HAD MANY QUESTIONS ABOUT THE NATURE OF THE STRANGE PLANET HE FOUND HIMSELF ON. ESPECIALLY IN REGARDS TO THE MYSTERIOUS MOUNTAIN HE WAS NOW HEADED TOWARD.
YET HE FELT LIKE HE HAD SOME INTRINSIC UNDERSTANDING OF THE WAR THAT WAS BEING FOUGHT THERE.
THE BATTLE BETWEEN THE DARK SIDE AND THE LIGHT WAS A UNIVERSAL ONE. AN ANCIENT AND PRIMAL ONE.
HOW ABOUT "FOOL"? HAVE YOU EVER BEEN CALLED THAT?
THAT WAS THE BATTLE THE JEDI MASTER SAW BEING WAGED AROUND HIM. EVEN THOUGH THESE PEOPLE HAD NEVER HEARD OF THE FORCE. LET ALONE OF THE JEDI.
BECAUSE THAT'S WHAT YOU ARE. A FOOL WALKING WILLFULLY TO HIS DEATH.
YOU REALLY THINK THE ROCKHAWKERS WILL SPARE YOU BECAUSE OF ME? HEH.
OR OF THE JEDI'S GREATEST RIVALS. THE SITH. THE SERVANTS OF THE DARK SIDE.
WELCOME TO THE SHADOW OF THE MOUNTAIN, YOU DEAD LITTLE FOOL.

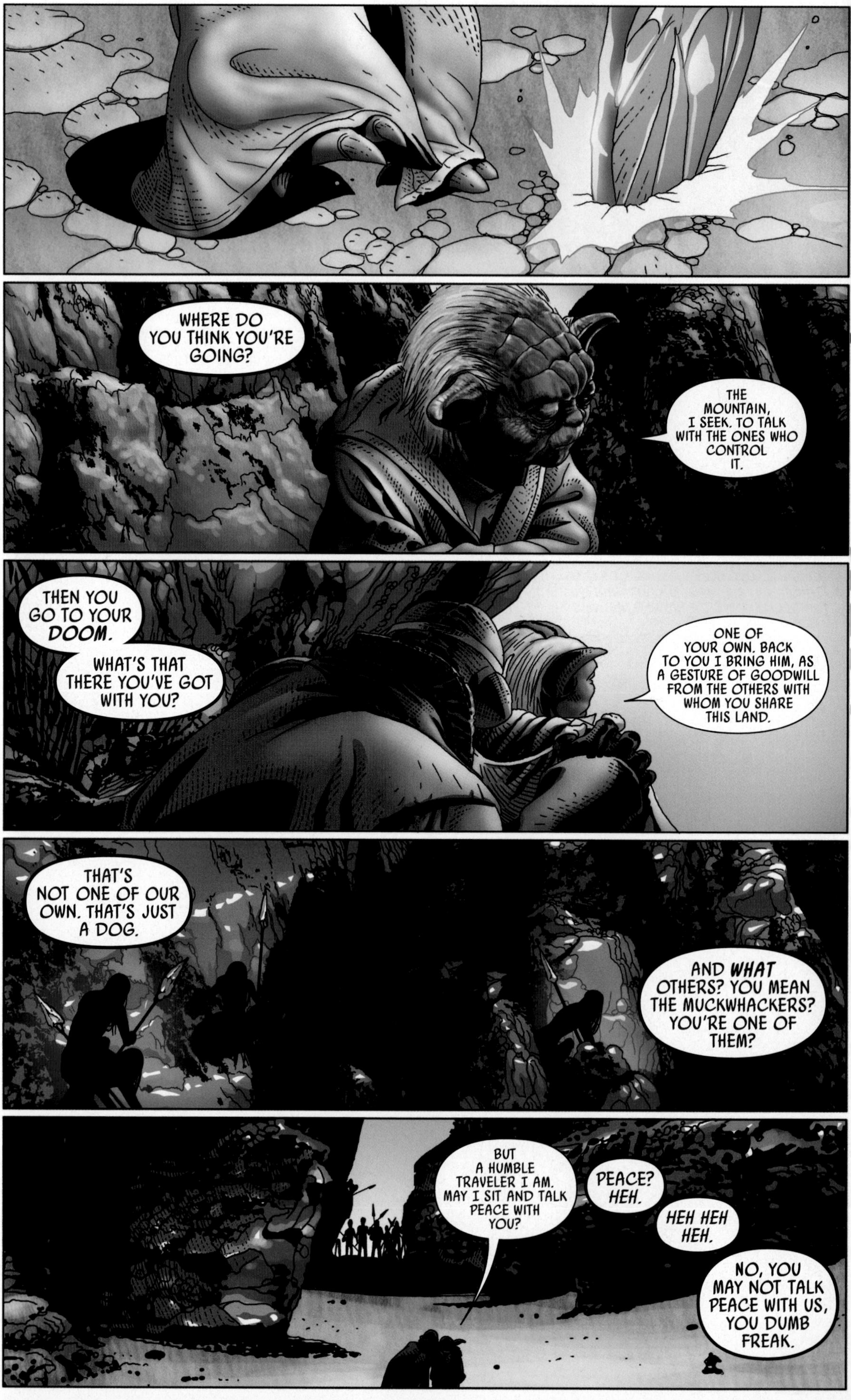
WHERE DO YOU THINK YOU'RE GOING?
THE MOUNTAIN, I SEEK. TO TALK WITH THE ONES WHO CONTROL IT.
THEN YOU GO TO YOUR DOOM.
WHAT'S THAT THERE YOU'VE GOT WITH YOU?
ONE OF YOUR OWN. BACK TO YOU I BRING HIM, AS A GESTURE OF GOODWILL FROM THE OTHERS WITH WHOM YOU SHARE THIS LAND.
THAT'S NOT ONE OF OUR OWN. THAT'S JUST A DOG.
AND WHAT OTHERS? YOU MEAN THE MUCKWHACKERS? YOU'RE ONE OF THEM?
BUT A HUMBLE TRAVELER I AM. MAY I SIT AND TALK PEACE WITH YOU?
PEACE? HEH.
HEH HEH HEH.
NO, YOU MAY NOT TALK PEACE WITH US, YOU DUMB FREAK.

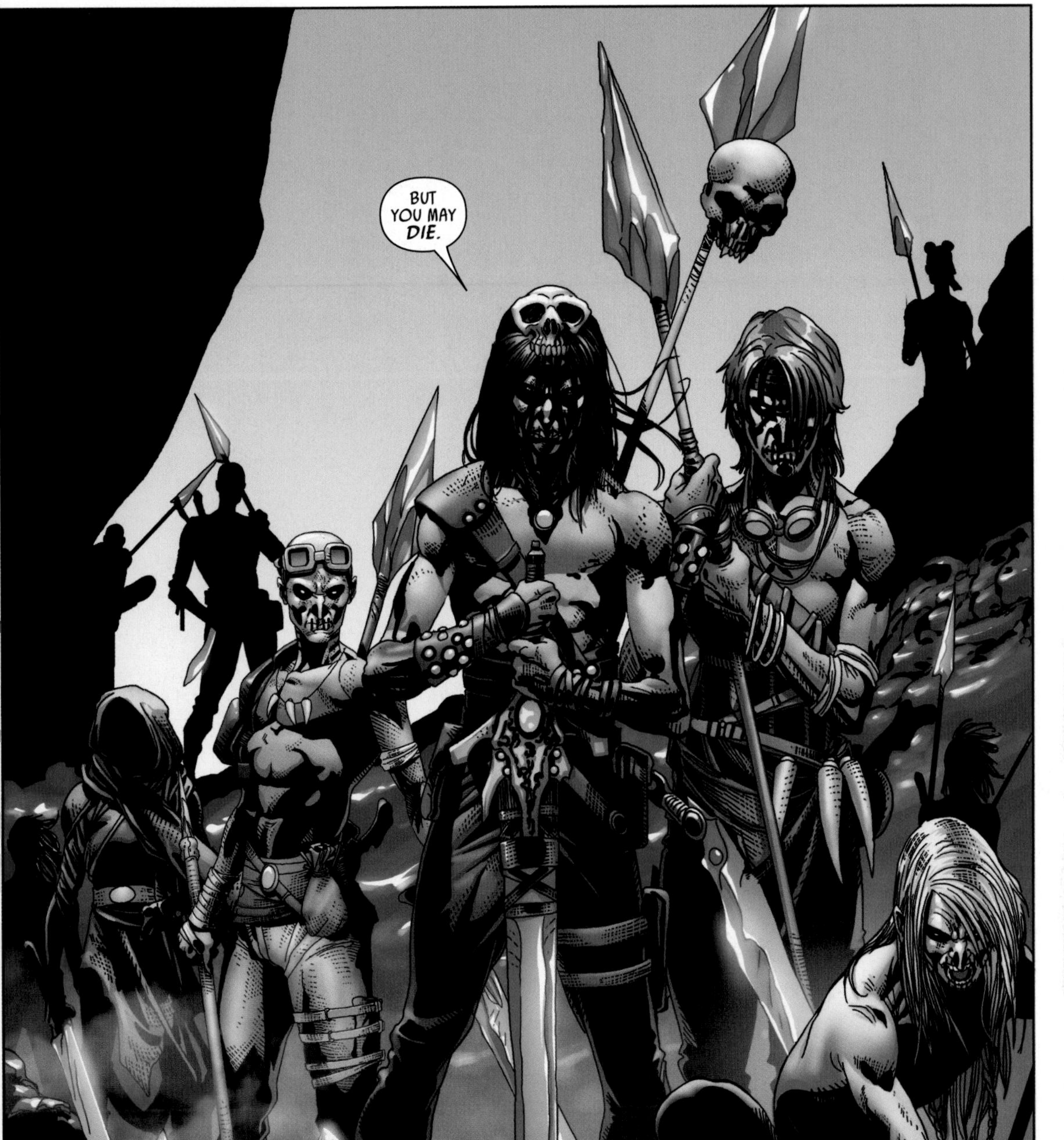
BUT YOU MAY DIE.

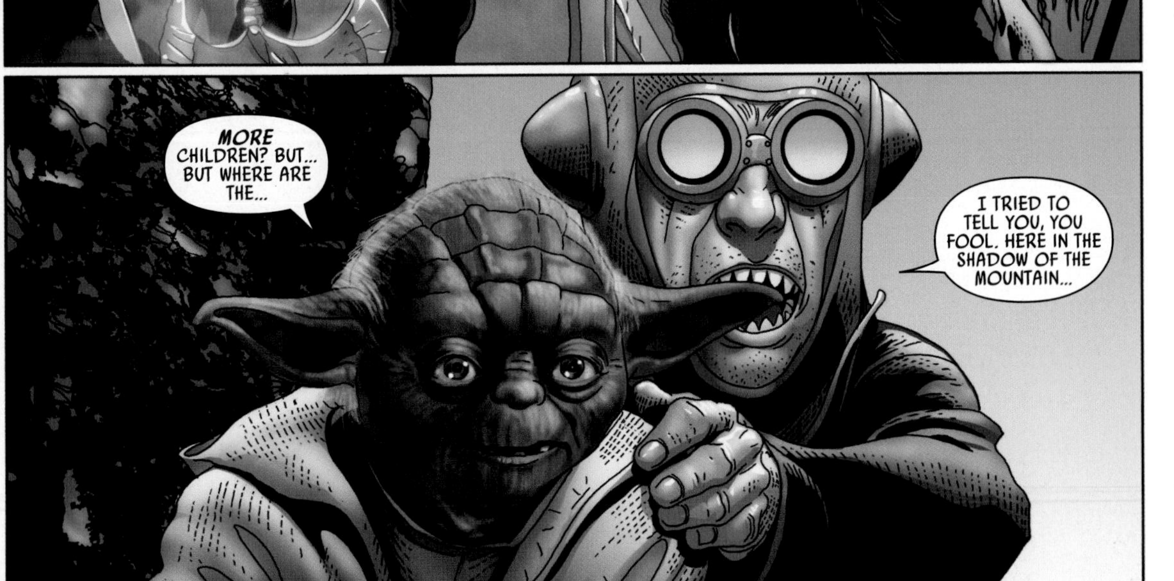
MORE CHILDREN? BUT... BUT WHERE ARE THE...
I TRIED TO TELL YOU, YOU FOOL. HERE IN THE SHADOW OF THE MOUNTAIN...

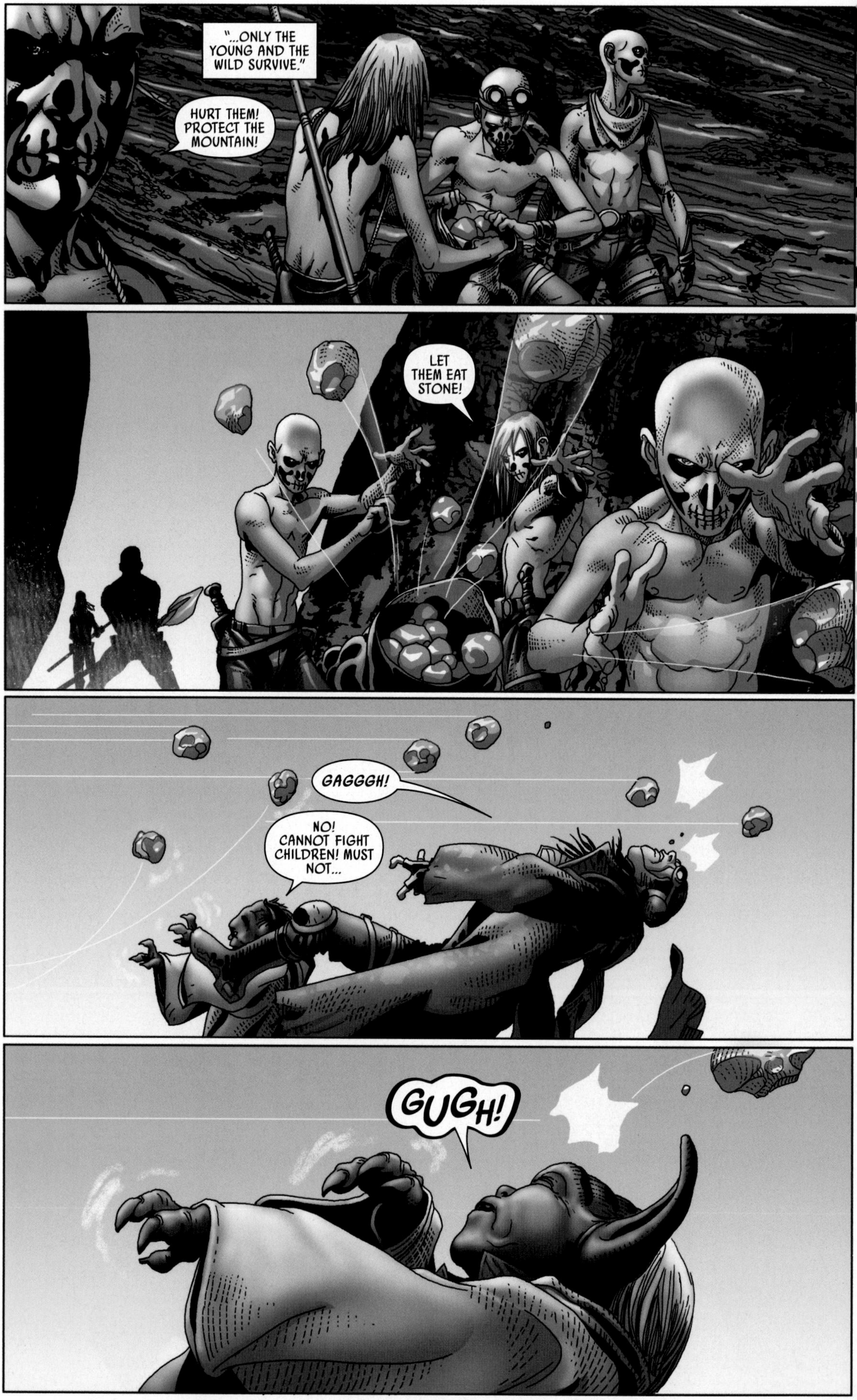
"...ONLY THE YOUNG AND THE WILD SURVIVE."
HURT THEM! PROTECT THE MOUNTAIN!
LET THEM EAT STONE!
GAGGGH!
NO! CANNOT FIGHT CHILDREN! MUST NOT...
GUGH!

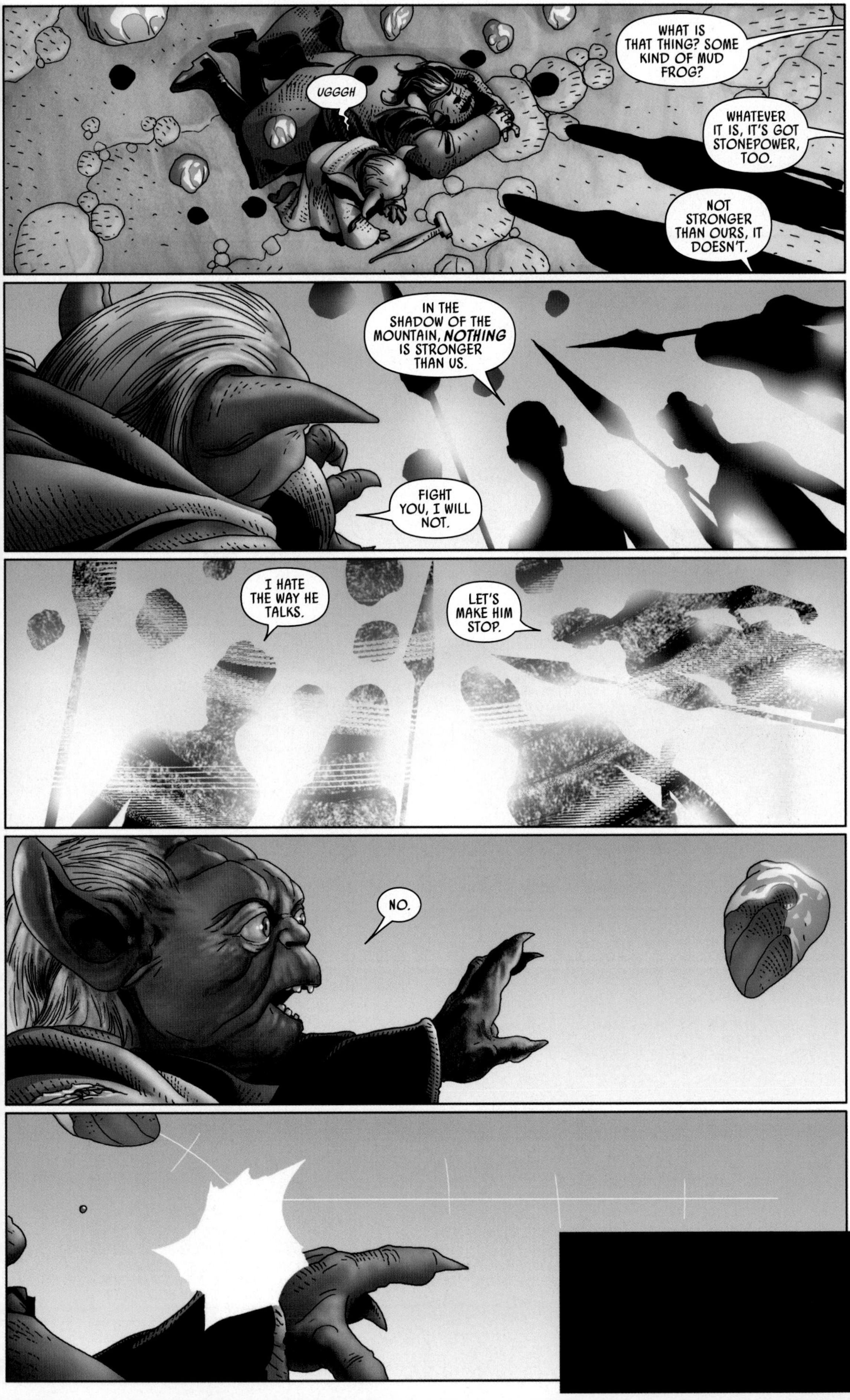

UGGGH
WHAT IS THAT THING? SOME KIND OF MUD FROG?
WHATEVER IT IS, IT'S GOT STONEPOWER, TOO.
NOT STRONGER THAN OURS, IT DOESN'T.
IN THE SHADOW OF THE MOUNTAIN, *NOTHING* IS STRONGER THAN US.
FIGHT YOU, I WILL NOT.
I HATE THE WAY HE TALKS.
LET'S MAKE HIM STOP.
NO.
[redacted]

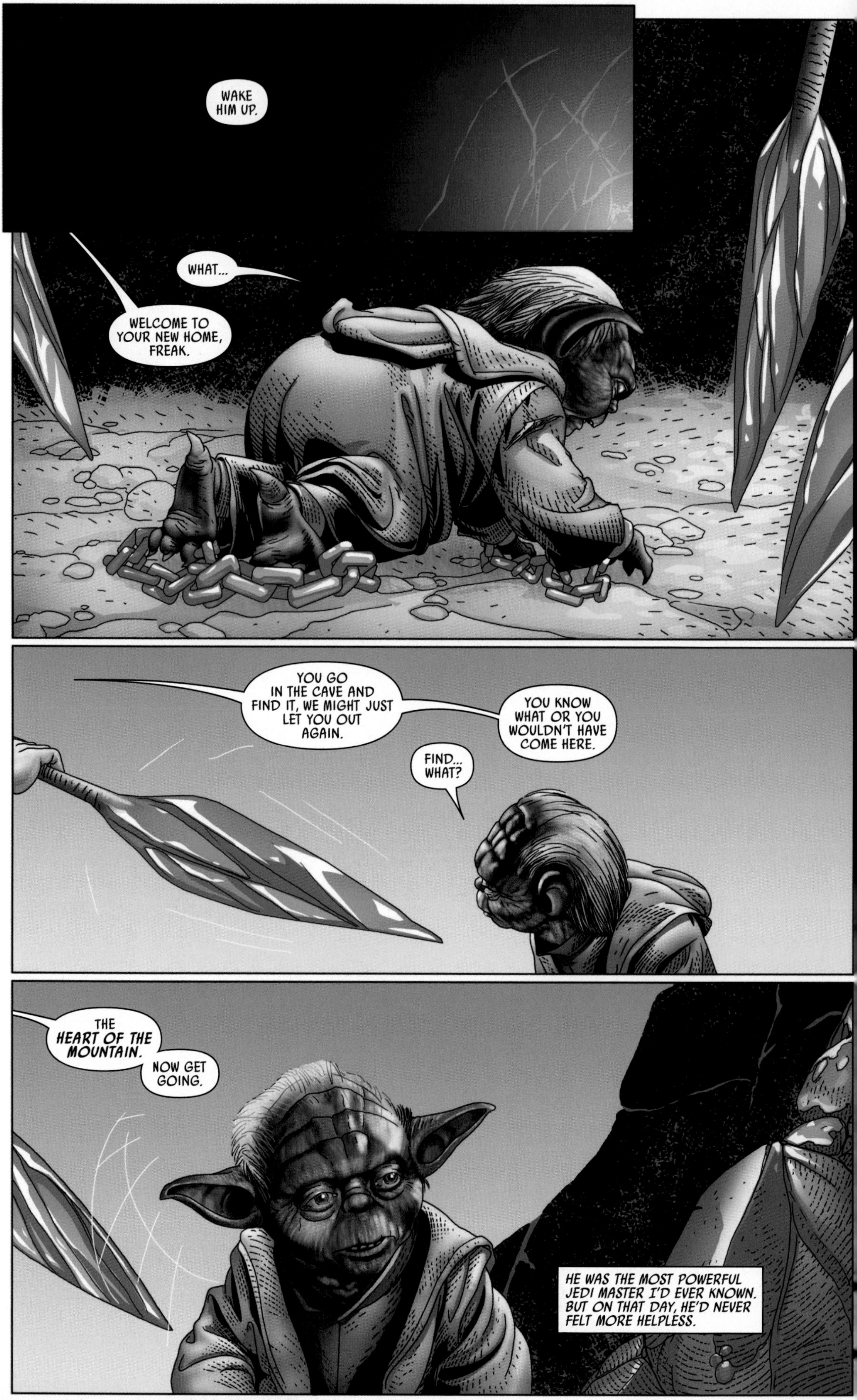
WAKE HIM UP.
WHAT...
WELCOME TO YOUR NEW HOME, FREAK.
YOU GO IN THE CAVE AND FIND IT, WE MIGHT JUST LET YOU OUT AGAIN.
YOU KNOW WHAT OR YOU WOULDN'T HAVE COME HERE.
FIND... WHAT?
THE HEART OF THE MOUNTAIN.
NOW GET GOING.
HE WAS THE MOST POWERFUL JEDI MASTER I'D EVER KNOWN. BUT ON THAT DAY, HE'D NEVER FELT MORE HELPLESS.

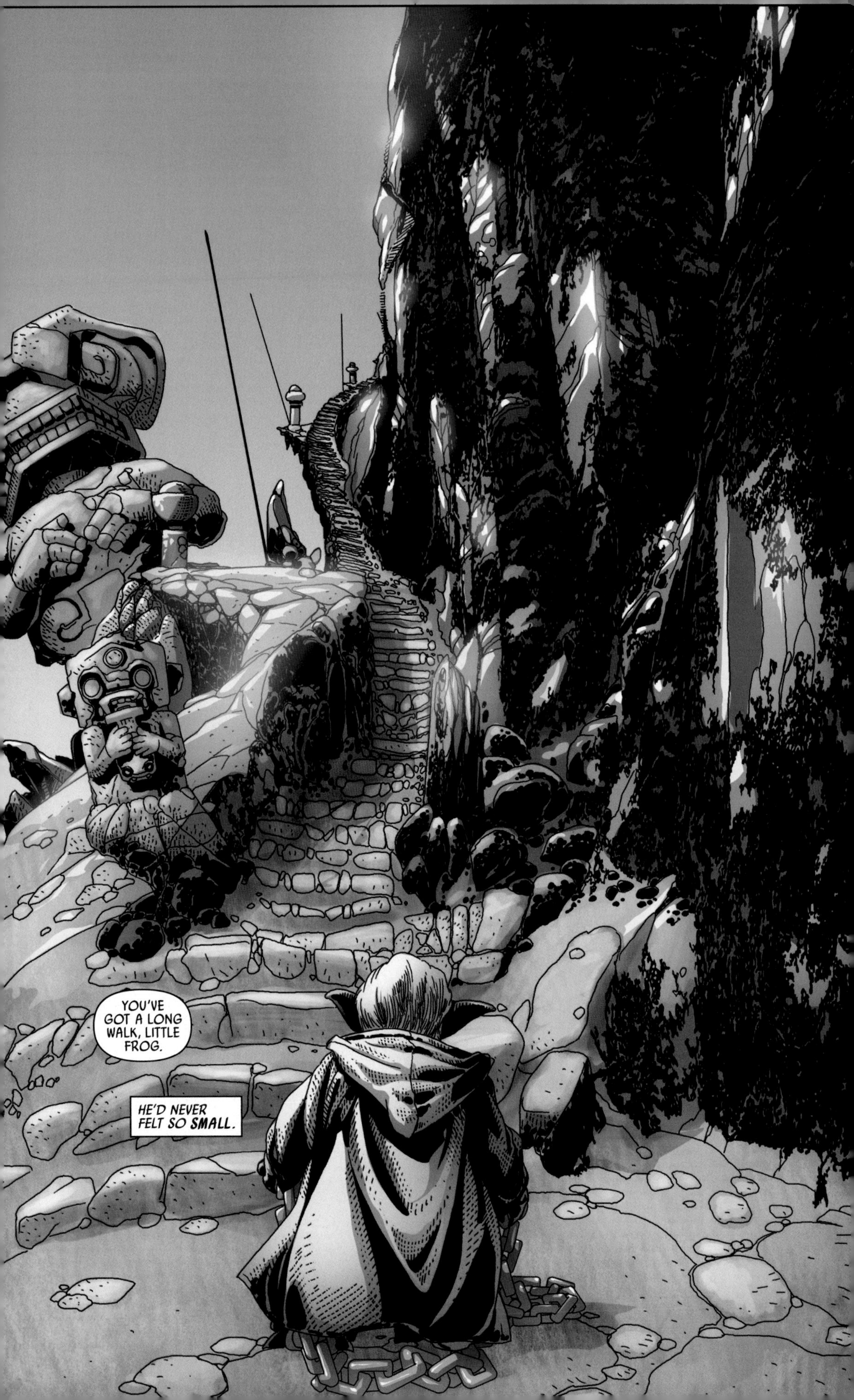
YOU'VE GOT A LONG WALK, LITTLE FROG.
HE'D NEVER FELT SO SMALL.

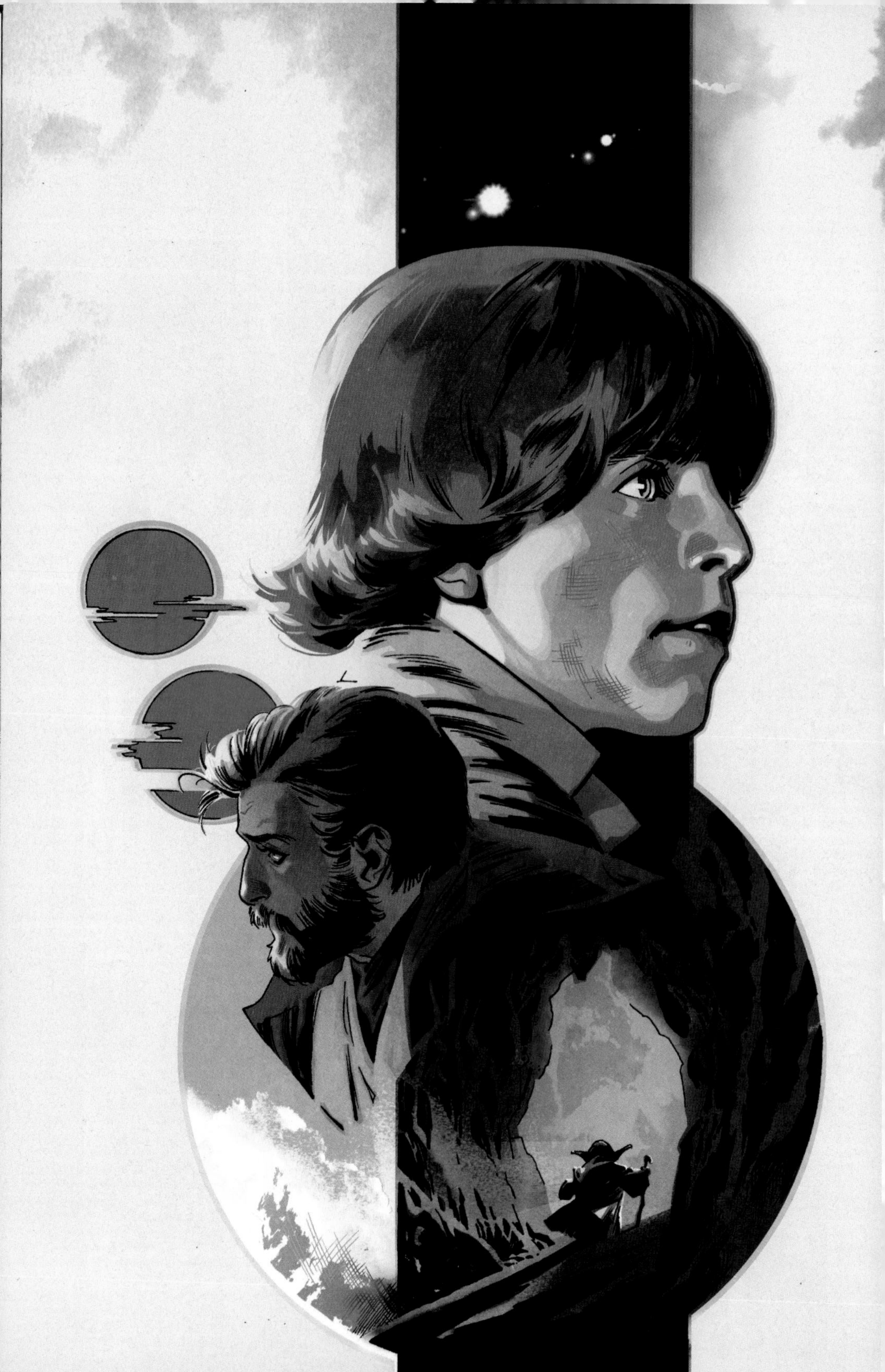

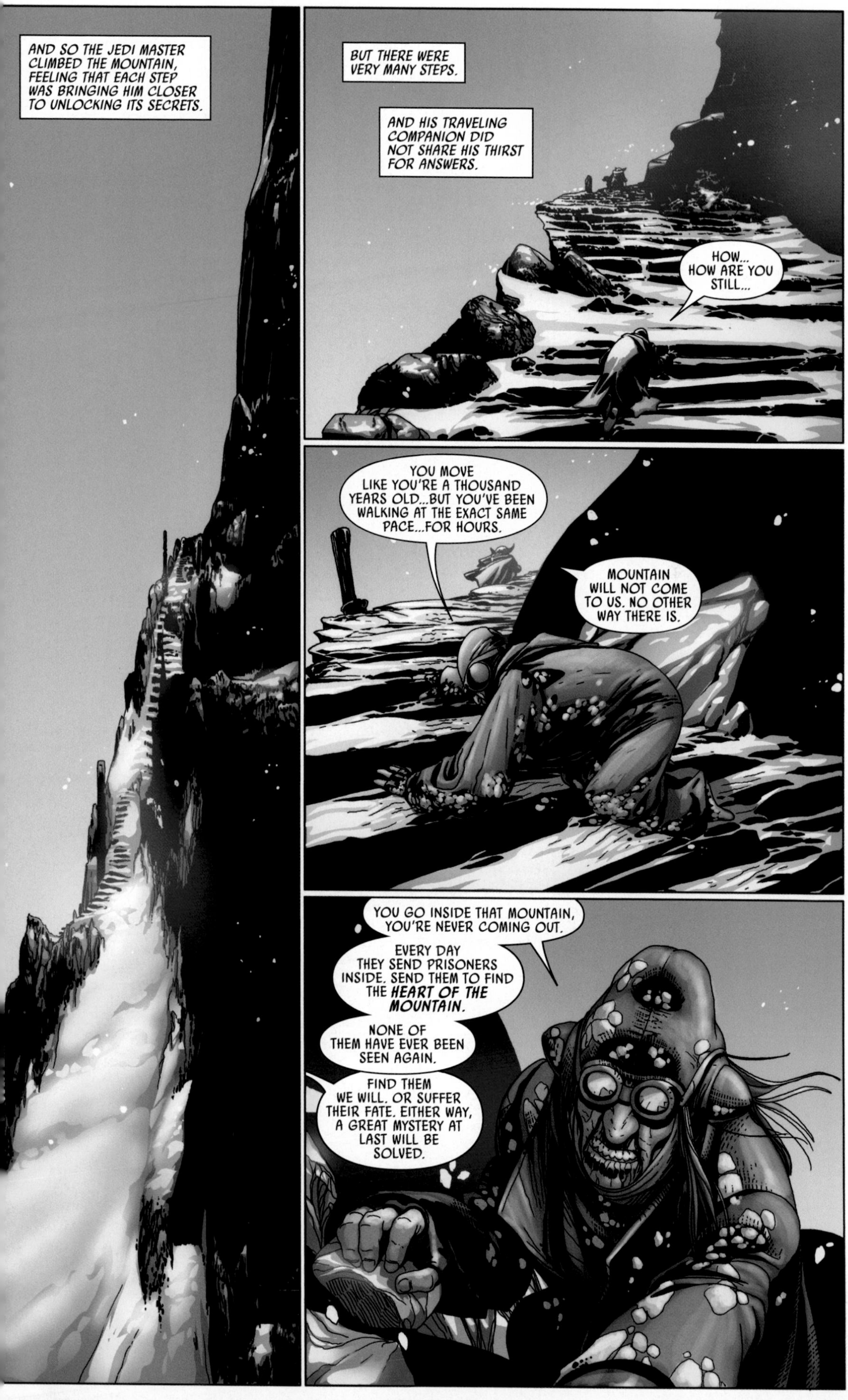
AND SO THE JEDI MASTER CLIMBED THE MOUNTAIN, FEELING THAT EACH STEP WAS BRINGING HIM CLOSER TO UNLOCKING ITS SECRETS.
BUT THERE WERE VERY MANY STEPS.
AND HIS TRAVELING COMPANION DID NOT SHARE HIS THIRST FOR ANSWERS.
HOW... HOW ARE YOU STILL...
YOU MOVE LIKE YOU'RE A THOUSAND YEARS OLD...BUT YOU'VE BEEN WALKING AT THE EXACT SAME PACE...FOR HOURS.
MOUNTAIN WILL NOT COME TO US. NO OTHER WAY THERE IS.
YOU GO INSIDE THAT MOUNTAIN, YOU'RE NEVER COMING OUT.
EVERY DAY THEY SEND PRISONERS INSIDE. SEND THEM TO FIND THE HEART OF THE MOUNTAIN.
NONE OF THEM HAVE EVER BEEN SEEN AGAIN.
FIND THEM WE WILL. OR SUFFER THEIR FATE. EITHER WAY, A GREAT MYSTERY AT LAST WILL BE SOLVED.

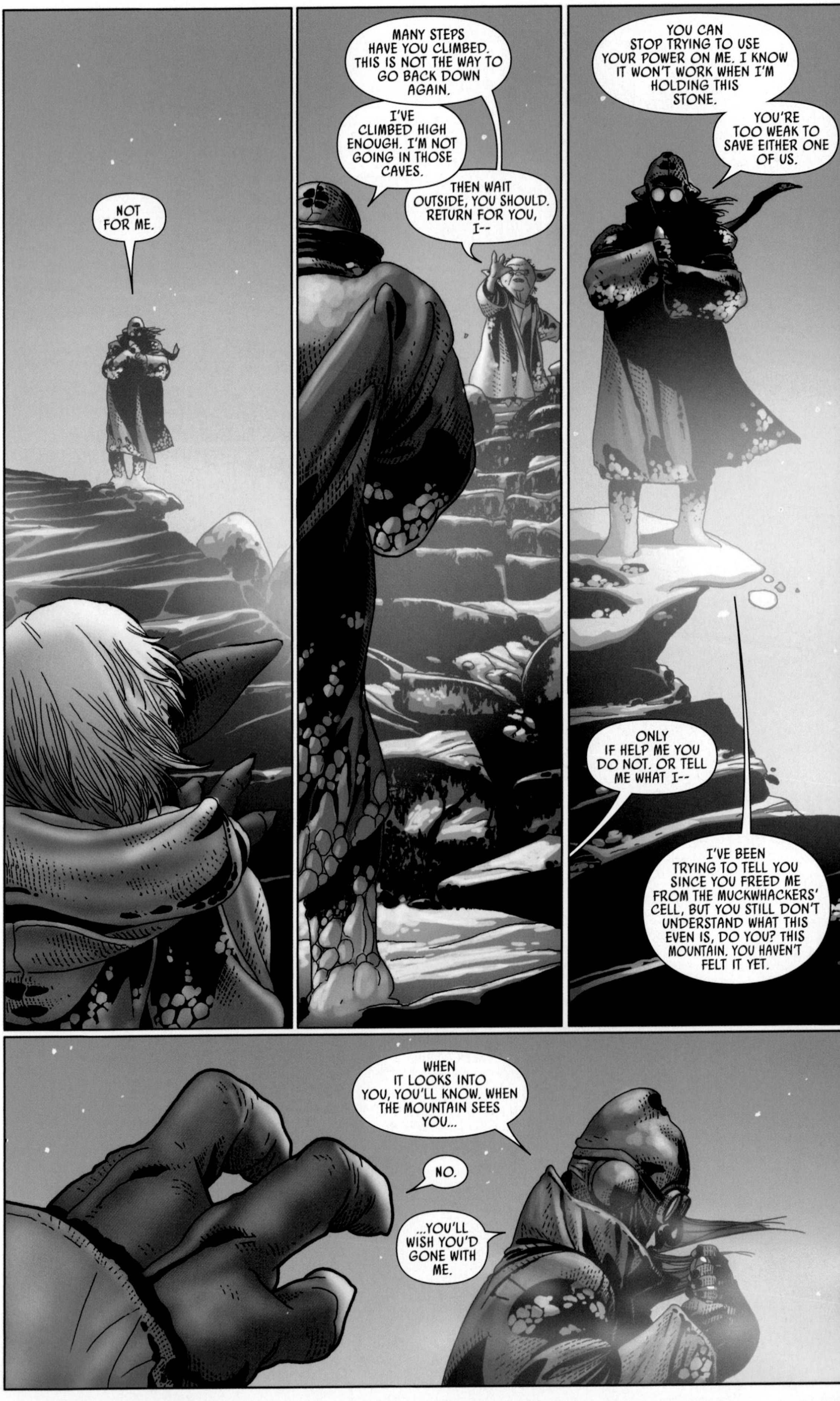
NOT FOR ME.
MANY STEPS HAVE YOU CLIMBED. THIS IS NOT THE WAY TO GO BACK DOWN AGAIN.
I'VE CLIMBED HIGH ENOUGH. I'M NOT GOING IN THOSE CAVES.
THEN WAIT OUTSIDE, YOU SHOULD. RETURN FOR YOU, I--
YOU CAN STOP TRYING TO USE YOUR POWER ON ME. I KNOW IT WON'T WORK WHEN I'M HOLDING THIS STONE.
YOU'RE TOO WEAK TO SAVE EITHER ONE OF US.
ONLY IF HELP ME YOU DO NOT. OR TELL ME WHAT I--
I'VE BEEN TRYING TO TELL YOU SINCE YOU FREED ME FROM THE MUCKWHACKERS' CELL, BUT YOU STILL DON'T UNDERSTAND WHAT THIS EVEN IS, DO YOU? THIS MOUNTAIN. YOU HAVEN'T FELT IT YET.
WHEN IT LOOKS INTO YOU, YOU'LL KNOW. WHEN THE MOUNTAIN SEES YOU...
NO.
...YOU'LL WISH YOU'D GONE WITH ME.

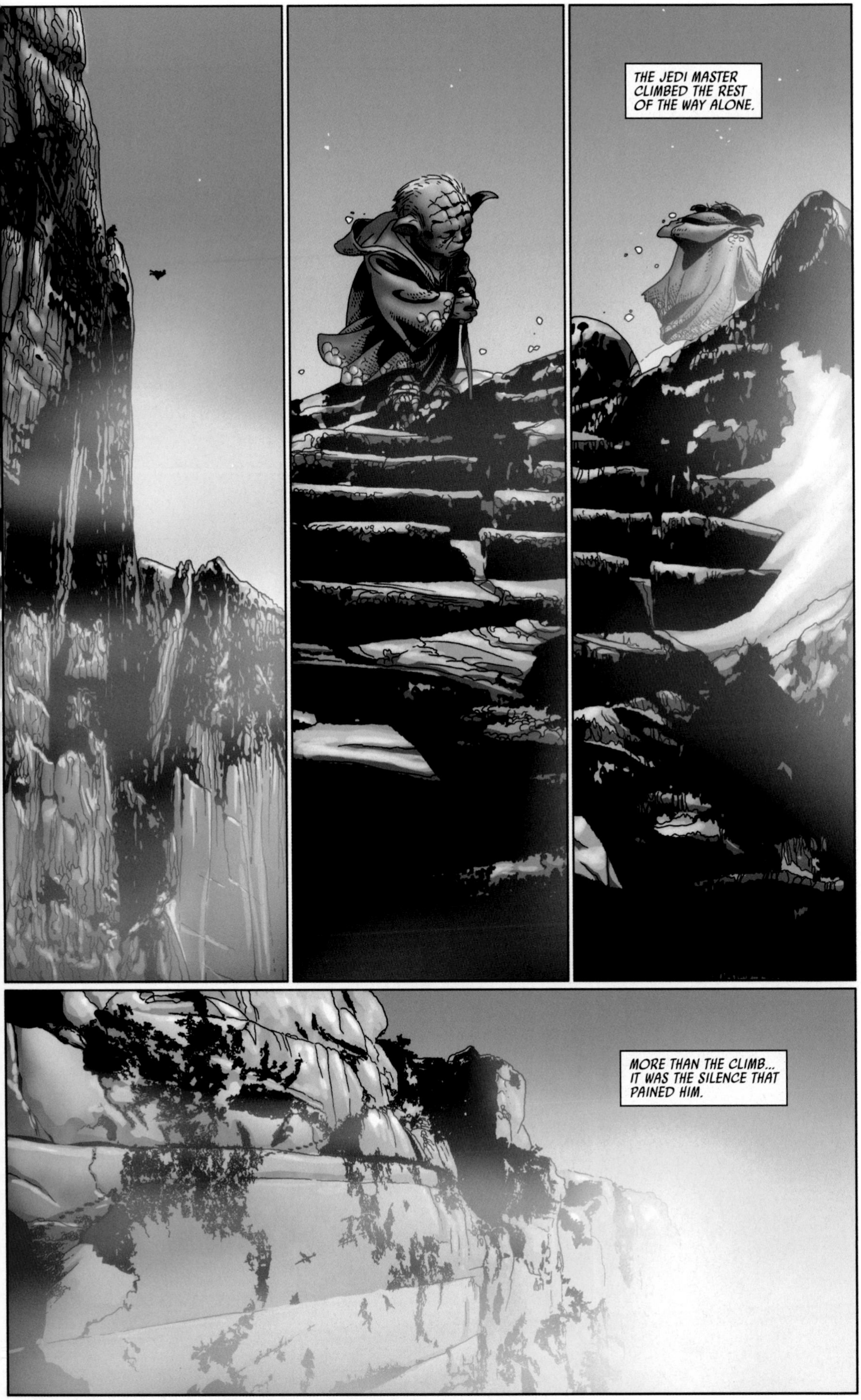
THE JEDI MASTER CLIMBED THE REST OF THE WAY ALONE.
MORE THAN THE CLIMB... IT WAS THE SILENCE THAT PAINED HIM.

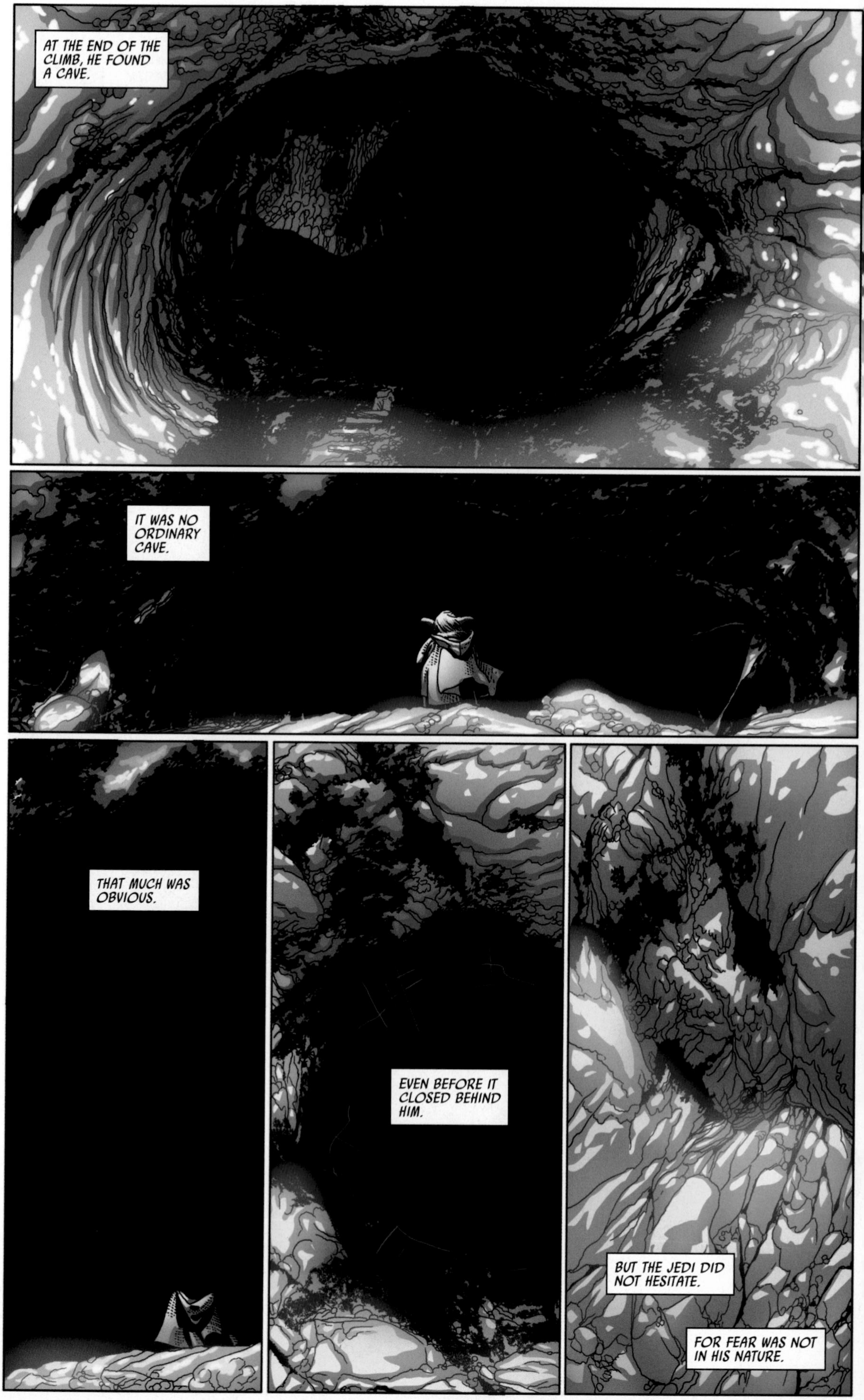
AT THE END OF THE CLIMB, HE FOUND A CAVE.
IT WAS NO ORDINARY CAVE.
THAT MUCH WAS OBVIOUS.
EVEN BEFORE IT CLOSED BEHIND HIM.
BUT THE JEDI DID NOT HESITATE.
FOR FEAR WAS NOT IN HIS NATURE.

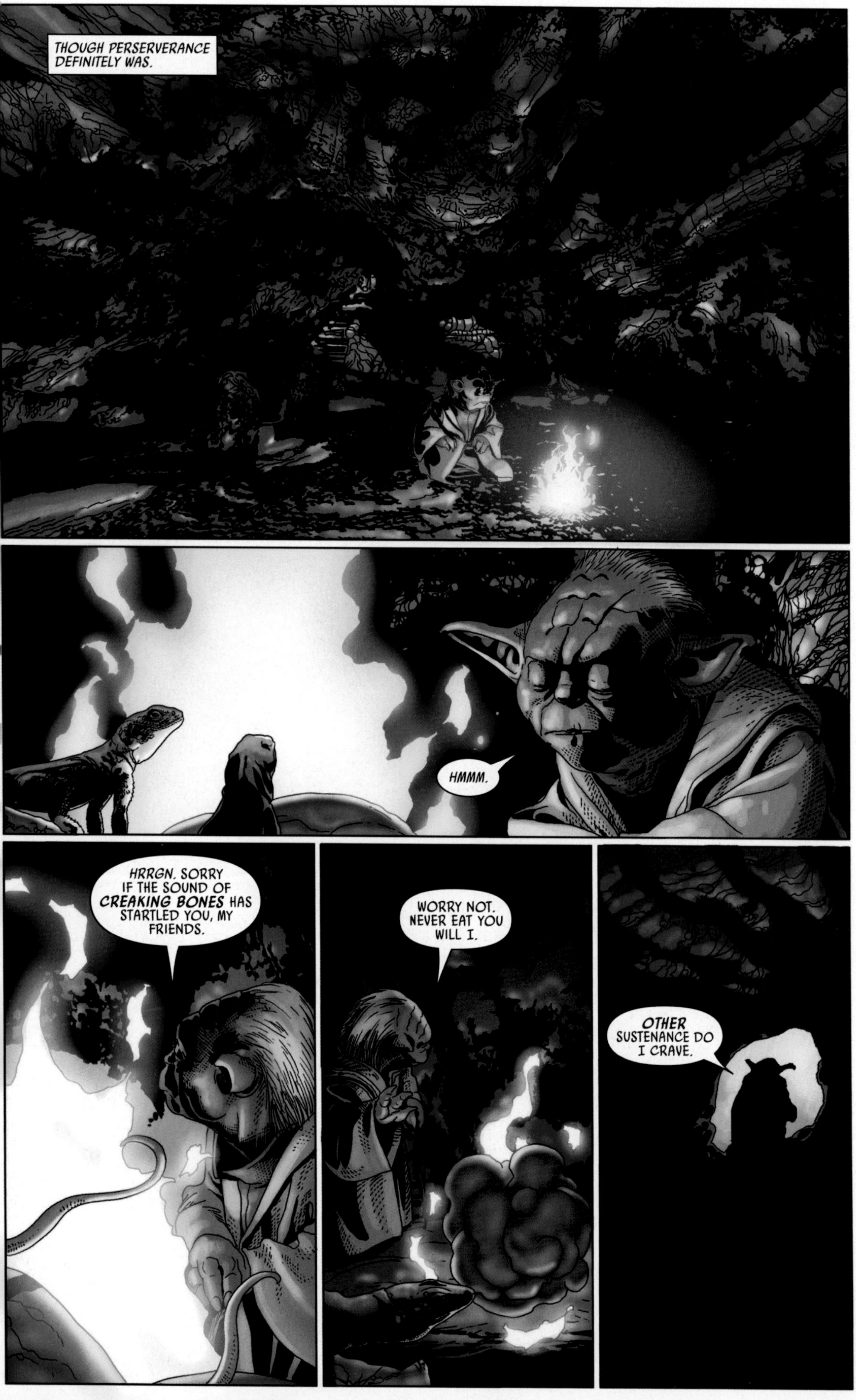
THOUGH PERSERVERANCE DEFINITELY WAS.
HMMM.
HRRGN. SORRY IF THE SOUND OF CREAKING BONES HAS STARTLED YOU, MY FRIENDS.
WORRY NOT. NEVER EAT YOU WILL I.
OTHER SUSTENANCE DO I CRAVE.

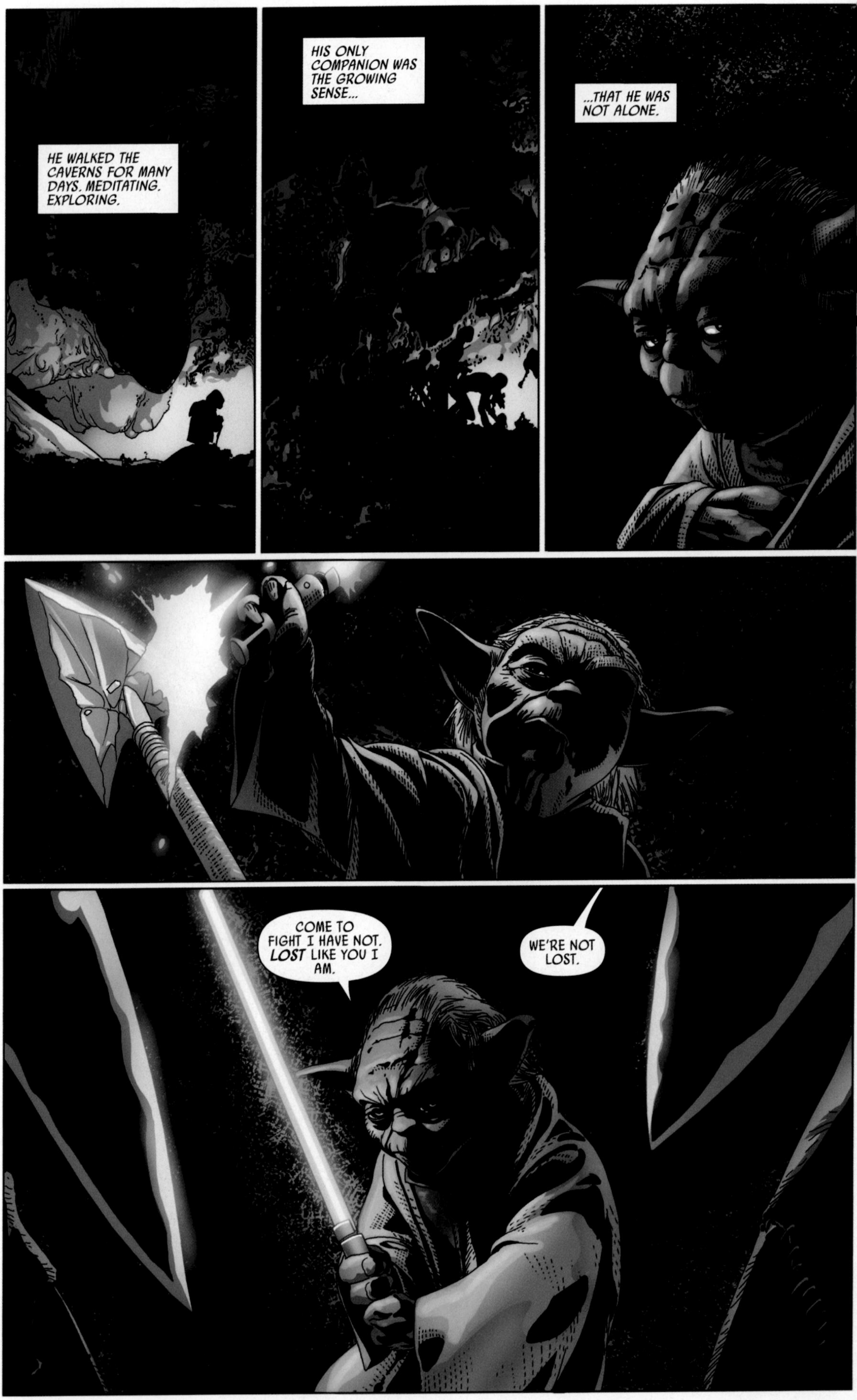
HE WALKED THE CAVERNS FOR MANY DAYS. MEDITATING. EXPLORING.
HIS ONLY COMPANION WAS THE GROWING SENSE...
...THAT HE WAS NOT ALONE.
COME TO FIGHT I HAVE NOT. LOST LIKE YOU I AM.
WE'RE NOT LOST.

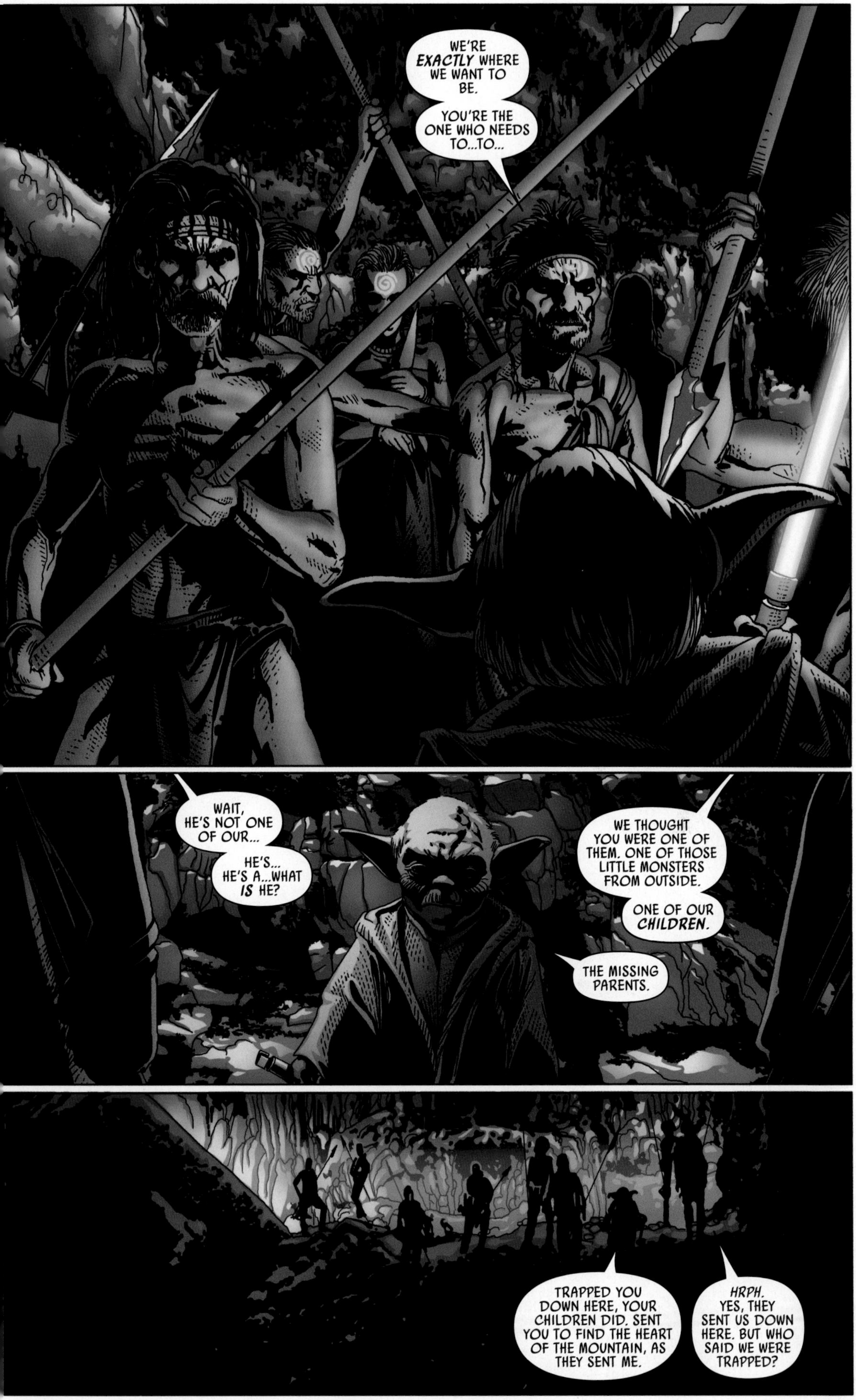
WE'RE EXACTLY WHERE WE WANT TO BE.
YOU'RE THE ONE WHO NEEDS TO...TO...
WAIT, HE'S NOT ONE OF OUR...
HE'S... HE'S A...WHAT IS HE?
WE THOUGHT YOU WERE ONE OF THEM. ONE OF THOSE LITTLE MONSTERS FROM OUTSIDE.
ONE OF OUR CHILDREN.
THE MISSING PARENTS.
TRAPPED YOU DOWN HERE, YOUR CHILDREN DID. SENT YOU TO FIND THE HEART OF THE MOUNTAIN, AS THEY SENT ME.
HRPH. YES, THEY SENT US DOWN HERE. BUT WHO SAID WE WERE TRAPPED?

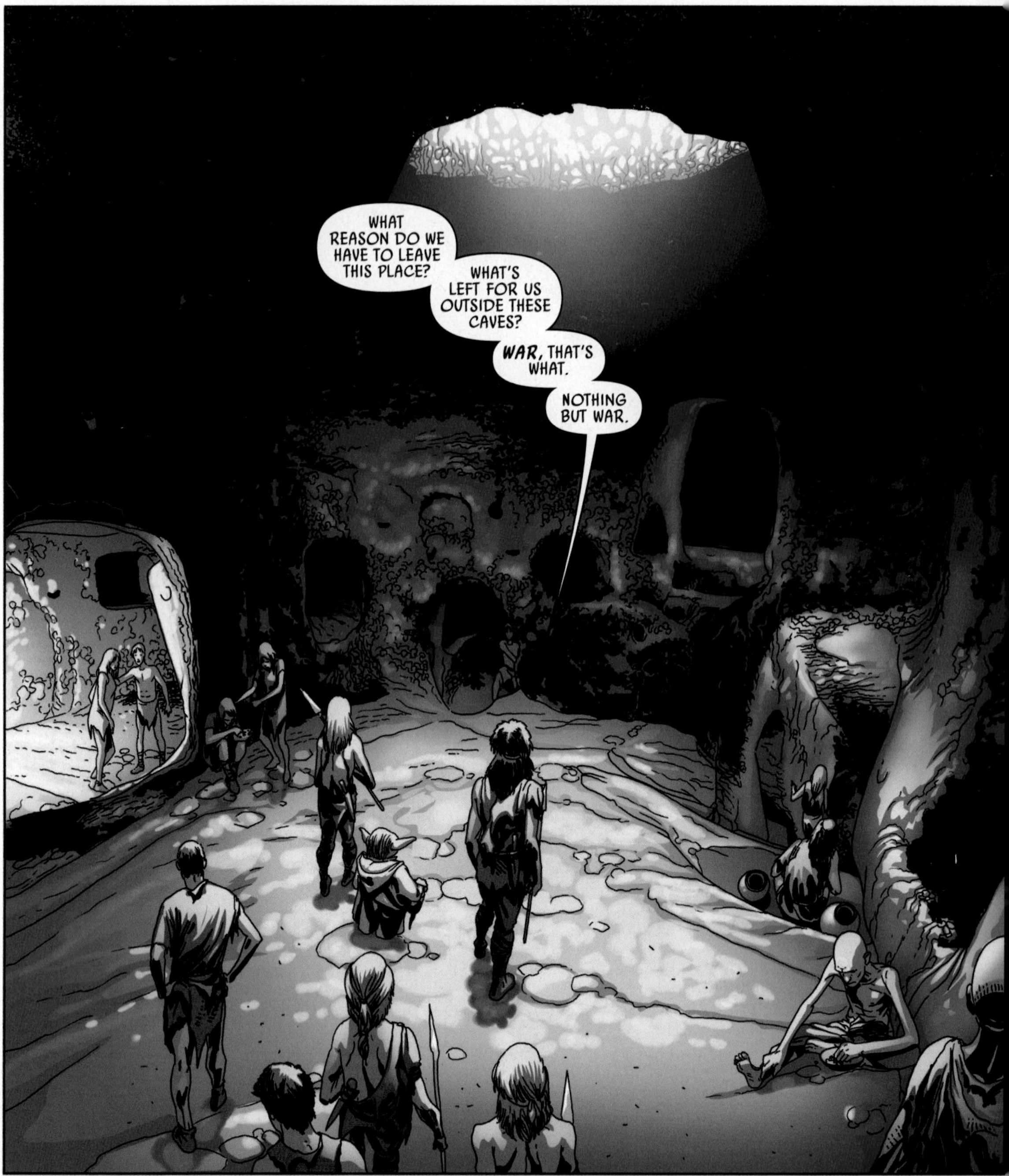
WHAT REASON DO WE HAVE TO LEAVE THIS PLACE?
WHAT'S LEFT FOR US OUTSIDE THESE CAVES?
WAR, THAT'S WHAT.
NOTHING BUT WAR.

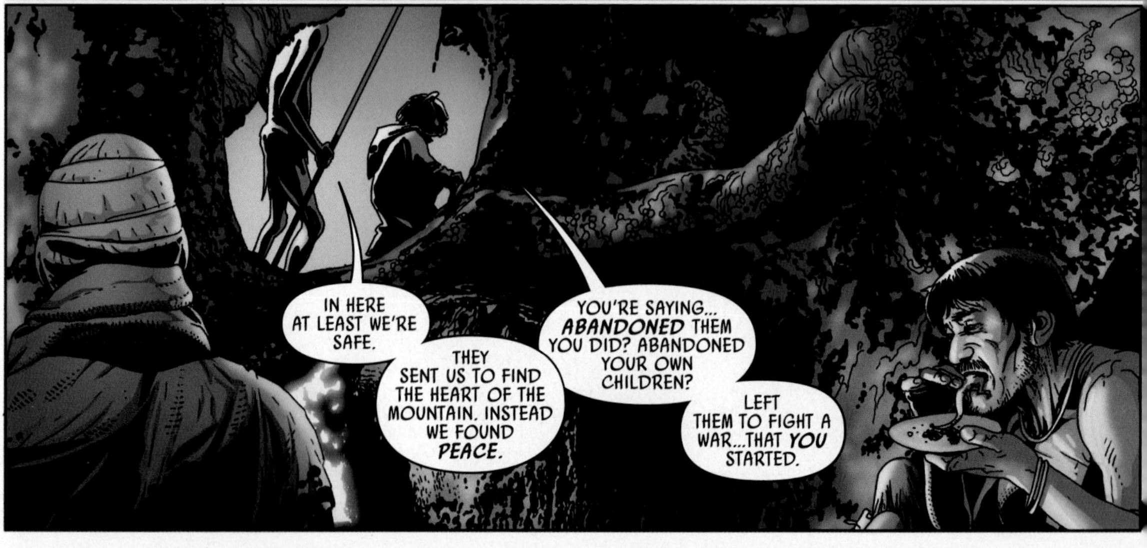
IN HERE AT LEAST WE'RE SAFE.
THEY SENT US TO FIND THE HEART OF THE MOUNTAIN. INSTEAD WE FOUND PEACE.
YOU'RE SAYING... ABANDONED THEM YOU DID? ABANDONED YOUR OWN CHILDREN?
LEFT THEM TO FIGHT A WAR...THAT YOU STARTED.

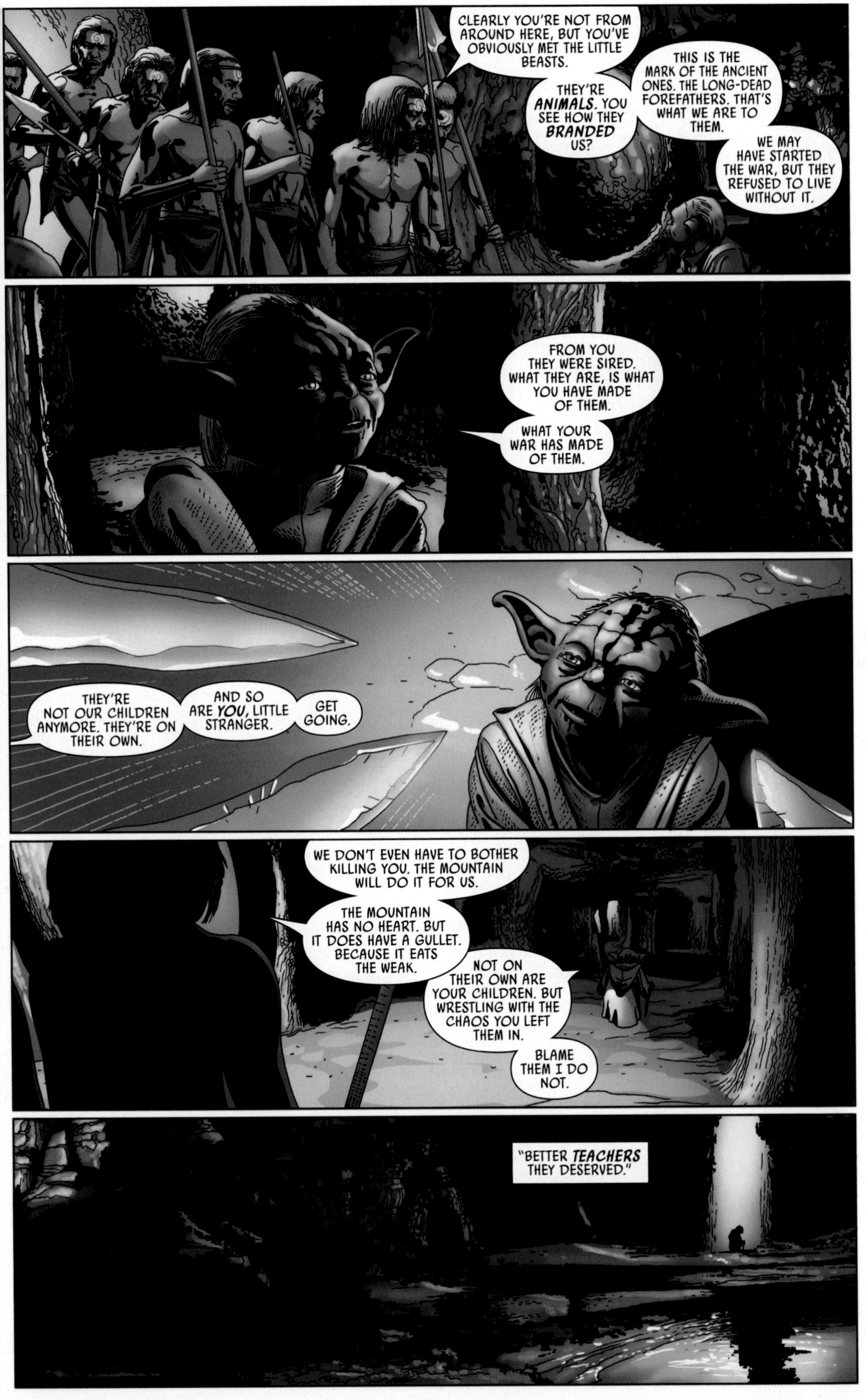
CLEARLY YOU'RE NOT FROM AROUND HERE, BUT YOU'VE OBVIOUSLY MET THE LITTLE BEASTS.
THEY'RE ANIMALS. YOU SEE HOW THEY BRANDED US?
THIS IS THE MARK OF THE ANCIENT ONES. THE LONG-DEAD FOREFATHERS. THAT'S WHAT WE ARE TO THEM.
WE MAY HAVE STARTED THE WAR, BUT THEY REFUSED TO LIVE WITHOUT IT.
FROM YOU THEY WERE SIRED. WHAT THEY ARE, IS WHAT YOU HAVE MADE OF THEM.
WHAT YOUR WAR HAS MADE OF THEM.
THEY'RE NOT OUR CHILDREN ANYMORE. THEY'RE ON THEIR OWN.
AND SO ARE YOU, LITTLE STRANGER.
GET GOING.
WE DON'T EVEN HAVE TO BOTHER KILLING YOU. THE MOUNTAIN WILL DO IT FOR US.
THE MOUNTAIN HAS NO HEART. BUT IT DOES HAVE A GULLET. BECAUSE IT EATS THE WEAK.
NOT ON THEIR OWN ARE YOUR CHILDREN. BUT WRESTLING WITH THE CHAOS YOU LEFT THEM IN.
BLAME THEM I DO NOT.
"BETTER TEACHERS THEY DESERVED."

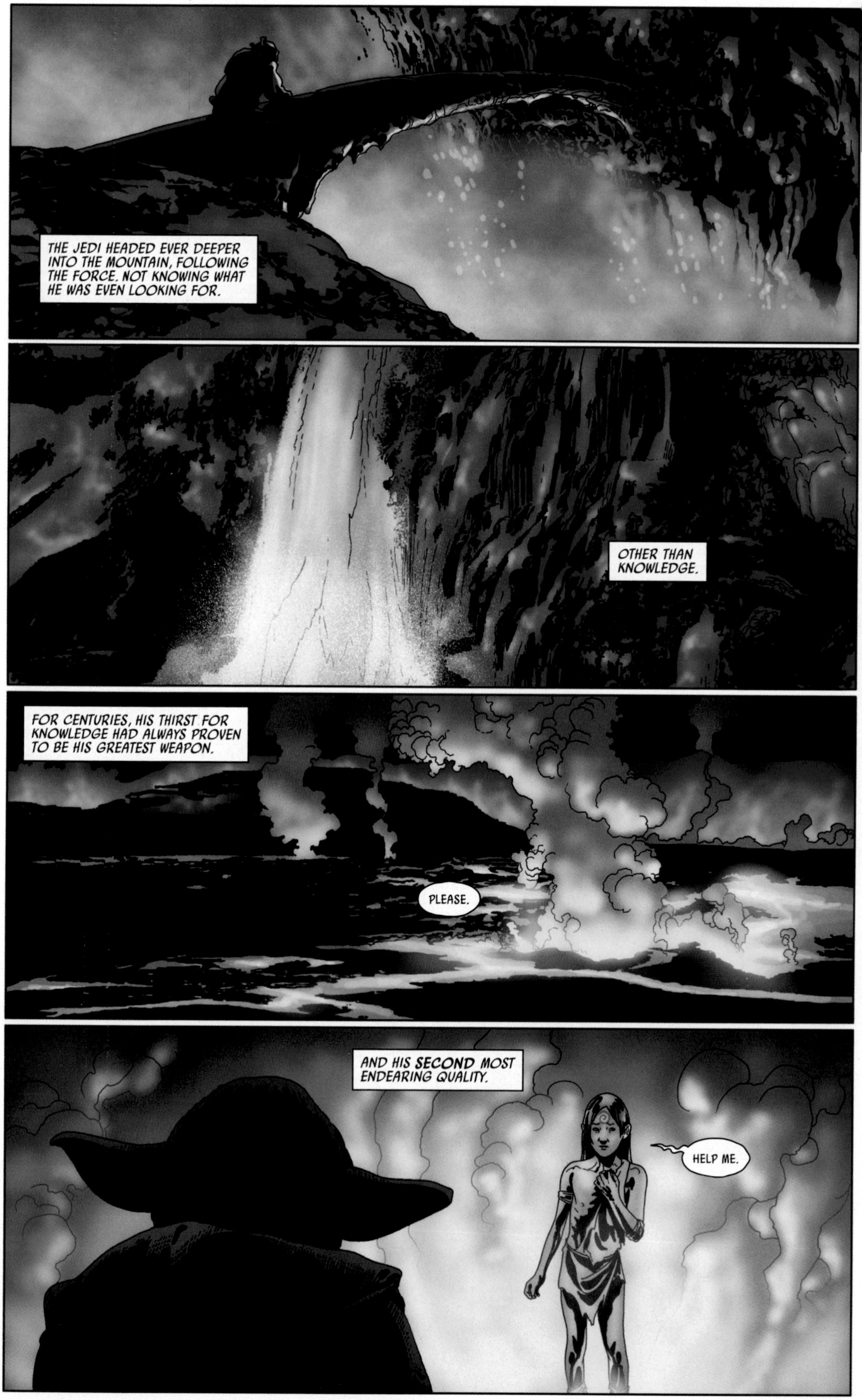
THE JEDI HEADED EVER DEEPER INTO THE MOUNTAIN, FOLLOWING THE FORCE. NOT KNOWING WHAT HE WAS EVEN LOOKING FOR.
OTHER THAN KNOWLEDGE.
FOR CENTURIES, HIS THIRST FOR KNOWLEDGE HAD ALWAYS PROVEN TO BE HIS GREATEST WEAPON.
PLEASE.
AND HIS SECOND MOST ENDEARING QUALITY.
HELP ME.

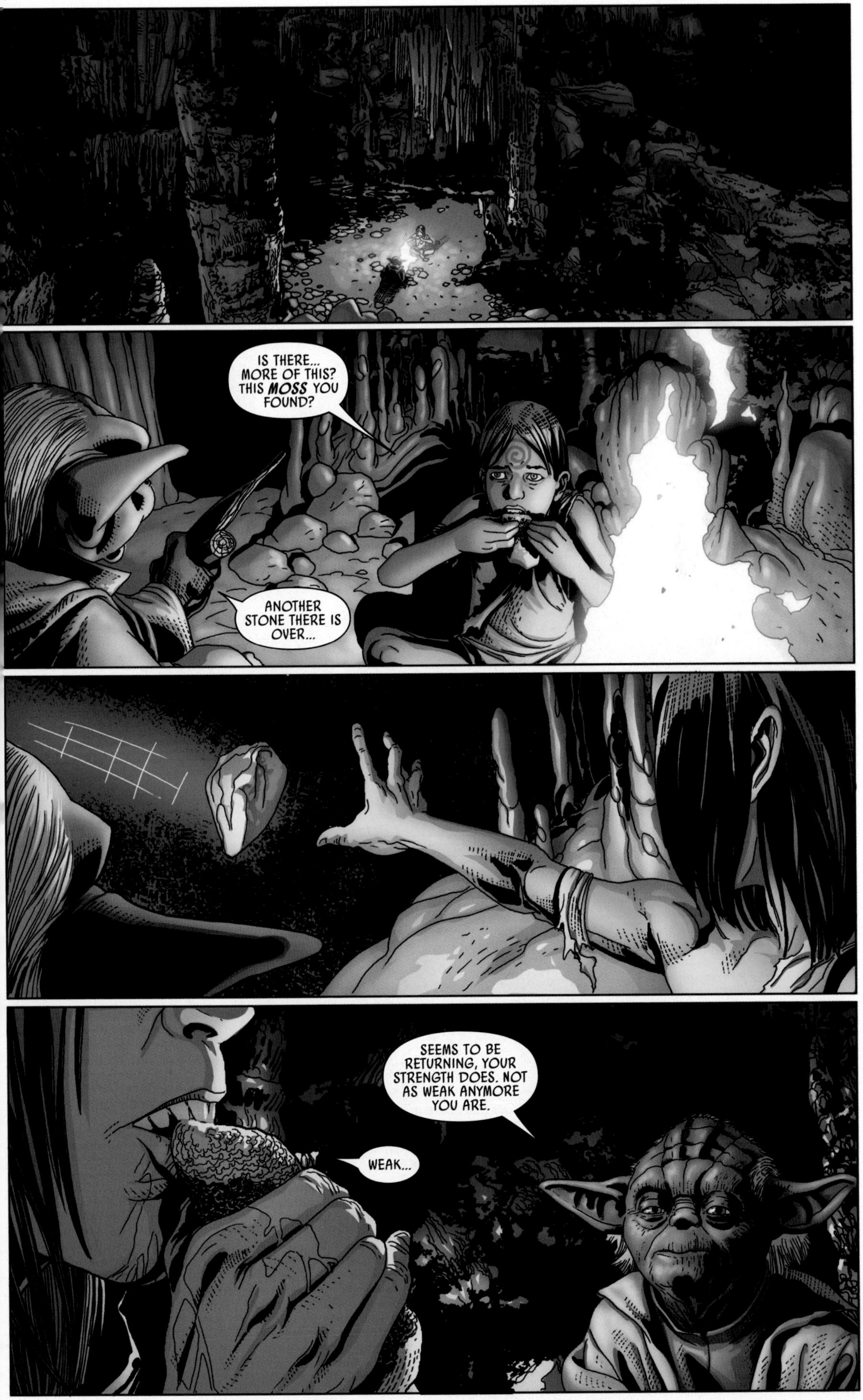
IS THERE... MORE OF THIS? THIS MOSS YOU FOUND?
ANOTHER STONE THERE IS OVER...
SEEMS TO BE RETURNING, YOUR STRENGTH DOES. NOT AS WEAK ANYMORE YOU ARE.
WEAK...

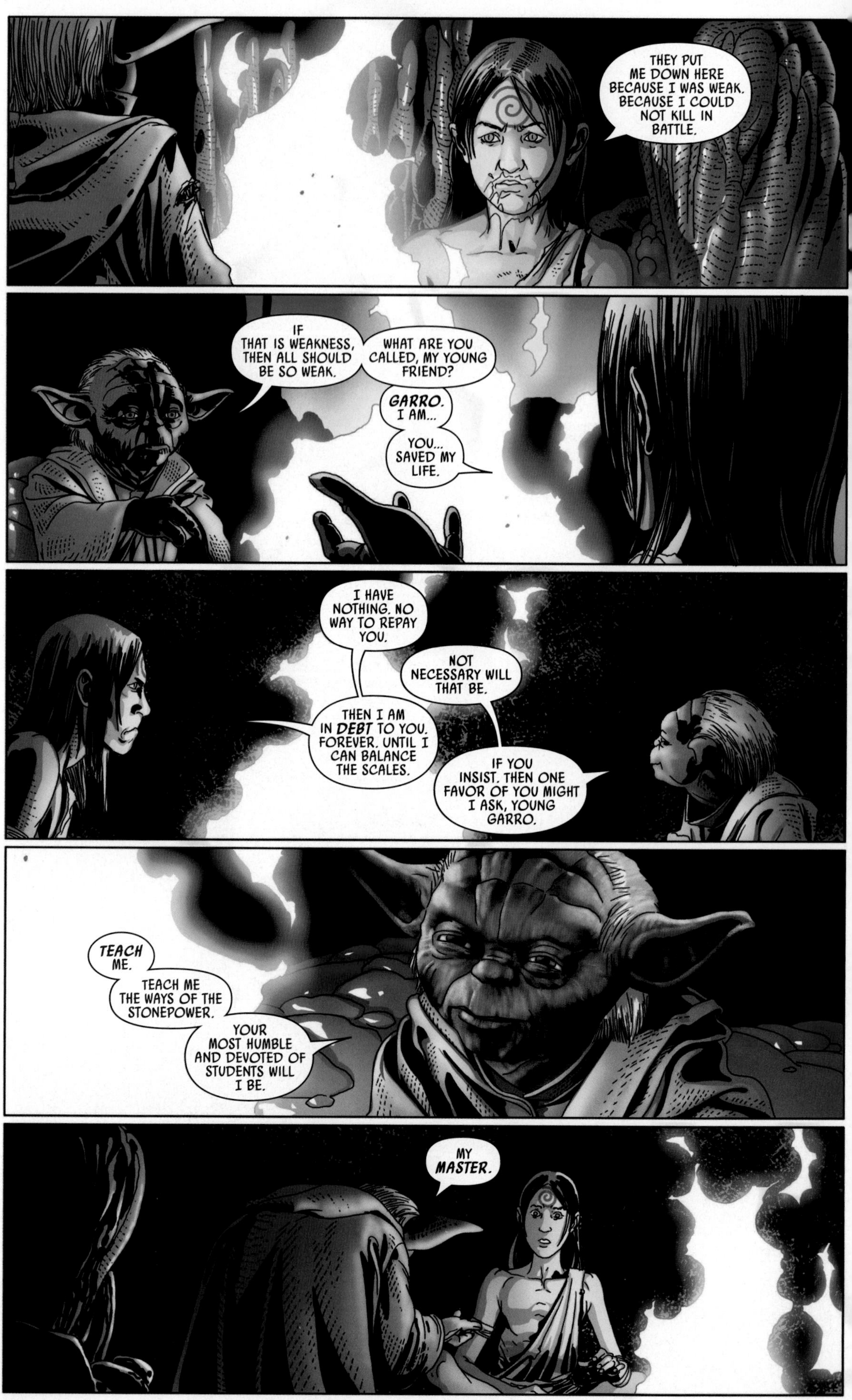
THEY PUT ME DOWN HERE BECAUSE I WAS WEAK. BECAUSE I COULD NOT KILL IN BATTLE.
IF THAT IS WEAKNESS, THEN ALL SHOULD BE SO WEAK.
WHAT ARE YOU CALLED, MY YOUNG FRIEND?
GARRO. I AM...
YOU... SAVED MY LIFE.
I HAVE NOTHING. NO WAY TO REPAY YOU.
THEN I AM IN DEBT TO YOU. FOREVER. UNTIL I CAN BALANCE THE SCALES.
NOT NECESSARY WILL THAT BE.
IF YOU INSIST. THEN ONE FAVOR OF YOU MIGHT I ASK, YOUNG GARRO.
TEACH ME.
TEACH ME THE WAYS OF THE STONEPOWER.
YOUR MOST HUMBLE AND DEVOTED OF STUDENTS WILL I BE.
MY MASTER.

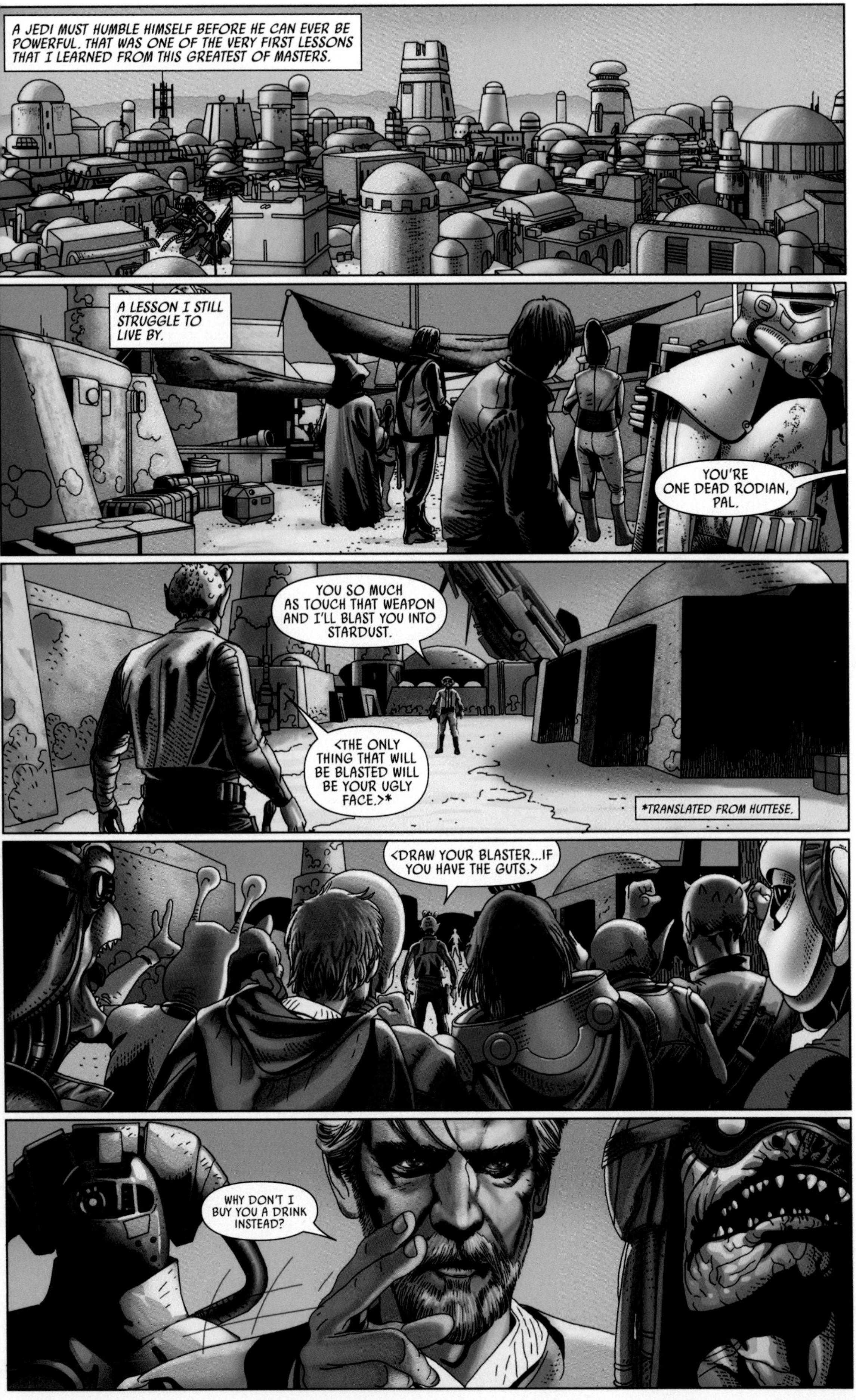
A JEDI MUST HUMBLE HIMSELF BEFORE HE CAN EVER BE POWERFUL. THAT WAS ONE OF THE VERY FIRST LESSONS THAT I LEARNED FROM THIS GREATEST OF MASTERS.
A LESSON I STILL STRUGGLE TO LIVE BY.
YOU'RE ONE DEAD RODIAN, PAL.
YOU SO MUCH AS TOUCH THAT WEAPON AND I'LL BLAST YOU INTO STARDUST.
<THE ONLY THING THAT WILL BE BLASTED WILL BE YOUR UGLY FACE.>*
*TRANSLATED FROM HUTTESE.
<DRAW YOUR BLASTER...IF YOU HAVE THE GUTS.>
WHY DON'T I BUY YOU A DRINK INSTEAD?

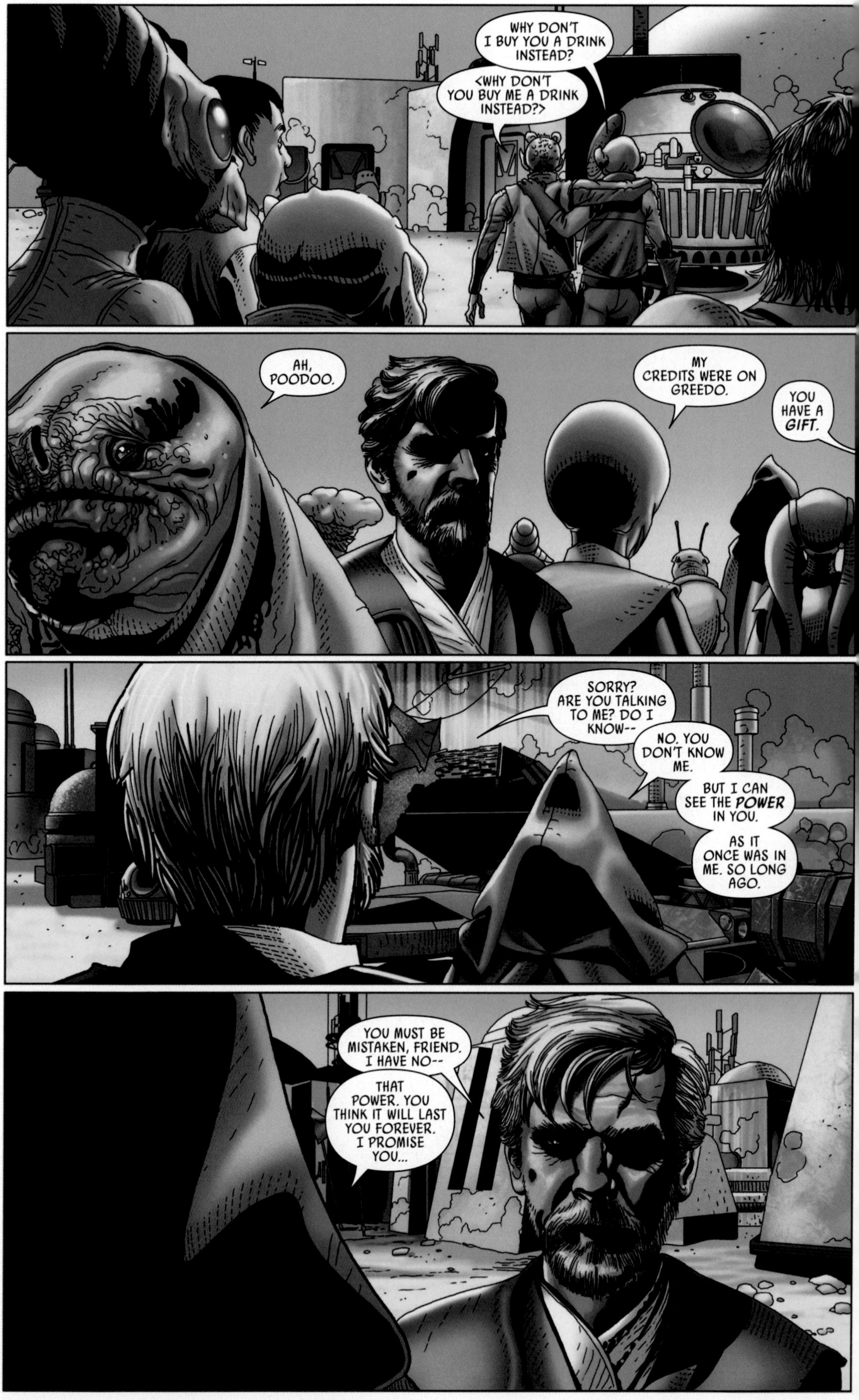
WHY DON'T I BUY YOU A DRINK INSTEAD?
<WHY DON'T YOU BUY ME A DRINK INSTEAD?>
AH, POODOO.
MY CREDITS WERE ON GREEDO.
YOU HAVE A *GIFT*.
SORRY? ARE YOU TALKING TO ME? DO I KNOW--
NO. YOU DON'T KNOW ME.
BUT I CAN SEE THE *POWER* IN YOU.
AS IT ONCE WAS IN ME. SO LONG AGO.
YOU MUST BE MISTAKEN, FRIEND. I HAVE NO--
THAT POWER. YOU THINK IT WILL LAST YOU FOREVER. I PROMISE YOU...

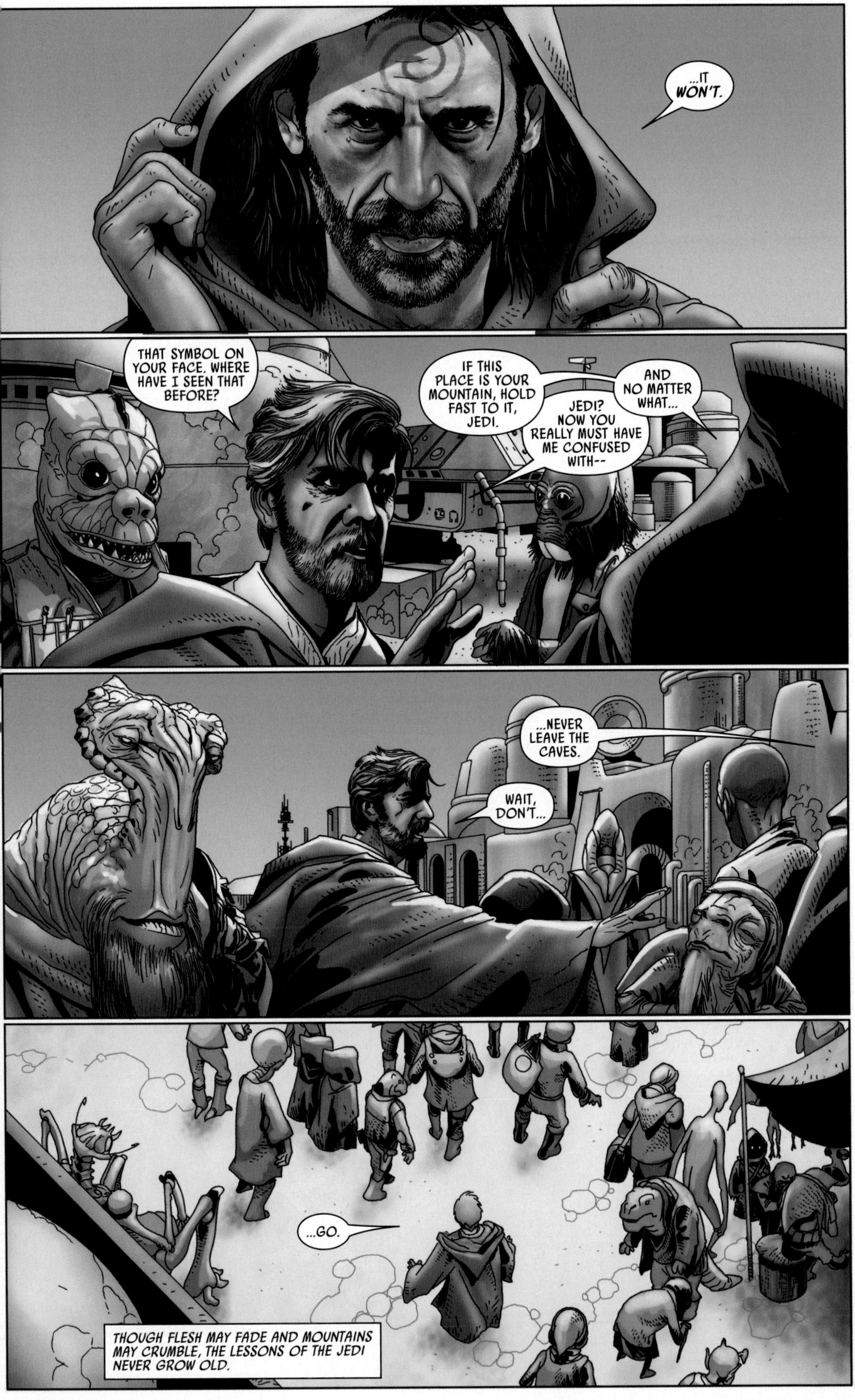
...IT WON'T.
THAT SYMBOL ON YOUR FACE. WHERE HAVE I SEEN THAT BEFORE?
IF THIS PLACE IS YOUR MOUNTAIN, HOLD FAST TO IT, JEDI.
JEDI? NOW YOU REALLY MUST HAVE ME CONFUSED WITH--
AND NO MATTER WHAT...
...NEVER LEAVE THE CAVES.
WAIT, DON'T...
...GO.
THOUGH FLESH MAY FADE AND MOUNTAINS MAY CRUMBLE, THE LESSONS OF THE JEDI NEVER GROW OLD.

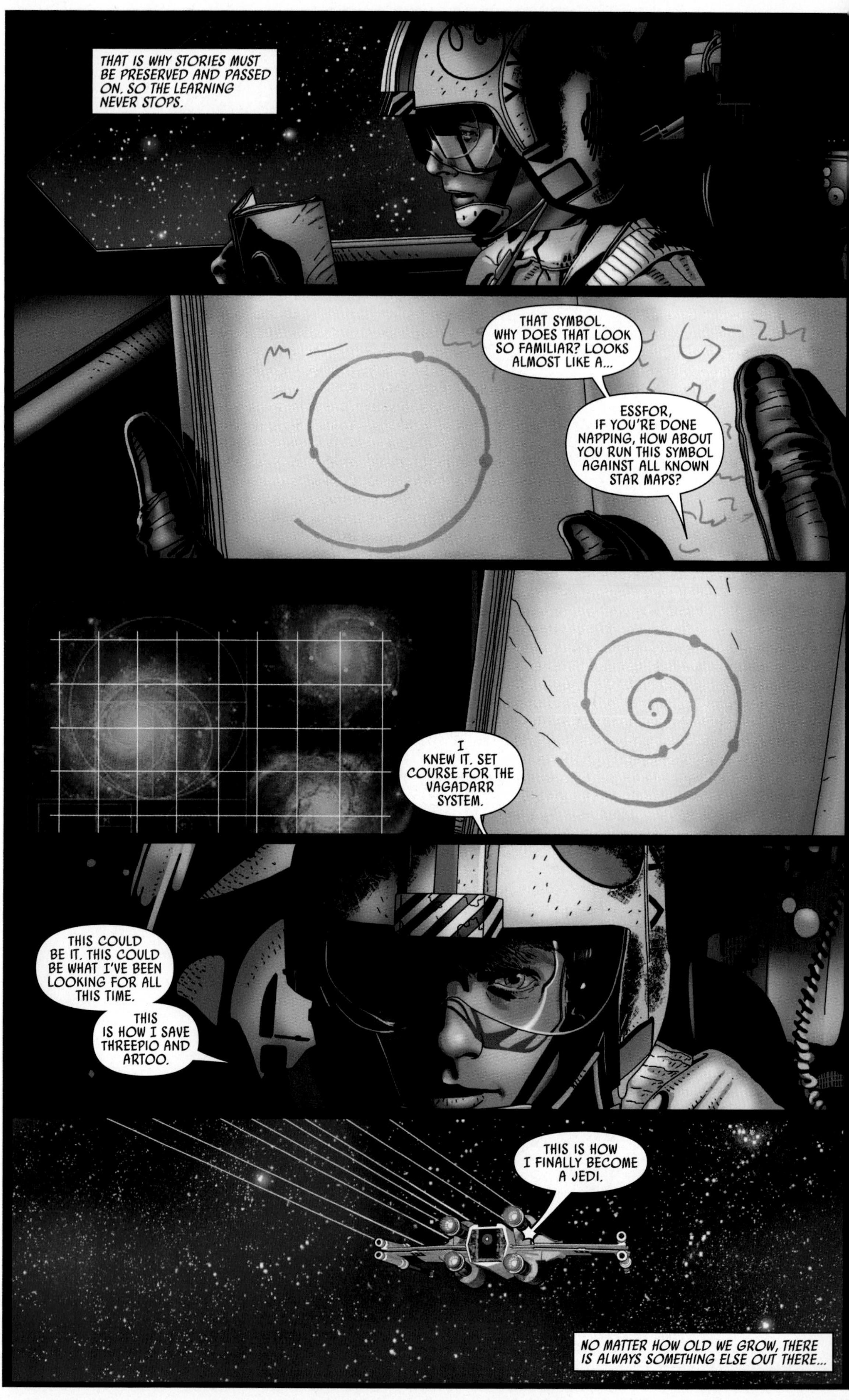
THAT IS WHY STORIES MUST BE PRESERVED AND PASSED ON. SO THE LEARNING NEVER STOPS.
THAT SYMBOL. WHY DOES THAT LOOK SO FAMILIAR? LOOKS ALMOST LIKE A...
ESSFOR, IF YOU'RE DONE NAPPING, HOW ABOUT YOU RUN THIS SYMBOL AGAINST ALL KNOWN STAR MAPS?
I KNEW IT. SET COURSE FOR THE VAGADARR SYSTEM.
THIS COULD BE IT. THIS COULD BE WHAT I'VE BEEN LOOKING FOR ALL THIS TIME.
THIS IS HOW I SAVE THREEPIO AND ARTOO.
THIS IS HOW I FINALLY BECOME A JEDI.
NO MATTER HOW OLD WE GROW, THERE IS ALWAYS SOMETHING ELSE OUT THERE...

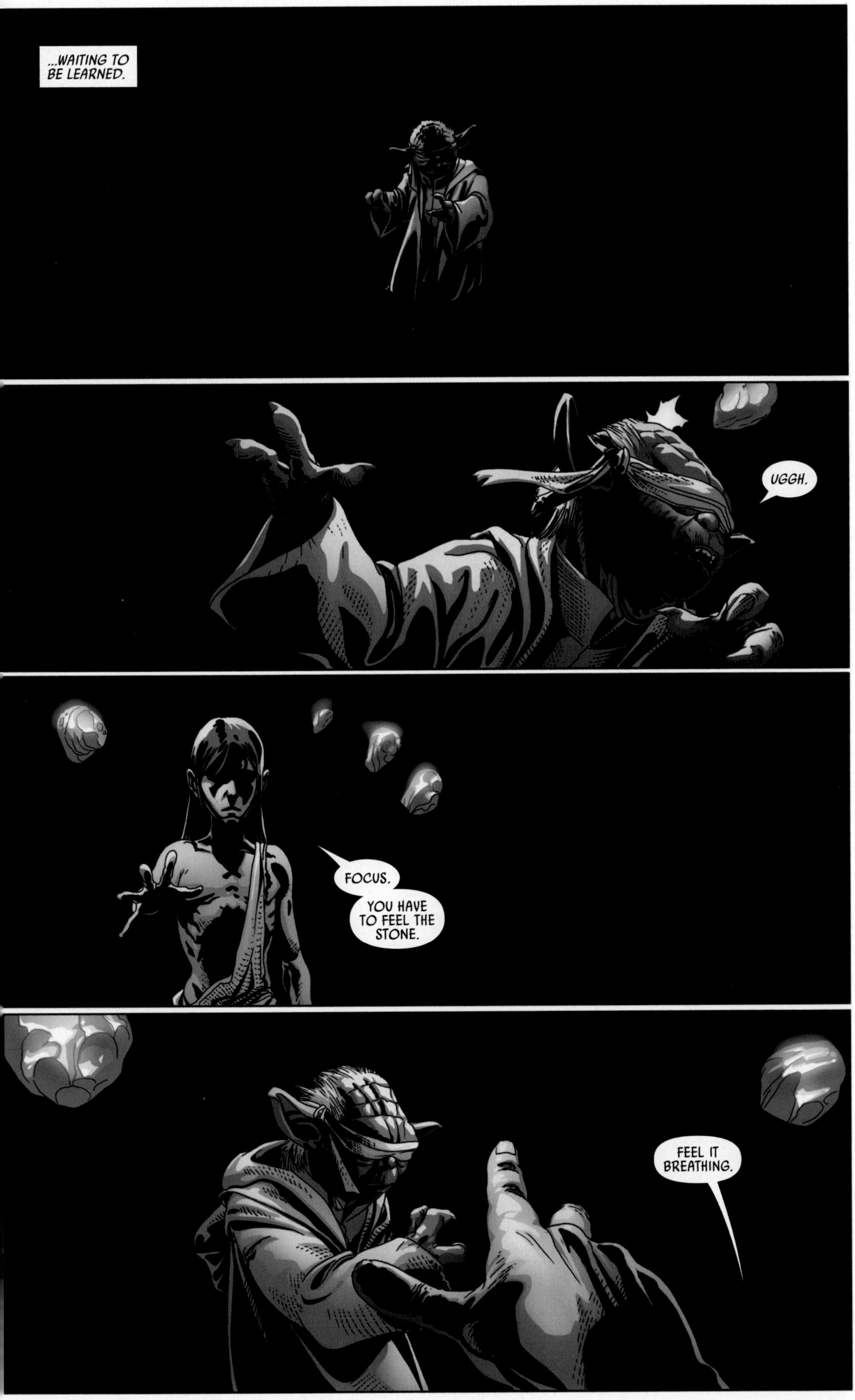
...WAITING TO BE LEARNED.
UGGH.
FOCUS.
YOU HAVE TO FEEL THE STONE.
FEEL IT BREATHING.

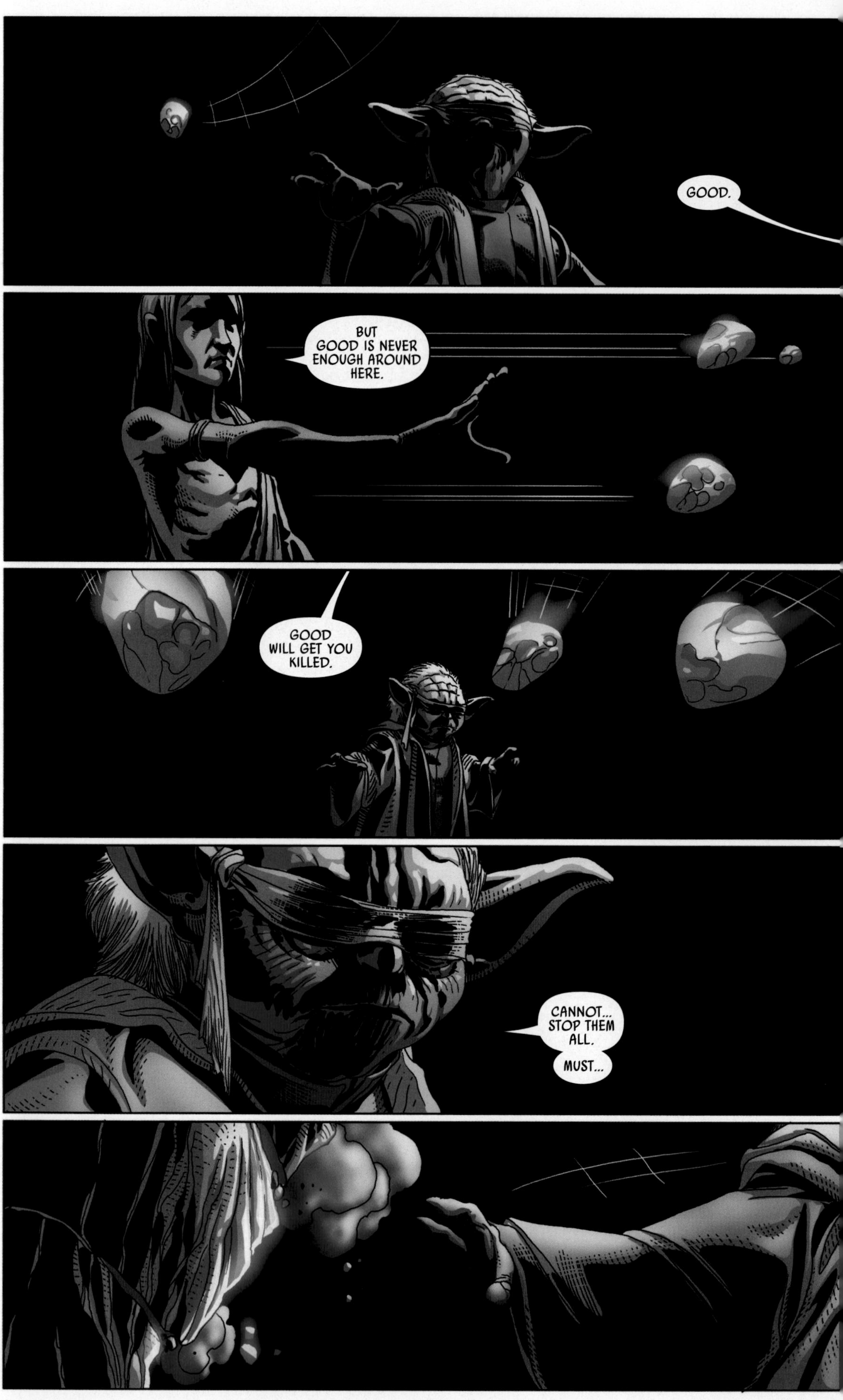
GOOD.
BUT GOOD IS NEVER ENOUGH AROUND HERE.
GOOD WILL GET YOU KILLED.
CANNOT... STOP THEM ALL.
MUST...

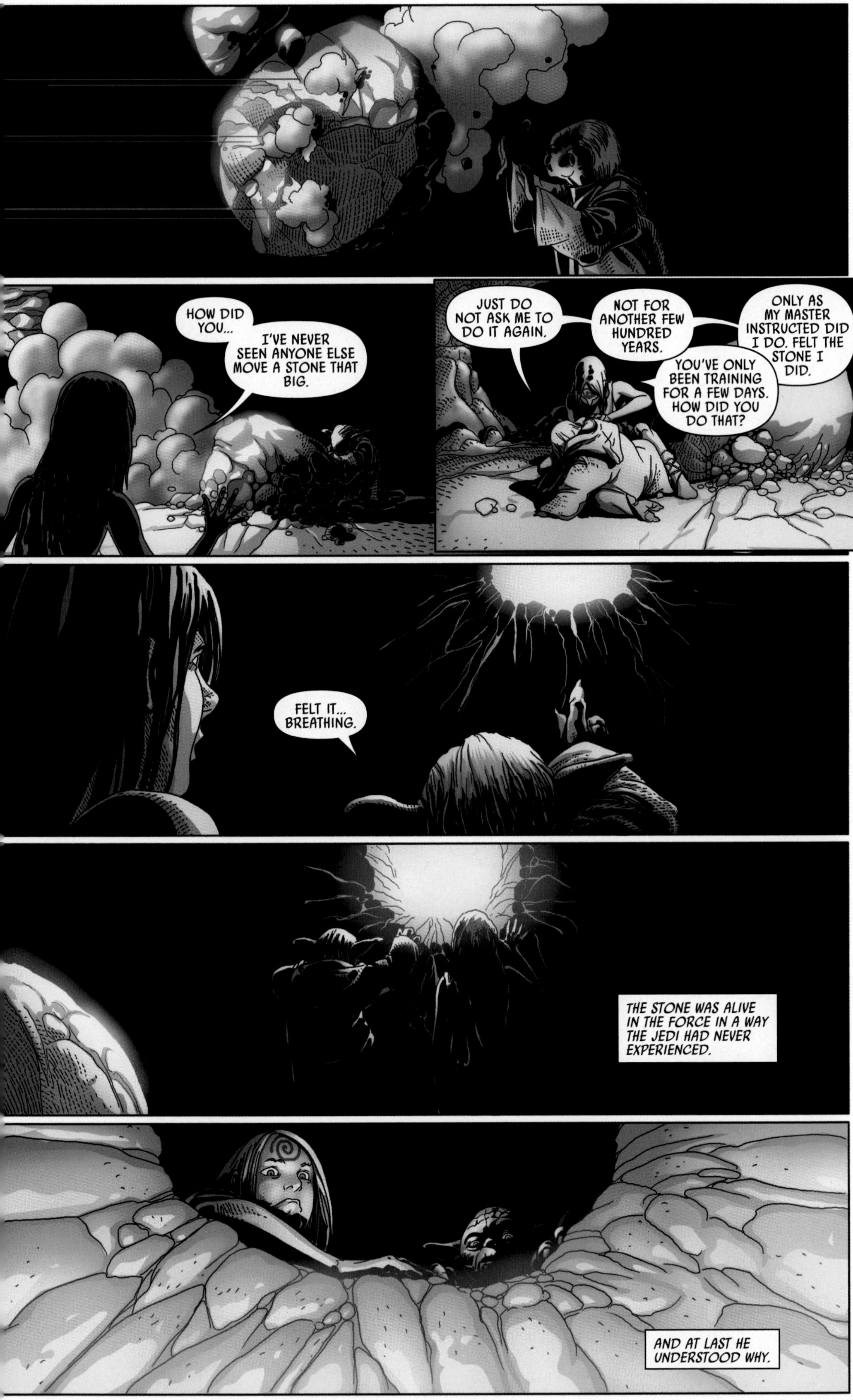
HOW DID YOU...
I'VE NEVER SEEN ANYONE ELSE MOVE A STONE THAT BIG.
JUST DO NOT ASK ME TO DO IT AGAIN.
NOT FOR ANOTHER FEW HUNDRED YEARS.
YOU'VE ONLY BEEN TRAINING FOR A FEW DAYS. HOW DID YOU DO THAT?
ONLY AS MY MASTER INSTRUCTED DID I DO. FELT THE STONE I DID.
FELT IT... BREATHING.
THE STONE WAS ALIVE IN THE FORCE IN A WAY THE JEDI HAD NEVER EXPERIENCED.
AND AT LAST HE UNDERSTOOD WHY.

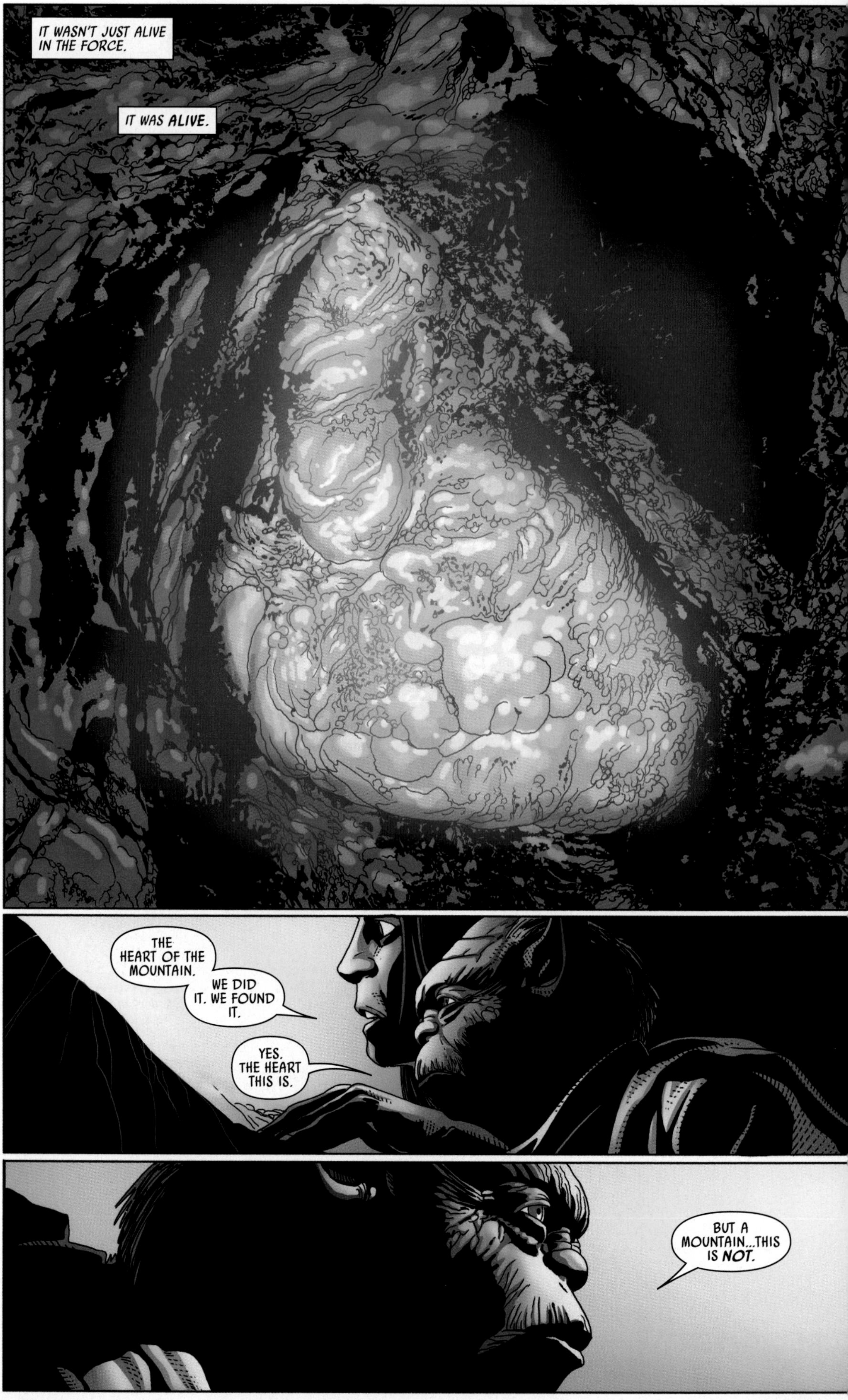
IT WASN'T JUST ALIVE IN THE FORCE.
IT WAS ALIVE.
THE HEART OF THE MOUNTAIN.
WE DID IT. WE FOUND IT.
YES. THE HEART THIS IS.
BUT A MOUNTAIN...THIS IS NOT.

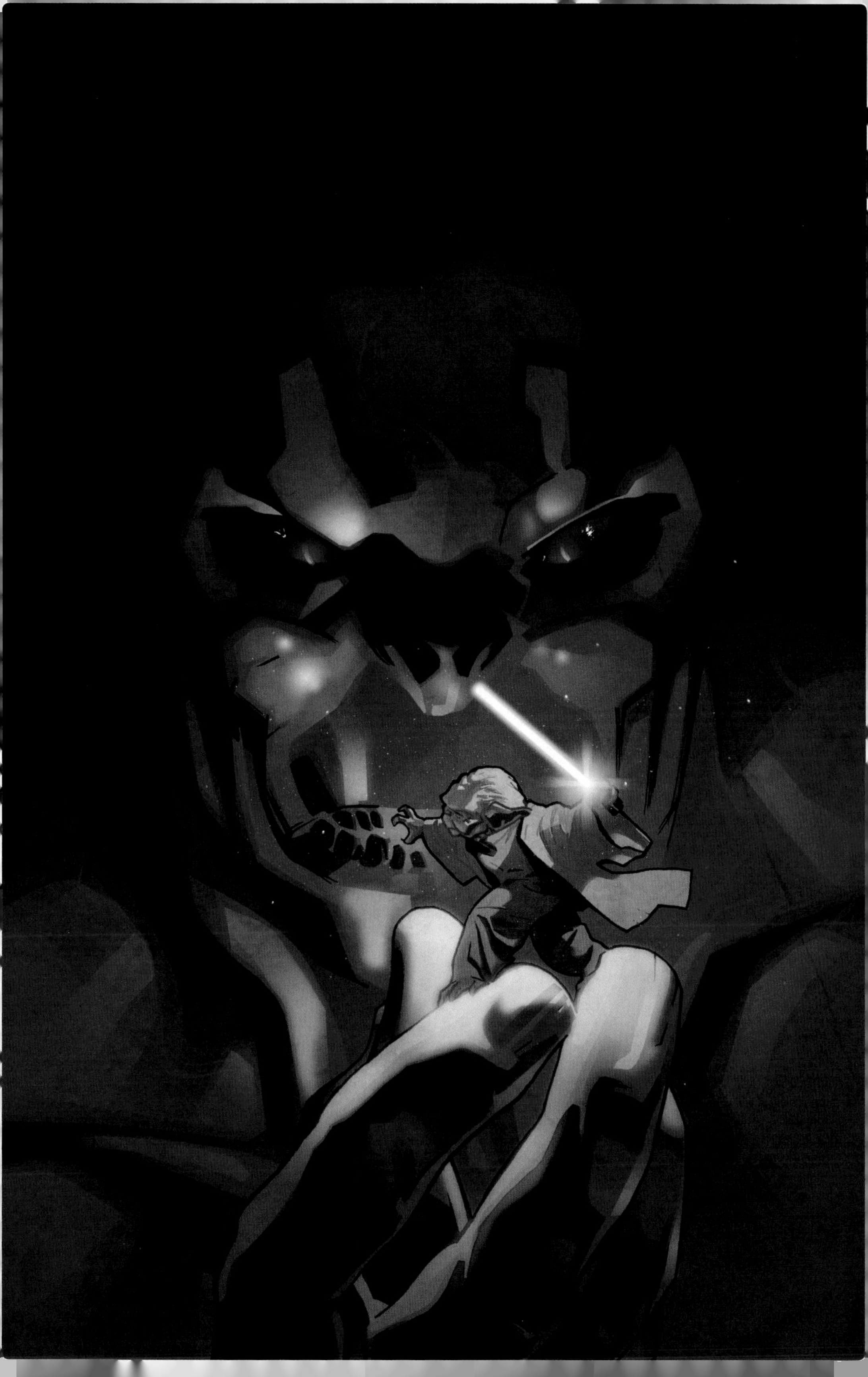

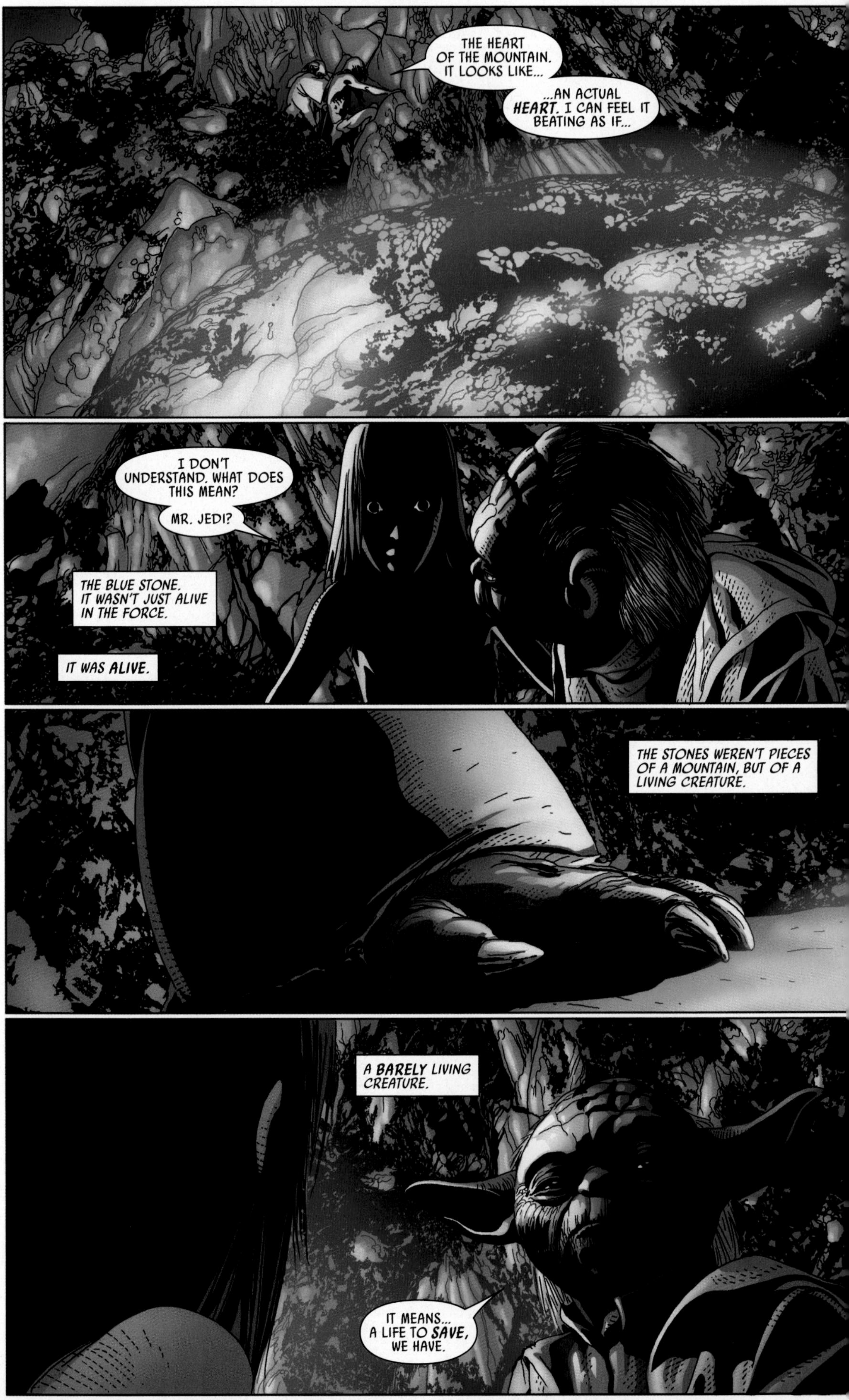
THE HEART OF THE MOUNTAIN. IT LOOKS LIKE...
...AN ACTUAL HEART. I CAN FEEL IT BEATING AS IF...
I DON'T UNDERSTAND. WHAT DOES THIS MEAN?
MR. JEDI?
THE BLUE STONE. IT WASN'T JUST ALIVE IN THE FORCE.
IT WAS ALIVE.
THE STONES WEREN'T PIECES OF A MOUNTAIN, BUT OF A LIVING CREATURE.
A BARELY LIVING CREATURE.
IT MEANS... A LIFE TO SAVE, WE HAVE.

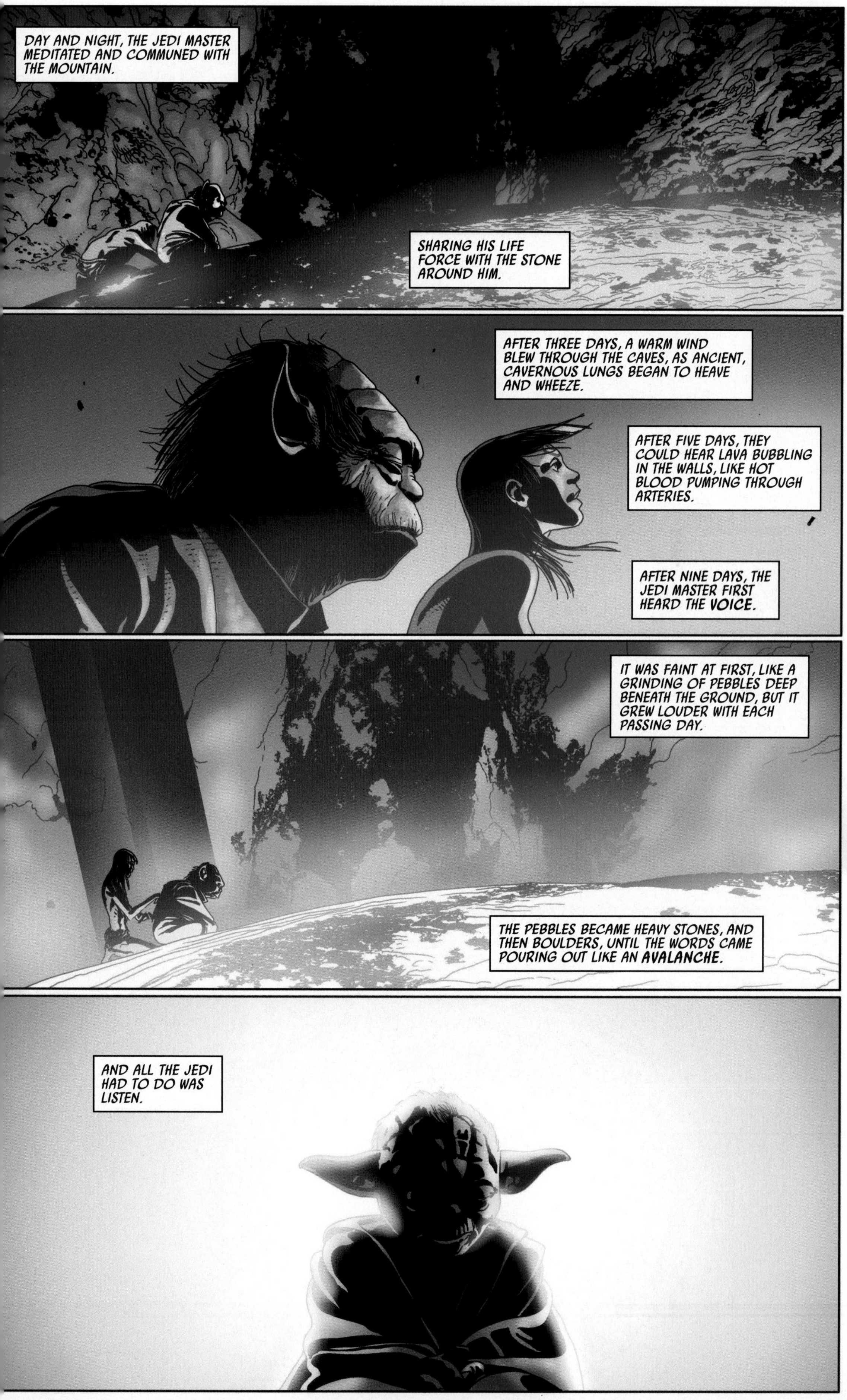
DAY AND NIGHT, THE JEDI MASTER MEDITATED AND COMMUNED WITH THE MOUNTAIN.
SHARING HIS LIFE FORCE WITH THE STONE AROUND HIM.
AFTER THREE DAYS, A WARM WIND BLEW THROUGH THE CAVES, AS ANCIENT, CAVERNOUS LUNGS BEGAN TO HEAVE AND WHEEZE.
AFTER FIVE DAYS, THEY COULD HEAR LAVA BUBBLING IN THE WALLS, LIKE HOT BLOOD PUMPING THROUGH ARTERIES.
AFTER NINE DAYS, THE JEDI MASTER FIRST HEARD THE **VOICE**.
IT WAS FAINT AT FIRST, LIKE A GRINDING OF PEBBLES DEEP BENEATH THE GROUND, BUT IT GREW LOUDER WITH EACH PASSING DAY.
THE PEBBLES BECAME HEAVY STONES, AND THEN BOULDERS, UNTIL THE WORDS CAME POURING OUT LIKE AN **AVALANCHE**.
AND ALL THE JEDI HAD TO DO WAS LISTEN.

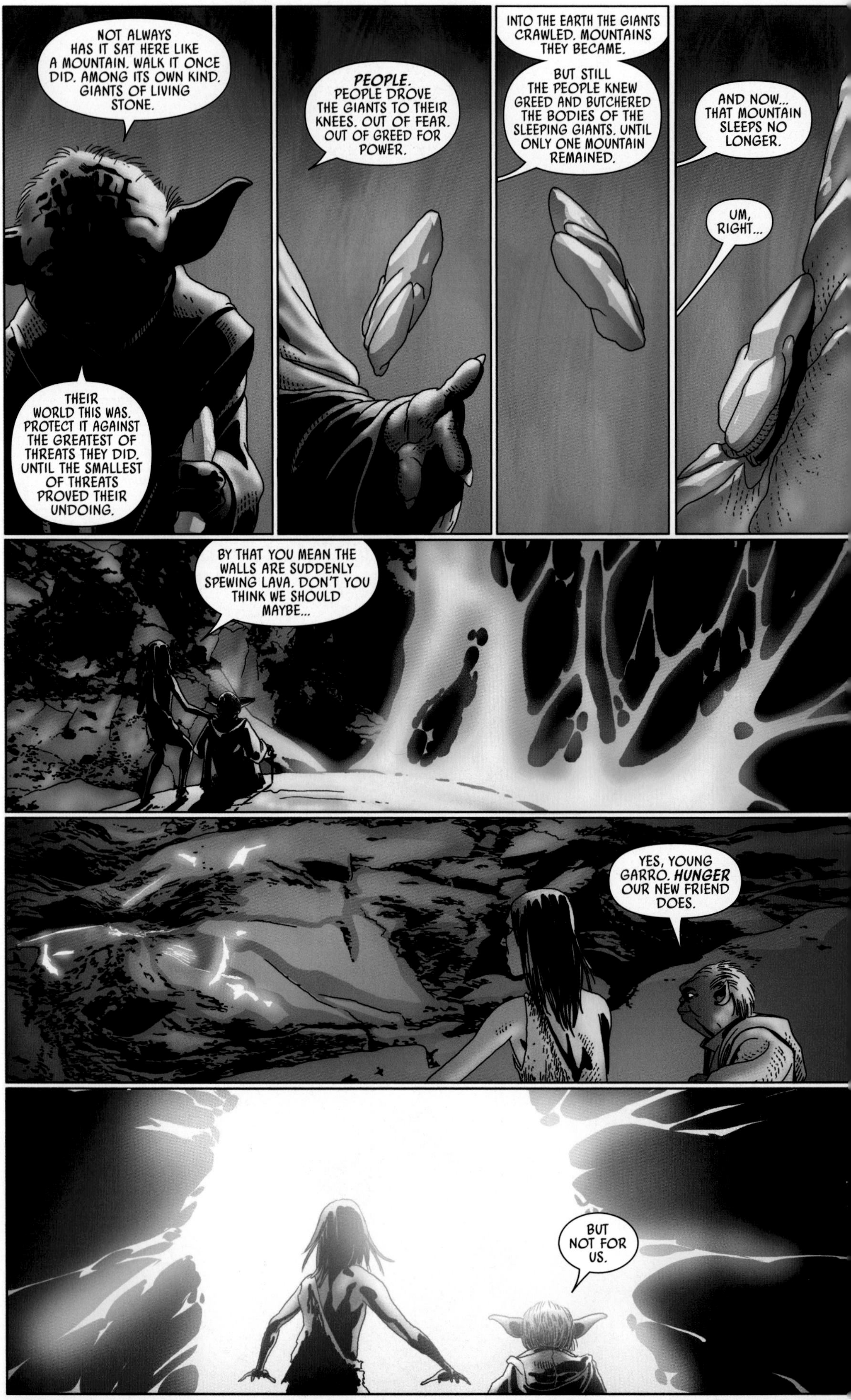
NOT ALWAYS HAS IT SAT HERE LIKE A MOUNTAIN. WALK IT ONCE DID, AMONG ITS OWN KIND. GIANTS OF LIVING STONE.
THEIR WORLD THIS WAS. PROTECT IT AGAINST THE GREATEST OF THREATS THEY DID. UNTIL THE SMALLEST OF THREATS PROVED THEIR UNDOING.
PEOPLE. PEOPLE DROVE THE GIANTS TO THEIR KNEES. OUT OF FEAR. OUT OF GREED FOR POWER.
INTO THE EARTH THE GIANTS CRAWLED. MOUNTAINS THEY BECAME.
BUT STILL THE PEOPLE KNEW GREED AND BUTCHERED THE BODIES OF THE SLEEPING GIANTS. UNTIL ONLY ONE MOUNTAIN REMAINED.
AND NOW... THAT MOUNTAIN SLEEPS NO LONGER.
UM, RIGHT...
BY THAT YOU MEAN THE WALLS ARE SUDDENLY SPEWING LAVA. DON'T YOU THINK WE SHOULD MAYBE...
YES, YOUNG GARRO. HUNGER OUR NEW FRIEND DOES.
BUT NOT FOR US.

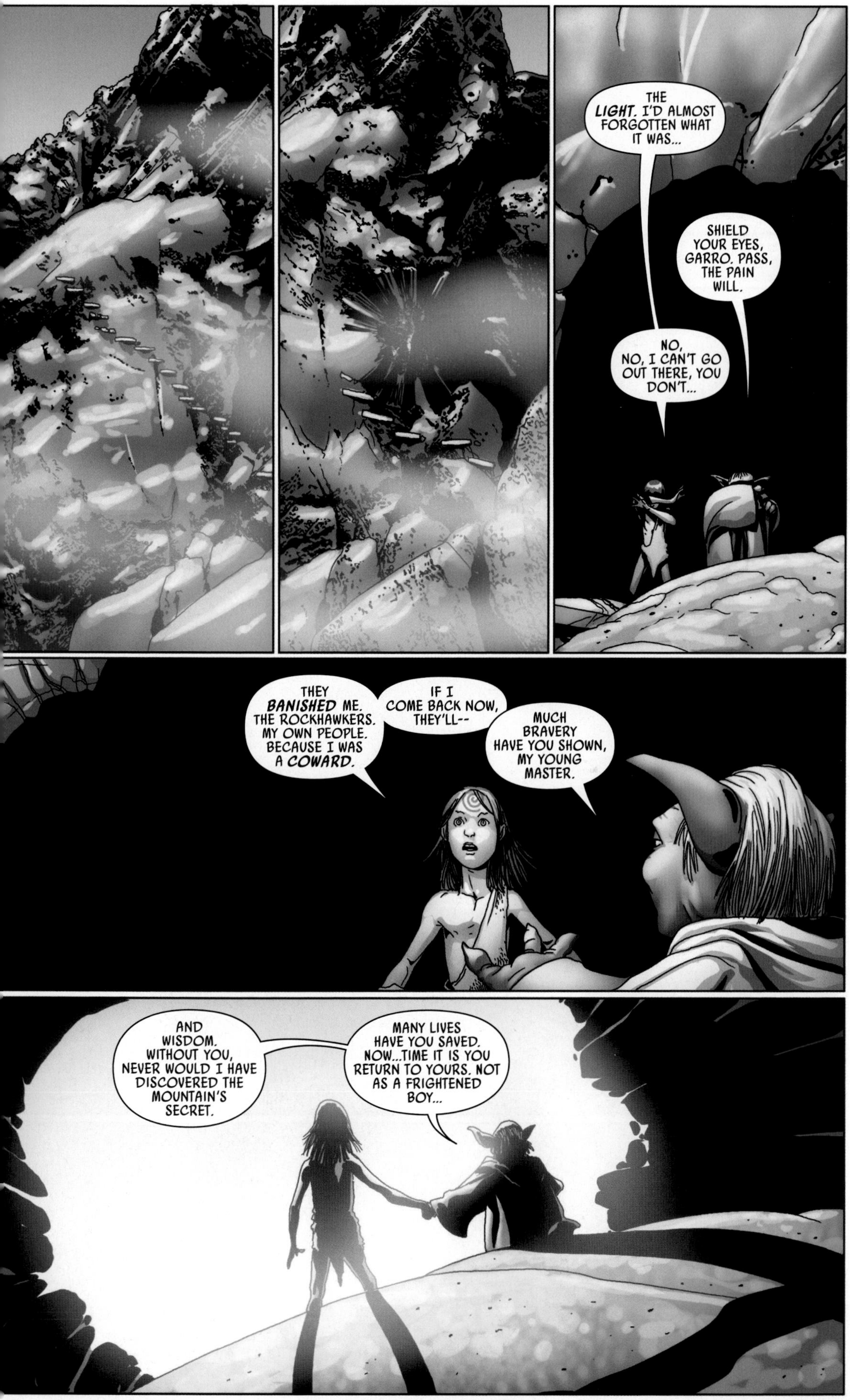
THE LIGHT. I'D ALMOST FORGOTTEN WHAT IT WAS...
SHIELD YOUR EYES, GARRO. PASS, THE PAIN WILL.
NO, NO, I CAN'T GO OUT THERE, YOU DON'T...
THEY BANISHED ME. THE ROCKHAWKERS. MY OWN PEOPLE. BECAUSE I WAS A COWARD.
IF I COME BACK NOW, THEY'LL--
MUCH BRAVERY HAVE YOU SHOWN, MY YOUNG MASTER.
AND WISDOM. WITHOUT YOU, NEVER WOULD I HAVE DISCOVERED THE MOUNTAIN'S SECRET.
MANY LIVES HAVE YOU SAVED. NOW...TIME IT IS YOU RETURN TO YOURS. NOT AS A FRIGHTENED BOY...

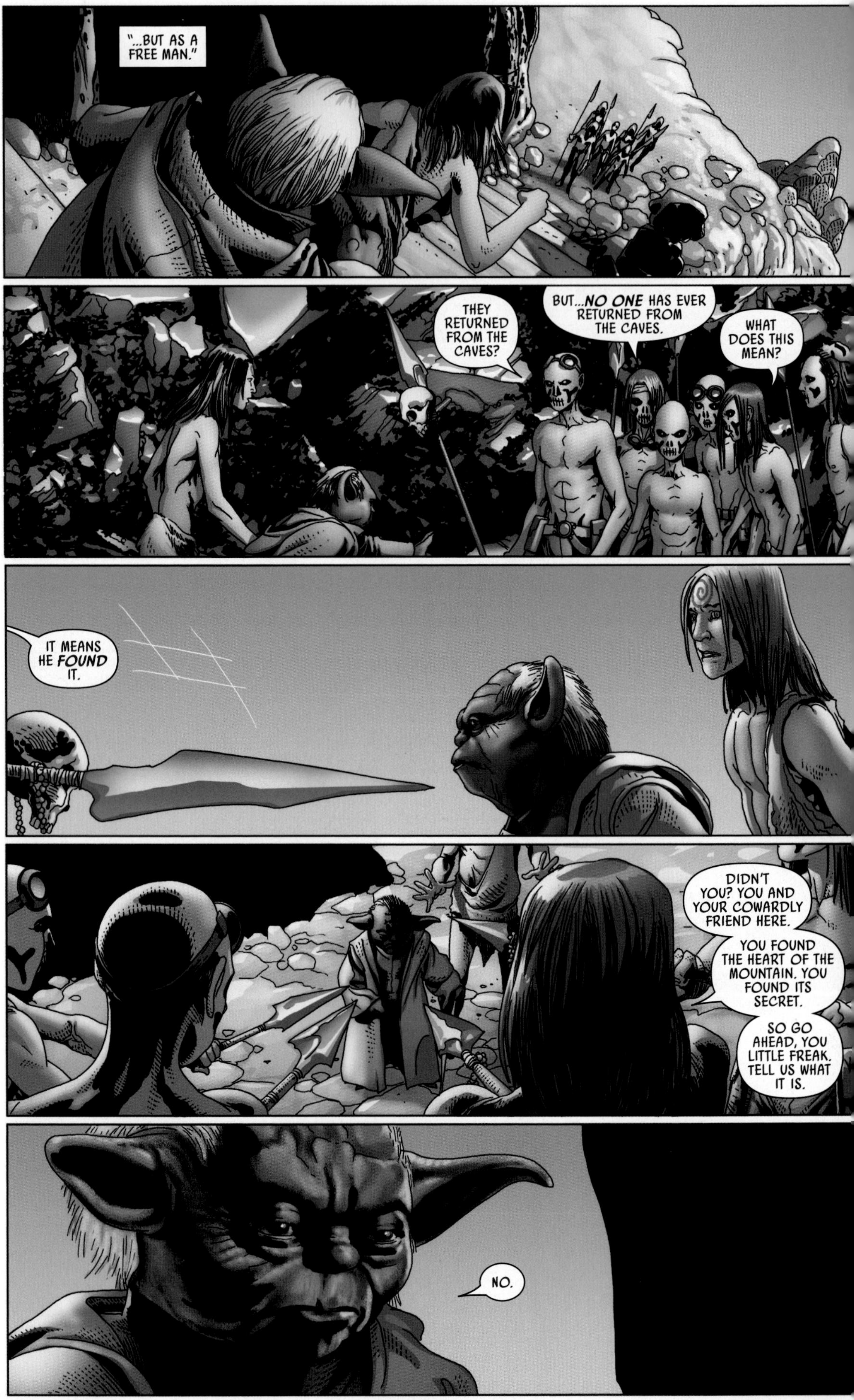
"...BUT AS A FREE MAN."
THEY RETURNED FROM THE CAVES?
BUT...NO ONE HAS EVER RETURNED FROM THE CAVES.
WHAT DOES THIS MEAN?
IT MEANS HE FOUND IT.
DIDN'T YOU? YOU AND YOUR COWARDLY FRIEND HERE.
YOU FOUND THE HEART OF THE MOUNTAIN. YOU FOUND ITS SECRET.
SO GO AHEAD, YOU LITTLE FREAK. TELL US WHAT IT IS.
NO.

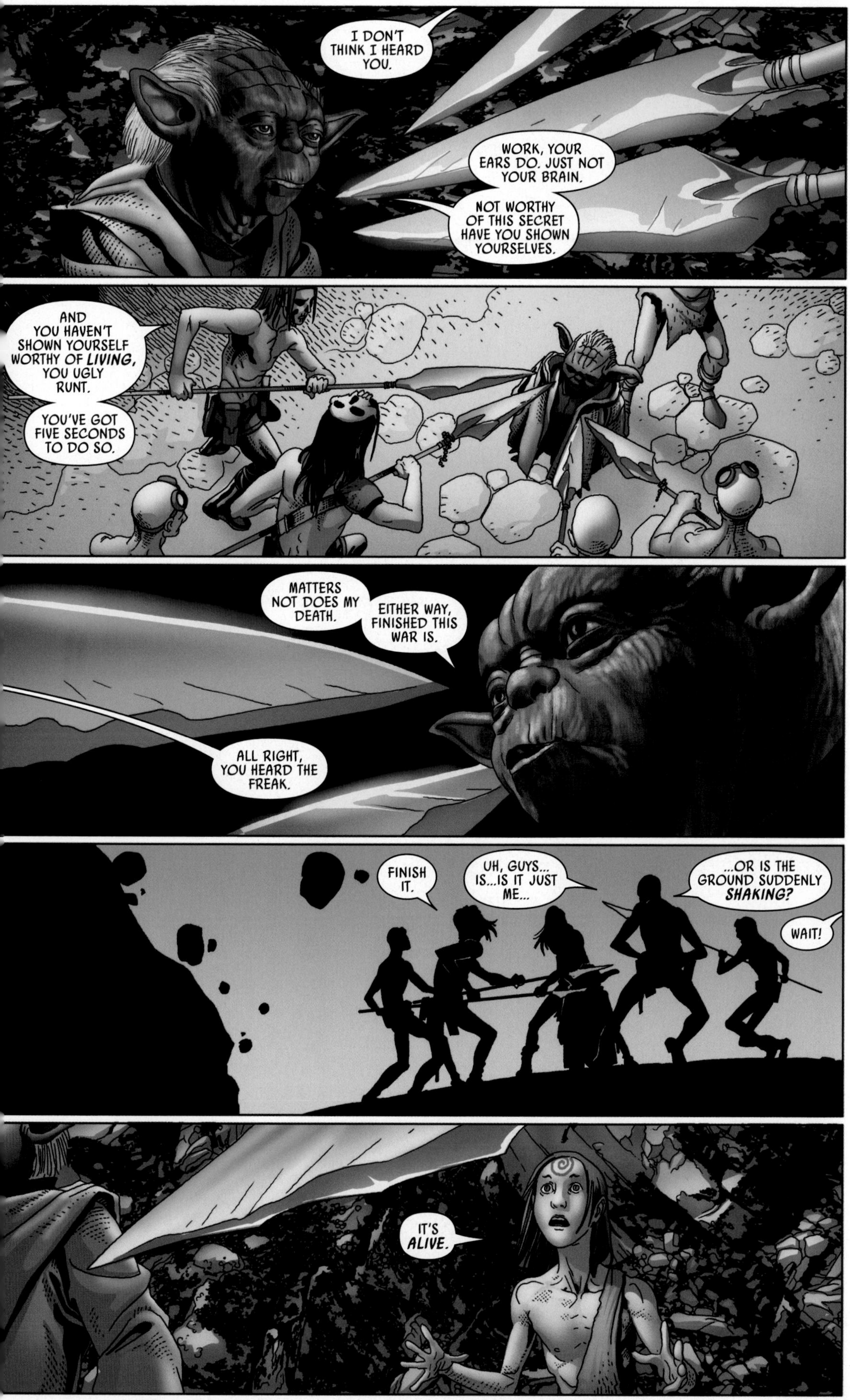
I DON'T THINK I HEARD YOU.
WORK, YOUR EARS DO. JUST NOT YOUR BRAIN.
NOT WORTHY OF THIS SECRET HAVE YOU SHOWN YOURSELVES.
AND YOU HAVEN'T SHOWN YOURSELF WORTHY OF LIVING, YOU UGLY RUNT.
YOU'VE GOT FIVE SECONDS TO DO SO.
MATTERS NOT DOES MY DEATH.
EITHER WAY, FINISHED THIS WAR IS.
ALL RIGHT, YOU HEARD THE FREAK.
FINISH IT.
UH, GUYS... IS...IS IT JUST ME...
...OR IS THE GROUND SUDDENLY SHAKING?
WAIT!
IT'S ALIVE.

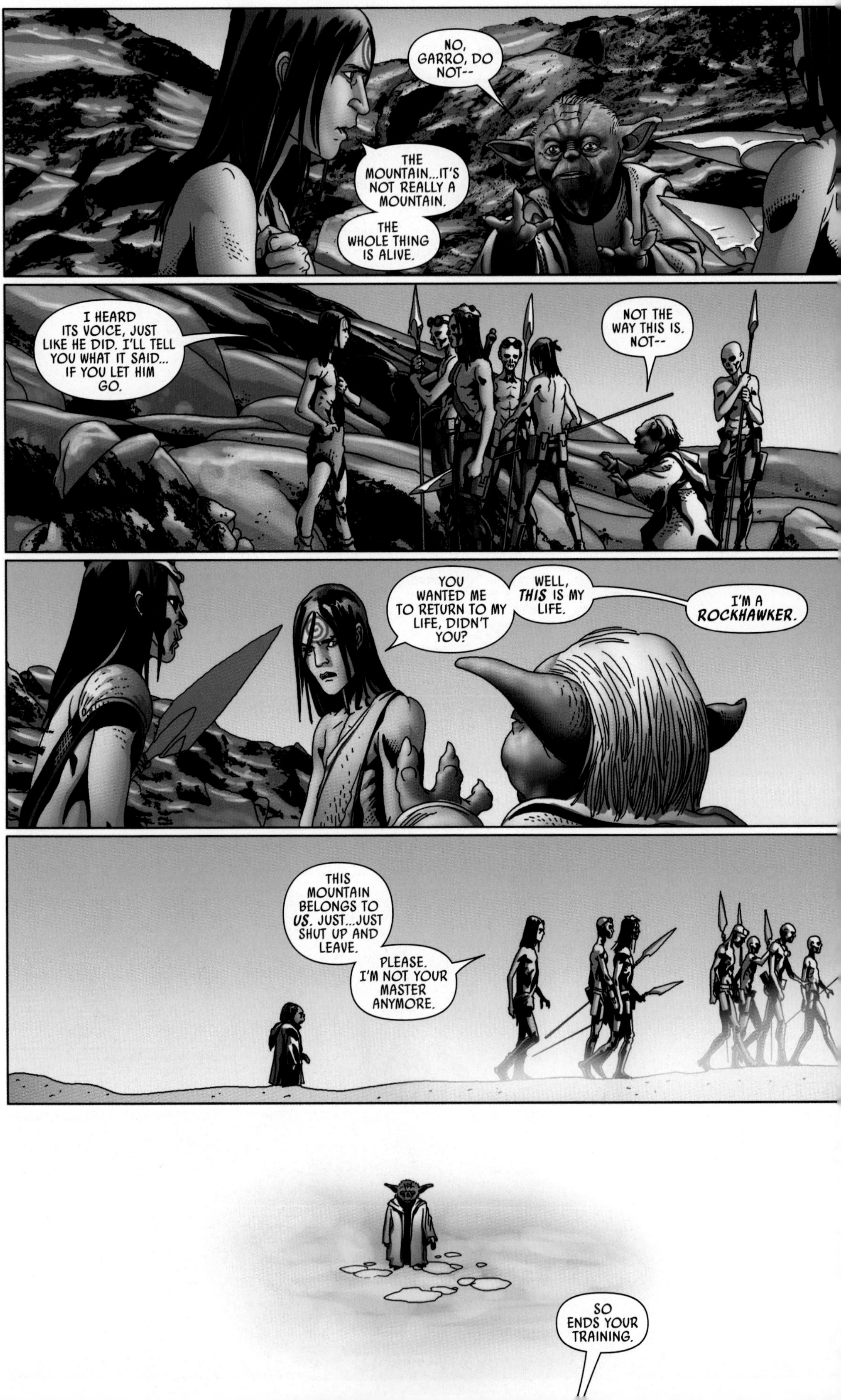
NO, GARRO, DO NOT--
THE MOUNTAIN...IT'S NOT REALLY A MOUNTAIN.
THE WHOLE THING IS ALIVE.
I HEARD ITS VOICE, JUST LIKE HE DID. I'LL TELL YOU WHAT IT SAID... IF YOU LET HIM GO.
NOT THE WAY THIS IS. NOT--
YOU WANTED ME TO RETURN TO MY LIFE, DIDN'T YOU?
WELL, *THIS* IS MY LIFE.
I'M A ***ROCKHAWKER***.
THIS MOUNTAIN BELONGS TO *US*. JUST...JUST SHUT UP AND LEAVE.
PLEASE. I'M NOT YOUR MASTER ANYMORE.
SO ENDS YOUR TRAINING.

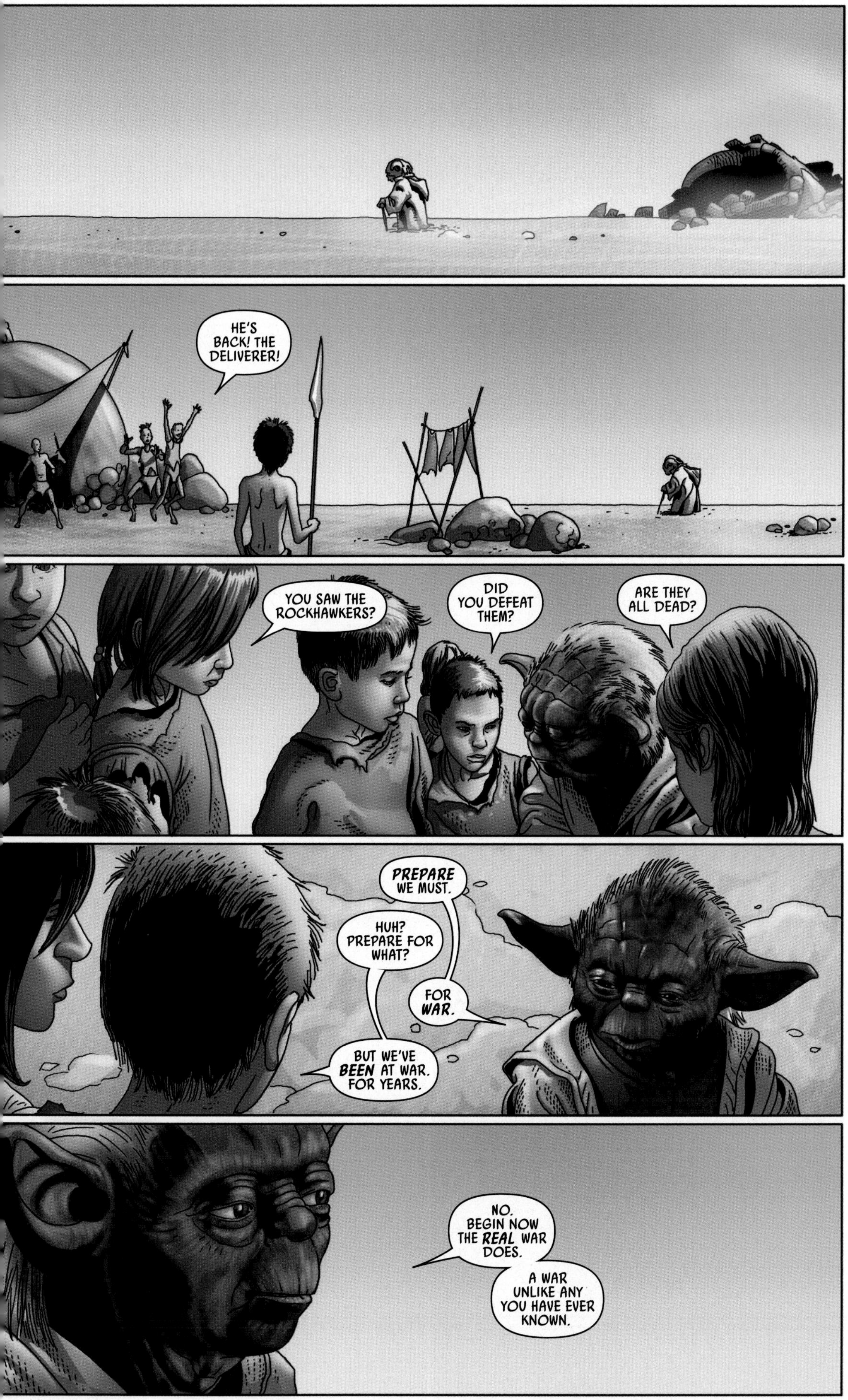
HE'S BACK! THE DELIVERER!
YOU SAW THE ROCKHAWKERS?
DID YOU DEFEAT THEM?
ARE THEY ALL DEAD?
PREPARE WE MUST.
HUH? PREPARE FOR WHAT?
FOR WAR.
BUT WE'VE BEEN AT WAR. FOR YEARS.
NO. BEGIN NOW THE REAL WAR DOES.
A WAR UNLIKE ANY YOU HAVE EVER KNOWN.

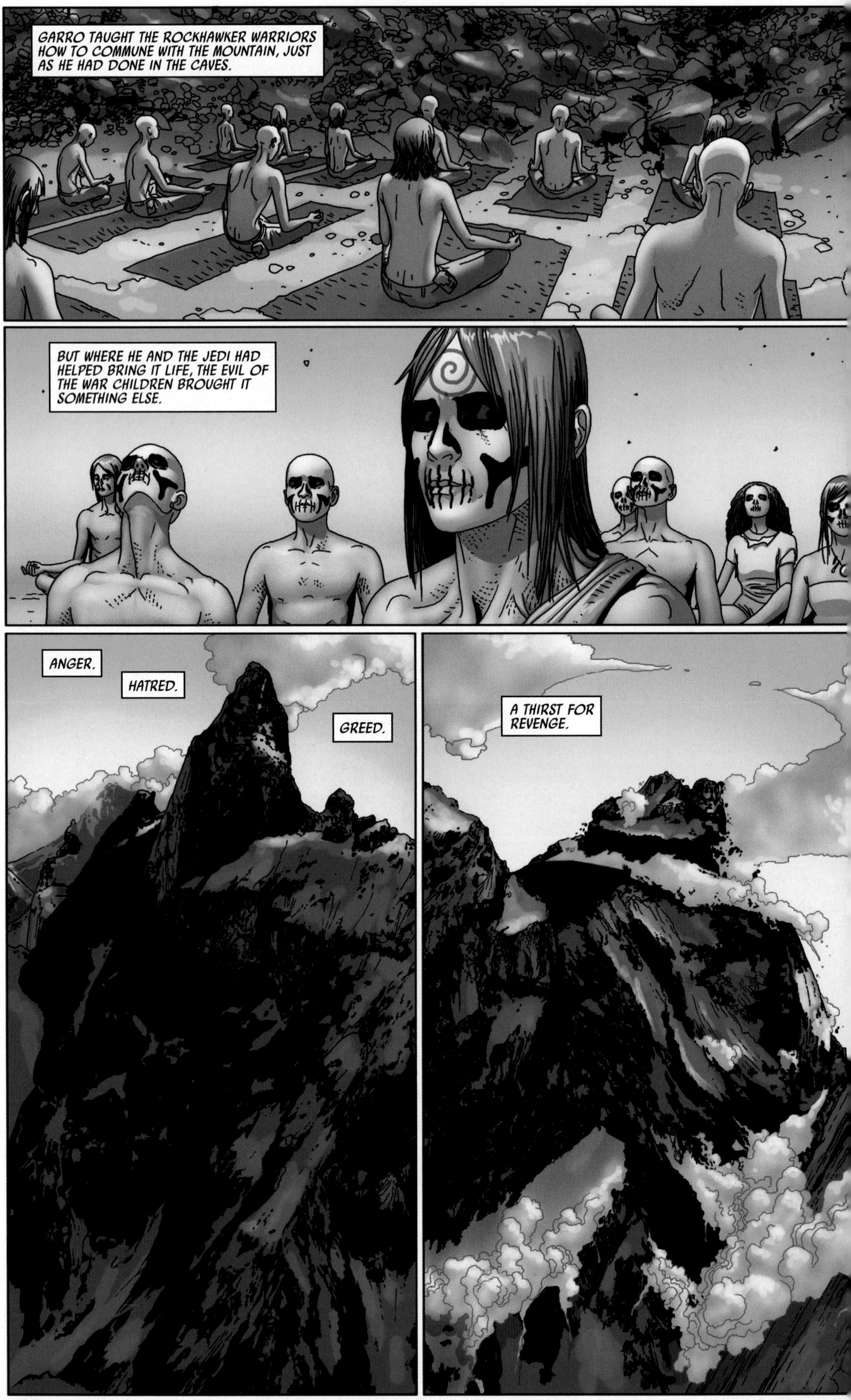
GARRO TAUGHT THE ROCKHAWKER WARRIORS HOW TO COMMUNE WITH THE MOUNTAIN, JUST AS HE HAD DONE IN THE CAVES.
BUT WHERE HE AND THE JEDI HAD HELPED BRING IT LIFE, THE EVIL OF THE WAR CHILDREN BROUGHT IT SOMETHING ELSE.
ANGER.
HATRED.
GREED.
A THIRST FOR REVENGE.

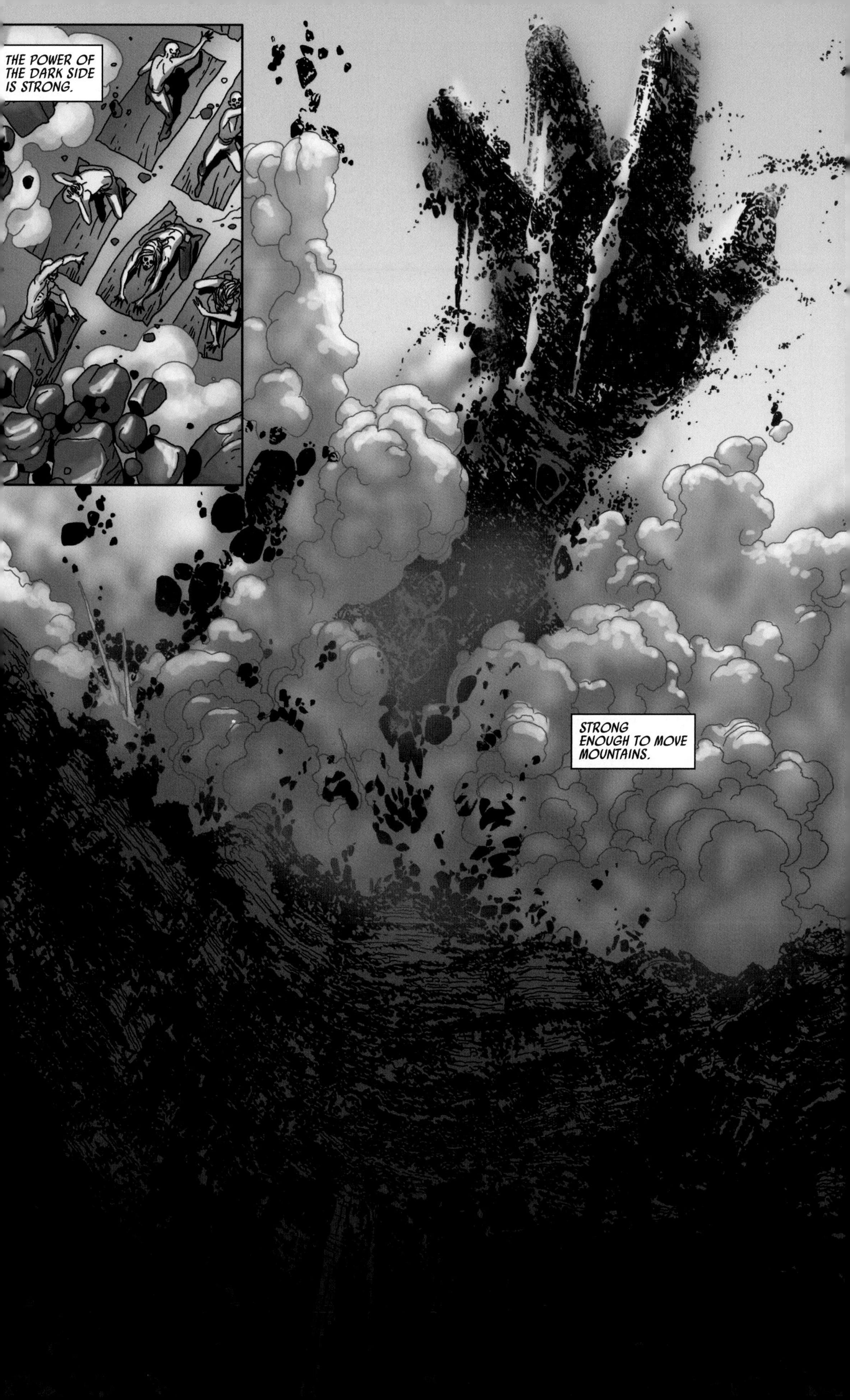
THE POWER OF THE DARK SIDE IS STRONG.
STRONG ENOUGH TO MOVE MOUNTAINS.

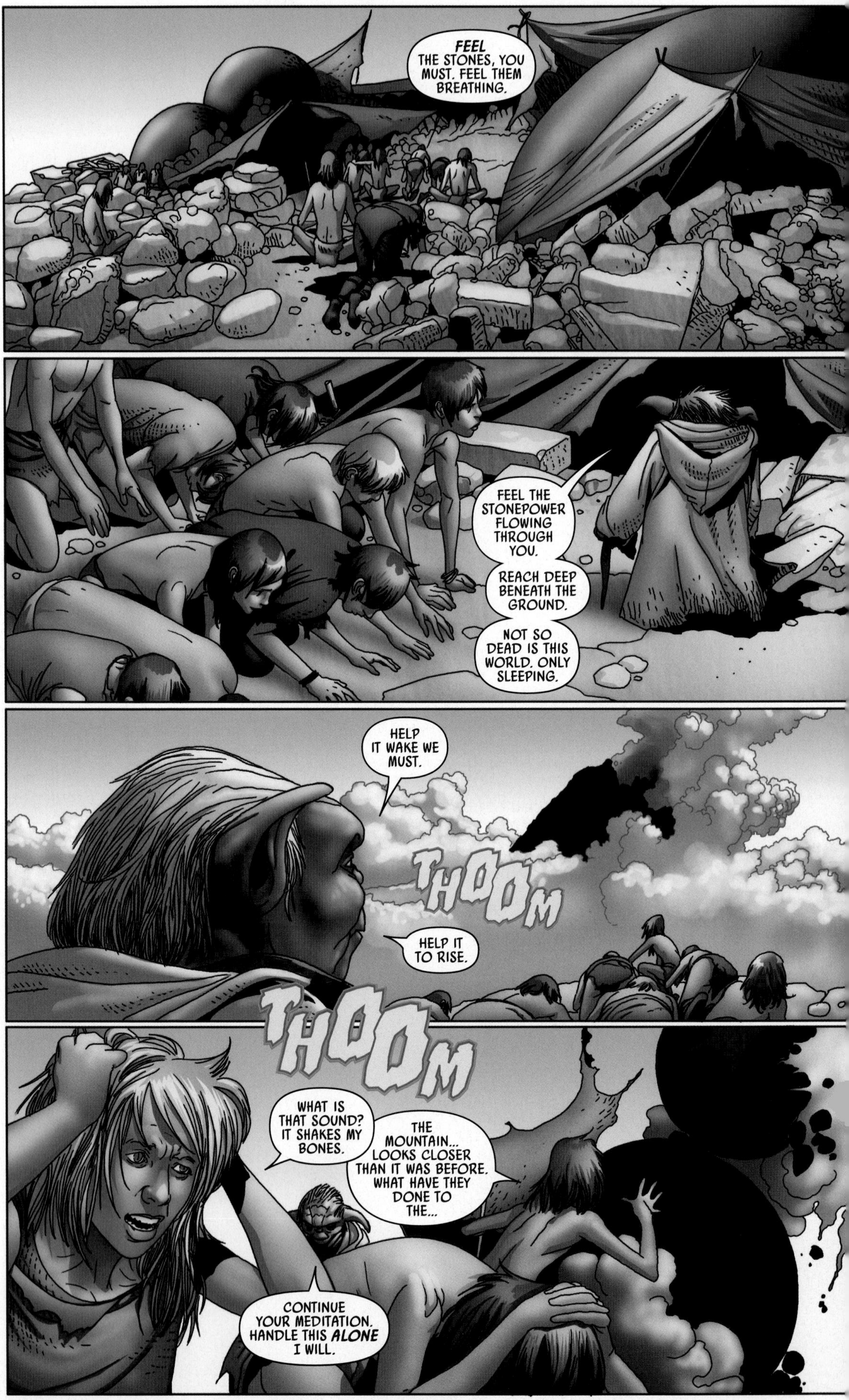
FEEL THE STONES, YOU MUST. FEEL THEM BREATHING.
FEEL THE STONEPOWER FLOWING THROUGH YOU.
REACH DEEP BENEATH THE GROUND.
NOT SO DEAD IS THIS WORLD. ONLY SLEEPING.
HELP IT WAKE WE MUST.
THOOM
HELP IT TO RISE.
THOOM
WHAT IS THAT SOUND? IT SHAKES MY BONES.
THE MOUNTAIN... LOOKS CLOSER THAN IT WAS BEFORE. WHAT HAVE THEY DONE TO THE...
CONTINUE YOUR MEDITATION. HANDLE THIS ALONE I WILL.

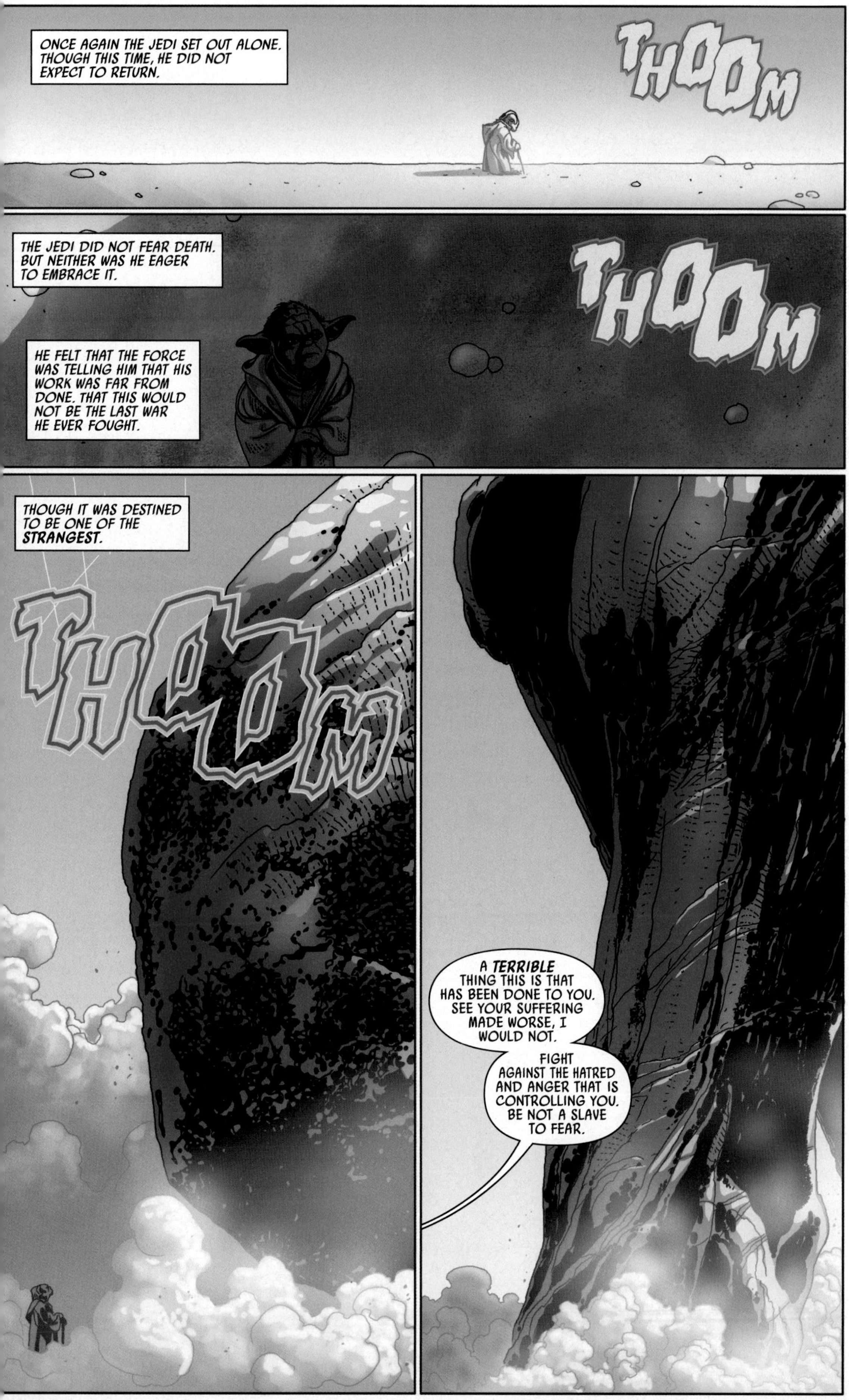
ONCE AGAIN THE JEDI SET OUT ALONE. THOUGH THIS TIME, HE DID NOT EXPECT TO RETURN.
THOOM
THE JEDI DID NOT FEAR DEATH. BUT NEITHER WAS HE EAGER TO EMBRACE IT.
THOOM
HE FELT THAT THE FORCE WAS TELLING HIM THAT HIS WORK WAS FAR FROM DONE. THAT THIS WOULD NOT BE THE LAST WAR HE EVER FOUGHT.
THOUGH IT WAS DESTINED TO BE ONE OF THE STRANGEST.
THOOM
A TERRIBLE THING THIS IS THAT HAS BEEN DONE TO YOU. SEE YOUR SUFFERING MADE WORSE, I WOULD NOT.
FIGHT AGAINST THE HATRED AND ANGER THAT IS CONTROLLING YOU. BE NOT A SLAVE TO FEAR.

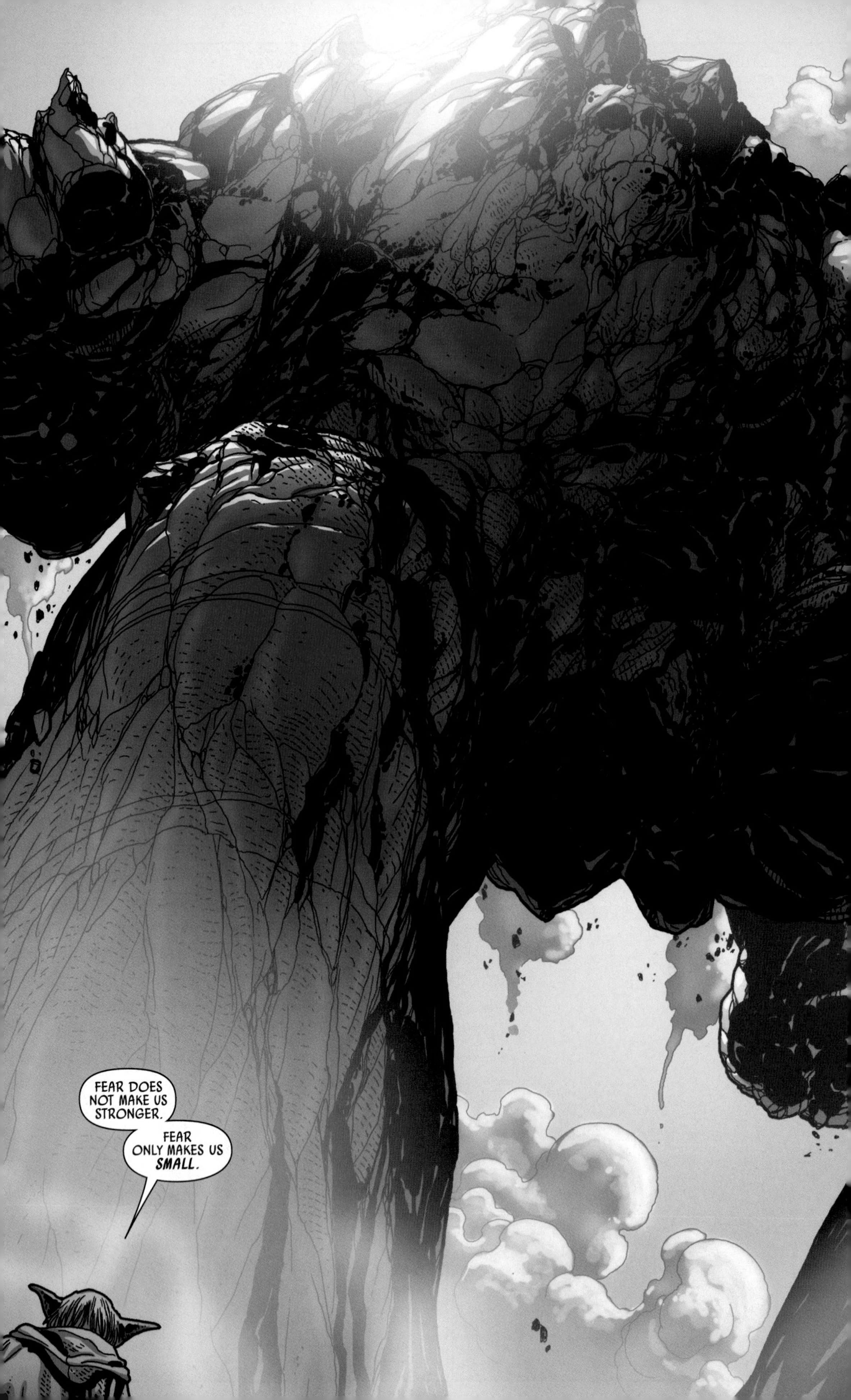
FEAR DOES NOT MAKE US STRONGER.
FEAR ONLY MAKES US SMALL.

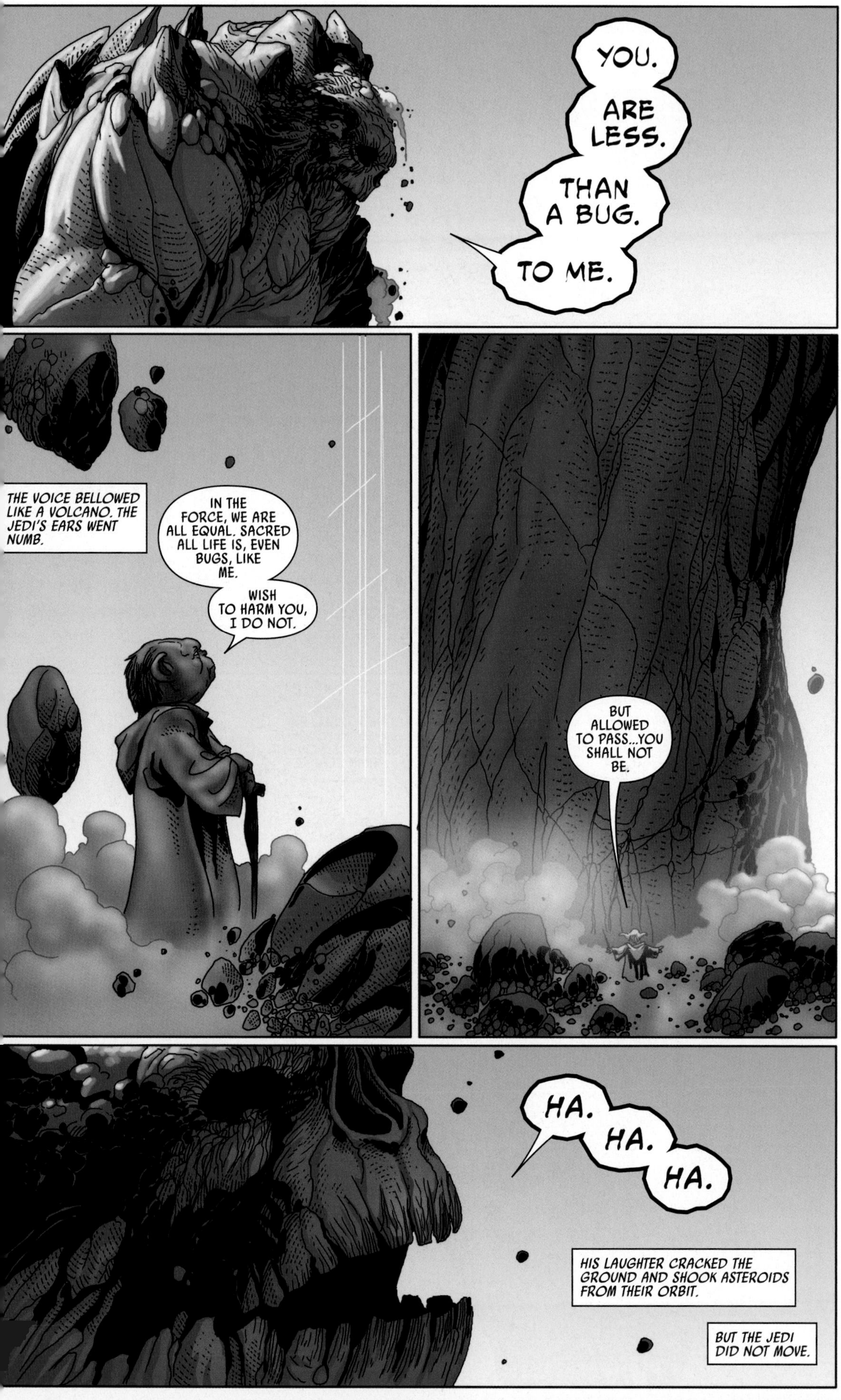
YOU.
ARE LESS.
THAN A BUG.
TO ME.
THE VOICE BELLOWED LIKE A VOLCANO. THE JEDI'S EARS WENT NUMB.
IN THE FORCE, WE ARE ALL EQUAL. SACRED ALL LIFE IS, EVEN BUGS, LIKE ME.
WISH TO HARM YOU, I DO NOT.
BUT ALLOWED TO PASS...YOU SHALL NOT BE.
HA.
HA.
HA.
HIS LAUGHTER CRACKED THE GROUND AND SHOOK ASTEROIDS FROM THEIR ORBIT.
BUT THE JEDI DID NOT MOVE.

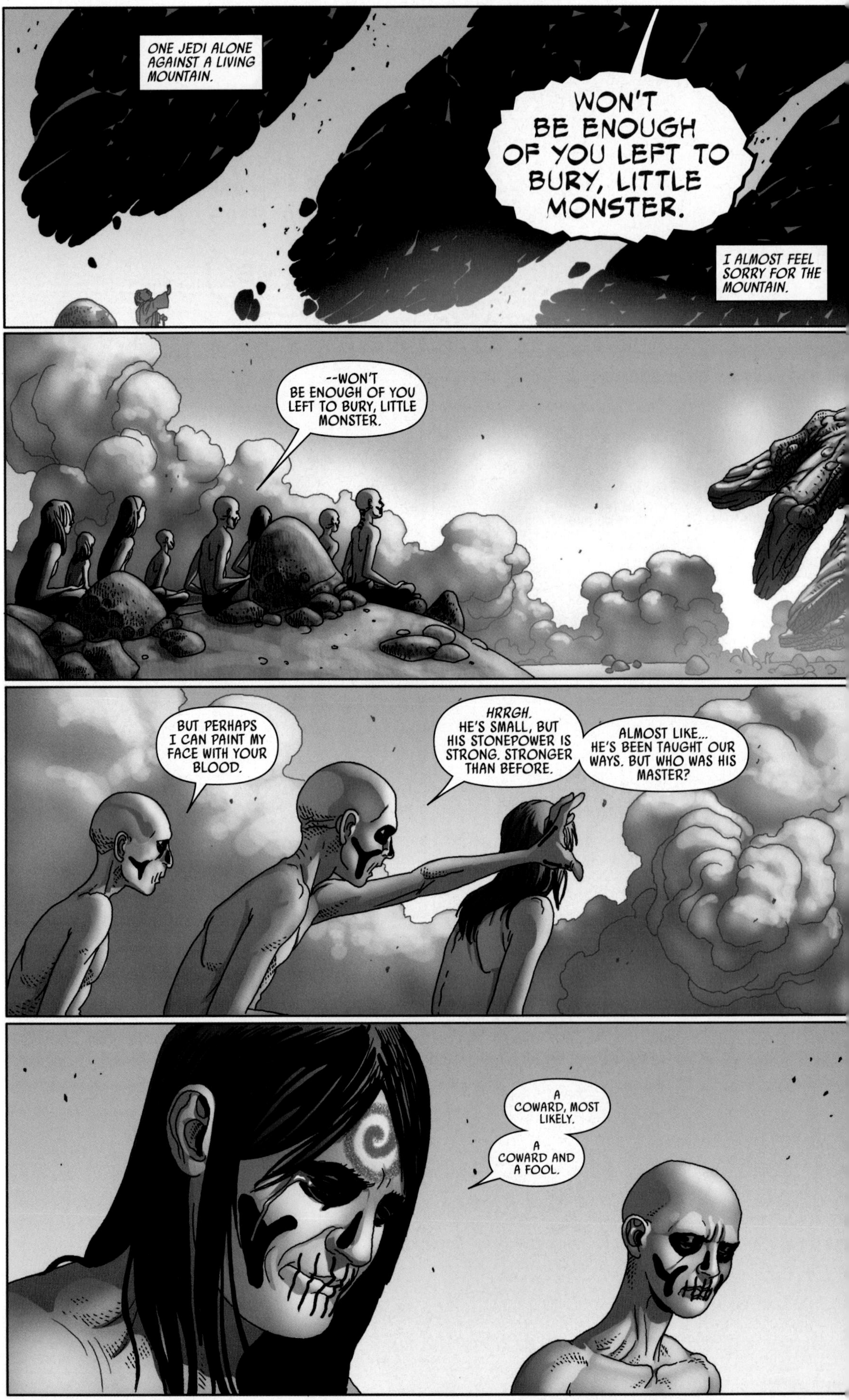
ONE JEDI ALONE AGAINST A LIVING MOUNTAIN.
WON'T BE ENOUGH OF YOU LEFT TO BURY, LITTLE MONSTER.
I ALMOST FEEL SORRY FOR THE MOUNTAIN.
--WON'T BE ENOUGH OF YOU LEFT TO BURY, LITTLE MONSTER.
BUT PERHAPS I CAN PAINT MY FACE WITH YOUR BLOOD.
HRRGH. HE'S SMALL, BUT HIS STONEPOWER IS STRONG. STRONGER THAN BEFORE.
ALMOST LIKE... HE'S BEEN TAUGHT OUR WAYS. BUT WHO WAS HIS MASTER?
A COWARD, MOST LIKELY.
A COWARD AND A FOOL.

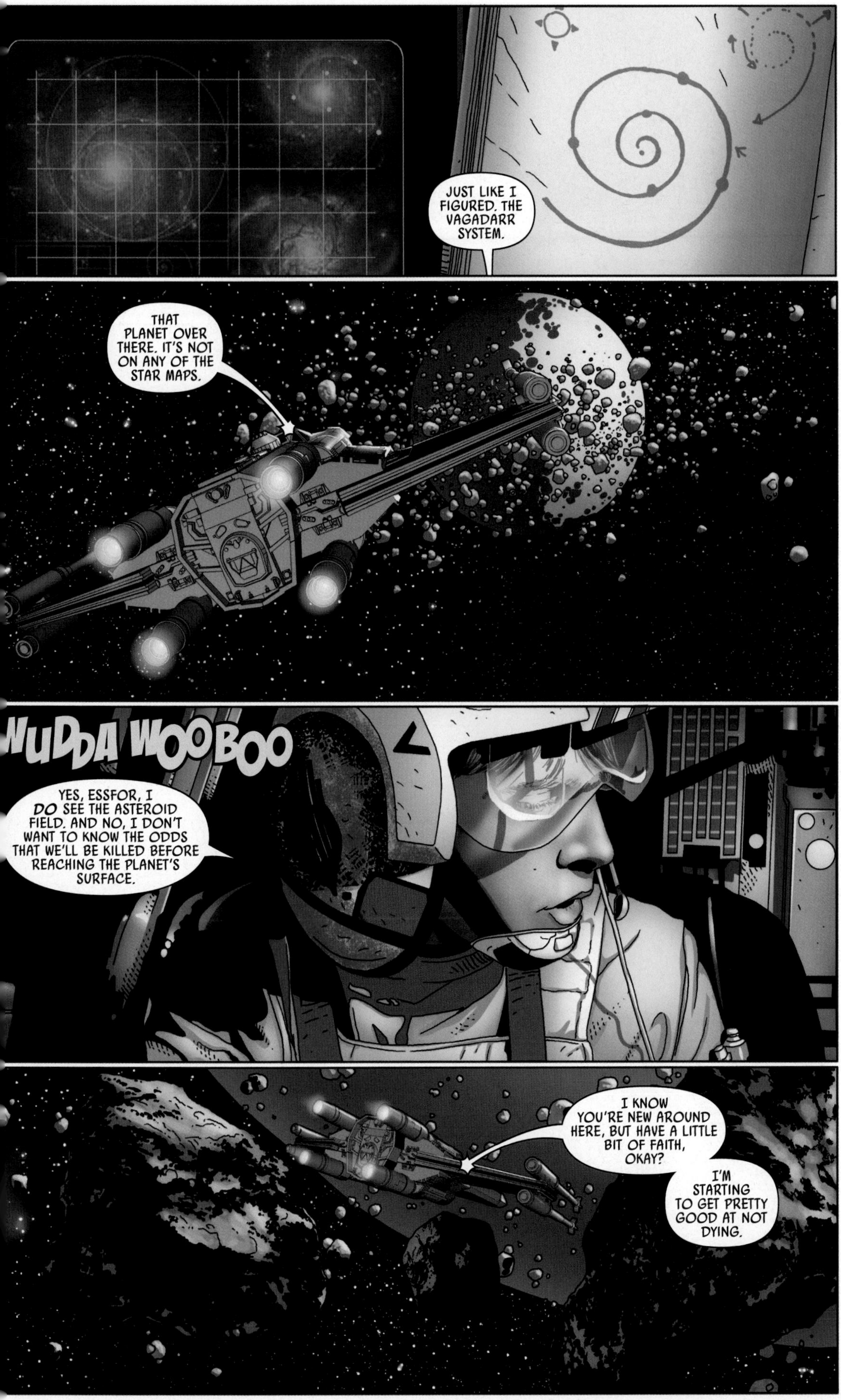
JUST LIKE I FIGURED. THE VAGADARR SYSTEM.
THAT PLANET OVER THERE. IT'S NOT ON ANY OF THE STAR MAPS.
NUDDA WOOBOO
YES, ESSFOR, I *DO* SEE THE ASTEROID FIELD. AND NO, I DON'T WANT TO KNOW THE ODDS THAT WE'LL BE KILLED BEFORE REACHING THE PLANET'S SURFACE.
I KNOW YOU'RE NEW AROUND HERE, BUT HAVE A LITTLE BIT OF FAITH, OKAY?
I'M STARTING TO GET PRETTY GOOD AT NOT DYING.

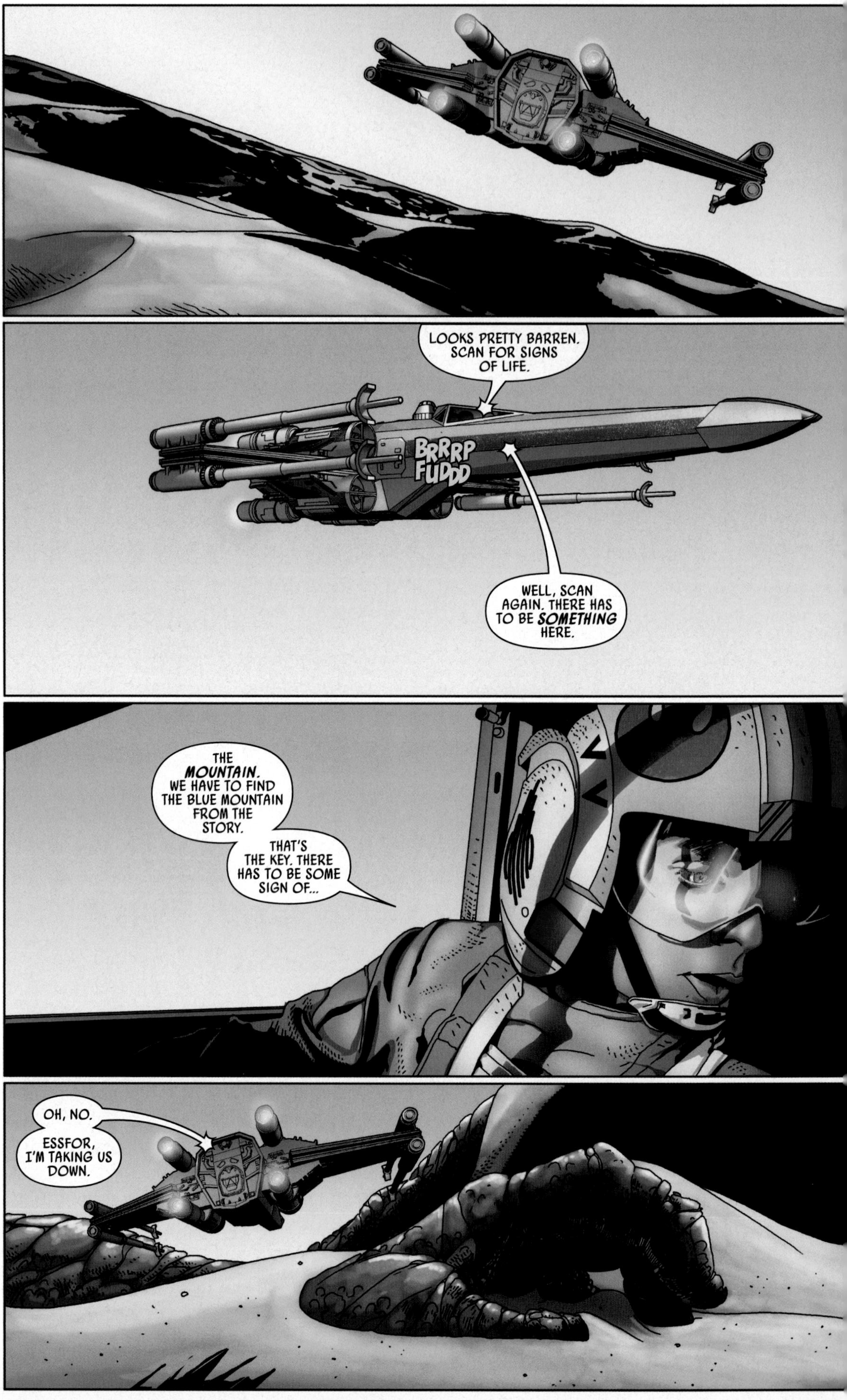
LOOKS PRETTY BARREN. SCAN FOR SIGNS OF LIFE.
BRRRP FUDDD
WELL, SCAN AGAIN. THERE HAS TO BE SOMETHING HERE.
THE MOUNTAIN. WE HAVE TO FIND THE BLUE MOUNTAIN FROM THE STORY.
THAT'S THE KEY. THERE HAS TO BE SOME SIGN OF...
OH, NO.
ESSFOR, I'M TAKING US DOWN.

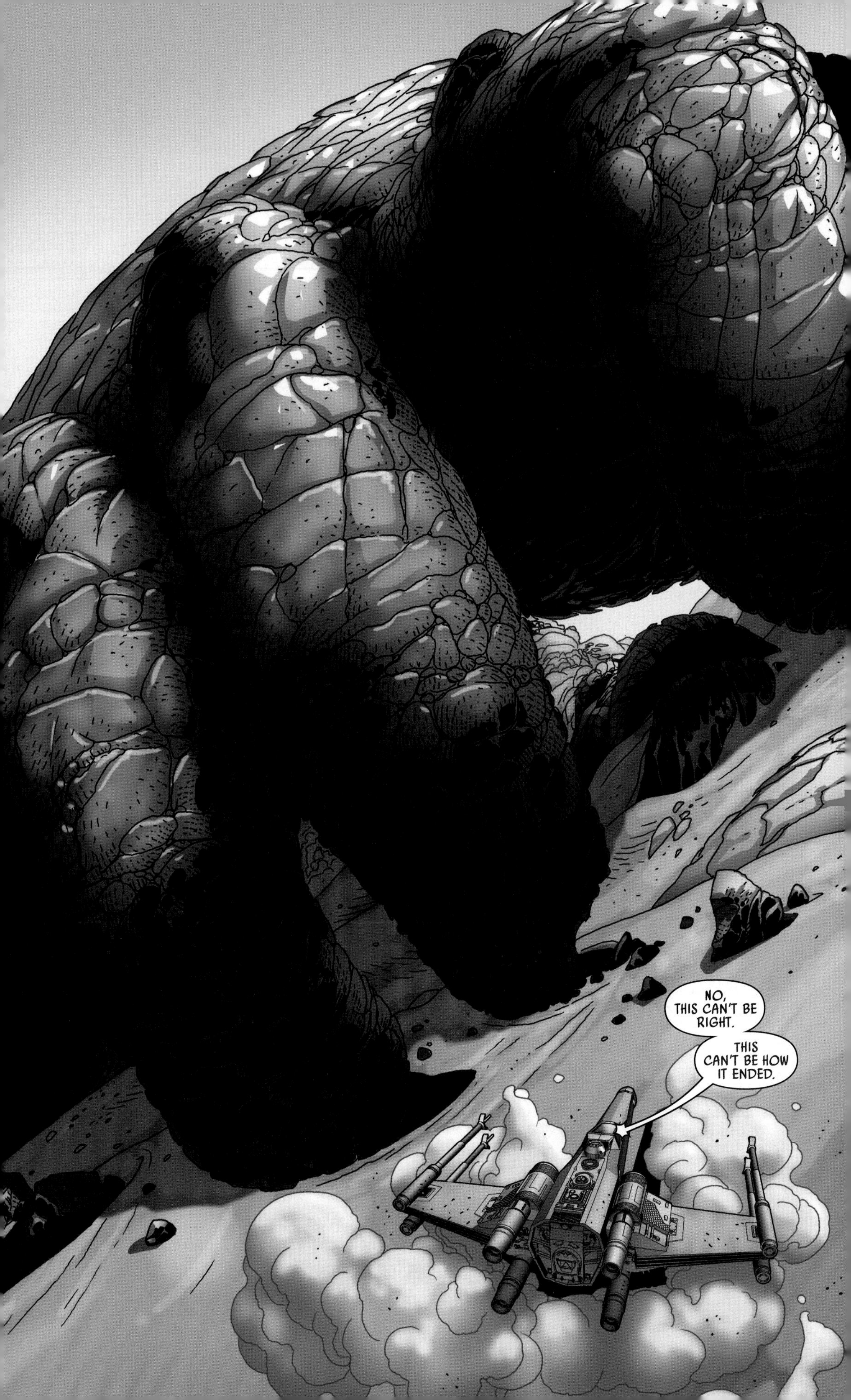
NO, THIS CAN'T BE RIGHT.
THIS CAN'T BE HOW IT ENDED.

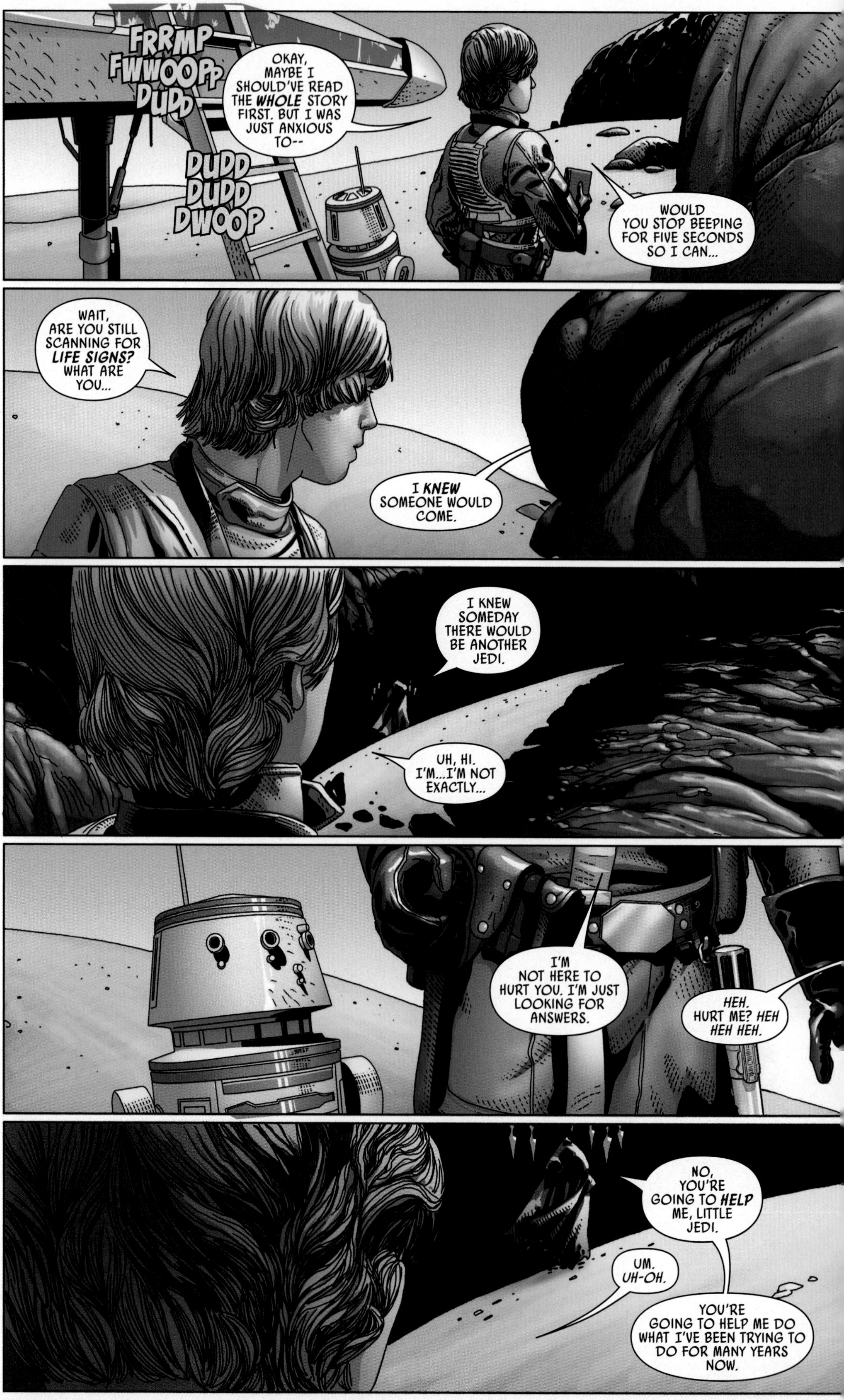
FRRMP FWWOOPP DUDD
OKAY, MAYBE I SHOULD'VE READ THE WHOLE STORY FIRST. BUT I WAS JUST ANXIOUS TO--
DUDD DUDD DWOOP
WOULD YOU STOP BEEPING FOR FIVE SECONDS SO I CAN...
WAIT, ARE YOU STILL SCANNING FOR LIFE SIGNS? WHAT ARE YOU...
I KNEW SOMEONE WOULD COME.
I KNEW SOMEDAY THERE WOULD BE ANOTHER JEDI.
UH, HI. I'M...I'M NOT EXACTLY...
I'M NOT HERE TO HURT YOU. I'M JUST LOOKING FOR ANSWERS.
HEH. HURT ME? HEH HEH HEH.
NO, YOU'RE GOING TO HELP ME, LITTLE JEDI.
UM. UH-OH.
YOU'RE GOING TO HELP ME DO WHAT I'VE BEEN TRYING TO DO FOR MANY YEARS NOW.

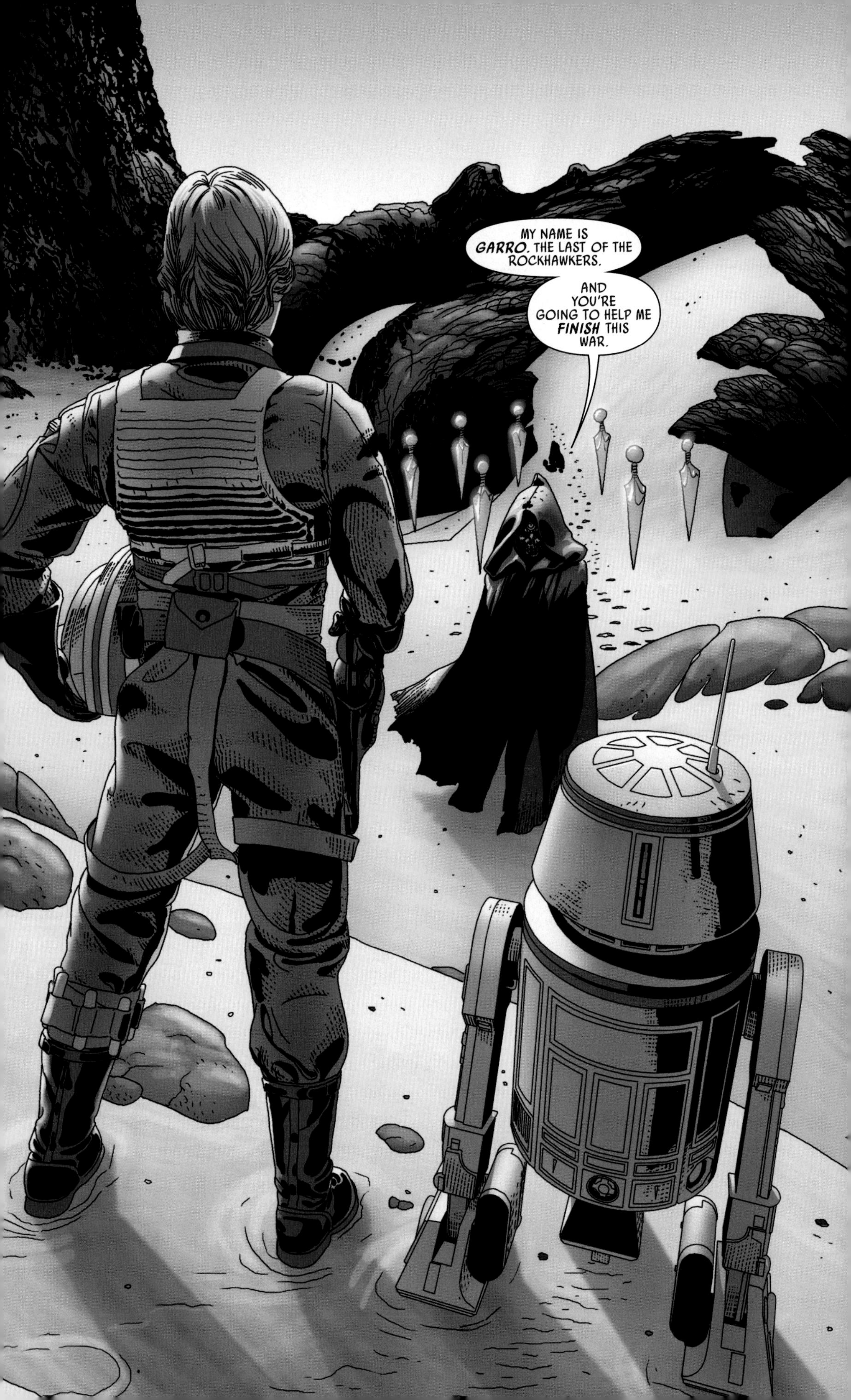
MY NAME IS GARRO. THE LAST OF THE ROCKHAWKERS.
AND YOU'RE GOING TO HELP ME FINISH THIS WAR.

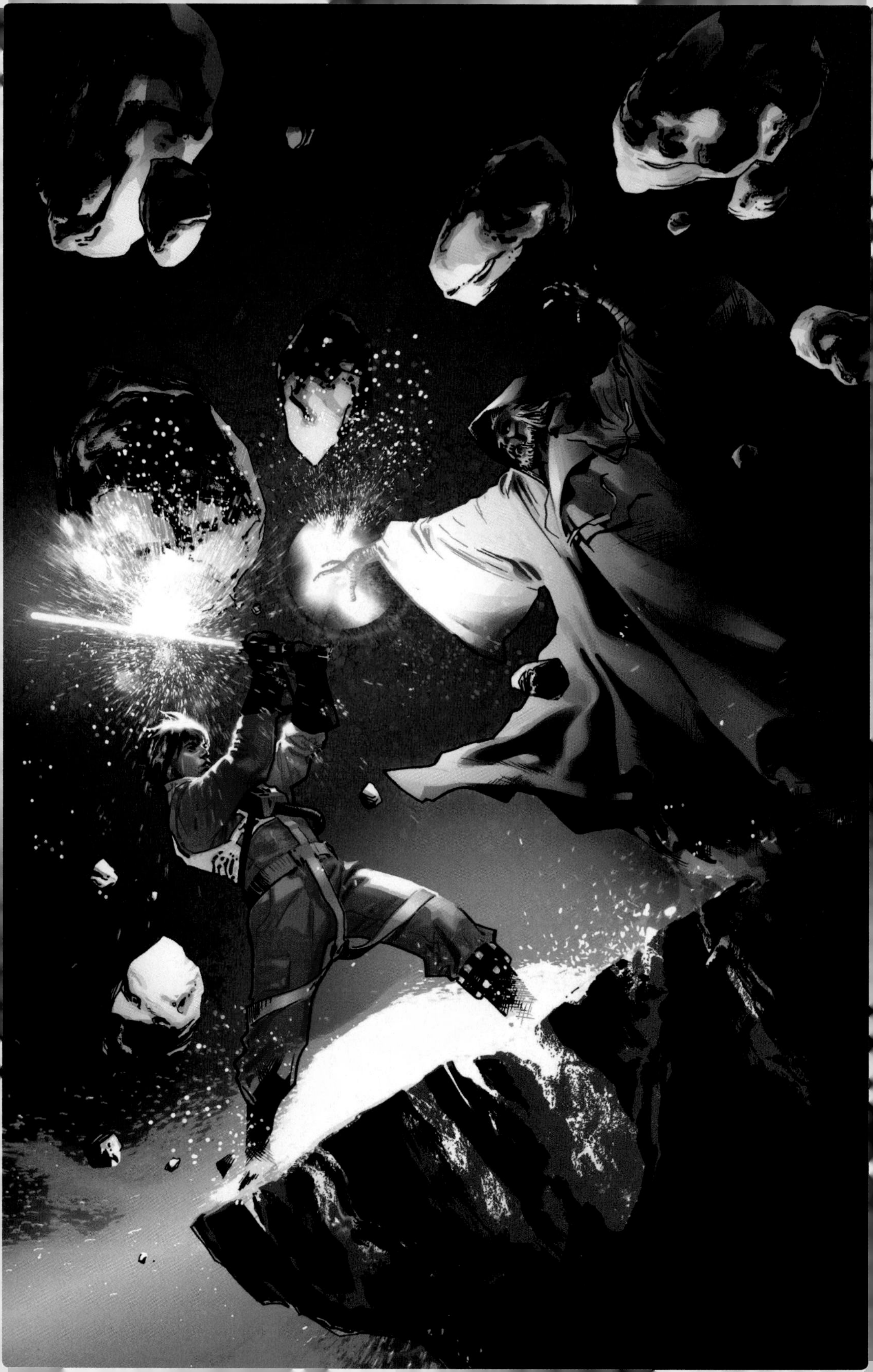

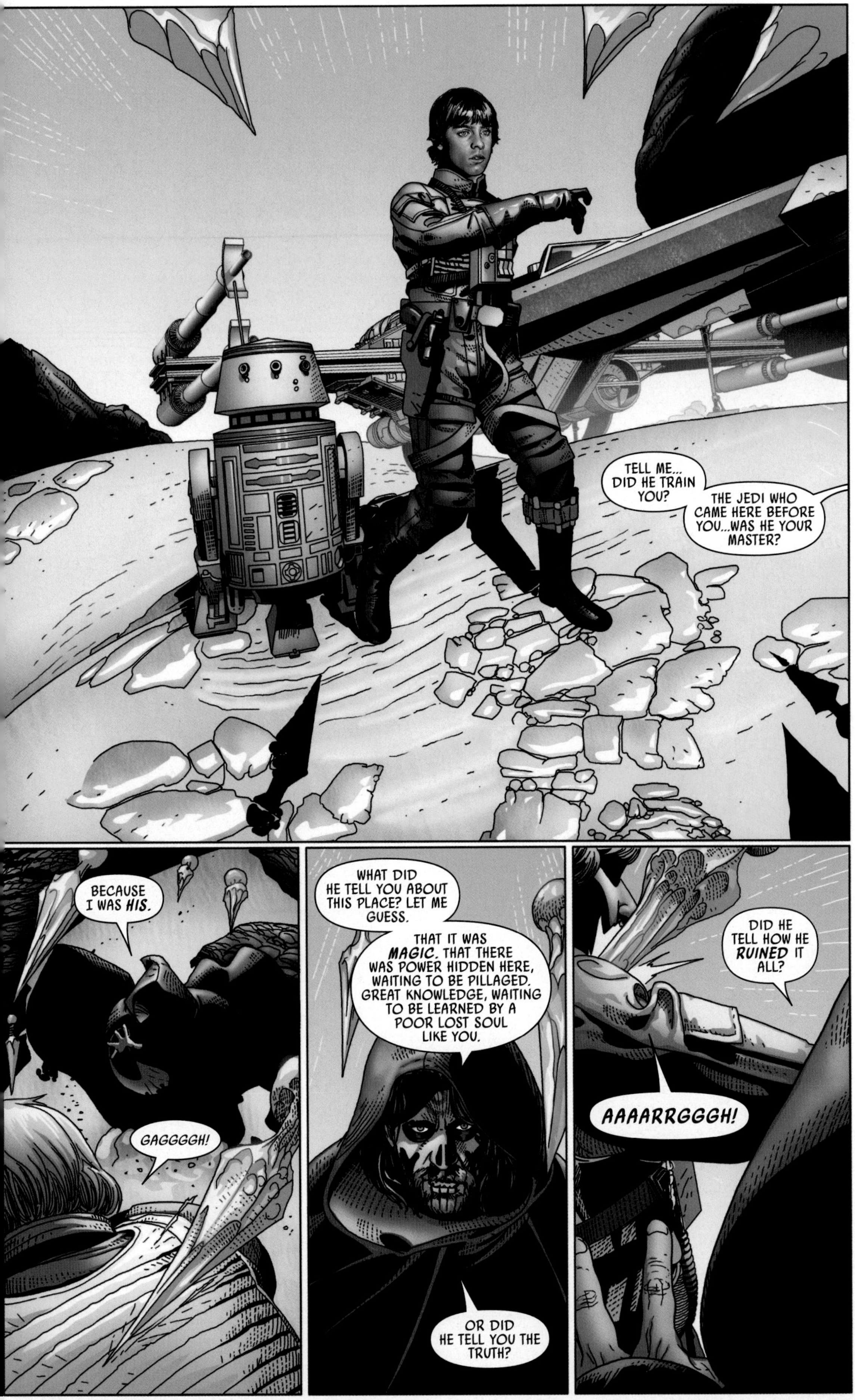
TELL ME... DID HE TRAIN YOU?
THE JEDI WHO CAME HERE BEFORE YOU...WAS HE YOUR MASTER?
BECAUSE I WAS HIS.
GAGGGGH!
WHAT DID HE TELL YOU ABOUT THIS PLACE? LET ME GUESS.
THAT IT WAS MAGIC. THAT THERE WAS POWER HIDDEN HERE, WAITING TO BE PILLAGED. GREAT KNOWLEDGE, WAITING TO BE LEARNED BY A POOR LOST SOUL LIKE YOU.
OR DID HE TELL YOU THE TRUTH?
DID HE TELL HOW HE RUINED IT ALL?
AAAARRGGGH!

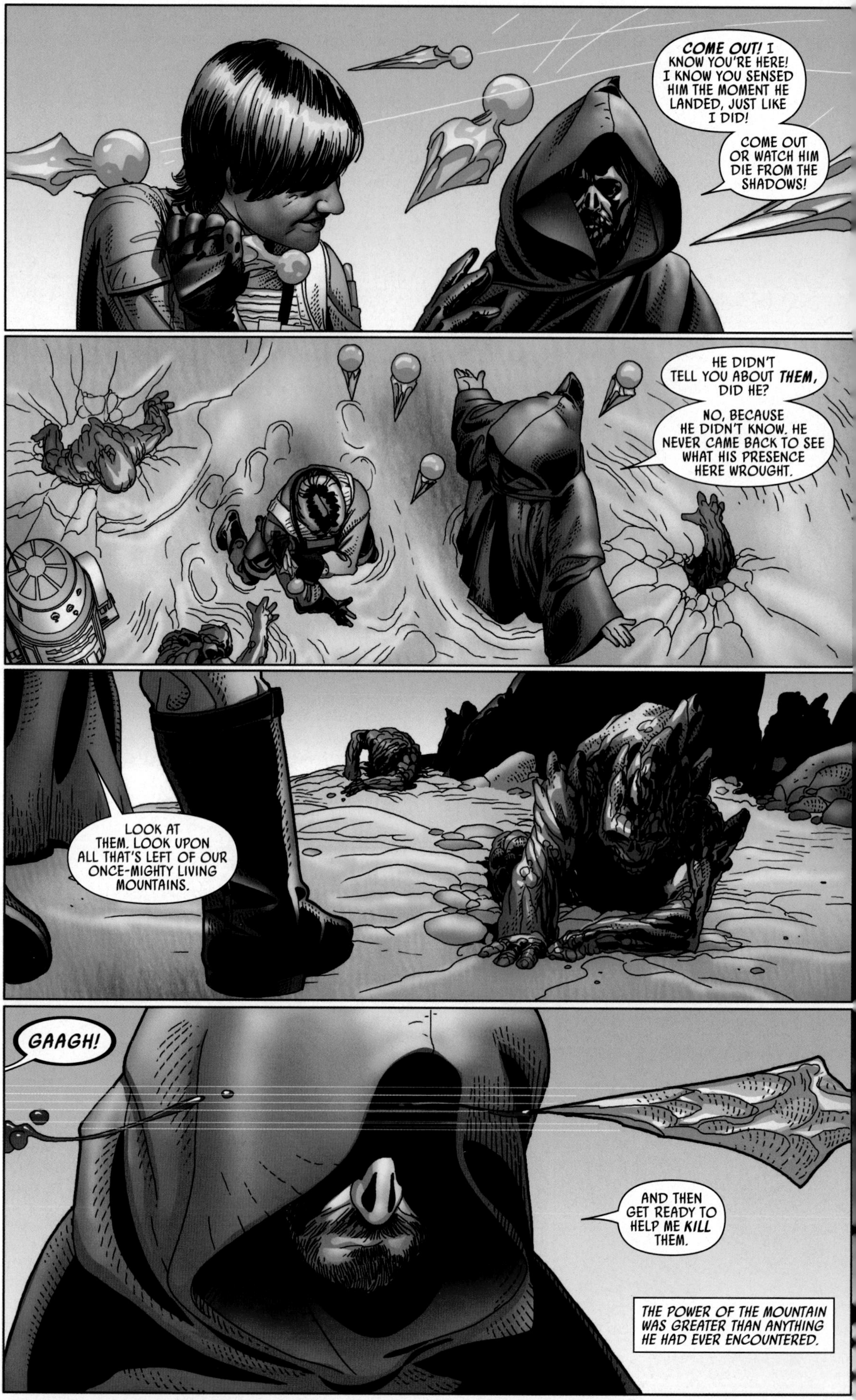
COME OUT! I KNOW YOU'RE HERE! I KNOW YOU SENSED HIM THE MOMENT HE LANDED, JUST LIKE I DID!
COME OUT OR WATCH HIM DIE FROM THE SHADOWS!
HE DIDN'T TELL YOU ABOUT THEM, DID HE?
NO, BECAUSE HE DIDN'T KNOW. HE NEVER CAME BACK TO SEE WHAT HIS PRESENCE HERE WROUGHT.
LOOK AT THEM. LOOK UPON ALL THAT'S LEFT OF OUR ONCE-MIGHTY LIVING MOUNTAINS.
GAAGH!
AND THEN GET READY TO HELP ME KILL THEM.
THE POWER OF THE MOUNTAIN WAS GREATER THAN ANYTHING HE HAD EVER ENCOUNTERED.

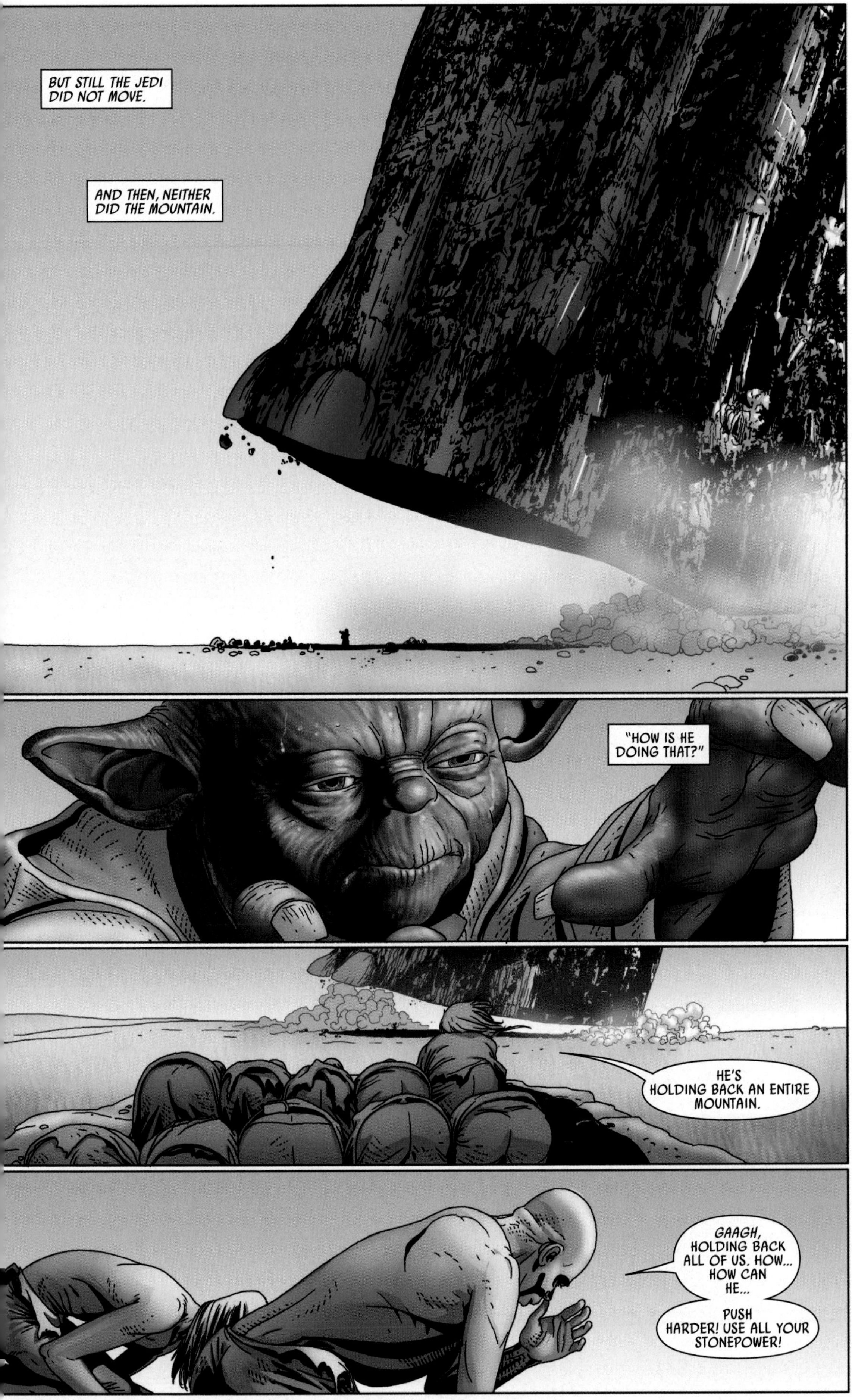
BUT STILL THE JEDI DID NOT MOVE.
AND THEN, NEITHER DID THE MOUNTAIN.
"HOW IS HE DOING THAT?"
HE'S HOLDING BACK AN ENTIRE MOUNTAIN.
GAAGH, HOLDING BACK ALL OF US. HOW... HOW CAN HE...
PUSH HARDER! USE ALL YOUR STONEPOWER!

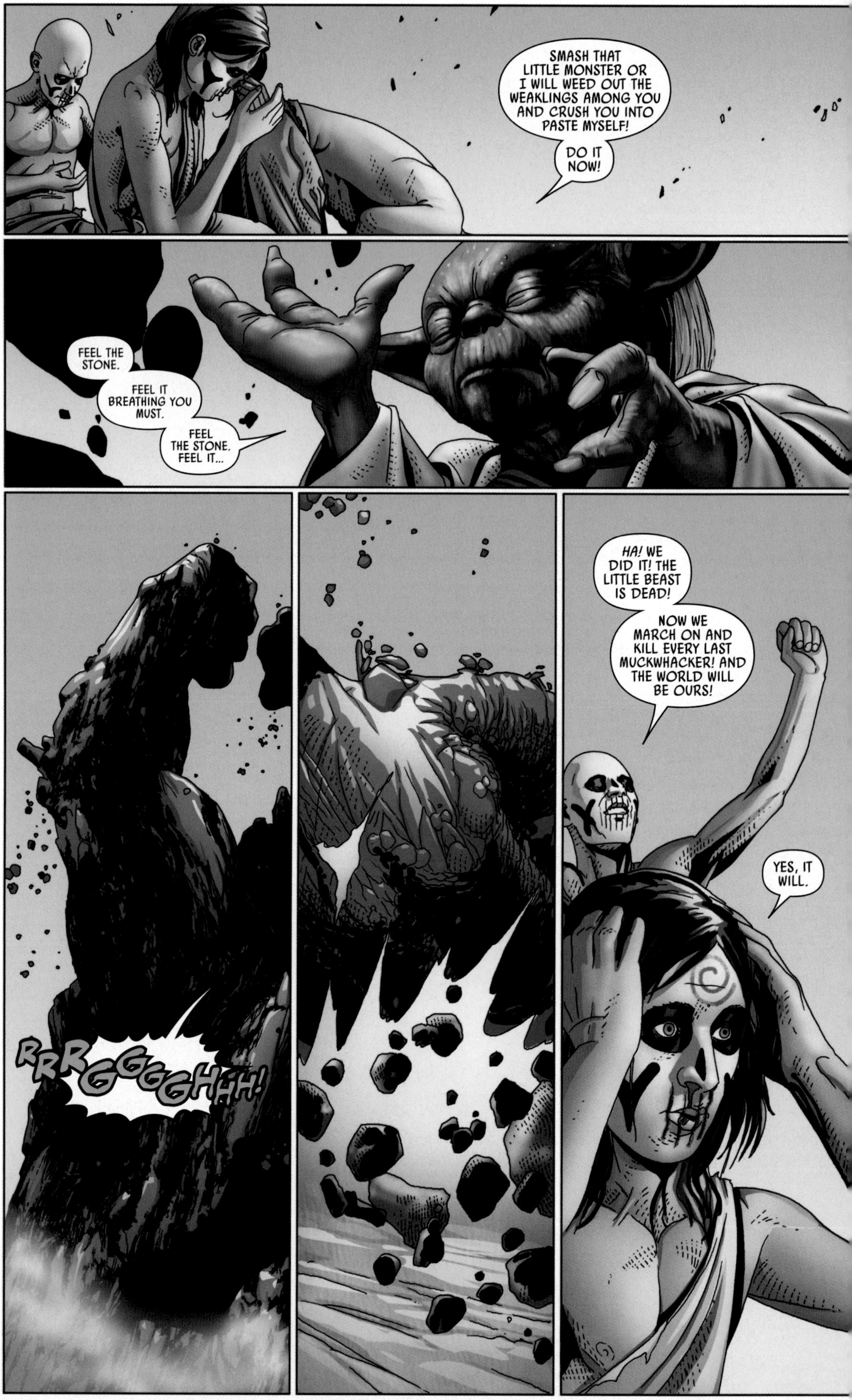
SMASH THAT LITTLE MONSTER OR I WILL WEED OUT THE WEAKLINGS AMONG YOU AND CRUSH YOU INTO PASTE MYSELF!
DO IT NOW!
FEEL THE STONE.
FEEL IT BREATHING YOU MUST.
FEEL THE STONE. FEEL IT...
RRRGGGGGHHH!
HA! WE DID IT! THE LITTLE BEAST IS DEAD!
NOW WE MARCH ON AND KILL EVERY LAST MUCKWHACKER! AND THE WORLD WILL BE OURS!
YES, IT WILL.

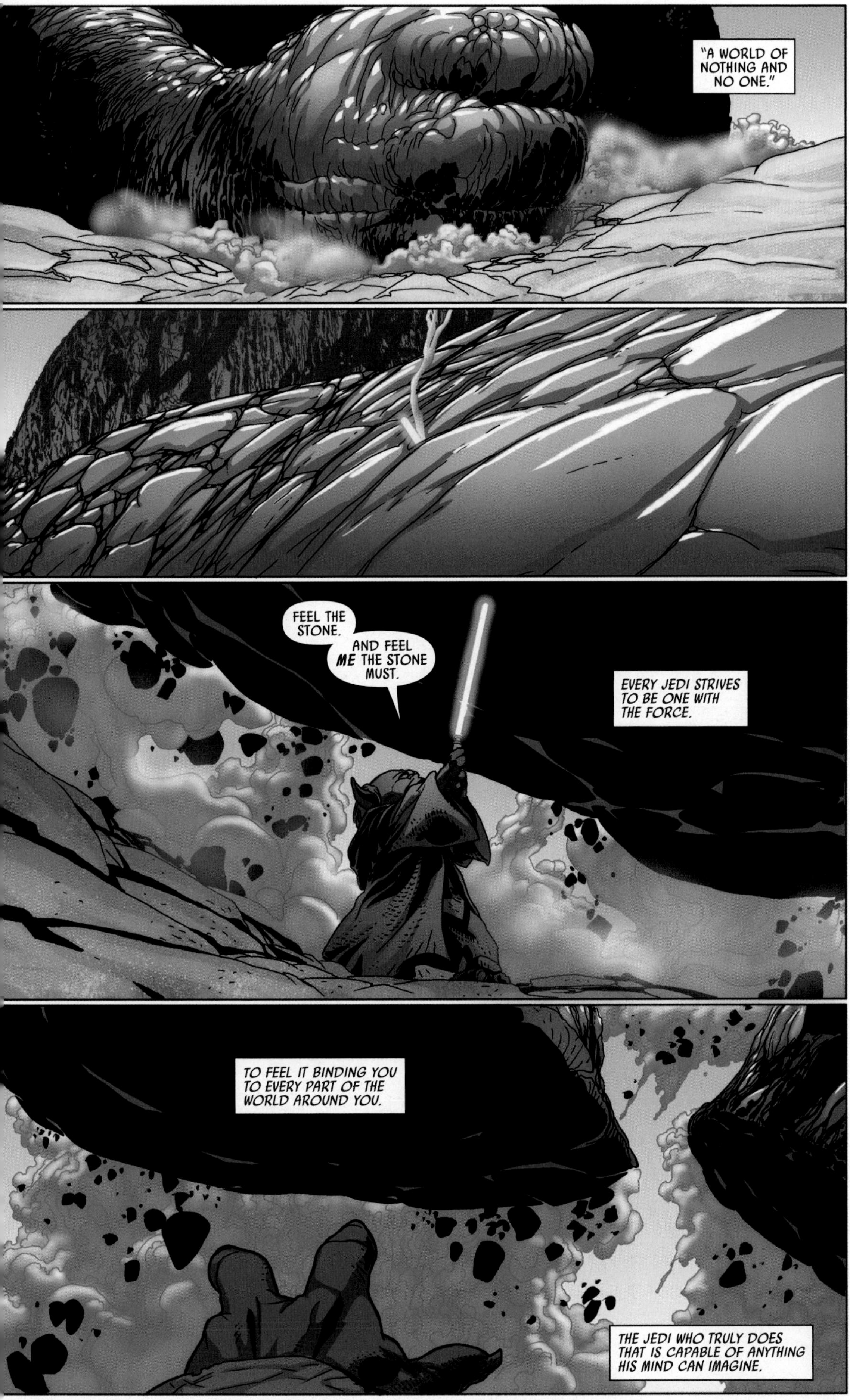
"A WORLD OF NOTHING AND NO ONE."
FEEL THE STONE.
AND FEEL *ME* THE STONE MUST.
EVERY JEDI STRIVES TO BE ONE WITH THE FORCE.
TO FEEL IT BINDING YOU TO EVERY PART OF THE WORLD AROUND YOU.
THE JEDI WHO TRULY DOES THAT IS CAPABLE OF ANYTHING HIS MIND CAN IMAGINE.

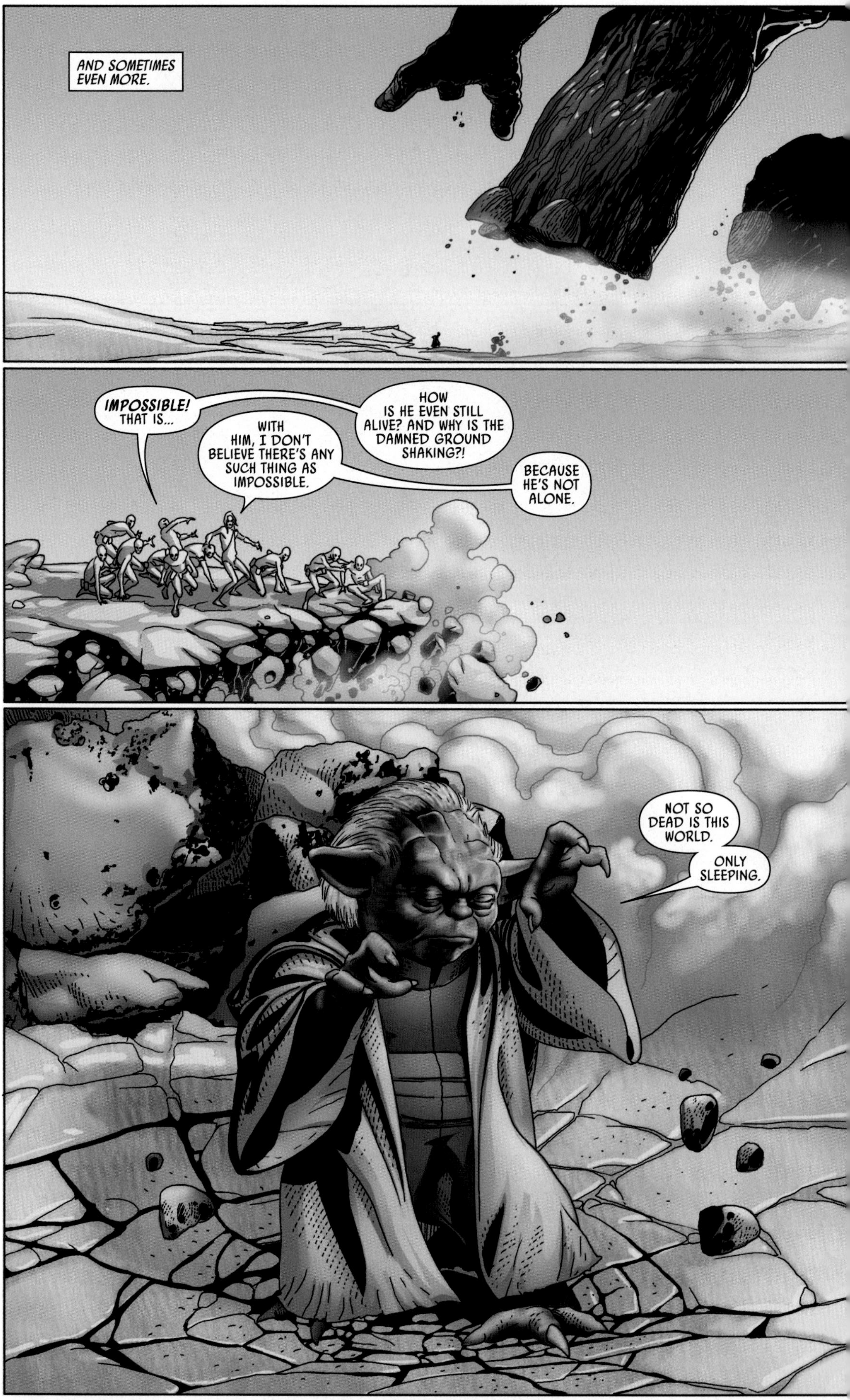
AND SOMETIMES EVEN MORE.
IMPOSSIBLE! THAT IS...
HOW IS HE EVEN STILL ALIVE? AND WHY IS THE DAMNED GROUND SHAKING?!
WITH HIM, I DON'T BELIEVE THERE'S ANY SUCH THING AS IMPOSSIBLE.
BECAUSE HE'S NOT ALONE.
NOT SO DEAD IS THIS WORLD.
ONLY SLEEPING.

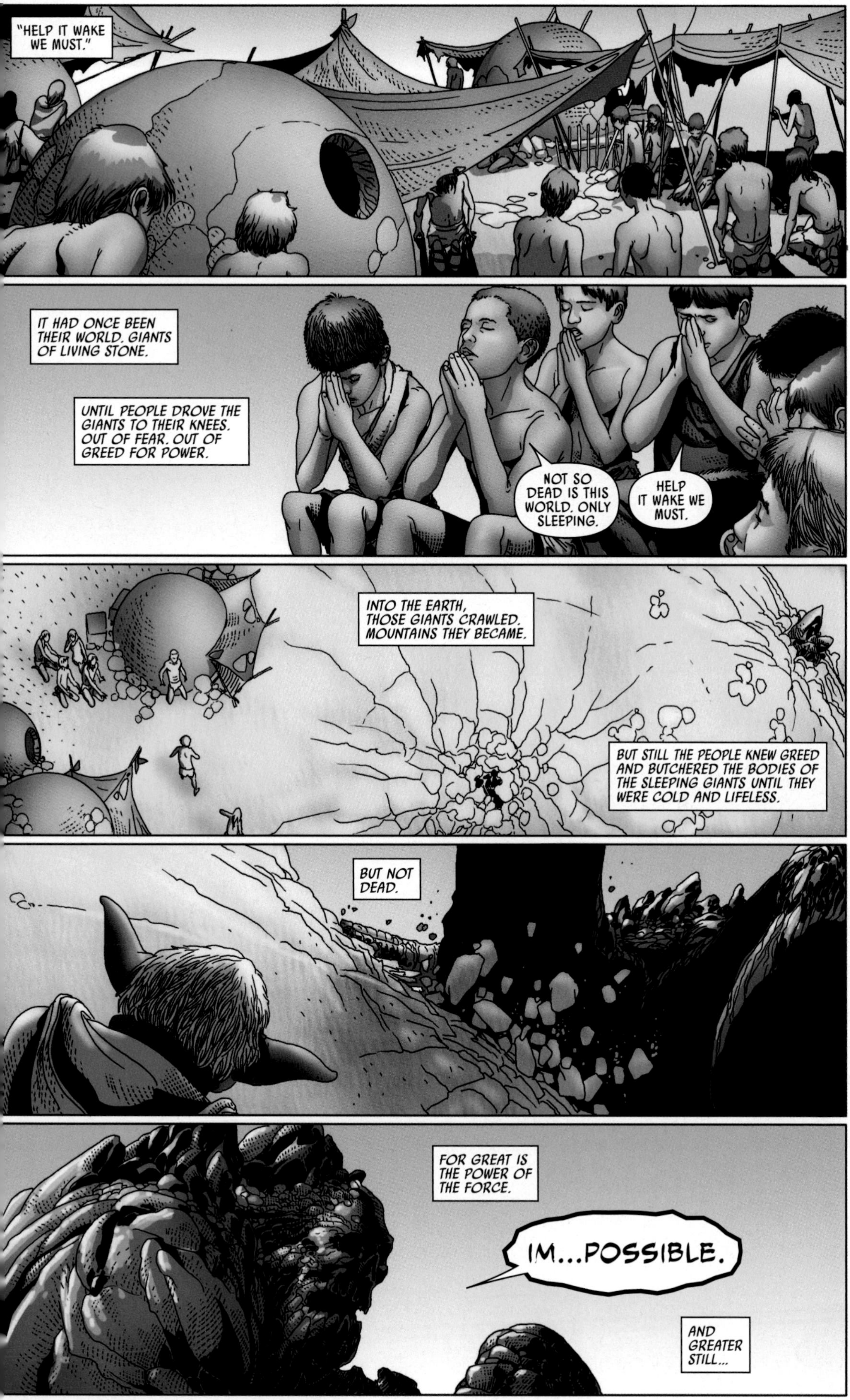
"HELP IT WAKE WE MUST."
IT HAD ONCE BEEN THEIR WORLD. GIANTS OF LIVING STONE.
UNTIL PEOPLE DROVE THE GIANTS TO THEIR KNEES. OUT OF FEAR. OUT OF GREED FOR POWER.
NOT SO DEAD IS THIS WORLD. ONLY SLEEPING.
HELP IT WAKE WE MUST.
INTO THE EARTH, THOSE GIANTS CRAWLED. MOUNTAINS THEY BECAME.
BUT STILL THE PEOPLE KNEW GREED AND BUTCHERED THE BODIES OF THE SLEEPING GIANTS UNTIL THEY WERE COLD AND LIFELESS.
BUT NOT DEAD.
FOR GREAT IS THE POWER OF THE FORCE.
IM...POSSIBLE.
AND GREATER STILL...

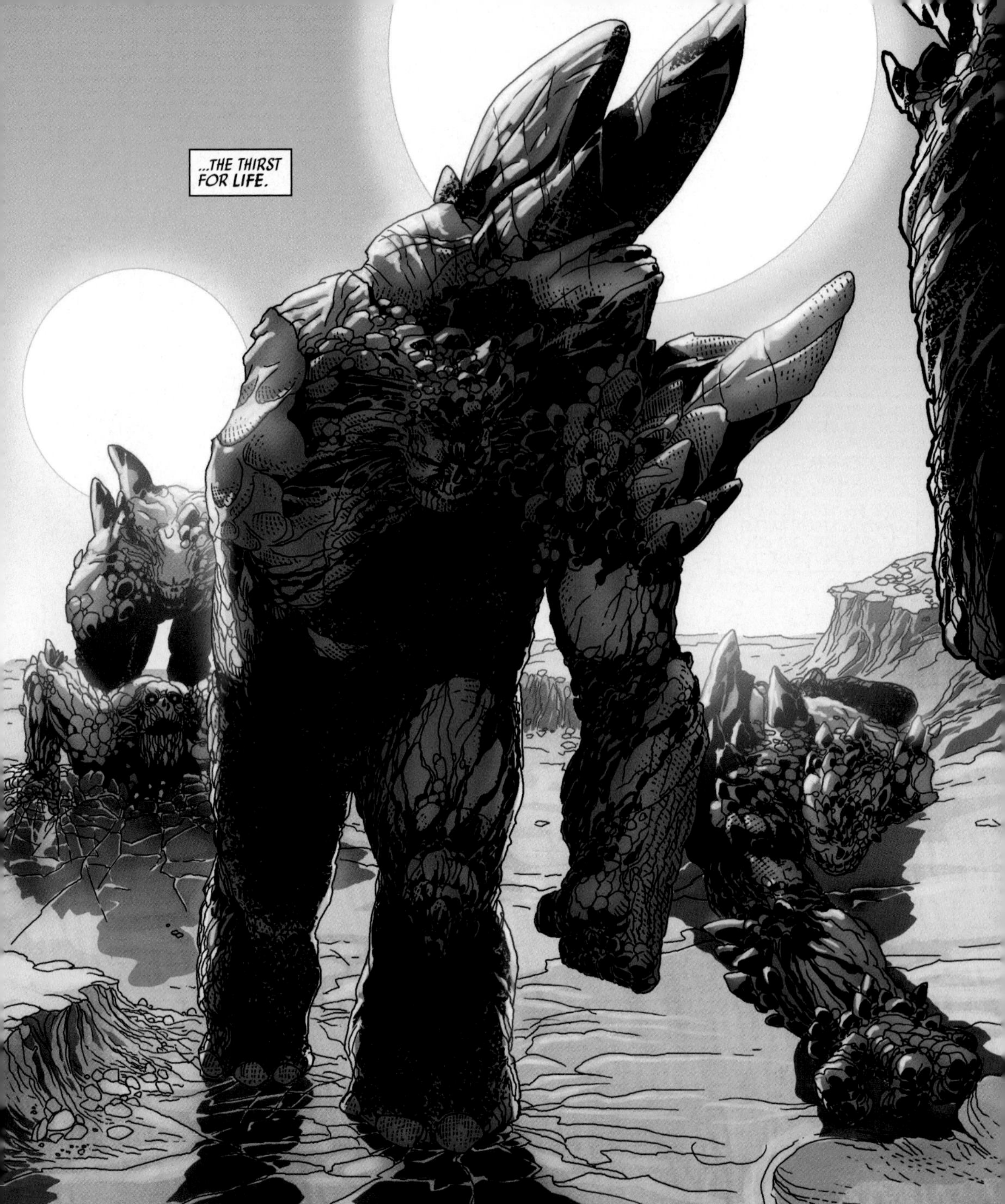
...THE THIRST
FOR LIFE.

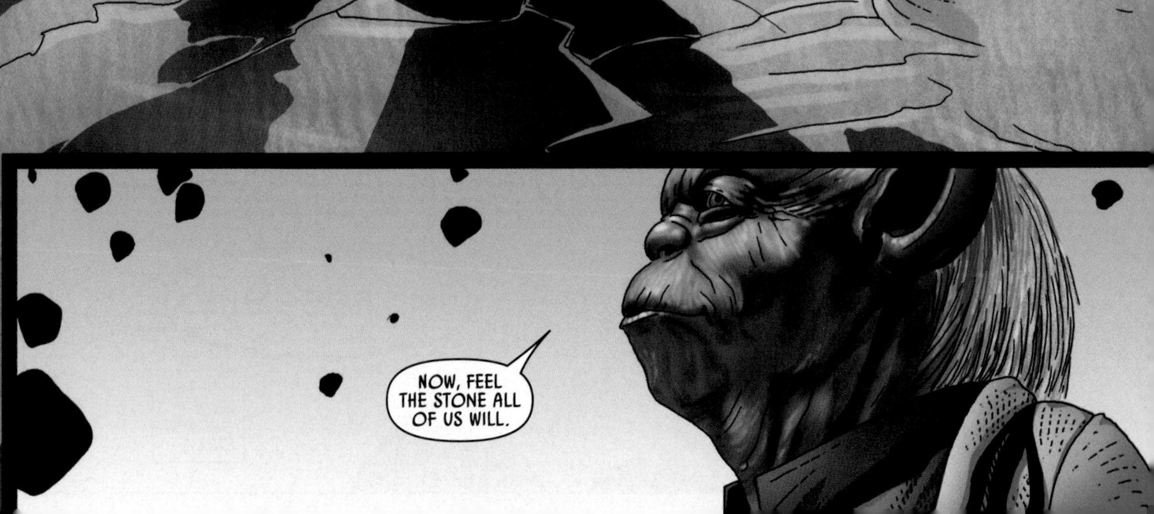
NOW, FEEL
THE STONE ALL
OF US WILL.

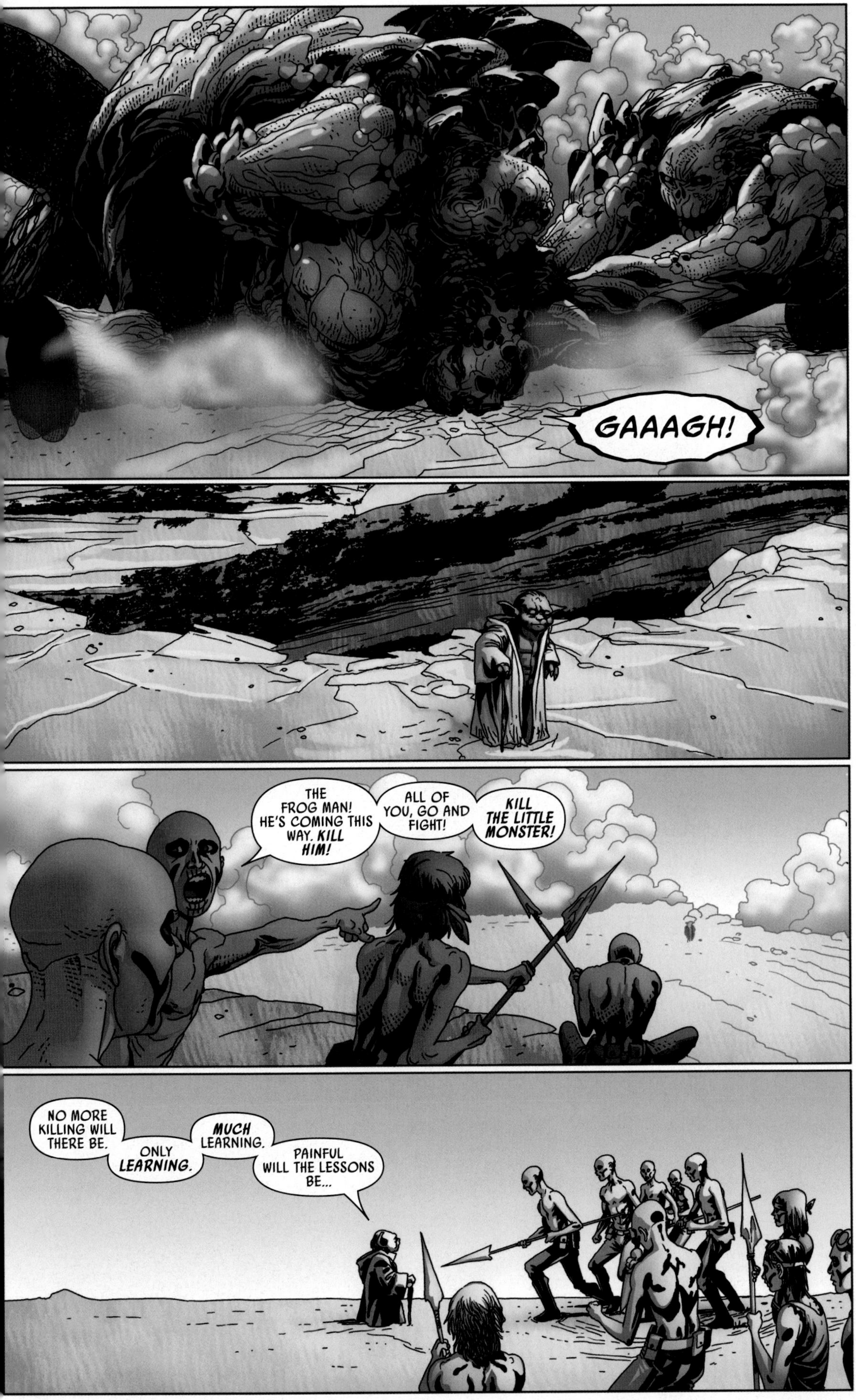
GAAAGH!
THE FROG MAN! HE'S COMING THIS WAY. KILL HIM!
ALL OF YOU, GO AND FIGHT!
KILL THE LITTLE MONSTER!
NO MORE KILLING WILL THERE BE.
ONLY LEARNING.
MUCH LEARNING.
PAINFUL WILL THE LESSONS BE...

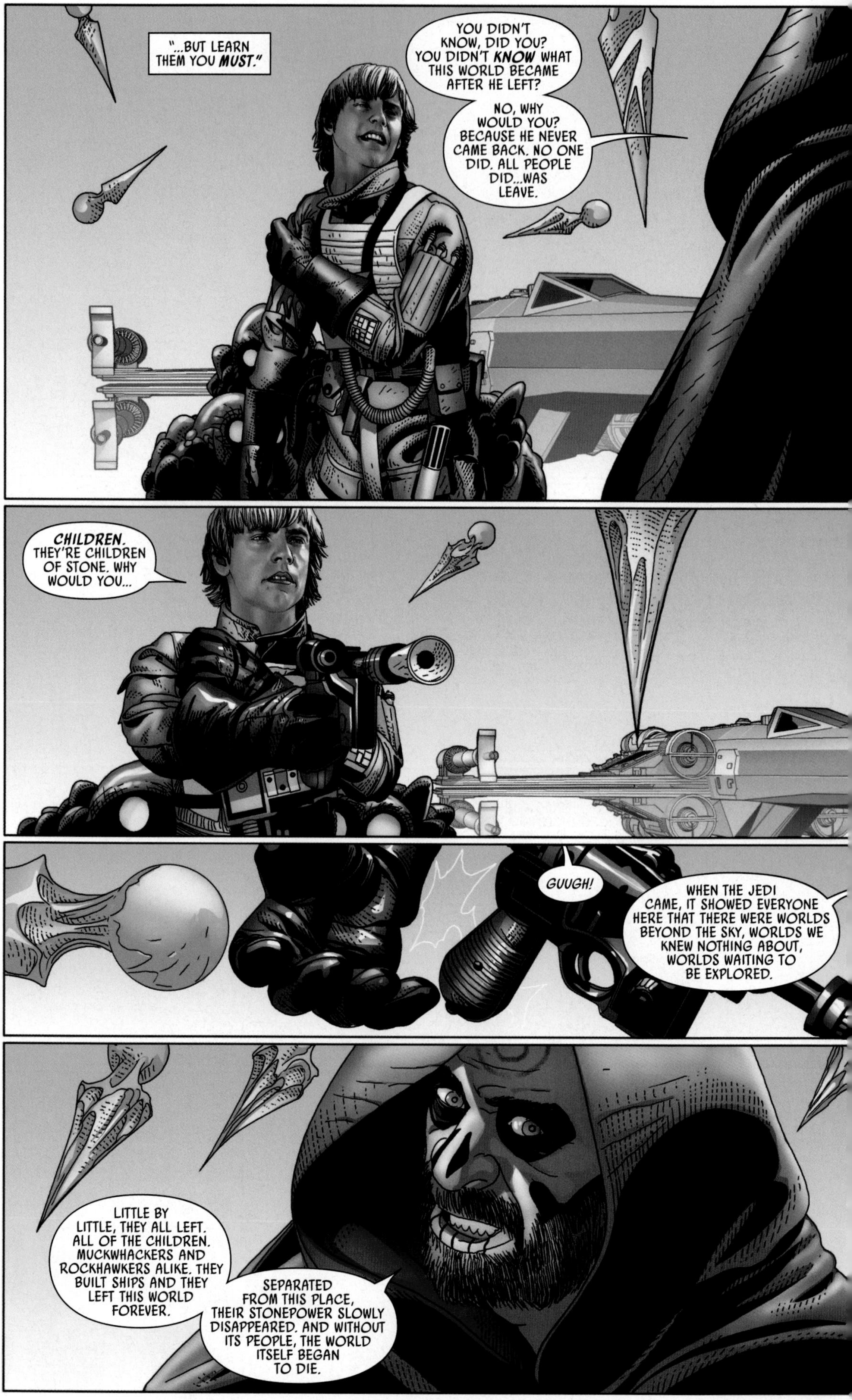
"...BUT LEARN THEM YOU MUST."
YOU DIDN'T KNOW, DID YOU? YOU DIDN'T KNOW WHAT THIS WORLD BECAME AFTER HE LEFT?
NO, WHY WOULD YOU? BECAUSE HE NEVER CAME BACK. NO ONE DID. ALL PEOPLE DID...WAS LEAVE.
CHILDREN. THEY'RE CHILDREN OF STONE. WHY WOULD YOU...
GUUGH!
WHEN THE JEDI CAME, IT SHOWED EVERYONE HERE THAT THERE WERE WORLDS BEYOND THE SKY, WORLDS WE KNEW NOTHING ABOUT, WORLDS WAITING TO BE EXPLORED.
LITTLE BY LITTLE, THEY ALL LEFT. ALL OF THE CHILDREN. MUCKWHACKERS AND ROCKHAWKERS ALIKE. THEY BUILT SHIPS AND THEY LEFT THIS WORLD FOREVER.
SEPARATED FROM THIS PLACE, THEIR STONEPOWER SLOWLY DISAPPEARED. AND WITHOUT ITS PEOPLE, THE WORLD ITSELF BEGAN TO DIE.

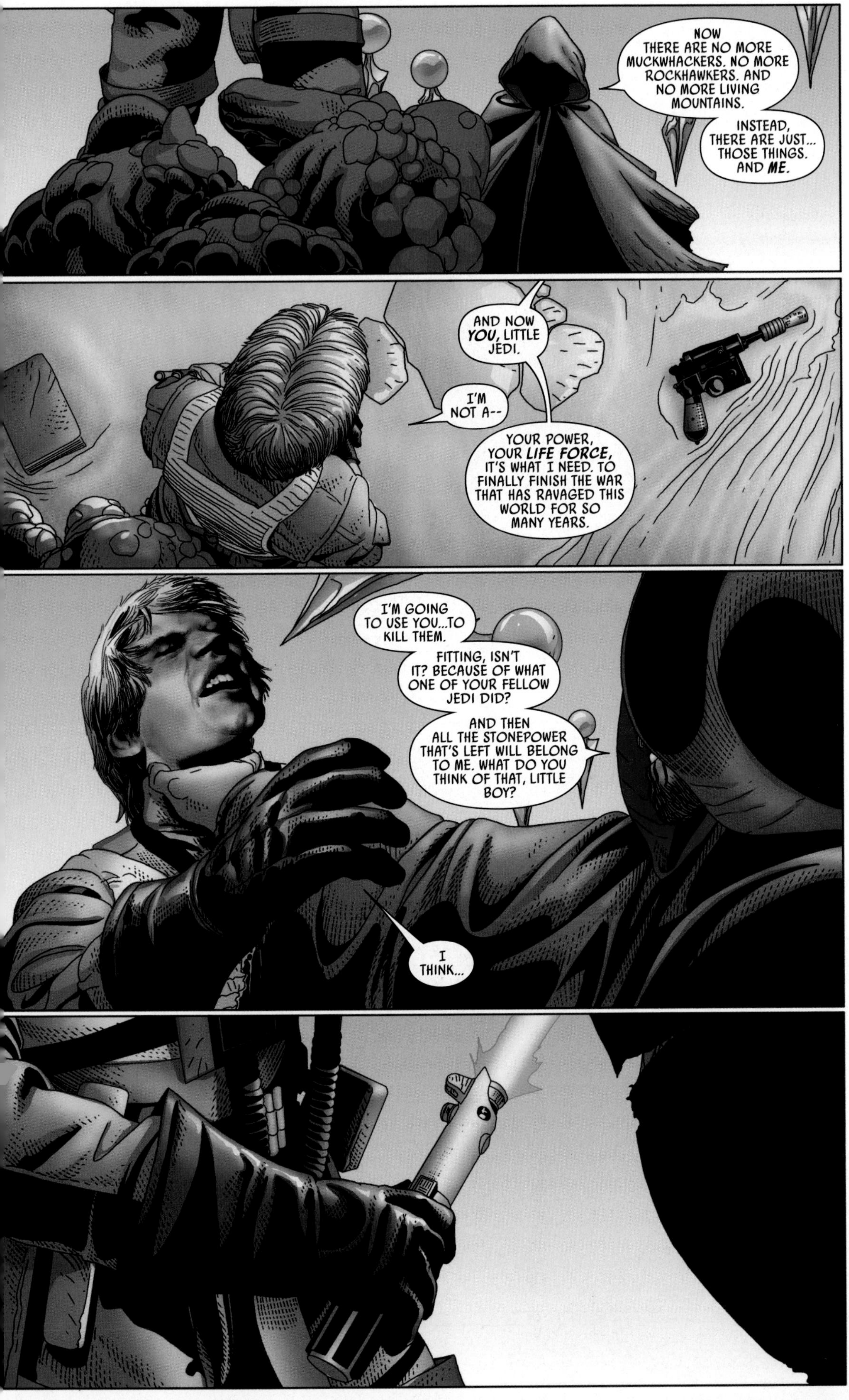
NOW THERE ARE NO MORE MUCKWHACKERS. NO MORE ROCKHAWKERS. AND NO MORE LIVING MOUNTAINS.
INSTEAD, THERE ARE JUST... THOSE THINGS. AND **ME.**
AND NOW **YOU,** LITTLE JEDI.
I'M NOT A--
YOUR POWER, YOUR **LIFE FORCE,** IT'S WHAT I NEED. TO FINALLY FINISH THE WAR THAT HAS RAVAGED THIS WORLD FOR SO MANY YEARS.
I'M GOING TO USE YOU...TO KILL THEM.
FITTING, ISN'T IT? BECAUSE OF WHAT ONE OF YOUR FELLOW JEDI DID?
AND THEN ALL THE STONEPOWER THAT'S LEFT WILL BELONG TO ME. WHAT DO YOU THINK OF THAT, LITTLE BOY?
I THINK...

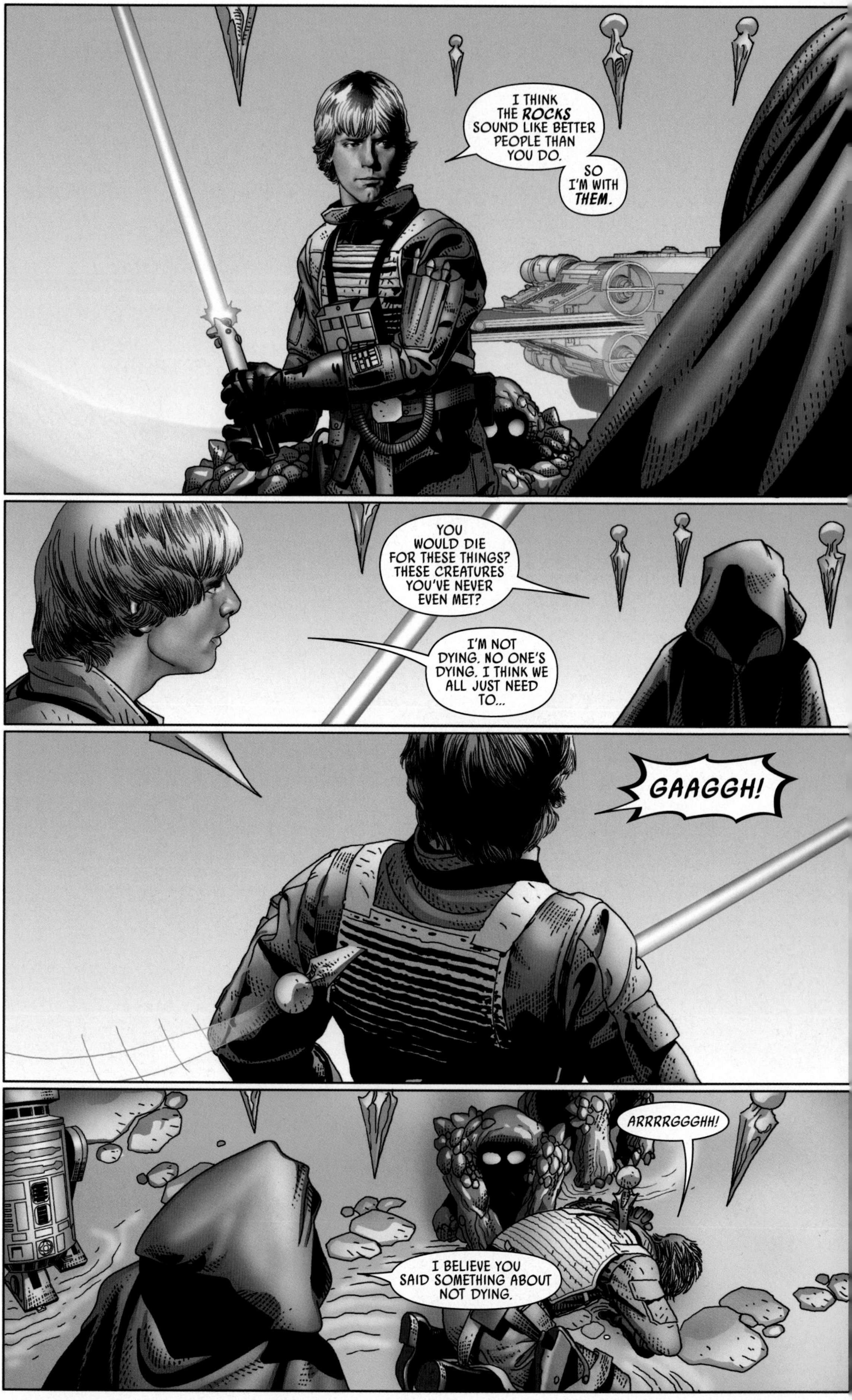
I THINK THE ROCKS SOUND LIKE BETTER PEOPLE THAN YOU DO.
SO I'M WITH THEM.
YOU WOULD DIE FOR THESE THINGS? THESE CREATURES YOU'VE NEVER EVEN MET?
I'M NOT DYING. NO ONE'S DYING. I THINK WE ALL JUST NEED TO...
GAAGGH!
ARRRRGGGHH!
I BELIEVE YOU SAID SOMETHING ABOUT NOT DYING.

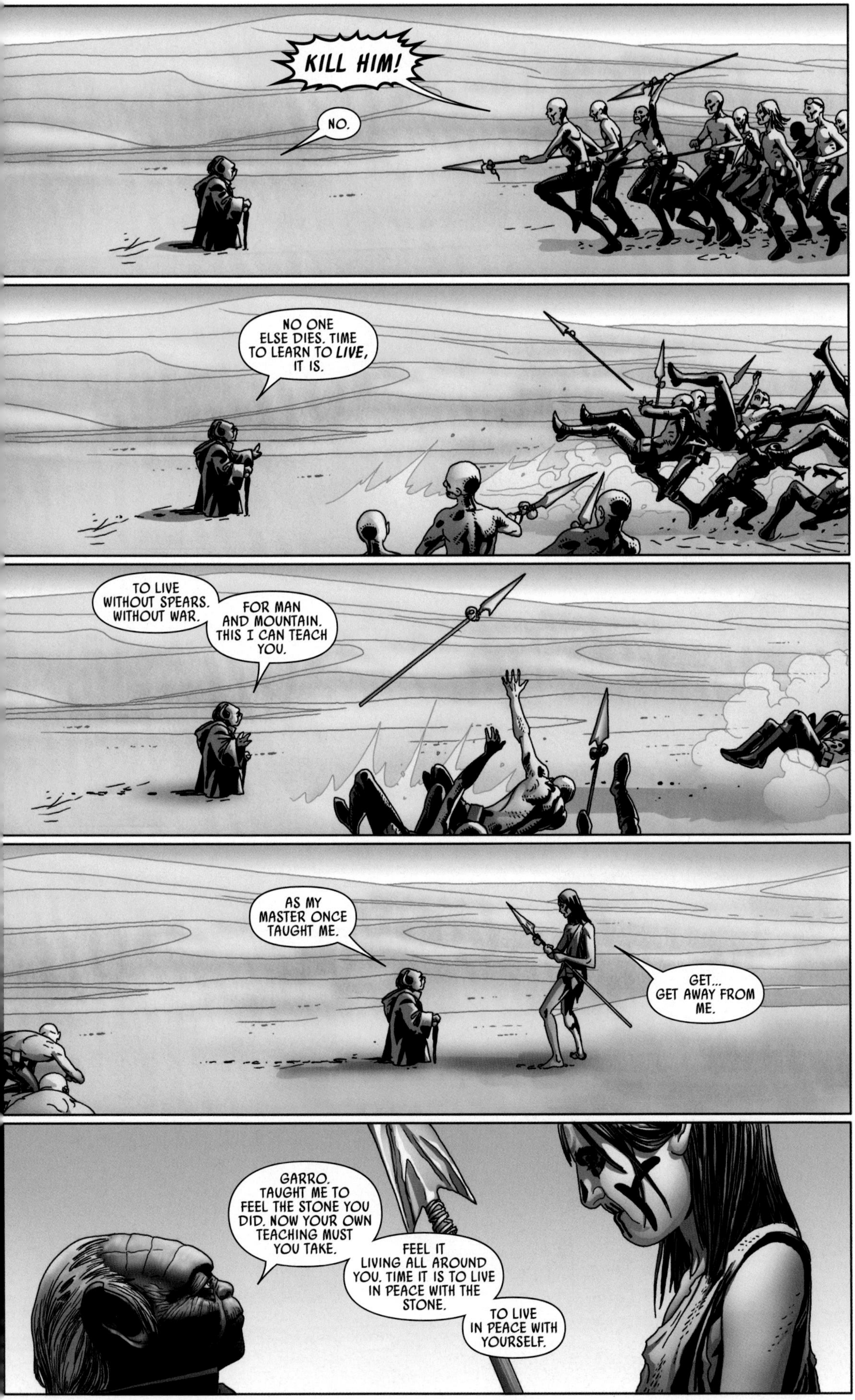
KILL HIM!
NO.
NO ONE ELSE DIES. TIME TO LEARN TO LIVE, IT IS.
TO LIVE WITHOUT SPEARS. WITHOUT WAR.
FOR MAN AND MOUNTAIN. THIS I CAN TEACH YOU.
AS MY MASTER ONCE TAUGHT ME.
GET... GET AWAY FROM ME.
GARRO. TAUGHT ME TO FEEL THE STONE YOU DID. NOW YOUR OWN TEACHING MUST YOU TAKE.
FEEL IT LIVING ALL AROUND YOU. TIME IT IS TO LIVE IN PEACE WITH THE STONE.
TO LIVE IN PEACE WITH YOURSELF.

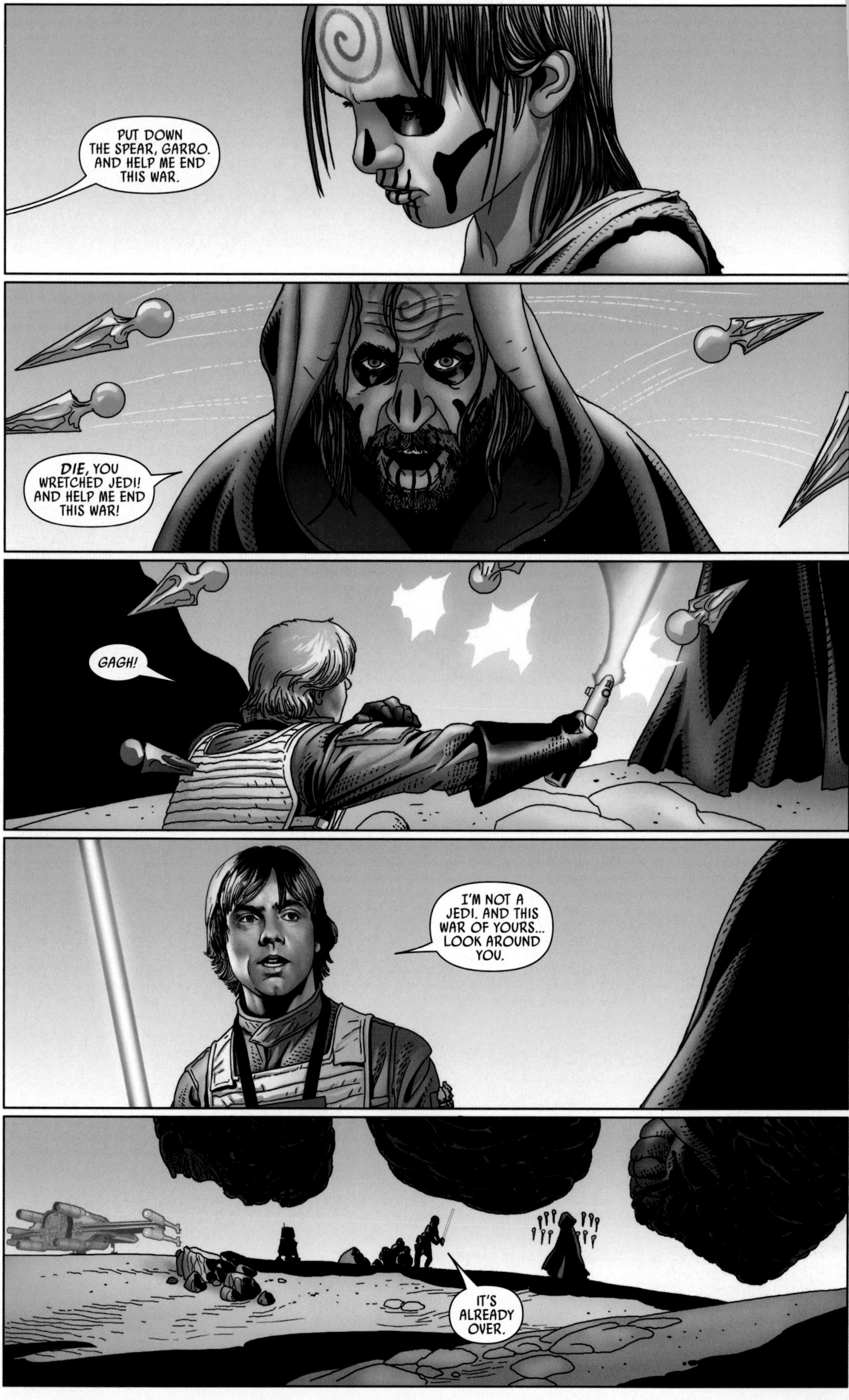
PUT DOWN THE SPEAR, GARRO. AND HELP ME END THIS WAR.
DIE, YOU WRETCHED JEDI! AND HELP ME END THIS WAR!
GAGH!
I'M NOT A JEDI. AND THIS WAR OF YOURS... LOOK AROUND YOU.
IT'S ALREADY OVER.

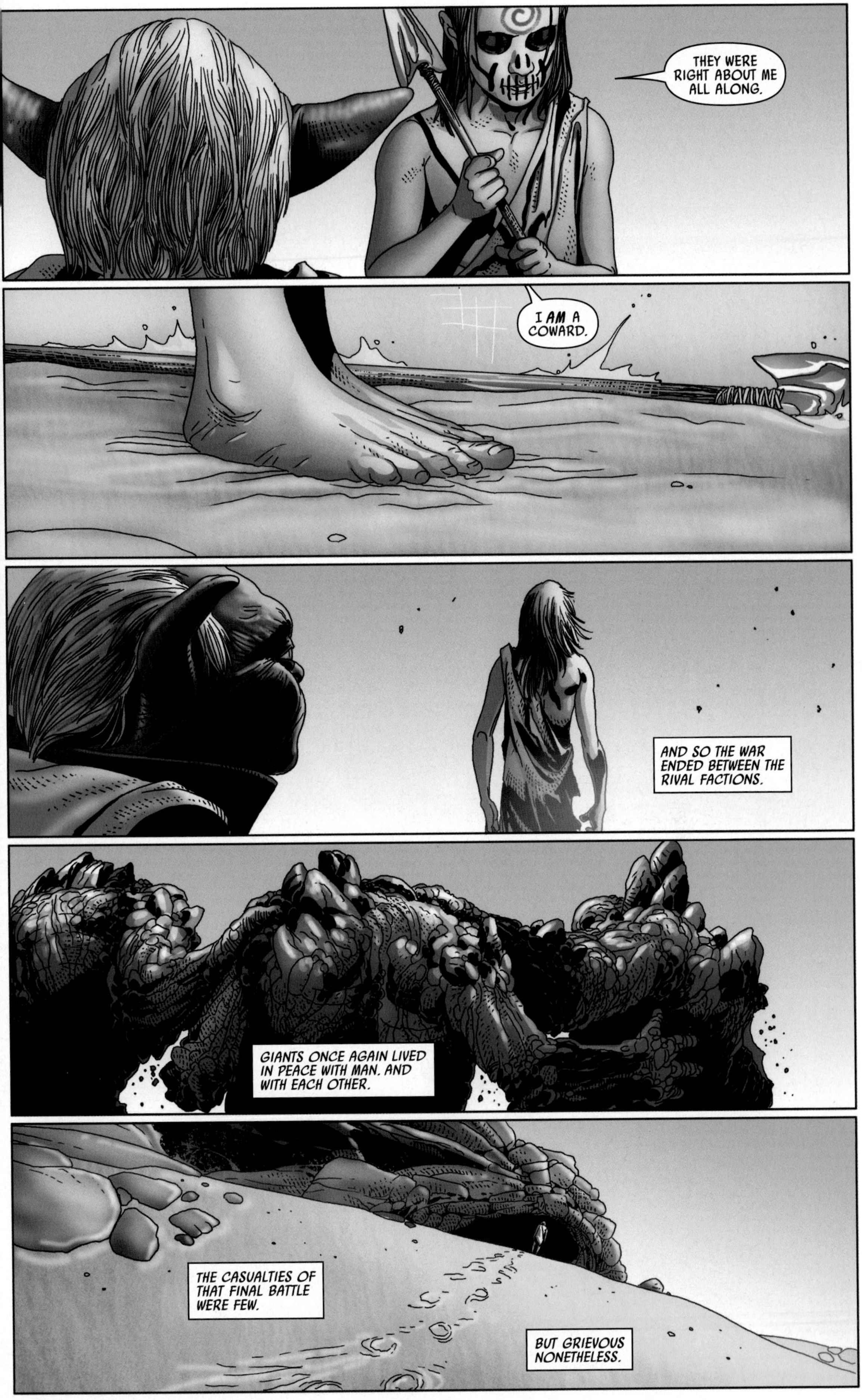
THEY WERE RIGHT ABOUT ME ALL ALONG.
I AM A COWARD.
AND SO THE WAR ENDED BETWEEN THE RIVAL FACTIONS.
GIANTS ONCE AGAIN LIVED IN PEACE WITH MAN. AND WITH EACH OTHER.
THE CASUALTIES OF THAT FINAL BATTLE WERE FEW.
BUT GRIEVOUS NONETHELESS.

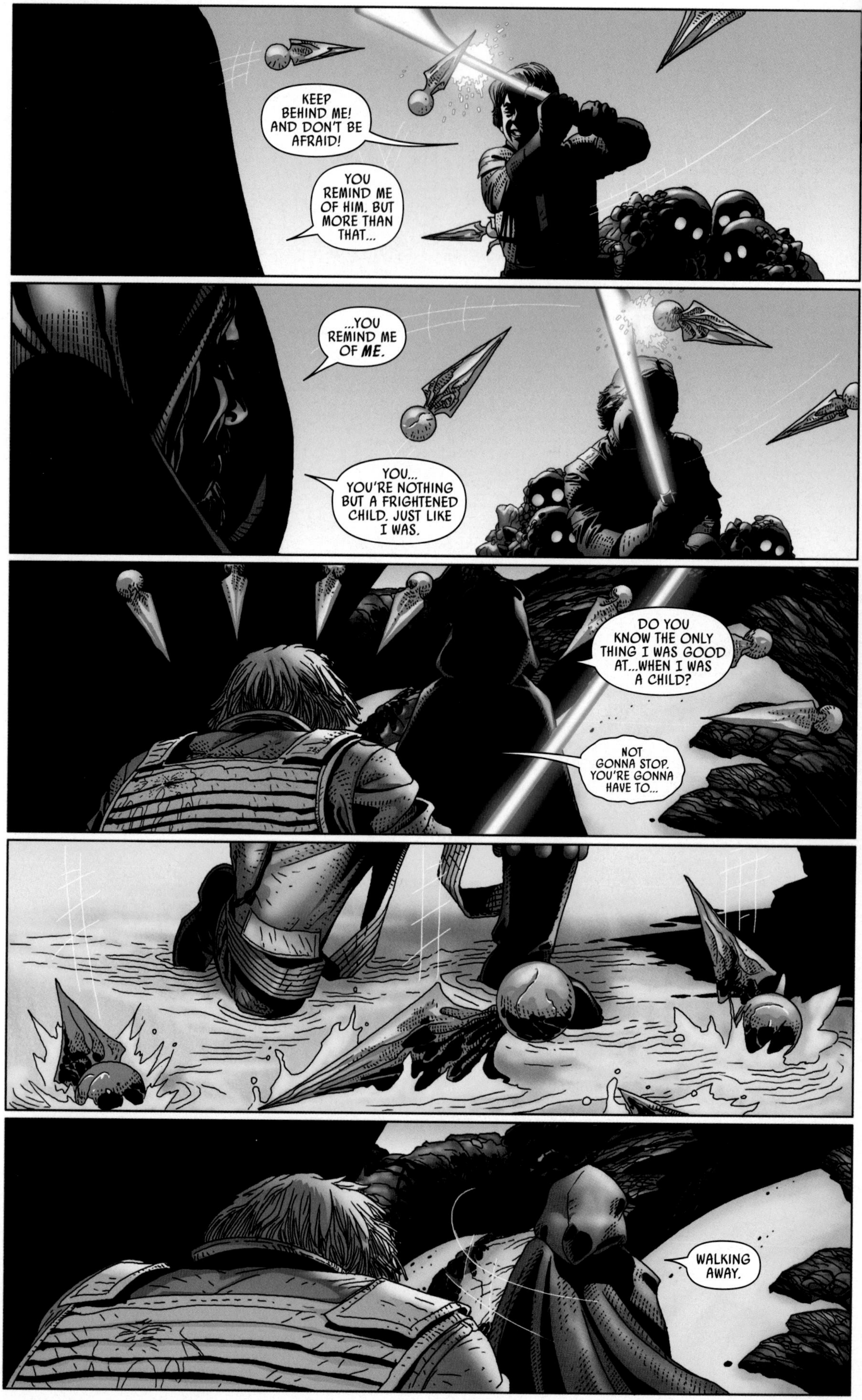
KEEP BEHIND ME! AND DON'T BE AFRAID!
YOU REMIND ME OF HIM. BUT MORE THAN THAT...
...YOU REMIND ME OF ME.
YOU... YOU'RE NOTHING BUT A FRIGHTENED CHILD. JUST LIKE I WAS.
DO YOU KNOW THE ONLY THING I WAS GOOD AT...WHEN I WAS A CHILD?
NOT GONNA STOP. YOU'RE GONNA HAVE TO...
WALKING AWAY.

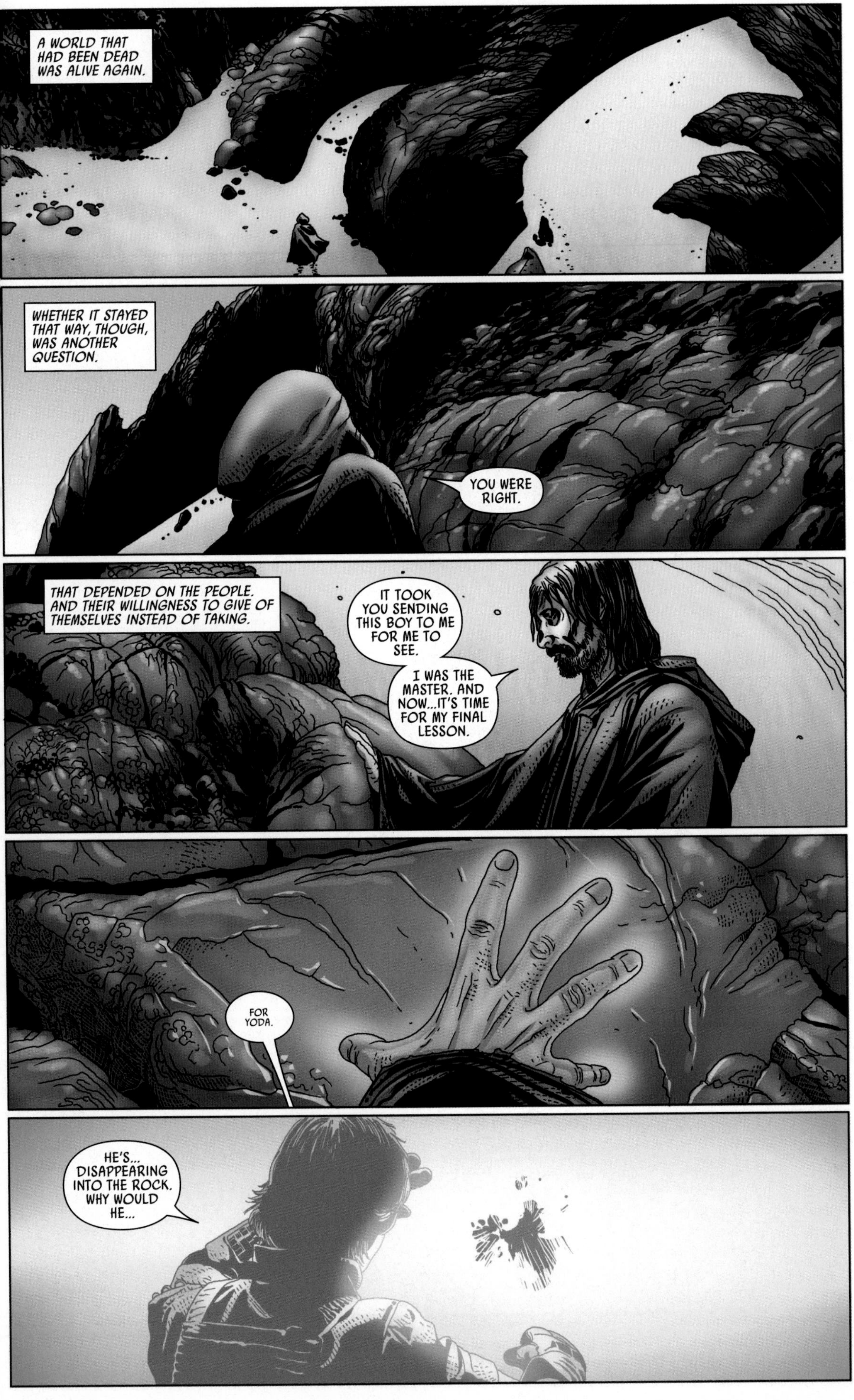
A WORLD THAT HAD BEEN DEAD WAS ALIVE AGAIN.
WHETHER IT STAYED THAT WAY, THOUGH, WAS ANOTHER QUESTION.
YOU WERE RIGHT.
THAT DEPENDED ON THE PEOPLE, AND THEIR WILLINGNESS TO GIVE OF THEMSELVES INSTEAD OF TAKING.
IT TOOK YOU SENDING THIS BOY TO ME FOR ME TO SEE.
I WAS THE MASTER. AND NOW...IT'S TIME FOR MY FINAL LESSON.
FOR YODA.
HE'S... DISAPPEARING INTO THE ROCK. WHY WOULD HE...

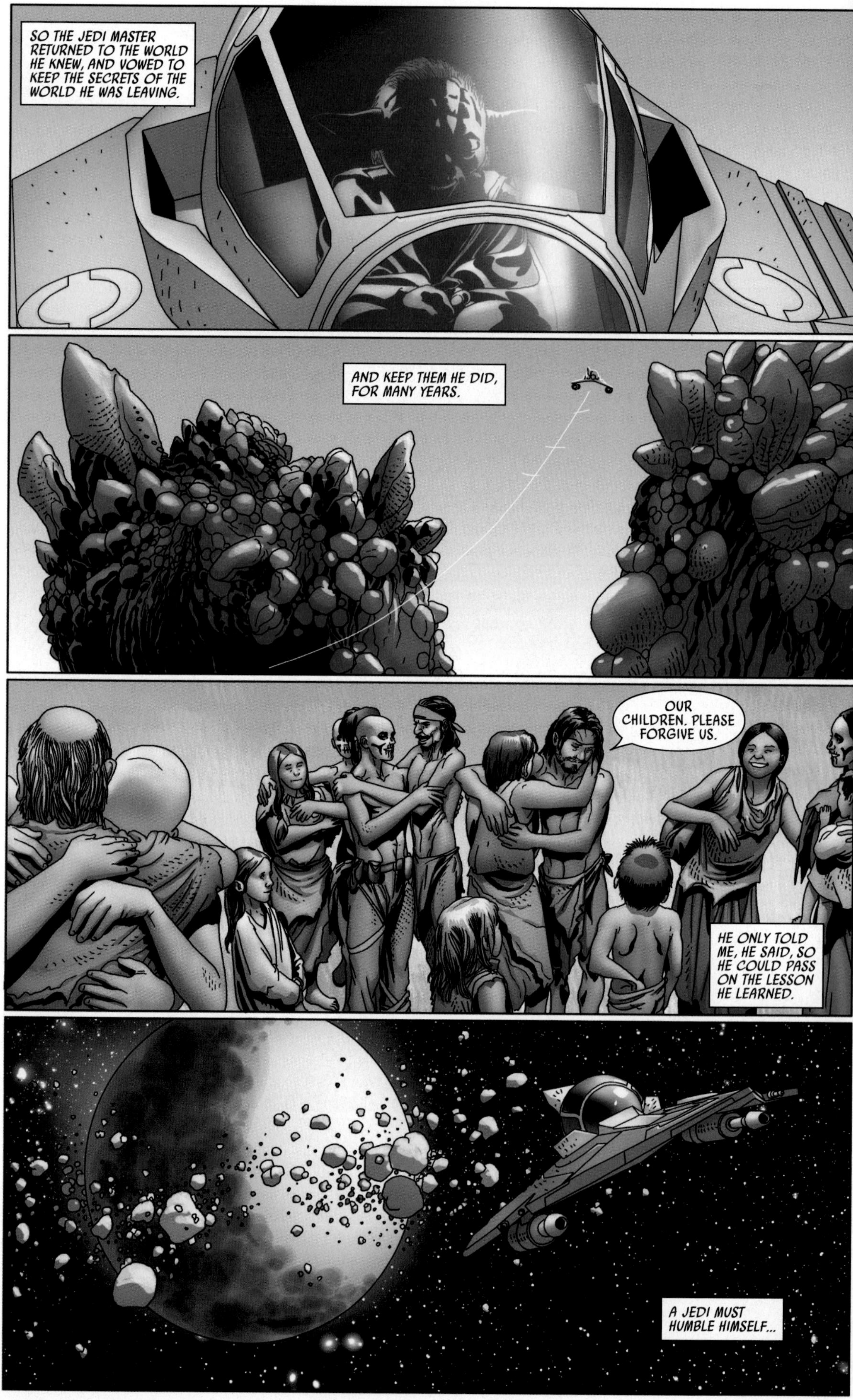
SO THE JEDI MASTER RETURNED TO THE WORLD HE KNEW, AND VOWED TO KEEP THE SECRETS OF THE WORLD HE WAS LEAVING.
AND KEEP THEM HE DID, FOR MANY YEARS.
OUR CHILDREN. PLEASE FORGIVE US.
HE ONLY TOLD ME, HE SAID, SO HE COULD PASS ON THE LESSON HE LEARNED.
A JEDI MUST HUMBLE HIMSELF...

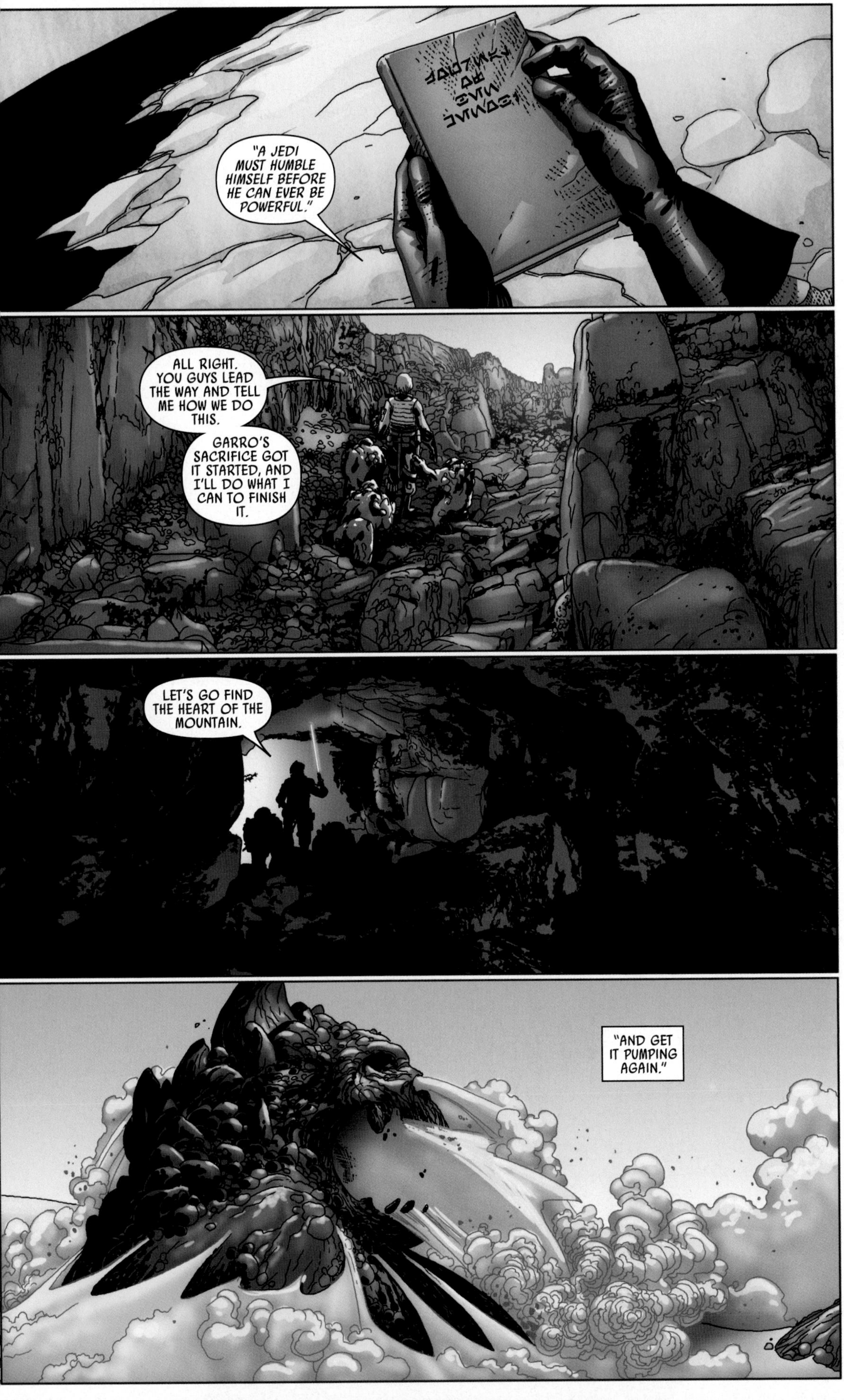
"A JEDI MUST HUMBLE HIMSELF BEFORE HE CAN EVER BE POWERFUL."
ALL RIGHT. YOU GUYS LEAD THE WAY AND TELL ME HOW WE DO THIS.
GARRO'S SACRIFICE GOT IT STARTED, AND I'LL DO WHAT I CAN TO FINISH IT.
LET'S GO FIND THE HEART OF THE MOUNTAIN.
"AND GET IT PUMPING AGAIN."

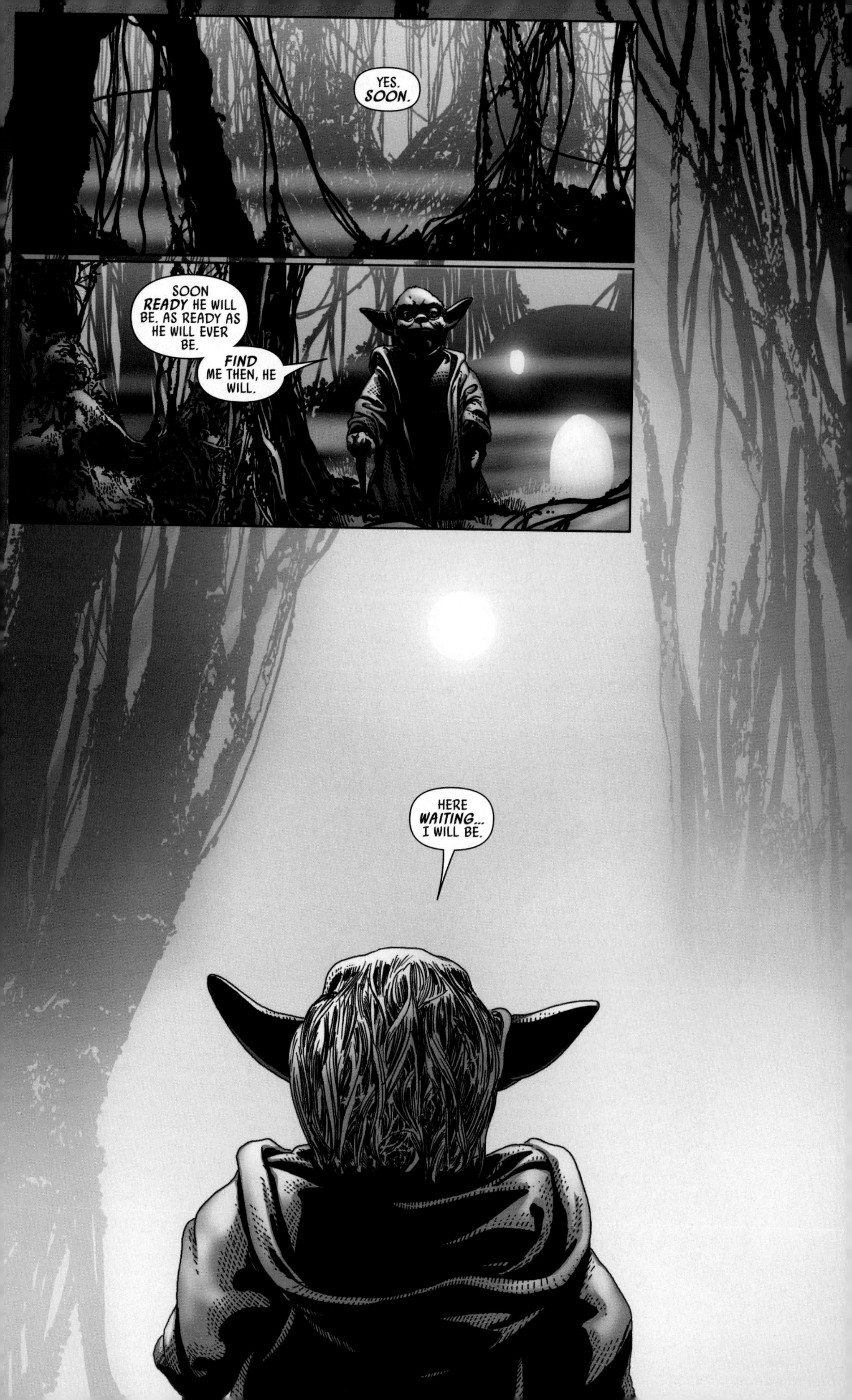
YES. SOON.
SOON READY HE WILL BE. AS READY AS HE WILL EVER BE.
FIND ME THEN, HE WILL.
HERE WAITING... I WILL BE.

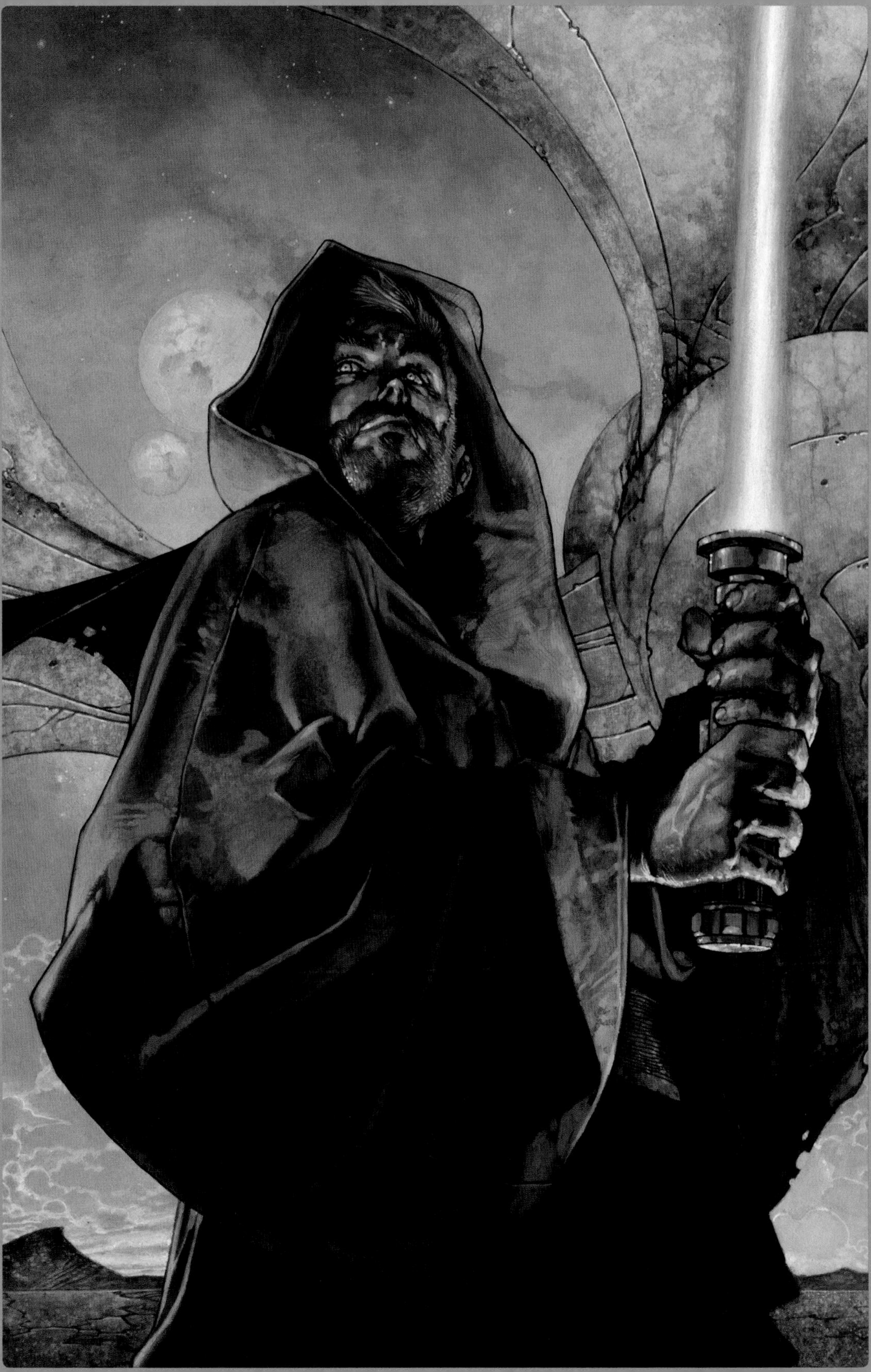

THE SAND WILL PROVIDE

It is a period of survival in the galaxy.
As war rages on between the Galactic
Empire and the Rebellion, the battle of
everyday survival continues for those
trying to live a normal life.

Between the scorching heat of the twin
suns on Tatooine and the vast deserts
of the Jundland Wastes, the life of a
Tusken Raider is not an easy one. But
when the world has turned its back on
the Tusken Raiders, they always have
the sand to call their home....

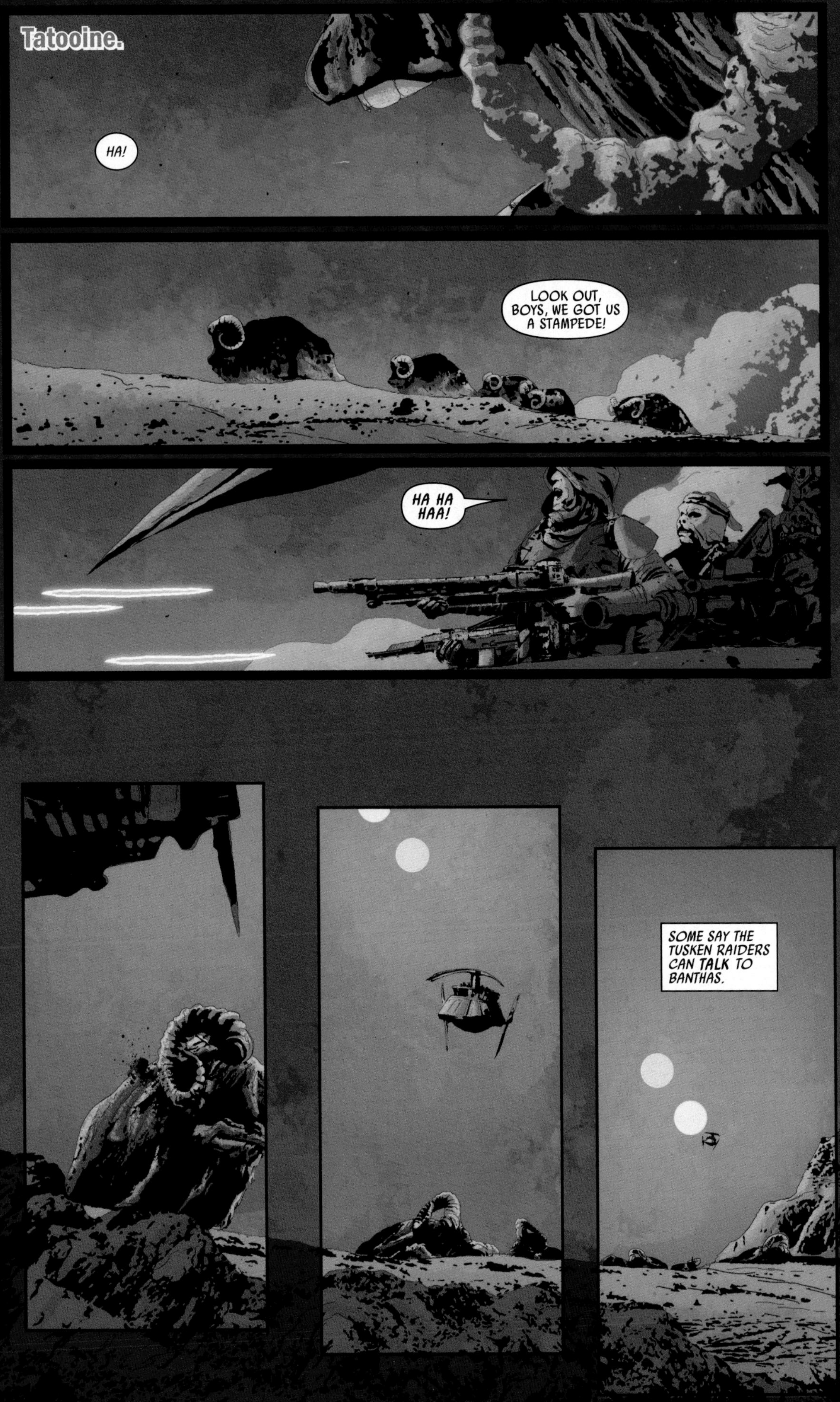
Tatooine.
HA!
LOOK OUT, BOYS, WE GOT US A STAMPEDE!
HA HA HAA!
SOME SAY THE TUSKEN RAIDERS CAN TALK TO BANTHAS.

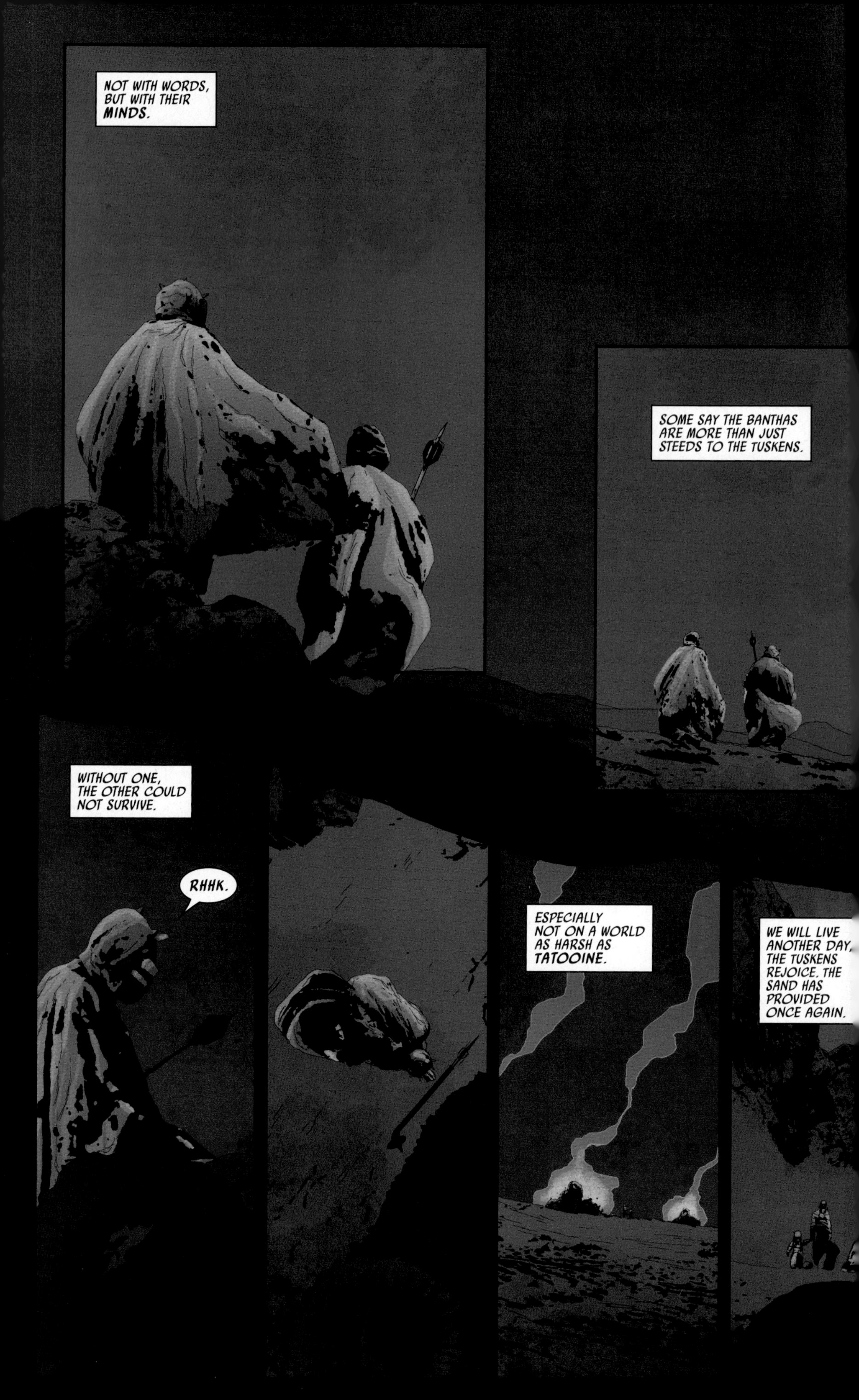
NOT WITH WORDS, BUT WITH THEIR MINDS.
SOME SAY THE BANTHAS ARE MORE THAN JUST STEEDS TO THE TUSKENS.
WITHOUT ONE, THE OTHER COULD NOT SURVIVE.
RHHK.
ESPECIALLY NOT ON A WORLD AS HARSH AS TATOOINE.
WE WILL LIVE ANOTHER DAY, THE TUSKENS REJOICE. THE SAND HAS PROVIDED ONCE AGAIN.

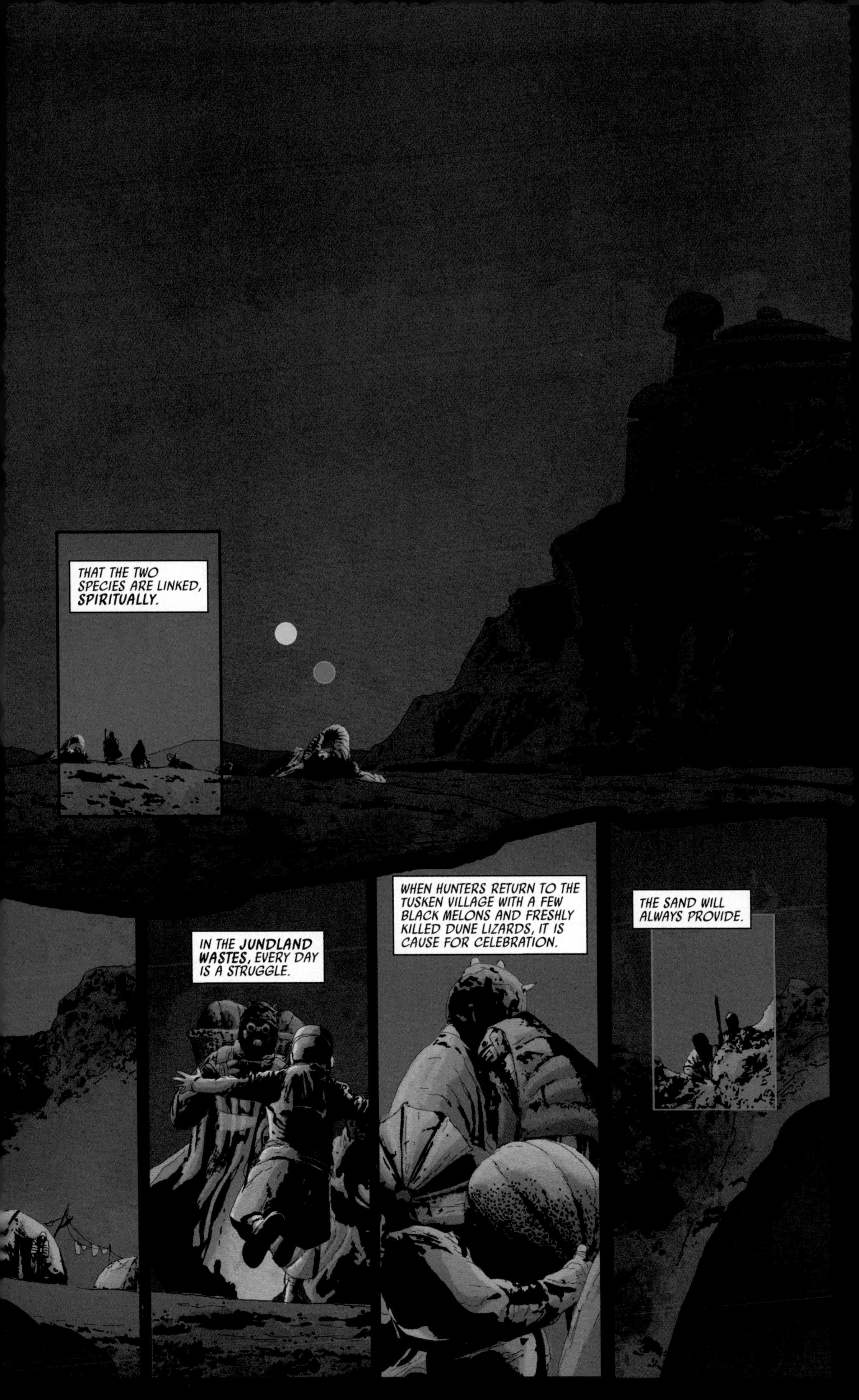
THAT THE TWO SPECIES ARE LINKED, SPIRITUALLY.
IN THE JUNDLAND WASTES, EVERY DAY IS A STRUGGLE.
WHEN HUNTERS RETURN TO THE TUSKEN VILLAGE WITH A FEW BLACK MELONS AND FRESHLY KILLED DUNE LIZARDS, IT IS CAUSE FOR CELEBRATION.
THE SAND WILL ALWAYS PROVIDE.

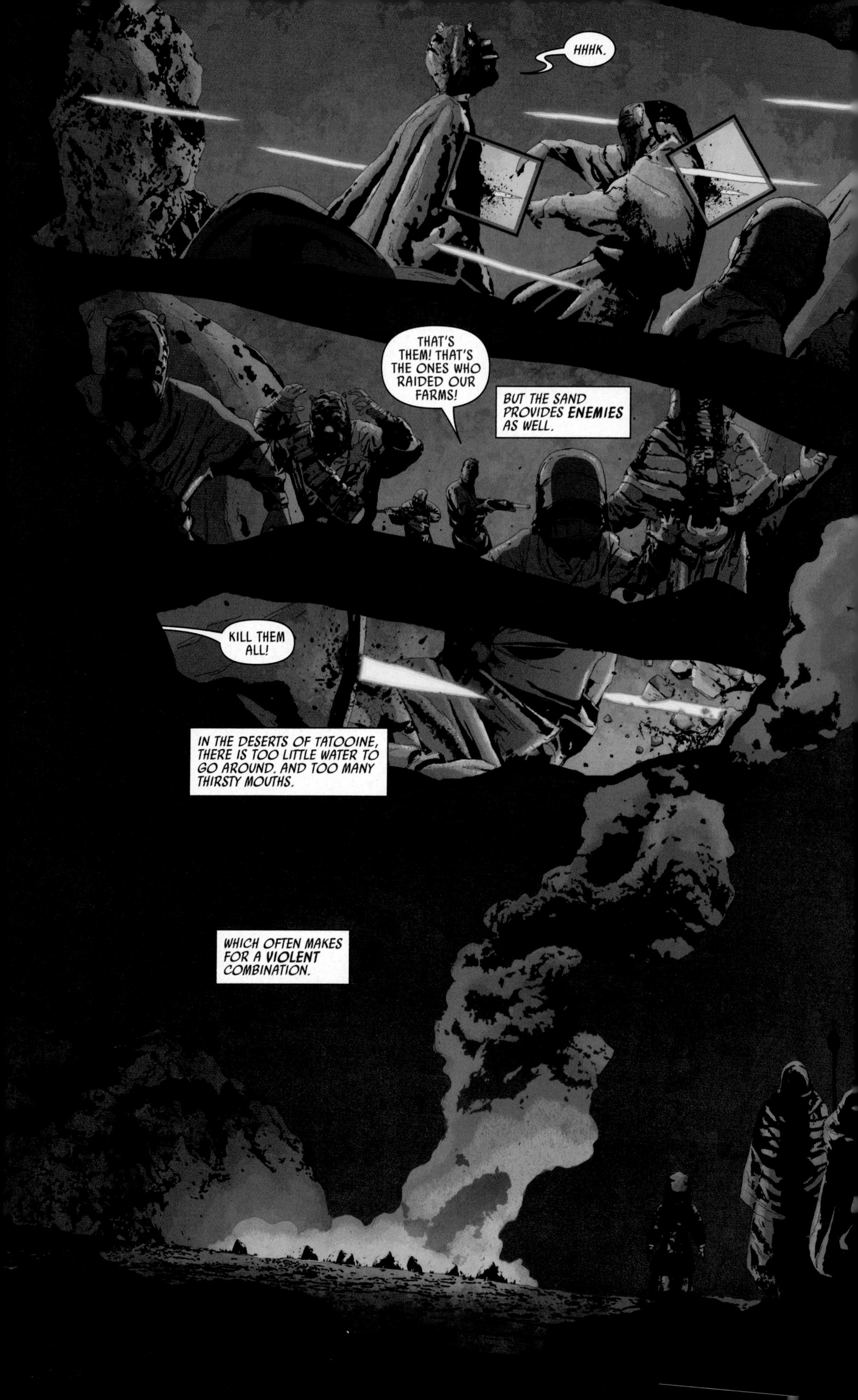
HHHK.
THAT'S THEM! THAT'S THE ONES WHO RAIDED OUR FARMS!
BUT THE SAND PROVIDES **ENEMIES** AS WELL.
KILL THEM ALL!
IN THE DESERTS OF TATOOINE, THERE IS TOO LITTLE WATER TO GO AROUND. AND TOO MANY THIRSTY MOUTHS.
WHICH OFTEN MAKES FOR A **VIOLENT** COMBINATION.

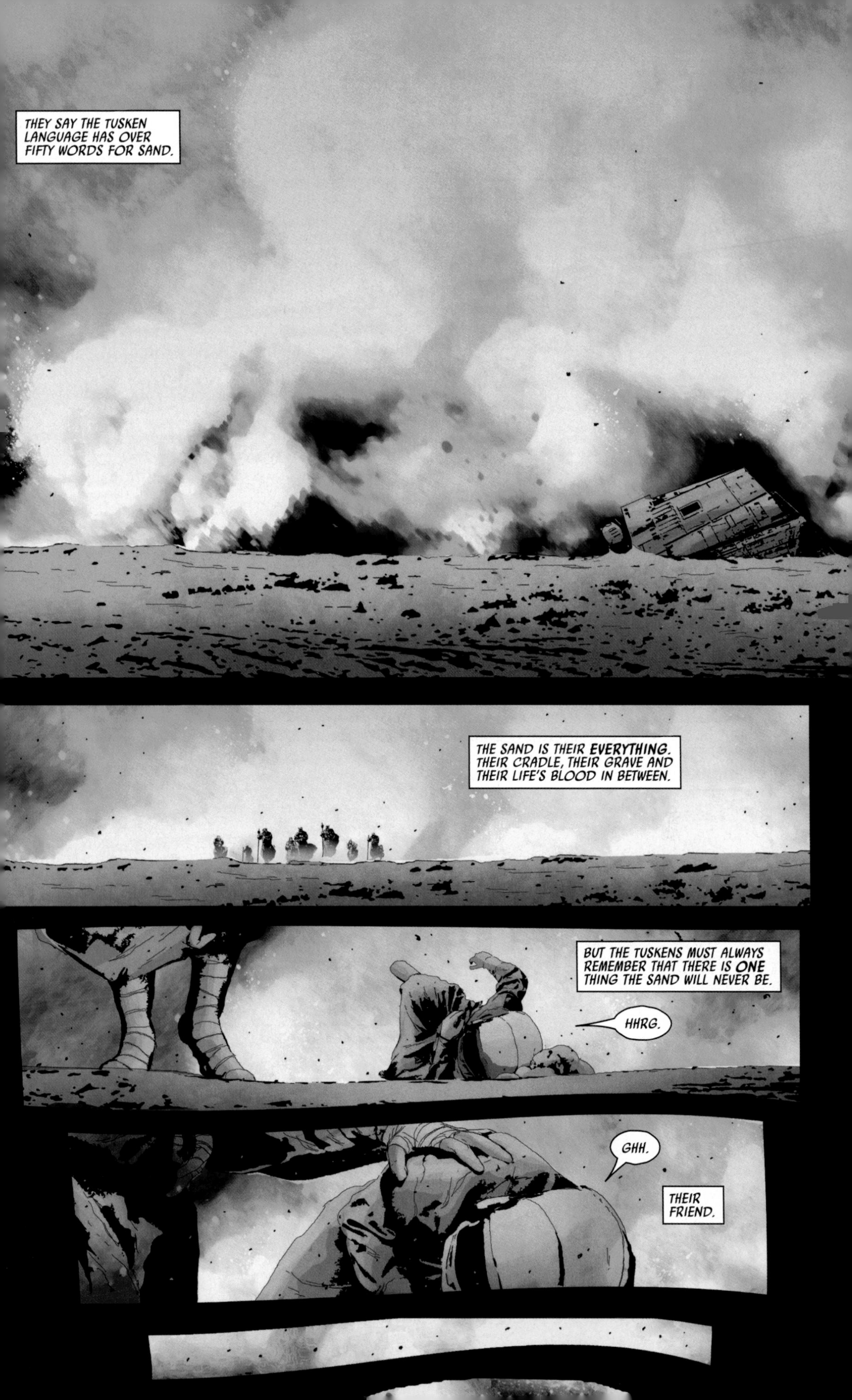
THEY SAY THE TUSKEN LANGUAGE HAS OVER FIFTY WORDS FOR SAND.
THE SAND IS THEIR EVERYTHING. THEIR CRADLE, THEIR GRAVE AND THEIR LIFE'S BLOOD IN BETWEEN.
BUT THE TUSKENS MUST ALWAYS REMEMBER THAT THERE IS ONE THING THE SAND WILL NEVER BE.
HHRG.
GHH.
THEIR FRIEND.

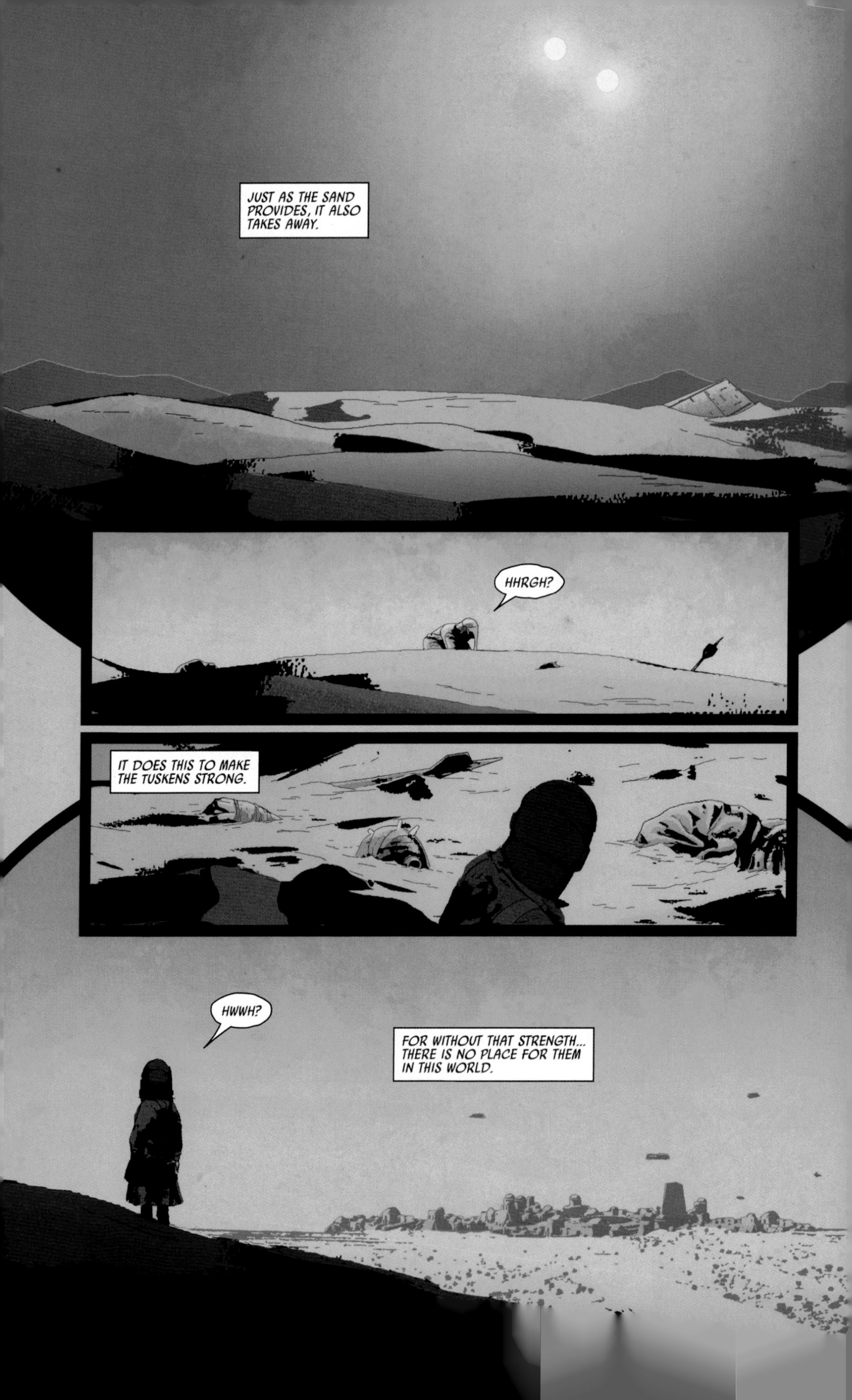
JUST AS THE SAND PROVIDES, IT ALSO TAKES AWAY.
HHRGH?
IT DOES THIS TO MAKE THE TUSKENS STRONG.
HWWH?
FOR WITHOUT THAT STRENGTH... THERE IS NO PLACE FOR THEM IN THIS WORLD.

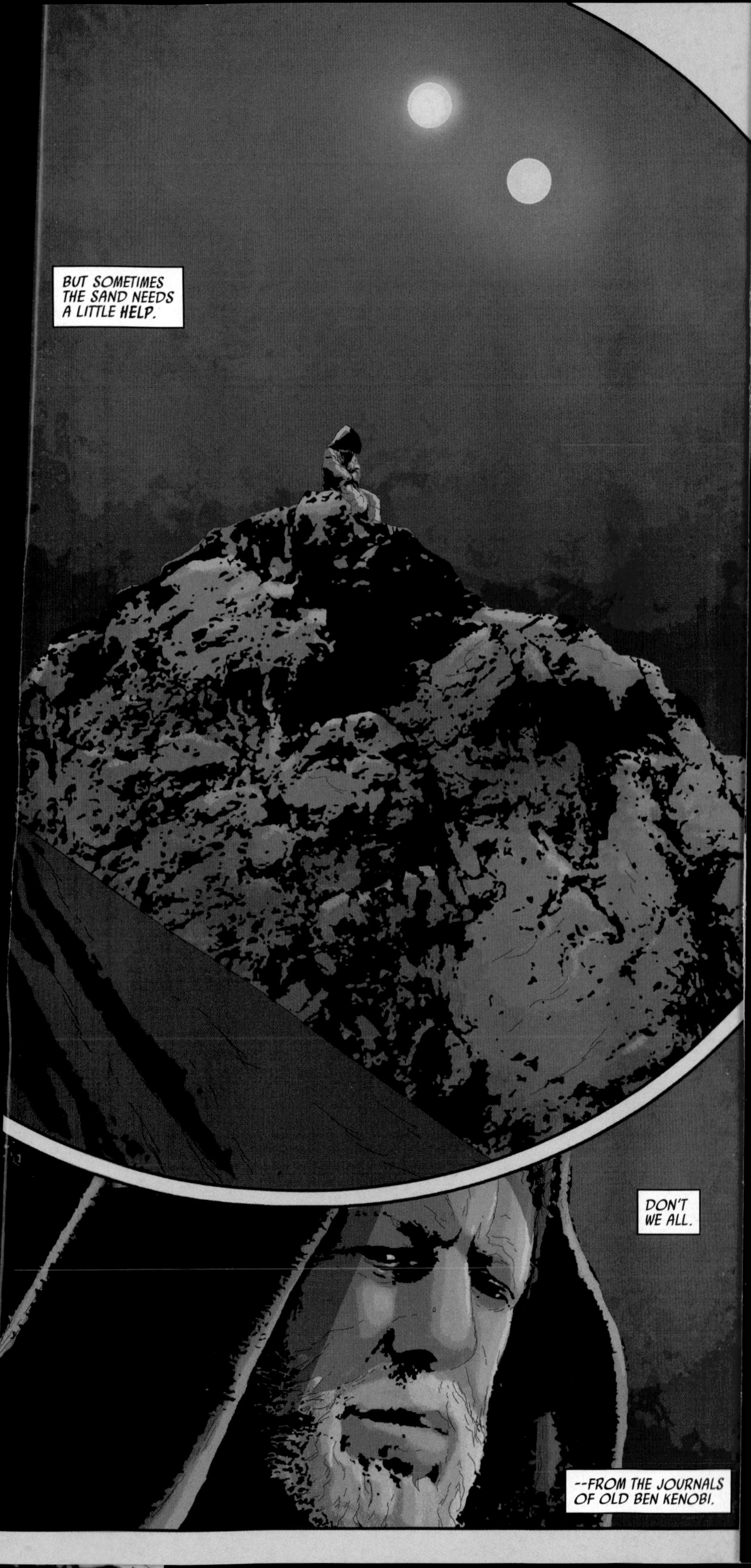
BUT SOMETIMES THE SAND NEEDS A LITTLE HELP.
DON'T WE ALL.
--FROM THE JOURNALS OF OLD BEN KENOBI.

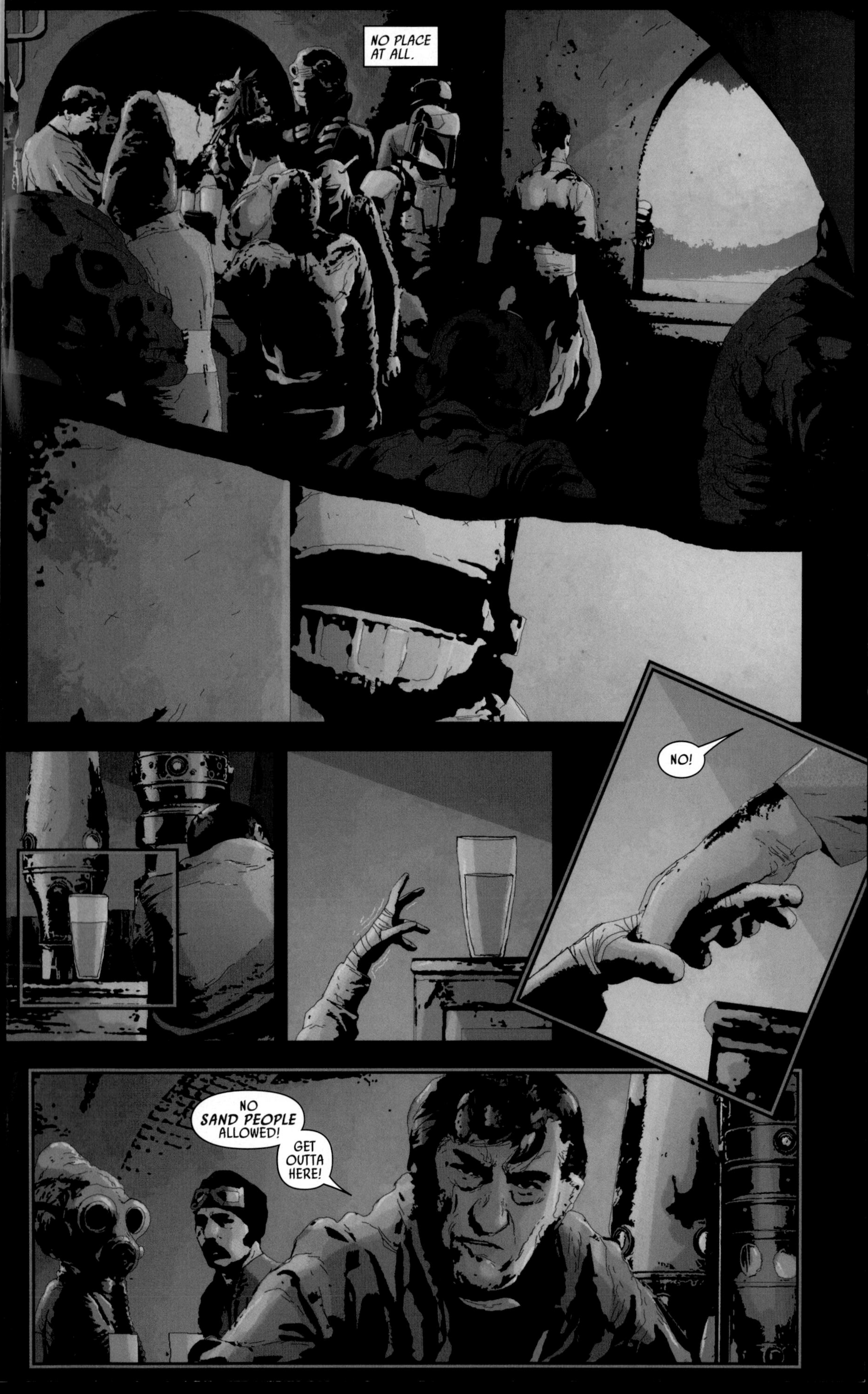
NO PLACE AT ALL.
NO!
NO SAND PEOPLE ALLOWED!
GET OUTTA HERE!

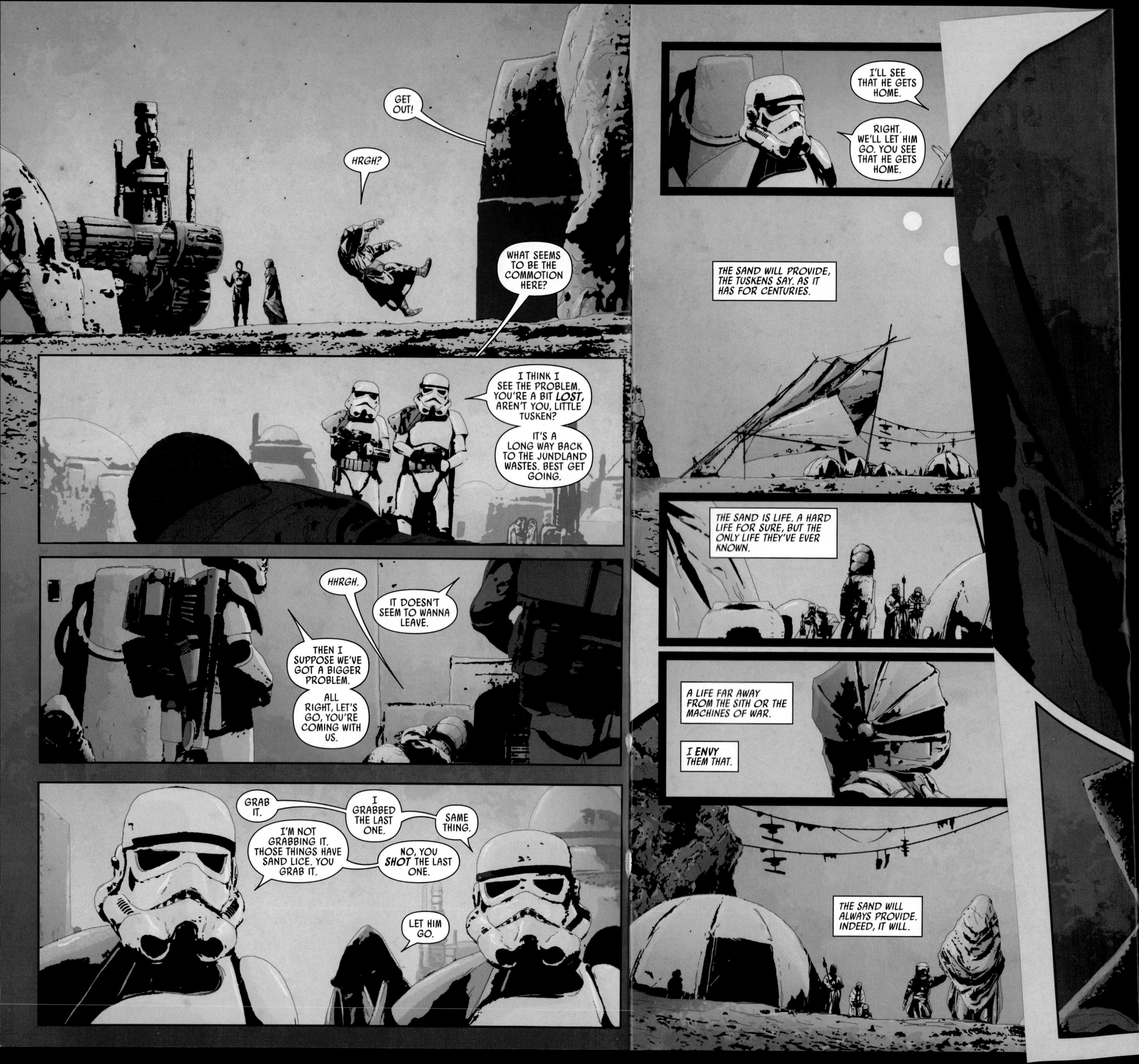
GET OUT!
HRGH?
WHAT SEEMS TO BE THE COMMOTION HERE?
I THINK I SEE THE PROBLEM. YOU'RE A BIT LOST, AREN'T YOU, LITTLE TUSKEN?
IT'S A LONG WAY BACK TO THE JUNDLAND WASTES. BEST GET GOING.
HHRGH.
IT DOESN'T SEEM TO WANNA LEAVE.
THEN I SUPPOSE WE'VE GOT A BIGGER PROBLEM.
ALL RIGHT, LET'S GO, YOU'RE COMING WITH US.
GRAB IT.
I GRABBED THE LAST ONE.
SAME THING.
I'M NOT GRABBING IT. THOSE THINGS HAVE SAND LICE. YOU GRAB IT.
NO, YOU SHOT THE LAST ONE.
LET HIM GO.
I'LL SEE THAT HE GETS HOME.
RIGHT. WE'LL LET HIM GO. YOU SEE THAT HE GETS HOME.
THE SAND WILL PROVIDE, THE TUSKENS SAY. AS IT HAS FOR CENTURIES.
THE SAND IS LIFE. A HARD LIFE FOR SURE, BUT THE ONLY LIFE THEY'VE EVER KNOWN.
A LIFE FAR AWAY FROM THE SITH OR THE MACHINES OF WAR.
I ENVY THEM THAT.
THE SAND WILL ALWAYS PROVIDE. INDEED, IT WILL.

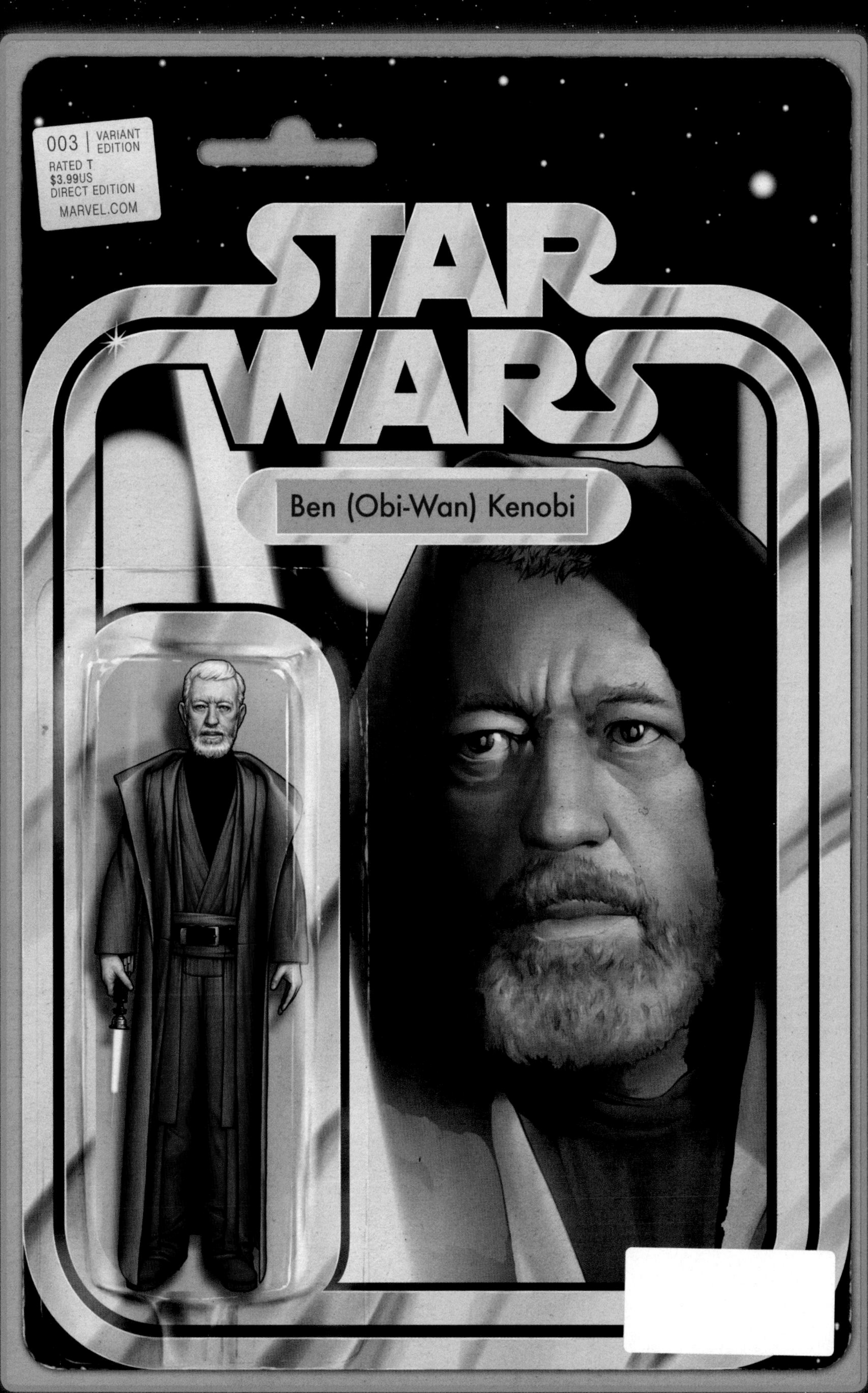
003 | VARIANT EDITION
RATED T
$3.99US
DIRECT EDITION
MARVEL.COM
STAR WARS
Ben (Obi-Wan) Kenobi

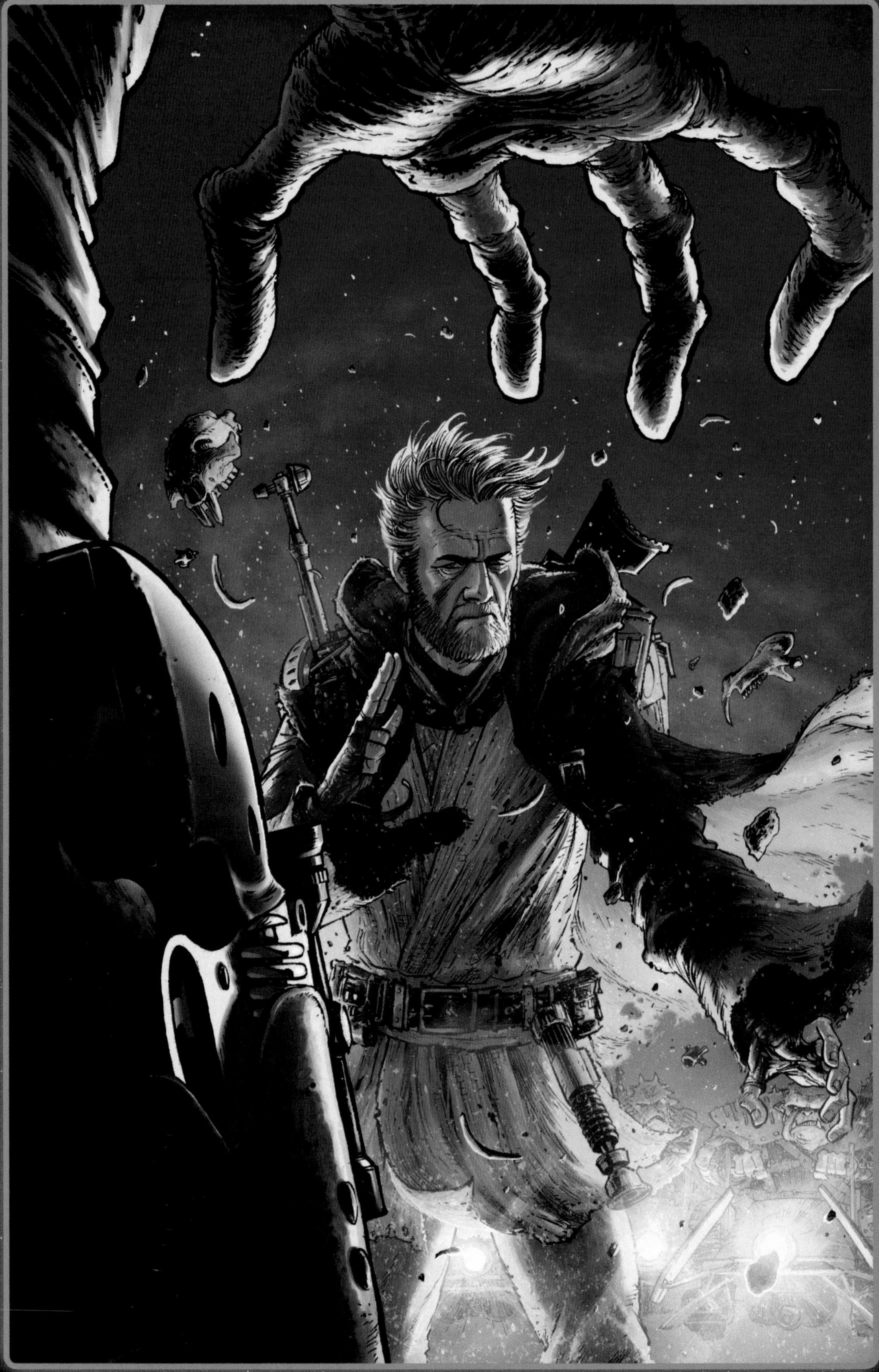

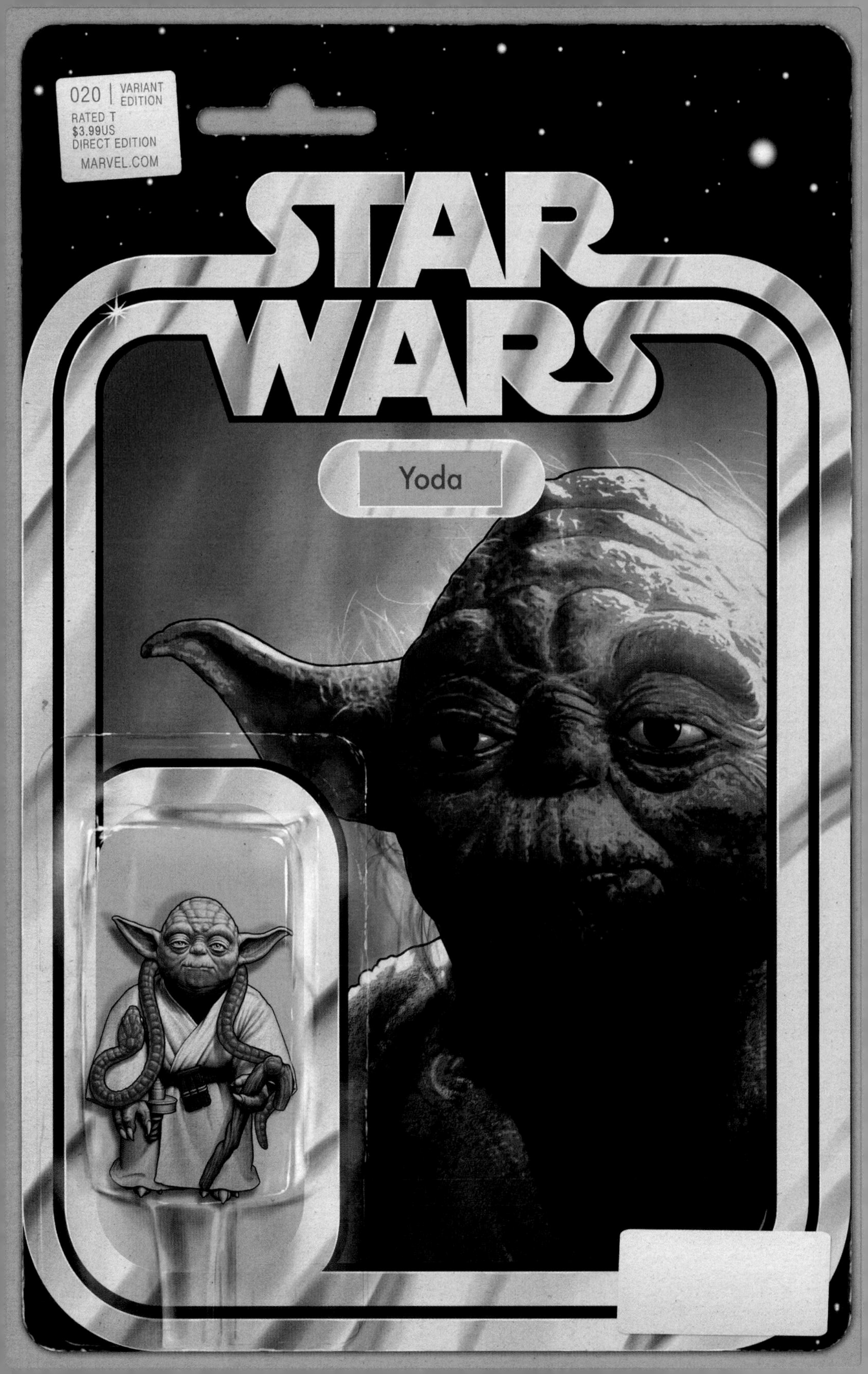
020 | VARIANT EDITION
RATED T
$3.99US
DIRECT EDITION
MARVEL.COM
STAR WARS
Yoda

STAR WARS

THERE ARE HEROES — AND VILLAINS — ON BOTH SIDES!

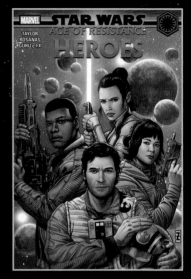

STAR WARS: AGE OF REPUBLIC – HEROES TPB
ISBN: 978-1302917104
ON SALE NOW!

STAR WARS: AGE OF REBELLION – HEROES TPB
ISBN: 978-1302917081
ON SALE NOW!

STAR WARS: AGE OF RESISTANCE – HEROES TPB
ISBN: 978-1302917128
NOVEMBER 2019

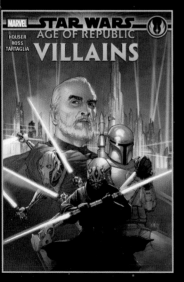

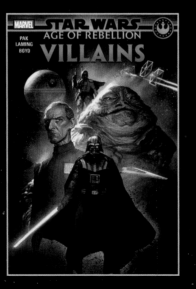

STAR WARS: AGE OF REPUBLIC – VILLAINS TPB
ISBN: 978-1302917296
ON SALE NOW!

STAR WARS: AGE OF REBELLION – VILLAINS TPB
ISBN: 978-1302917296
ON SALE NOW!

STAR WARS: AGE OF RESISTANCE – VILLAINS TPB
ISBN: 978-1302917302
NOVEMBER 2019

IN PRINT AND DIGITAL WHEREVER BOOKS ARE SOLD.
TO FIND A COMIC SHOP NEAR YOU, **VISIT COMICSHOPLOCATOR.COM.**

DISNEP · LUCASFILM MARVEL

ROGUE ARCHAEOLOGIST DOCTOR APHRA THIEVES HER WAY ACROSS THE GALAXY!

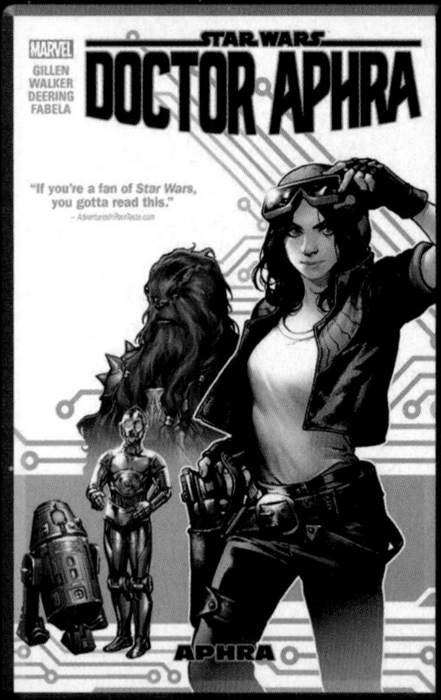
MARVEL
STAR WARS
DOCTOR APHRA
GILLEN
WALKER
DEERING
FABELA
"If you're a fan of Star Wars, you gotta read this."
APHRA

STAR WARS: DOCTOR APHRA VOL. 1 – APHRA TPB
ISBN: 978-1302913212

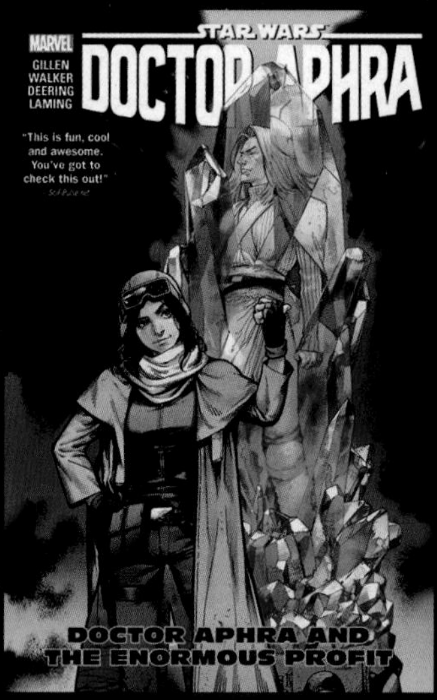
MARVEL
STAR WARS
DOCTOR APHRA
GILLEN
WALKER
DEERING
LAMING
"This is fun, cool and awesome. You've got to check this out!"
DOCTOR APHRA AND THE ENORMOUS PROFIT

STAR WARS: DOCTOR APHRA VOL. 2 – DOCTOR APHRA AND THE ENORMOUS PROFIT TPB
ISBN: 978-1302907631

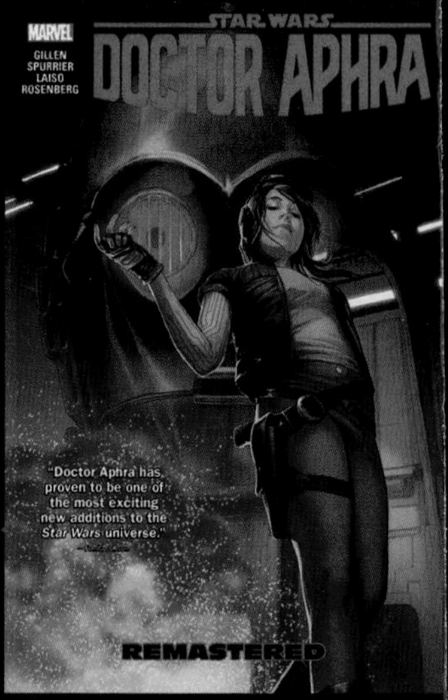
MARVEL
STAR WARS
DOCTOR APHRA
GILLEN
SPURRIER
LAISO
ROSENBERG
"Doctor Aphra has proven to be one of the most exciting new additions to the Star Wars universe."
REMASTERED

STAR WARS: DOCTOR APHRA VOL. 3 – REMASTERED TPB
ISBN: 978-1302911522

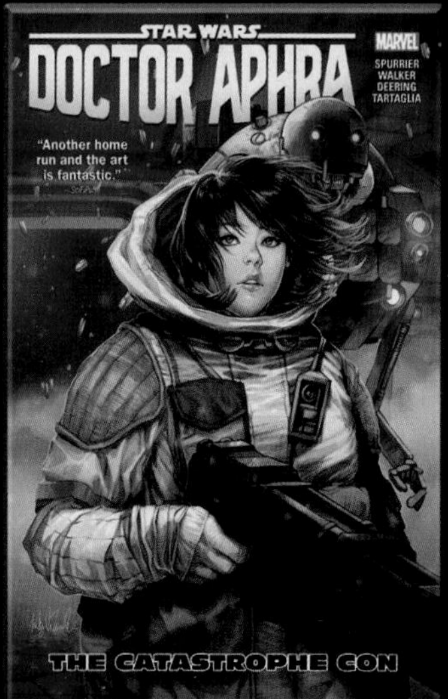
STAR WARS
DOCTOR APHRA
MARVEL
SPURRIER
WALKER
DEERING
TARTAGLIA
"Another home run and the art is fantastic."
THE CATASTROPHE CON

STAR WARS: DOCTOR APHRA VOL. 4 – THE CATASTROPHE CON TPB
ISBN: 978-1302911539

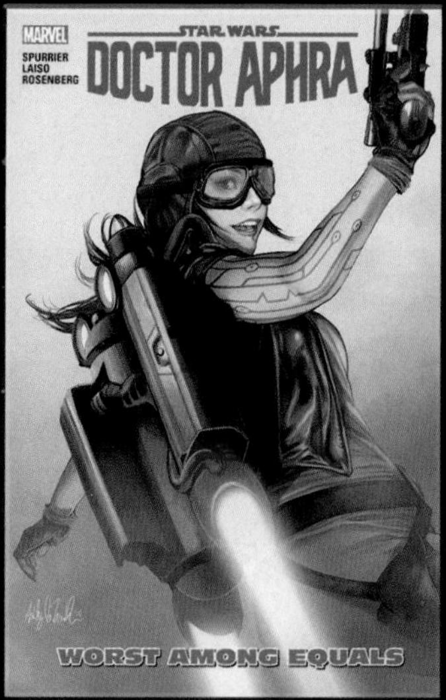
MARVEL
SPURRIER
LAISO
ROSENBERG
STAR WARS
DOCTOR APHRA
WORST AMONG EQUALS

STAR WARS: DOCTOR APHRA VOL. 5 – WORST AMONG EQUALS TPB
ISBN: 978-1302914875

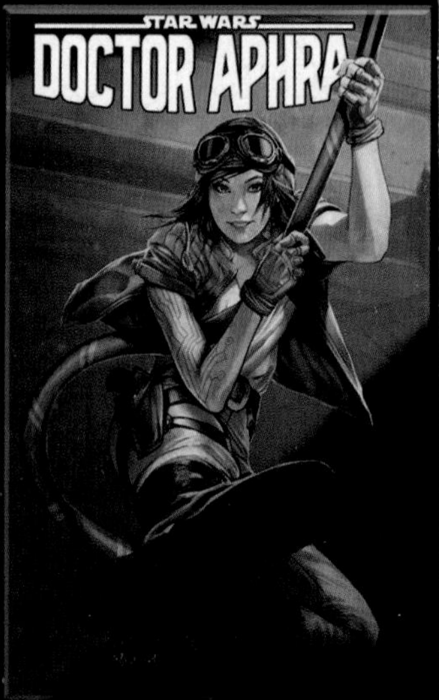
STAR WARS
DOCTOR APHRA

STAR WARS: DOCTOR APHRA VOL. 6 – UNSPEAKABLE REBEL SUPERWEAPON TPB
ISBN: 978-1302914882

ON SALE NOW
AVAILABLE IN PRINT AND DIGITAL
WHEREVER BOOKS ARE SOLD

TO FIND A COMIC SHOP NEAR YOU,
VISIT COMICSHOPLOCATOR.COM.